ELITE RECRUITMENT IN DEMOCRATIC POLITIES

ELITE RECRUITMENT IN DEMOCRATIC POLITIES

Comparative Studies Across Nations

Edited by

HEINZ EULAU

Stanford University

and

MOSHE M. CZUDNOWSKI

Northern Illinois University

SAGE PUBLICATIONS

Halsted Press Division
JOHN WILEY & SONS
New York — London — Sydney — Toronto

Distributed by Halsted Press, a Division of
John Wiley & Sons, Inc., New York

JC
330
,E43

Printed in the United States of America

Library of Congress Cataloging in Publication Data
Main entry under title:

Elite recruitment in democratic polities.

   1. Elite (Social sciences)—Addresses, essays, lectures. 2. Elections—Addresses, essays, lectures. 3. Comparative government—Addresses, essays, lectures. 4. Democracy—Addresses, essays, lectures. I. Eulau, Heinz, 1915-
    II. Czudnowski, Moshe M., 1924-
JC330.E43   301.5'92   76-2698
ISBN 0-470-15056-4

FIRST PRINTING

CONTENTS

PREFACE

Fifteen years separate the publication of the first cross-national symposium on political recruitment (Dwaine Marvick, ed., *Political Decision-makers: Recruitment and Performance*, 1961) from this second effort to present to the student of politics an updated view of some of the thematic, theoretical, and methodological concerns in the empirical study of elites. These fifteen years have witnessed, in particular, a developing interest in the *recruitment process*, documented in the continuing contributions of such scholars as James D. Barber, Mattei Dogan, Lewis J. Edinger, Samuel J. Eldersveld, Allan Kornberg, Dwaine Marvick, Samuel C. Patterson, Kenneth Prewitt, Austin Ranney, Joseph A. Schlesinger, Lester G. Seligman, and others. The subject of political recruitment has now received formal recognition of its place in political science by the inclusion of a separate chapter on empirical recruitment studies in a recently published comprehensive inventory of the discipline (Moshe M. Czudnowski, "Political Recruitment," in Fred I. Greenstein and Nelson W. Polsby, eds., *Handbook of Political Science*, Vol. II, 1975).

Yet, this volume did not originate from an abundance of recruitment studies in search of a publisher. In fact, what had attracted us some years ago to this enterprise was curiosity about what was going on by way of empirical research on elite recruitment as much as a feeling for the need of making more visible what we sensed to exist as an "invisible college" of scholars. But if we had thought that we could fill up the projected volume in a hurry, we were sadly in error. We had to learn, though we should have known it before starting the project, that elite studies are time-consuming and costly undertakings, and that only a relatively small group of scholars has been in a position to maintain a continuing *research involvement* in this field. In some Western European countries, we were unable to find ongoing research on elite *recruitment* (though there is much interest in the *composition* of elites), and on the American scene only a few scholars were engaged either in expanding the range of research or in testing new ideas on data collected in the sixties. However, this volume also shows that the period of scholarly apprenticeship in research on elite recruitment has not been excessively long: In several chapters of this symposium, a second generation of researchers is firmly establishing its presence in the field, either independently or in collaboration with others.

One obvious consequence for this volume of the relative scarcity of recent research is perhaps an unrepresentative sample of foci of interest if set against the many dimensions, levels, stages, and aspects that characterize the recruitment process across democratic polities. No scholar's contribution is more relevant in regard to the latter than Harold D. Lasswell's. As becomes clear in Eulau's revisit of Lasswell's writings concerning elites and their recruitment (Chapter 1), this seminal political scientist not only anticipated, as he did on so many other occasions, the course of empirical recruitment research but also provided an agenda of possible topics that has as yet remained unexploited. Although the final title of Eulau's essay is "Elite Analysis and Democratic Theory," the original title, "The Reception of Elite Analysis in the United States," conveys more accurately the intellectual debt that scholars in the field owe to HDL.

Although elite analysis like other fields of social research has not been immune from discontinuity stemming from shifting fads or generational change, there are invariably knowledgeable custodians who are sensitive to continuities in theory and research that will escape the novice. Dwaine Marvick, in "Continuities in Recruitment Theory and Research" (Chapter 2), makes creative use of a variety of old and new hypotheses concerning recruitment to speculate about the interactive process that links the recruit to the established apparatus into which he is recruited. The process is not, as has been traditionally assumed, one-directional. Just as the recruit will adapt to the existing cadre, the cadre will adjust to the recruit. In developing his model, Marvick does not present a routine review of past research but critically utilizes the research tradition, and in doing so conveys a sense of intellectual continuity and richness often absent in the work of those either ignorant or forgetful of a research tradition.

Recruitment research penetrates levels of analysis as deeply as research instruments permit. In "Aspiring and Established Politicians: The Structure of Value Systems and Role Profiles" (Chapter 3), Czudnowski uses personality-determined, sociopsychological, and political variables to explore differences between aspiring and established politicians. Distinguishing between instrumental and terminal values for the person, and terminal political values and political issue positions, Czudnowski illustrates the complexity of motivations in the recruitment process, which is further complicated by situational conditions such as the incumbent/challenger status of candidatures or the degree of competition in the political structure. By combining Milton Rokeach's work on value systems with recruitment theory and investigating resultant motivational profiles at different levels of involvement, Czudnowski reconfirms

Lasswell's insistence on the importance of personality and culture in the study of political phenomena.

Acknowledged continuity in a different genre of theory and research is evident in "Partisanship in the Recruitment and Performance of American State Legislators" (Chapter 4) by Chong Lim Kim, Justin Green, and Samuel C. Patterson. In building on the research tradition initiated by John C. Wahlke and his associates in *The Legislative System* (1962), the Iowa group constructs an imaginative typology of recruits into the legislature variously called party agent, careerist, coopted candidate, and entrepreneur, in order to examine and assess the impact of *party* recruitment on partisan behavior in legislative decision-making. Symptomatic of the advance made in legislative recruitment research in the last fifteen years or so is this study's primary concern with the consequences of different recruitment paths on role performance. But, again, there is frank recognition that contextual factors like district typicality and competitiveness reduce the power of recruitment as a variable to explain variance in legislative behavior.

The effect of partisanship on the composition and transformation of executive elites at the national level as against the effect of secular trends occasioned by society's functional requirements is examined in Kenneth Prewitt and William McAllister's "Changes in the American Executive Elite— 1930-1970." Whereas, in the period covered, the parties continued to react differentially to changes in the representational demand structure associated with the existence of a system of stratification in various societal sectors like religion or education, they were "powerless" (if the proverb is permissible) in the face of the "skill revolution" that seems to be an immanent feature of societal development in this age of high technology. It comes as something of a shock to learn that the ratio of federal executives who had a law degree to those who held a doctoral degree had dropped from 7.00 in the Hoover and even second Eisenhower administrations to 1.73 in the first Nixon administration. Prewitt and McAllister offer a number of ingenious interpretations in tracing the flow of recruitment over time.

Compared with the political environment of the United States, the politics of campaigning in India would seem to constitute a milieu in which isolating the process of recruitment is truly a tour de force. And such, indeed, is Dwaine Marvick's "Recruitment Patterns of Campaign Activities in India" (Chapter 6). A purposive sample of different types of campaign activists permits Marvick to examine, along with other aspects of the recruitment process, what he felicitously calls "careers in orbit" and "careers in transit." A typology of activists—localists, dualists, and translocalists—serves him both to observe differing career paths and to estimate probabilities of success in moving into various middle-level posts of the political system.

Galen A. Irwin's "Party, Accountability and the Recruitment of Municipal Councilmen in the Netherlands" (Chapter 7) is probably the first genuinely cross-national replication of an elaborate recruitment study. Although one can hardly imagine political environments as different as Dutch cities, on the one hand, and cities in the San Francisco Bay area, on the other hand, Irwin's comparison of Dutch and American city councilmembers highlights the possibilities of what has come to be called a "most-different-systems" research design by demonstrating the impact of different recruitment mechanisms on otherwise relatively similar elites. This study confirms the tenet that to do comparison across nations is to compare what is comparable rather than to camouflage non-comparables in esoteric nomenclature (as in some structural-functional formulations) so abstract as to obscure just what it is that is or is not being compared.

There will surely be the critical charge that this collection is a "non-book," as are so many other symposia of similar design. The trouble with this criticism is that it is so easy to make and that it is so often made. But at issue is not really the diversity of representations of reality in a collective volume such as this but the diversity of the reality itself. That this volume is not "representative" of the diverse reality in recruitment practices across polities we take for granted; but insofar as it approximates diversity we need not be apologetic. For, in fact, this volume also displays a conspicuous skewness in the distribution of subjects of investigation which is probably symptomatic of a substantively relevant focus of interest: The last three chapters are explicitly or implicitly concerned with crisis recruitment and its impact on the composition of elites, their attitudes and behavior.

The concept of crisis recruitment and relevant empirical observations are explicit in "Crisis Recruitment and the Political Involvement of Local Elites" (Chapter 8) by Sidney Tarrow and V. Lamonte Smith. In their genuinely comparative analysis of recruitment among French and Italian local elites, Tarrow and Smith apply a kind of generational cohort analysis that has been all too rare in political science. Equally admirable is their self-conscious reliance on three models of the polity which they characterize as subcultural model, exchange model, and institutional constraints model. Guided by these models, Tarrow and Smith are able to make sense of differences in the conduct of Italian and French crisis- and noncrisis-recruited elites and, at the same time, to draw cross-level inferences from individual to systemic behavior that would otherwise escape the analytic net.

Crisis recruitment is less a characteristic of the German elites reported on by Werner Kaltefleiter in "The Recruitment Market of the German Political Elite" (Chapter 9) than it is of their parents, most of whom must have been of political age during the years of Weimar (1918-1932) and Hitler (1933-1945). Given these periods—and especially the latter—we find it rather unconvincing that, as Kaltefleiter reports, "In the perception of the present elite, there was no significant sympathy for National Socialism among their parents." One must surely doubt the accuracy of the respondents in recollecting their parents' political orientations. It is, of course, impossible to say whether some of the respondents were lying outright, conveniently forgetful, inadvertently mis-recollecting, or simply not knowledgeable about their parents' political orientations. The research dilemma revealed here is common to much survey research that relies on recollections. On the other hand, in tracing the career paths of the German elite across different recruitment sectors Kaltefleiter can rely not only on more trustworthy data but is also able to make a significant contribution by using the interchange ratio among the different sectors to divide them into "elite sellers," "elite buyers," and "self-sufficient systems."

The hazards of survey research are absent from Michael King's and Lester Seligman's "Critical Elections, Congressional Recruitment and Public Policy" (Chapter 10) which relates electoral outcomes over a period of more than eighty years to data about congressional careers. By doing so, King and Seligman make a contribution both to the theory of elections and to the theory of political recruitment. What makes a critical election critical is not just some new realignment of voters but also the emergence of new leadership and subsequent changes in public policy. What makes possible the circulation of the elite is, of course, precisely that realignment of the voters that electoral theory seeks to explain. Although the causal sequence in the election-recruitment-policy series of events is far from clear, King and Seligman have made a most important contribution to the linkage of electoral and recruitment theory.

Since the concept of crisis-recruitment implies that the processes of elite transformation are perceived as dependent variables, crisis recruitment provides the student of elites with an almost unique quasi-experimental design in which he or she can test hypotheses relating the various stages of recruitment to the sociopolitical environment both under crisis conditions and under those prevailing in the pre-crisis situation. Furthermore, the student can study the effects of such elite transformations on attitudes, behavior, and policy. These effects complete the cycle in the function of recruitment as a reciprocal link between society and polity. One of the issues raised but not resolved by the research reported here is the question of whether crisis recruitment has only a short-term or also a long-term impact on crisis recruited cohorts. To the extent that inferences can be made from a comparison of only three studies which inquire into different aspects of recruitment, it seems that differences in political structures and sociopolitical environments are at least as important as the nature and resolution of a crisis in determining differences between patterns of change in the composition and performance of elites. This inference, however, may be merely one way of acknowledging the scarcity of guiding hypotheses that could be tested across nations. We believe these studies have contributed important elements for the development of such hypotheses.

One of the fundamental human needs in society is the need for a modicum of predictability in the behavior of others. For this purpose, constitutions have been written, laws enacted, courts established, and leaders elected, appointed, or otherwise accepted to implement an expected pattern of predictability. The patterns and rules of eligibility and selection in the recruitment of these leaders also determine, in the last analysis, their responsiveness and accountability for the manner and the degree to which this expectation has been fulfilled. At the time of writing, if we are to believe opinion pollsters in the largest and ideologically most committed democracy, the United States, only a small percentage of the citizenry have confidence in the ability of the political elites to fulfill their task. This is likely to be the single most dramatic crisis in the trust in public officials that has been documented so far. To the political scientist, this is a crisis in the performance of the recruitment function. If a modicum of predictability is to prevail, we expect that in the near future both practitioners and students will devote far more attention to recruitment than they have in the past.

Heinz Eulau
Moshe M. Czudnowski

November 7, 1975

Chapter 1

ELITE ANALYSIS AND DEMOCRATIC THEORY:
THE CONTRIBUTION OF HAROLD D. LASSWELL

HEINZ EULAU

Stanford University

Discontinuity in scientific development is a chronic curse of the social studies. No model of knowledge-making in the social sciences can therefore bypass the problem of discontinuity—the apparently immutable circumstance that yesteryear's ideas or findings are all too often forgotten or neglected, only to be rediscovered in innocence and at considerable cost. This explains, perhaps, why Thomas Kuhn's theory of "scientific revolutions" has been so popular among at least some, and usually younger, social scientists.[1] Because the intellectual memory is short or, as I have reason to believe, the homework has not always been properly done, what is only rediscovery rather than discovery is taken as an indication that "normal science" is in crisis, and that some fundamental change in "scientific paradigm" is just around the corner. When, some years ago, David Easton announced a "new revolution in political science," he not only invoked the authority of Kuhn's theory but also ignored Harold Lasswell and those in the Lasswellian mode who for thirty years prior to the new revelation had labored in the Augean stable of policy science.[2] But Kuhn's is only a theory that may or may not explain scientific development in the natural and physical disciplines; whether it "fits" the social sciences remains an open question.[3]

A plausible model of development in the study of man and society is not linear, nor cyclical, nor cataclysmic. It is spiral. Intellectual development in the social sciences seems to resemble the roller coaster—there are ups and downs and levels, except that beginnings are difficult to pinpoint and ends are not in sight. William Bennett Munro put it this way:

History never repeats itself. Or history always repeats itself. Both these assertions are half true, half false. The course of history does not run in cycles on a plane surface. It does not bring us back to where we were before. Rather it follows the windings of a spiral, up or down. We come back to what looks like the same place, but we are on a higher or a lower level.[4]

A case in point is the reception of elite analysis in the United States. One opens a recent book on the theory of elites and searches in vain for the name of Harold D. Lasswell in the "Name Index" or the "Selected Bibliography."[5] How can it be? Is it an oversight? Is it poor scholarship? Is it willful neglect? It is none of these things. Rather, it seems to be something that is "built in" the social sciences—the curse of discontinuity.

I cannot recall hearing about "elites" in my college courses in political science, back in the thirties; and while I would not want to say, without further study, that the term was never used before 1935 or so in the American literature on politics, I am quite sure that it would have been rarely used. This is not to say that the phenomena to which the term refers were not investigated. But if one goes, for instance, to the writings of Walter Lippmann, the American political theorist who perhaps more than any other was sensitive to the differentiation between elite and mass, and to the problematics this differentiation creates for democracy, one does not encounter the term.[6] Harold Lasswell's use of the elite concept in his early writings was, therefore, quite novel. Indeed, it meant the reception of elite analysis, long a preoccupation of European social scientists, in the United States.

THE METHODOLOGICAL STANCE

Extracting Lasswell's conception of elite from the corpus of his writings involves the danger of distortion, and there have been such distortions. I shall not claim immunity if my interpretation is judged deficient, but I offer three points of circumspection. In the first place, Lasswell's uses of the elite concept are embedded in an extraordinarily complex vision of politics so that extraction is risky. In this vision, the outstanding events of modern world history—those "world revolutions" like the French of 1789 or the Russian of 1917 whose effects pervade space and time, or the "skill revolution" of our own time—are linked to the most intimate details in the psychological make-up and life experiences of individual actors, elites and masses alike. If one reads with care the work in which Lasswell spelled out this vision, *World Politics and Personal Insecurity*,[7] one is sensitized to the easy possibility of vulgarization. For instance, by making Lasswell's elite analysis the core of a critique that failed to comprehend the total vision, David Easton could characterize Lasswell's intellectual development as having moved from an "elitist amoral phase" to a "decisional moral phase."[8] However, a much harsher critic, Robert Horwitz, comes to the opposite conclusion in characterizing Lasswell's early thought as "positive liberalism."[9] Whatever the truth, and I am inclined in this connection to side with Horwitz rather than Easton, it is clear that in concentrating on Lasswell's elite analysis out of the total intellectual context of his work one is likely to misunderstand it.

Second, although Lasswell's theoretical framework from his earliest writings to his latest has remained basically unchanged, it has also undergone a variety of elaborations themselves so intertwined that it is difficult to specify what he "really means" at any one time. The resultant ambiguity is something that Lasswell has in common with the two social theorists who more than any others shaped his thinking, Marx and Freud. The strategy of unravelling intellectual ambiguity cannot be simple exegesis of successive elaborations, on the assumption that what is said later somehow supervenes or supplements what has been said earlier. Rather, the appropriate strategy of dealing with ambiguity is to move both forward and backward simultaneously—to seek understanding of what was said earlier in terms of what is said later, and to interpret what is said later in light of what was said earlier. The task, then, is plausible reconstruction of the analysis as a whole as it might have been undertaken if omniscience were human. This type of integrative reconstruction is all the more necessary because Lasswell's style and language are rarely conducive to immediate comprehension.

Finally, there are Lasswell's own guidelines for the analysis of political phenomena. These guidelines are likely to befuddle the reader who comes to his work for the first time, but I want to quote a relevant passage because it is an economical way to present his overall approach and style:

> The statements which have been offered about the composition of the elite and their methods have been developed in connection with the application of two supplementary modes of analysis and attitudes of mind to the problem of correct self-orientation in the all-embracing continuum in which we find our unfolding way. Both developmental and equilibrium modes of analysis, and contemplative and manipulative attitudes of approach, are comprehended within the configurative method of political orientation. The provisional findings of the present will be constantly reconsidered in the light of new details about the past, and new emergents through the future.[10]

Let me translate this passage into my own language: "To understand something ('correct self-orientation') like the composition of the elite and their methods over time ('the all-embracing continuum in which we find our unfolding way'), it is necessary to look at past, present and future ('developmental analysis') and the conditions under which causes have effects ('equilibrium analysis'); it is also important to be both an objective and disinterested observer ('contemplative attitude') and to take the standpoint of an activist and purposive participant ('manipulative attitude'). This multifaceted approach is called the configurative method. Moreover, what we know of the present is provisional and subject to revision as more is learned about the past, and as new phenomena occur in a future that is not as yet known ('new emergents through the future')."[11]

Given Lasswell's unorthodox strategy of inquiry, systematic reconstruction of his analysis that does not follow his guidelines is likely to be truncated. Yet, I see no alternative if what Lasswell has to say about elite phenomena is to be absorbed into a constantly emergent political science. For, as Lasswell himself might say, his approach, though that of a master, is only one event in the manifold of intellectual events that constitute the science of politics.

THE RESEARCH CONTEXT

The not uncommon but, as I already suggested, false identification of Lasswell as an "elitist," whatever this might mean, seems to stem in large part from the attention given to his highly succinct *Politics: Who Gets What, When, How?* (1936) rather than to the discursive *World Politics and Personal Insecurity* (1935). However, it is the earlier work rather than the later that harnesses Lasswell's approach as a whole, and that sets the agenda for a life time of scholarship. *Politics* is at best a primer, while *World Politics* is a treatise. And whereas the primer oversimplifies, the treatise overcomplicates.

Comparing the opening sentences of the two books is revealing. The first chapter of *Politics* is entitled "Elite" and opens with the direct and provocative assertion that "the study of politics is the study of influence and the influential."[12] By way of contrast, the first chapter of *World Politics* is called "The Configurative Analysis of the World Value Pyramids," and the first sentence states that "political analysis is the study of changes in the shape and composition of the value patterns of society."[13] If a reading of *Politics* gives the impression that Lasswell is fascinated by the elite phenomenon as such, the impression is not altogether unfounded. But whatever the bias of this fascination, the elite concept is only a tool in the analysis of world politics which "implies the consideration of the shape and composition of the value patterns of mankind as a whole."[14] It is this task—"to describe and explain the 'world revolution of our time,' " as Lasswell puts it later [15]—that "necessitates the comparison of world elites in terms of social origins, special skills, personal traits, subjective attitudes, and sustaining assets, such as symbols, goods, and violence."[16]

In a more mundane research context, the social characteristics of elites and their governing strategies are treated, in the language of statistical science, as "independent" variables; they are assumed to explain those changes in values (the "dependent" variables) from which, in turn, the transformation of world revolutionary patterns can be inferred. This is not to say that changes in elites might not also be considered worthy of explanation as an intrinsic interest. "Large changes in the composition of the elite," Lasswell notes, "may be treated as functions of large changes in the prevailing division of labor; hence, through any time section, the probability of elite alterations will be increased if the processes of production have notably altered."[17] Indeed, *The Comparative Study of Elites* (1952), introducing the empirical elite studies undertaken by project RADIR, [18] suggests various hypotheses "to explain the changes of elite structure that can be discerned in our period." [19] But this is a secondary objective. Rather, "by learning the nature of the elite, we learn much about the nature of society. Changes in the elite structure are . . . indexes of revolution. By determining what is happening to the elites of societies around the globe, therefore, we can test the underlying hypothesis . . . that a 'world revolution is under way during our epoch.' "[20]

Elite analysis is for Lasswell an attractive research strategy not because he holds some preconceived notions about elites as either virtuous or vicious, but because he is interested in the *distribution* of values in society. Although crisp statements in *Politics* like "the influential are those who get most of what there is to get," or "those who get the most are *elite*; the rest are *mass*," [21] have a tantalizing and almost doctrinaire ring, no dogmatic assumptions are made. The existence of elites that grab most of what there is to grab is not the starting point; rather, the starting point is the differential distribution of multiple values in the community that is implicit is the structure of elites and the functions they perform. Unless one recognizes and accepts Lasswell's research approach for what it is—explicitly naturalistic and strictly heuristic—it is impossible to understand his (I think successful) reconciliation of elite notions with assumptions about democracy.

Unlike his European predecessors or some of his American successors, Lasswell does not praise or condemn the formation and existence of elites. There is no doubt, and Robert Horwitz has amply demonstrated this, that Lasswell's own preferences, his posture of scientific disinterestedness notwithstanding, have always been in favor of a wide sharing of those values that a community has to distribute among its people. But Lasswell does not permit these preferences to bias his naturalistic bent of seeing things as they are. Although differentiation in social and political structures may be so self-evident as to be accepted as axiomatic, it is always something to be investigated rather than presupposed: "The division into elite and mass can be made wherever there are any differences—whether as to weight, scope, or domain—in the amount of power enjoyed by various persons in the group. Nothing more is presupposed by the concept as here defined than the existence of some such difference."[22]

Commenting on elite studies some thirty years after his own first formulation, Lasswell is both generous, as he always is in regard to the work of others, and yet critical: "Contemporary studies of elite phenomena in politics are enormously diversified in conception and procedure. The field has abounding intellectual vigor, despite, or because of, its conspicuous lack of elegant intellectual unity."[23] What Lasswell finds lacking in the study of elites is some broad frame of reference that can only be had by the elaboration of developmental constructs, like his own construct of the "garrison state," against which changes in the recruitment and circulation of elites can be assessed. And because it is the frame of reference as defined by a developmental construct rather than elite phenomena as such that gives meaning to political analysis, Lasswell's formal definition of political elite, like Pareto's, can be unashamedly tautological: "What is said, in effect, is that every people is ruled—by rulers."[24] The definition makes sense only in the broad research context envisaged for the study of world revolutionary transformations; out of this context, it has no meaning at all. Yet, the characterization of Lasswell as an "elitist" commits precisely the error of non-contextuality.[25]

THE DISTRIBUTIVE APPROACH

If, within the Lasswellian research context, the existence of rulers and ruled is treated as axiomatic, the existence of particular types of elite is not. What elites exist is a matter of inquiry into the distribution of values in a society. It is the shape of the curves describing the distribution that expresses various social structures. Although Lasswell originally assumes, and demonstrates, that in most societies "the pattern of any value resembles a pyramid,"[26] his approach does not preclude the discovery of alternative patterns in the distribution of values:

> It should be clear that nothing inherent in the geometry of power restricts power to the pyramid. . . . When effective participation is widely dispersed it is more accurate to redraw the pyramid into a squat figure resembling a "flattop" or a western "mesa." The group at the very bottom of the heap may be small, rather than large, so that the bottom of the pryamid must be pinched together and the whole figure redrawn nearer to the shape of a carrot. In any case the significant point is that the elite patterns are to be discovered by research and not settled by arbitrary definition.[27]

However, Lasswell does not pursue the logic of this observation. If the distribution of a given value is no longer pyramidical or otherwise asymmetrical but approximates a plane, what has disappeared is precisely that "inequality of distance" which is a necessary condition of elite formation.[28] The distribution of power, of course, is never likely to be egalitarian in any absolute sense, for then the only possible decision rule in a society would have to be unanimity, something hardly feasible except in very small face-to-face groups. In other words, equality stops short of the leveling of power and is constrained by what Dahrendorf calls "the structural limit of equality."[29]

Whatever the shape of the distribution, the important point is that the operational definition of elite, in contrast to a nominal definition, treats the values that give rise to social differentiation as what in statistics are called "continuous variables." Being continuous variables, values permit of varying cutting points by which to classify those who get more and those who get less of what there is to get. Of course, some values, like wealth or education, are easier to measure than values like power or respect, but the latter are in principle measurable. In any case, the cutting points needed for identifying an elite or other social strata are given by the distribution of values in a population, but they are not absolutely dictated by the distribution. Even if the distribution index is relatively low—that is, the resultant social structure is highly pyramidical—it still remains a matter of analytic judgment where the cutting points are made, and that judgment in turn is made in terms of some primitive assumptions that should be plausible. The conceptual distinction Lasswell makes between elite and "rank and file" (in *World Politics*) or between elite and "mass" (in *Politics*) may seem arbitrary. But there is nothing inherent in the distributive approach to the discovery of social or political structures that requires this kind of dichotomized treatment. Indeed, Lasswell at times speaks of a trichotomized power structure in which "the elite are those with most power in the group; the mid-elite, those with less power; the mass, least power.[30] What is significant in the distributive approach to social differentiation is that it removes the false dualism that the use of an elite terminology seems to postulate.

There are, of course, as many social structures as there are values to be distributed in a society and, consequently, as many elites. In his earliest work, Lasswell introduces safety, income, and deference as "representative values." By "representative," Lasswell simply means that these values are not exclusive. Political analysis "could make use of other combinations, and the resulting elite comparisons would differ."[31] Indeed, the list was gradually expanded. The RADIR project includes power, respect, well-being, and safety. The final list is composed of eight values classified in two sets: "deference values" including power, respect, rectitude, and affection; and "welfare values" including well-being, wealth, skill, and enlightenment.[32] Presumably Lasswell considers these values as universal, though not all of them may be available for distribution in every society. But neither the composition of the list nor its universality is particularly important. What is important is that Lasswell's approach to elite analysis is not only distributive but also pluralistic. Whatever the cutting points made for the purpose of identifying the elite as "those who get the most" of any *one* value, it is the plurality of values to be distributed that precludes a single elite from getting the lion's share of *all* values:

It is plain, however, that no simple index can be profitably used to measure influence and the influential. One aspect of influence is the relative sharing of values. *An elite of deference is not necessarily an elite of safety*. . . . Whatever the list, the items may be differently combined, thus reaching different results to correspond to varying judgments of *the* elite. New results may be obtained by defining influence in other terms than relative share of values. The term may be used to indicate a judgment of how values *might* be influenced if there were conflicts about them. Thus financial capitalists may be judged to be stronger or weaker than industrial capitalists in case of a hypothetical collision.[33]

An elite, then, is not some reified entity, but a social formation that changes as new value criteria are applied in order to identify it:

From analysis, then, we can expect no static certainty. It is a constant process of reexamination which brings new aspects of the world into the focus of critical attention. The unifying frame of reference for the special student of politics is the rich and variable meaning of "influence and the influential," "power and the powerful."[34]

Elites, for Lasswell, are not monolithic structures that take on a life of their own—in the imagination of some a conspiratorial life; rather, they are kaleidoscopic formations in constant flux whose identity cannot be taken for granted but is subject to incessant discovery.

Pluralism as a way of looking at social and political change has been criticized as tending to be conservative and oriented toward the status quo. Implicit in this criticism is the presupposition that only the *distribution* of values matters, and that only evidence of redistribution of values in favor of those who get less or least of what there is to get can be accepted as indicative of "progressive" social change. Lasswell's multivariate approach suggests that redistribution is not the only avenue of social change and may, in fact, be the conservative way. Social change may occur, and with it a change in the recruitment and composition of elites, if one or several values are replaced by others over time. In other words, the evaluation of values is itself not immutable, and different types of value are likely to be differentially valued as a result of cultural and technological changes. The erosion of one value and its replacement by another in the scheme of values is probably more indicative of fundamental social change than is the redistribution of current values. For instance, the replacement of land by capital as an indicator of status, or the incipient replacement of financial property by management skill may usher in more fundamental shifts in the composition of elites than the redistribution of land or capital.[35]

ELITE FORMATION

The value-distributive approach to the identification of elites would seem to yield only statistical or categoric groupings of those who get most of what there is to get. As categoric groups, elites and their behavior can only be investigated at the micro level of the individual or at the macro level of the statistical aggregate. Yet, clearly, social theorists think of elites as something more than aggregates of individuals. They think of them as interactive formations or "real groups." If one were to limit the identification of elites to the distribution of individuals on different values alone, one would have to conclude that any one person's position in different value hierarchies is a sufficient condition of elite status. Obviously, more is involved when one speaks of elites.

Moreover, there are operational obstacles that make it difficult to pursue the value-distributive approach in practice. While it is feasible to determine any one person's location on different values in relatively small groups,[36] it is practically impossible to do so in a population of millions. It is for this reason that most elite analysts invariably fall back on a "positional approach," on the assumption that those in conventionally agreed-on high-status positions do indeed constitute *the* elite. For these persons—say, cabinet ministers, legislative leaders, heads of corporations, Nobel Prize winners, university presidents, symphony conductors, high labor union officials, popular novelists, and so on—are easy to identify. No wonder, then, that when Lasswell has to face the task of empirical research, he is forced to adopt a positional approach: "Since the true decision-makers are not necessarily known at the beginning of research the investigator can select government in the conventional sense as a convenient starting point."[37] Even though the procedure is not theoretically elegant, it is probably the only procedure open to those who reject a simplistic reputational approach to the identification of elites.[38] There is no guarantee, of course, that there may not be elites whom the positional approach will miss. It must be supplemented, therefore, by a strategy of cumulative approximation that may possibly round out the picture of elite formation. Lasswell provides some suggestive leads.

In the first place, a person's presumptive location in various value hierarchies is a necessary but certainly not a sufficient condition of elite status. What similar location facilitates is interaction as a further condition for elite formation. This is not to say that an elite—say, a ruling elite—is a cohesive group. But similarity of position in the distributive scheme of things is fair presumptive evidence that there will be contact at least among those who give leadership in a given society. Whether contact and interaction actually occur is, of course, an empirical matter that is yet to be determined. But speaking of "the official elite," Lasswell describes it as

usually bound by ties of upbringing and specific advantage to the prevailing property system, and the exercise of official discretion follows the general pattern appropriate to the time and place. Since the official, propertied, and cultured elites are
partially coincident, ties of family association and friendship operate selectively
upon the versions of reality which are circulated among them. People of "standing"
who are "accepted" are listened to, with little attention paid to the possibility that
their behavior may be governed by the conscious pursuit of material advantage, or
by insidious unconscious adaptation to courses of action which advance material
interests.[39]

Lasswell continues suggesting that "this sort of inter-relationship can be given
flesh and blood by means of specific instances," but he is careful to point out
that "it is extraordinarily difficult to work out a valid method of sampling the
relative intensity of such influence in numerous situations."[40] In another
connection, speaking of the intellectual elite, he writes:

> Those who declare that they want truth and are indifferent to control may, indeed,
> get truth; they are bound to have some control. *The mere fact of persisting in a net-
> work of interpersonal relations* means that one finds a place in, and partly modifies
> the shape and composition of the current value pyramid, whether one keeps this in
> mind or not.[41]

One may question whether these formulations solve the problem of identifying
elites and specifying their functions. Indeed, one may ask whether the elite
concept is useful in social and political analysis. Lasswell evidently thought so
when introducing it into American political science, for he believed that "the elite
concept fills a blank in the language of science and policy."[42] The blank filled
is the absence of a term "to cover both leadership and the strata of society from
which leaders usually come."[43] As an example, Lasswell mentions Winston
Churchill, clearly a "leader" even when not in office: "Nevertheless, even when
too young to take part in public affairs, Churchill belonged to the political elite
of his country, since he was born into one of the ruling families."[44]

The justification is not very convincing. "Elite" evidently refers not only to
"leaders" but also to what Prewitt calls "the pool of eligibles" from which
leaders are recruited.[45] But the pool of eligibles is at best a categoric grouping
in the distribution of values and not necessarily an interactive unit, though
belonging to the pool opens up possibilities of contact in the recruitment process
to positions of leadership. Covering both "leadership" and "the strata of society
from which leaders usually come" by the concept of elite should lead to the
conclusion that because not all eligibles can enter the leadership, there is an elite
within the elite, and that is precisely where Lasswell seems to come out. If, in the
political realm for instance, the rulers are "the most active and powerful
members of the elite,"[46] they are surely an elite within an elite, and the elite
concept yields little by way of explanatory power.

Lasswell's paradigmatic exposition in *Power and Society* is not very helpful. In part this is due to the frequently indiscriminate use of terms like "leaders," "rulers," "most powerful," "ruling class," and so on. For instance, having characterized the "rulers" as "the most active and powerful members of the elite," reference is made in the next sentence to "the ruling class" as "the effective constituency of the rulers."[47] In other words, elite is now synonymous with ruling class. Both rulers and ruling class are elite because, by definition, both get most of what there is to get, but rulers get evidently more (of power, for instance) than the ruling class from which they are recruited and which is their effective constituency. But, by definition also, if rulers alone are elite, the pool of eligibles—the strata from which rulers come—cannot be elite, at least if the original definition is to hold. If it cannot hold, the elite concept would seem to be expendable in social and political analysis.

If elite-relevant and class-relevant terms are treated as interchangeable, as Lasswell's discussion at times would seem to suggest, the heuristic quality of either set of concepts is lost. This is inevitable if both elite and class formulations are made in terms of the prevailing distribution of values. Referring to "ruling class," for instance, Lasswell writes: "But the definition is of a social class, that is, a class specified with regard to both welfare and deference values. It enjoys a preferential share not only of power but of the other values as well."[48] In other words, the same method is used to differentiate between elite and mass, on the one hand, and between social classes, on the other hand. Yet, Lasswell is concerned with the question of how a class, any class, may become a ruling class:

> In the preceding section the hypothesis was formulated that a class *becomes* a ruling class in proportion to its importance in the production of the important values. In the converse direction, the elite strengthens predispositions favorable to the value on which its power is based.[49]

If it is to be explained how a class rises to power status in a society so that it may be considered an elite or ruling class, it would seem necessary to discriminate between class terms of discourse and elite terms by way of different operations and indicators. Indeed, elsewhere Lasswell distinguishes very clearly between elite and class concepts in order to compare different elites in terms of their class bases and to explain the replacement of elites, notably in revolutionary situations. For this purpose, class is not defined in terms of the distribution of values but rather as a "major social group of similar function, status, and outlook."[50] A revolution, in turn, is characterized as "a shift in the class composition of elites."[51] By calling attention to the class origins of elites, it is possible to say whether the circulation of elites has been revolutionary—whether there has not only been a redistribution of values but also a substitution of one value or more by another value or several in the valuational scheme of things of a society. Put differently, in observing the changing social composition of elites it is possible to explain social and political change. The obverse—namely, that revolutionary change occasioned by the replacement of one ruling class by another (say, of the bourgeoisie by the proletariat, or of capitalists by technocrats) brings about a change in the elite structure is not really very interesting—for it is a foregone conclusion given the transformation in the class basis of society.

Social stratification in conventional class terms is not the sole basis of elite formation. Although Lasswell considers "skill" as one of the values by which an elite can be identified, he evidently accepts different *types* of skill—skill in fighting, skill in organization, skill in interpersonal relations, skill in symbol manipulation, skill in bargaining, and so on—as autonomous bases of elite formation. Like class, skill is a multidimensional phenomenon that varies in response to societal requirements over time. It is evidence of Lasswell's high degree of imaginitive sensitivity to social transformation that he was one of the first social scientists to suggest that skill may be the most pervasive and critical value in the emerging present and future—what we now call post-industrial or technetronic society.[52] And if this is so, classes in the conventional sense may well be replaced by "skill groups" as fundamental social phenomena.[53] Elites will be recruited from those skill groups whose expertise is in special demand at a particular time to meet the increasingly technical problems of modern society.

Other bases of elite formation suggested by Lasswell are more psychological than sociological in character. Picking up his interest in clinical psychology, he suggests that elites can be grounded in personality types because some such types "are predisposed by nature and by early nurture to find satisfaction in playing particular roles on the stage of politics."[54] Finally, what he calls "attitude groups" can serve as bases of influence and movement into elite positions: "The world is divided among those who are influential on the basis of shared symbols of loyalty to nation, class, occupation, person."[55] But, more important, these bases of elite formation—class, skill, personality, and attitude groups—are not mutually exclusive and can cut across each other, and the various bases may exist without being fully developed:

> At any given time the members of a skill or class group may not have risen to full skill or class consciousness. Although an objective observer may be able to consider the meaning of events for their relative success or failure, the members of the skill or class group may talk the language of patriotism, and have no common symbol of class or skill.[56]

ELITE ANALYSIS AND DEMOCRACY: ACCOUNTABILITY

The axiom of the inevitable co-existence of rulers and ruled creates intellectual problems for theories of democracy even in the distributive and pluralistic haven of Lasswell's analysis. There are, of course, two "easy" solutions for removing the evident contradiction between the ineluctable fact of rulership and various requisites of democratic governance. One of these solutions is simply to deny the possibility of democracy. Although Sorel, Pareto, and even Mosca have been occasionally interpreted as coming to this conclusion, it is a misconception of their analytic intentions. Only Michels probably drew this ultimate inference.[57] The other solution, proposed by Easton, is to eliminate the term "elite" from the vocabulary of political science.[58] Easton's recommendation was made almost twenty-five years ago, but elite terminology and elite analysis flourish more than ever. It is doubtful that the term's elimination would remove the conceptual and practical problems it creates for thinking about democratic government in the age of the skill revolution.[59] The problems with which elite analysis deals will not go away simply because the term is eliminated. On the contrary, as Suzanne Keller suggests,

> Because of the characteristics of industrial societies, the social significance of elites is growing, as is the difference between them and ruling classes. One of the striking trends in these societies is not, as many would suppose, toward a decline of elite groups, but toward their proliferation, greater variety, and more extensive powers.[60]

Not the least difficult problem for the elite approach to democracy stems from the tension between the shorthand language of theoretical discourse and the longhand language of empirical analysis. Because Lasswell is committed to the longhand language of empiricism, but because theorizing is necessarily shorthand, the process of translating empirically viable formulations into the abstract language of theory is hazardous. For instance, as already hinted, Lasswell injects the notion of a "mid-elite" to characterize those with "less power" than the elite and "more power" than the mass. Even this language, introduced for the purpose of theorizing, is essentially shorthand: It barely disguises the implicitly continuous character of the phenomenon to which the terms elite, mid-elite, and mass refer. Yet, it is precisely at the intersection of where the "many" become "few," and where the "few" become "many," that the politically crucial issue of democracy—the distribution and control of power—remains unresolved.

To say that "power" is one of the most bewildering concepts in the language of the social sciences has become trite. It is a concept which, as James G. March concludes, "gives us surprisingly little purchase in reasonable models of complex systems of social choice."[61] Yet, it is a concept political science can evidently not do without. The phenomena to which the concept refers are manifold and all too visible. In the decades in which Lasswell evolved his orientation to politics, power was a pervasive feature of national and international politics. His attempt to relate the assumptions and findings of elite analysis to a conception of democracy is predicated on the special use he makes of the concept of power.

Lasswell's early definition of power is an adaptation of Max Weber's formulation to the task of personality analysis: "The essence of power is understood to be the capacity, and usually the will, to impose one's own values as permanent or transitory motives upon others."[62] In *Politics* and *World Politics*, the concept of power is used only incidentally and remains undefined: "The unifying frame of reference for the special student of politics is the rich and variable meaning of 'influence and the influential,' 'power and the power-ful' "[63] Lasswell does, however, introduce the notion of "relative sharing" of values as the critical test for discriminating between elite and mass. On the one hand, "influence is determined on the basis of shares in the values which are chosen for purposes of analysis. . . . No single index is wholly satisfactory as a gauge of influence, but situations may be clarified by the successive application of specific standards."[64] On the other hand, concentrating "upon the influential does not imply the neglect of the total distribution of values throughout the community. *It is impossible to locate the few without considering the many*."[65] Assuming that power is a value that can be operationalized and measured independently of the influence an elite may have as a result of its control over other values, the notion of power-sharing calls attention to the need for measuring the degree of power available to the elite and to the mass. The problem of democracy is to determine how much power with respect to control over other values is to be shared by the elite and how much by the mass, keeping in mind that elite and mass are used as relative terms to characterize differentiation along what in reality is a continuum. The notion that power is shared rather than exclusively allocated also calls attention to the bondedness of those who share more or less— elite and mass. If power were not divisible, if politics were a zero-sum power struggle, and if all power were allocated to the elite, democracy would be impossible. The distributive and relational aspects of power are crucial properties of democratic organization:

> Because of organization, power cannot be conceived as a unilateral relationship. Both the subject (READ: ruled) and power groups (READ: elites) participate in the making of decisions, though with different weights. The distinction between them is relative, being based on the comparatively greater power in the hands of one group; it is not a distinction between the group having all the power and the group having none.[66]

At the theoretical (rather than operational) level of discourse, Lasswell conceives of elite and mass as *role concepts* rather than as status or categorical concepts. While the empirical discovery of elite and mass involves either the positions they occupy in the institutional realm or their location in the hierarchies of societal values, elite and mass now appear to be "role partners" neither of whom can do without the other. Role is eminently a linkage concept that calls attention to the nature of the relationship of, minimally, two persons rather than to their categoric or idiosyncratic attributes.[67] It is therefore a concept that is theoretically useful for understanding the nature of the elite-mass relationship in a democracy. The view of elite and mass as role partners explains, I think, why Lasswell can conclude, quite logically, that the axiom "every people is ruled—by rulers" does not conflict with the democratic postulate of power sharing:

> The point is important in the light of the common supposition that to put the concept of elite to the fore in political science is to deny from the outset the possibility of democratic institutions. But whether a social structure is democratic depends not on whether or not there is an elite, but on the relations of the elite to the mass—how it is recruited and how it exercises its power.[68]

Once attention is focused on the *relationship* between elite and mass, the *number* of the few who govern the many is immaterial for it "does not settle the question of degree of democracy"; and, moreover, "a society may be democratic and express itself through a small leadership." Instead, *"the key question turns on accountability."*[69]

This is hardly a startling statement, were it not for Lasswell's coupling of accountability and influence: "To be accountable is to be influenced."[70] Although Lasswell, at this point of the discussion, simply lists the familiar means of democratic rule like freedom of organization, free elections, and so on, it is the logic implicit in his linking accountability and influence that is noteworthy. All of the constitutional methods of democracy are of no avail in ensuring accountability unless the rulers can in fact be influenced. But they cannot be influenced unless those to whom they are to be accountable have at least some share in power. A democratic government, then,

> can be defined in terms of shared power. . . . What are the limits within which sharing may vary in a government or in a society that is entitled to be called "democratic"? With respect to power, we may stipulate that a democratic government authorizes majority participation in the making of important decisions. . . . The majority must participate actively.[71]

If rulers and ruled are linked in a system of accountability, and if accountability is predicated on a sufficient sharing in power by the ruled, the cutting point in discriminating between elite and mass is just the point where, in the distribution of power, any increment of power on one or the other side of the dividing line will make a significant difference. Yet, having defined power as "participation in the making of important decisions," Lasswell insists that "the extent of power sharing must be determined in every situation by research, since there is no universal pattern of power."[72] The theory defines a democratic polity as one in which the ruled share that minimum of power necessary to hold the rulers accountable, but the minimum cannot be theoretically deduced from the postulate of accountability. Put differently, the theory of accountability has low predictive potential. It stipulates that a political elite will be held accountable if, and only if, the mass has a sufficient share of power; but it cannot predict what precise amount of power sharing is needed for accountability to occur.

In Lasswell's theory, power sharing is nonequalitarian by definition, for by definition the rulers or elite have more power than the ruled. Democracy requires only that the mass share enough power to influence the rulers and thereby hold them accountable; equal power sharing is, therefore, not a necessary condition of democracy: "If political equality were defined so as to exclude the existence of an elite, the concept [of elite] would be vacuous."[73] By minimizing political equality in the conventional sense as a necessary condition of democracy, Lasswell opens himself up to the charge of "elitism." But any just reading of what he has to say about power sharing, accountability, and democracy, unbiased by preconceived notions about equality, suggests that his theory of democracy, operational difficulties notwithstanding, probably more approximates real-life conditions in complex modern societies than do the utopian theories of democracy that are regurgitated so much that they sound like self-evident truths which they conspicuously are not. In pointing to the relationship between accountability and the distribution of influence, Lasswell raises a sophisticated question that remains to be answered in contemporary research on the role of elites in a democracy.[74]

ELITE ANALYSIS AND DEMOCRACY: RECRUITMENT

Accountability as a means of democratic control is not sufficient to close the gap between rulers and ruled because its corollary, power, is not equally shared by elite and mass. But power sharing is not the only criterion of democracy. In a democratic commonwealth, Lasswell writes, "power is not only shared but subordinated to respect for the dignity of human personality."[75] Respect for the dignity of human personality as a value superior to power implies that precisely because in practice power cannot be equally shared by all, an effort must be made to make it possible for all to have access to positions of power even if equality in sharing power is impossible.

It is this normative view that directs Lasswell to elite recruitment as a critical aspect of democracy. "A rule is defined to be equalitarian, not in the degree to which *power* is equally distributed, but rather *access* to power. Power is never equally distributed: there is always an elite."[76] The principles of elite recruitment practiced in a society are important, then, because they may "provide equal opportunity for acquisition of power, or [because] they may severely restrict its acquisition in various ways."[77] Political equality is not a matter of equal power sharing but "a matter of equal eligibility to power status (of course, effective and not merely formal eligibility)."[78] In turn, presumably, equal eligibility to power status is predicated on equal access to the skills of rulership; only then is the goal of human dignity being approximated.

To meet the definition of democracy as a commonwealth that subordinates power to respect for human dignity, Lasswell requires that "leaders must be drawn from the community at large, rather than from a few social strata." The requirement seems clear enough, except that Lasswell does not indicate what he means by "community at large." And one cannot assume that he means "mass," though this interpretation is plausible. For he retains the notion of "elite" to designate "the social formation from which leaders are recruited." This formulation creates conceptual difficulties. Leaders are to be drawn from the "community at large, rather than from a few social strata," but the social formation from which they are in fact drawn constitutes an elite. Democratic leadership, Lasswell continues,

> is selected from a broad base and remains dependent upon the active support of the entire community. With few exceptions every adult is eligible to have as much of a hand in the decision-making process as he wants and for which he is successful in winning the assent of his fellow citizens. There is no monopoly of power in a ruling caste when such conditions prevail, and the whole community is a seedbed from which rulers and governors come. The elite of democracy ("the ruling class") is society-wide.[79]

It is difficult to interpret this formulation. It seems to hold that in a democracy "community at large" and "elite" are the same thing, and that the distinction between elite and mass is only applicable in political orders other than democracy.

Lasswell is sensitive to the possibility of this interpretation. He asserts, therefore, that "the distinction between leaders and the elite enables us to avoid the confusion that often arises when someone points out that government is always government by the few, whether carried on in the name of the *few* or the *one* or the *many*.[80]

He cites in this connection James Bryce's famous empirical observation:

> In all assemblies and groups and organized bodies of men, from a nation down to a committee of a club, direction and decisions rest in the hands of a small percentage, less and less in proportion to the larger size of the body, till in a great population it becomes an infinitessimally small proportion of the whole number. This is and always has been true of all forms of government, though in different degrees.

Lasswell argues that Bryce's proposition is correct if understood to mean that "government is always government by a few *leaders*"; but false if understood to mean that "government is always government by a highly restricted *elite*" (which would mean that "democracy is by definition impossible").[81]

The conceptual difficulty, however, does not lie in Bryce's alleged failure to distinguish between the governing few and the elite from which they are recruited; rather, it lies in Lasswell's broadening of the concept "elite" to include the "community at large." If Lasswell were correct in this connection, one might well recommend elimination of the term "elite" from the vocabulary of descriptive political science. However, Lasswell is not correct. I suspect that the trouble lies in Lasswell's ignoring the complexity of the recruitment *process* that, in a democracy, may enable persons at the bottom of the social structure to reach the "political elite" or what Lasswell elsewhere refers to as "the top power class."[82] This process, in turn, is not predicated on direct and equal access to power positions by the community at large as a *result* of recruitment, but on an "opportunity structure"[83] that makes it possible for members of the community at large to move into the "pool of eligibles" from which rulers are recruited. Now, this pool of eligibles is largely determined by societal requirements—the kind of persons needed to conduct a society's public affairs in a given stage of its development.

What values are cherished in a given society—power, respect, rectitude, affection, well-being, wealth, skill, or enlightenment—is clearly not unrelated to the kind of persons who are thought competent to direct society toward their maximization. That those called on to give leadership and direction also come to be the main beneficiaries of the social order is a highly probable consequence of their recruitment and should be a surprise only if it did not occur. But, over time, elites succeed each other as new values conducive to the satisfaction of societal needs come to the fore. The process of elite formation, then, is dictated by societal requirements for those with the "right" values and supportive skills and attitudes to move into positions of rulership. Elites as such are not "recruited" but *emerge* in the process of societal transformation as new values come to constitute the bases of power. The process of elite emergence is universal, though it may be facilitated or impeded by the prevailing opportunity structure. That structure is of course not neutral and is itself a function of the distribution of values at a given time. Democracy presumably differs from other forms of rule in that it seeks to reduce the bias inherent in the opportunity structure.

To recognize bias in the opportunity structure is the first step to its reduction. But "equal access" to positions of rulership can only mean that the value biases of the opportunity structure are not absolute barriers to elite recruitment. It cannot mean that every person has exactly the same probability of being recruited. For the very meaning of something being valued is that there is *more or less* of this "something" to go around. Given this axiomatic propostion, Lasswell's bothersome statement that "the elite of democracy ('the ruling class') is society-wide," can have no other *scientific* meaning but that the pool of eligibles for elite positions expands as bias in the opportunity structure is reduced through wider sharing of those particular values in terms of which an elite is constituted. To expect more is unrealistic. Lasswell's distributive-pluralistic approach to elite analysis provides the empirical foundations for a theory of democracy that is congenial to those who see the recruitment process as critical in linking rulers and ruled as well as closing the gap between them.

CONCLUSION

Any theory of political recruitment takes it as axiomatic, even if the axiom is not explicitly acknowledged, that elites seek to perpetuate themselves, their goals and their ways of doing things. This axiom of elite succession is as applicable to constitutionally oligarchic societies where political elites maintain themselves by arbitrary rule as to democratic societies were multiple elites compete for control of the policy-making process by mobilizing multiple electorates and seeking their support. Political elites are interested in having a hand in their own succession because, being policymakers, they are shaping the future, and because, as a corollary, they have a stake in the future. Political elites are necessarily interested in the maintenance and continuation of the policies that they have shaped, tried to shape, or still hope to shape. There are, of course, differences of degree among elites in this respect, but without this interest it would be absurd for an elite to be involved in the policy process. Indeed, without a long-term commitment to giving policy leadership and direction to a society, a political elite would lose its reason for being. If an elite were to take the position of *après nous le déluge,* it would lose its legitimacy and authority.

One can invert the axiom of elite succession and make it a theorem derived from system maintenance assumptions. By this reasoning, any political community, to remain a community, is predicated on a certain degree of continuity in its public policies. Radical shifts and changes in public policies will undermine the stability of the community; but as the notion of community involves the existence of stable relationships made possible by consistent public policies, the continuity of policies is a necessary condition for the maintenance of the community. As policies are made by elites, the self-perpetuation of political elites is a prerequisite of both policy continuity and community stability.

Both the behavioral and the functional formulations are plausible but not convincing. While they postulate elite self-perpetuation as a prerequisite of policy continuity, they cannot assert it as a necessary condition. It can be demonstrated that policy continuity may be secured by political strategies other than elite self-perpetuation.

Nevertheless, the methods of elite recruitment and succession partly define the nature of the regime and its policies. Where elites open up opportunities for non-elites to reach positions of rulership, where elites are willing to expose themselves to competitive challenges from counter-elites and are willing to leave the determination of "who shall rule" to citizens deciding in free elections, and where there is relatively little risk involved in challenging incumbent elites, the regime can be defined as democratic and policies are likely to be responsive to a wide range of political interests. Where the opposite conditions prevail, the regime must be defined as oligarchic and policies are likely to be restrictive.

Elite recruitment is of interest because the kind of elites attracted to politics, and the ways in which they are attracted, are revealing indicators of the regime and its policies. If one treats elite recruitment as the independent variable of political analysis, the strategies employed by elites to perpetuate themselves in power and to secure their policies become a major research concern. These strategies have not been thoroughly or systematically explored, either by Lasswell or by his European predecessors or his American successors.[84]

NOTES

1. Thomas S. Kuhn, *The Structure of Scientific Revolutions* (Chicago: University of Chicago Press; Phoenix Edition, 1964).

2. David Easton, "The new revolution in political science," American Political Science Review 63 (December 1969): 1051-1061.

3. See Martin Landau, "Objectivity, neutrality, and Kuhn's paradigm," in *Political Theory and Political Science* (New York: Macmillan, 1972), pp. 43-77.

4. William Bennett Munro, "Jackson and Smith," *The Century Magazine* (October 1928): 641.

5. See Kenneth Prewitt and Alan Stone, *The Ruling Elites: Elite Theory, Power, and American Democracy* (New York: Harper & Row, 1973).

6. See especially the following of Lippmann's works: *A Preface to Politics* (New York: Kennerley, 1913); *Public Opinion* (New York: Macmillan, 1922); and *The Phantom Public* (New York: Harcourt, Brace, 1925).

7. (New York: McGraw-Hill, 1935). The edition used in this article was republished in 1950 by the Free Press as part of a volume entitled *A Study of Power* which also includes books by Charles E. Merriam and T.V. Smith.

8. David Easton, "Harold Lasswell: policy scientist for a democratic society," Journal of Politics 12 (August 1950): 450-477.

9. Robert Horwitz, "Scientific propaganda: Harold D. Lasswell," in Herbert J. Storing, ed., *Essays on the Scientific Study of Politics* (New York: Holt, Rinehart & Winston, 1962), pp. 225-304.

10. Lasswell, *World Politics*, p. 282.

11. See Heinz Eulau, "H.D. Lasswell's developmental analysis," Western Political Quarterly 11 (June 1958): 229-242; and Heinz Eulau, "The maddening methods of Harold D. Lasswell: some philosophical underpinnings," Journal of Politics 30 (February 1968): 3-24. Both essays are reprinted in Heinz Eulau, *Micro-Macro Political Analysis: Accents of Inquiry* (Chicago: Aldine, 1969), pp. 105-137.

12. Harold D. Lasswell, *Politics: Who Gets What, When, How* (New York: McGraw-Hill, 1936). The edition used here is found in *The Political Writings of Harold D. Lasswell* (New York: Free Press, 1951), p. 295.

13. *World Politics*, p. 3.

14. Ibid., p. 3.

15. Harold D. Lasswell, Daniel Lerner and C. Easton Rothwell, *The Comparative Study of Elites* (Stanford: Stanford University Press, 1952), p. 1.

16. *World Politics*, p. 3.

17. Ibid., p. 5.

18. The project on Revolution and the Development of International Relations (RADIR) was conducted by Lasswell and his associates at the Hoover Institution on War, Revolution, and Peace at Stanford University.

19. *Comparative Study*, p. 1.

20. Ibid., p. 1.

21. *Politics*, p. 295.

22. Harold D. Lasswell and Abraham Kaplan, *Power and Society* (New Haven: Yale University Press, 1950), p. 202.

23. Harold D. Lasswell, "Agenda for the Study of Political Elites," in Dwaine Marvick, ed., *Political Decision-makers* (New York: Free Press, 1961), p. 264.

24. *Power and Society*, p. 202.

25. See, for instance, Peter Bachrach, *The Theory of Democratic Elitism* (Boston: Little, Brown, 1967), pp. 65-82.

26. *World Politics*, p. 3.

27. *Comparative Study*, p. 13.

28. See Kenneth Prewitt, "Schooling, Stratification, Equality: Notes for Research," in Michael W. Kirst, *State, School, and Politics* (Lexington, Mass.: D.C. Heath, 1972), p. 113.

29. Ralf Dahrendorf, *Class and Class Conflict in Industrial Society* (Stanford: Stanford University Press, 1959), pp. 241 ff.

30. *Power and Society*, p. 201.

31. *World Politics*, p. 3; *Politics*, p. 297.

32. *Comparative Study*, p. 1; *Power and Society*, p. 72.

33. *Politics*, pp. 305-306.

34. Ibid., p. 306.

35. See especially Chapter X, "Process," in *Power and Society*, pp. 240-284.

36. See, for instance, Heinz Eulau, "Bases of authority in legislative bodies: a comparative analysis," Administrative Science Quarterly 7 (December 1962): 309-321.

37. *Comparative Study*, p. 8.

38. The approach is examplified by Floyd Hunter, *Community Power Structure* (Chapel Hill: University of North Carolina Press, 1953). For a critique, see Nelson W. Polsby, *Community Power and Political Theory* (New Haven: Yale University Press, 1963), pp. 47-53.

39. *World Politics*, p. 150.

40. Ibid., pp. 150-151. Italics added.

41. Ibid., pp. 20-21.

42. *Comparative Study*, p. 6.

43. Ibid., p. 6.

44. Ibid., p. 6.

45. Kenneth Prewitt, *The Recruitment of Political Leaders: A Study of Citizen-Politicians* (Indianapolis: Bobbs-Merrill, 1970).

46. *Power and Society*, p. 206.

47. Ibid., p. 206.

48. Ibid., p. 206.

49. Ibid., p. 214. Italics added.

50. *Politics*, p. 299.

51. Ibid., p. 392.

52. See Daniel Bell, *The Coming of Post-Industrial Society*, (New York: Basic Books, 1973); Zbigniew Brzezinski, *Between Two Ages: America's Role in the Technetronic Era* (New York: Viking, 1970).

53. Harold D. Lasswell, "Skill Politics and Skill Revolution," in *The Analysis of Political Behavior* (New York: Oxford, 1948), pp. 133-145.

54. *Politics*, p. 303.

55. Ibid., p. 305.

56. Ibid., p. 305.

57. See Geraint Parry, *Political Elites* (London: Allen & Unwin, 1969).

58. Easton, "Harold Lasswell," p. 475.

59. See Heinz Eulau, "Skill revolution and consultative commonwealth," American Political Science Review 67 (March 1973): 169-191.

60. Suzanne Keller, *Beyond the Ruling Class* (New York: Random House, 1963), p. 5.

61. James G. March, "The Power of Power," in David Easton, ed., *Varieties of Political Theory* (Englewood Cliffs, N.J.: Prentice-Hall, 1966), p. 70.

62. Harold D. Lasswell, *Psychopathology and Politics* (Chicago: University of Chicago Press, 1930). The edition used here is in *The Political Writings*, p. 50.

63. *Politics*, p. 306.

64. Ibid., p. 309.

65. Ibid., p. 309. Italics added.

66. *Power and Society*, p. 201.

67. See Heinz Eulau, *The Behavioral Persuasion in Politics* (New York: Random House, 1963), pp. 39-46.

68. *Power and Society*, p. 202.

69. *Comparative Study*, p. 7. Italics added.

70. Ibid., p. 11.

71. Harold D. Lasswell, "The Developing Science of Democracy," in *Political Behavior*, p. 8.

72. *Comparative Study*, p. 13.

73. *Power and Society*, p. 226.

74. But see, for an exception, Heinz Eulau and Kenneth Prewitt, *Labyrinths of Democracy* (Indianapolis: Bobbs-Merrill, 1973), Parts III-V.

75. Harold D. Lasswell, *Power and Personality* (New York: W.W. Norton, 1948), p. 108.

76. *Power and Society*, p. 226.

77. Ibid., p. 227.

78. Ibid., p. 227.

79. This and immediately preceding quotes are from *Power and Personality*, p. 109.

80. Ibid., p. 109.

81. Ibid., p. 110.

82. *Comparative Study*, p. 13.

83. See Joseph A. Schlesinger, *Amibition and Politics: Political Carrers in the United States* (Chicago: Rand McNally, 1966), pp. 11-21.

84. But for a perceptive analysis of recruitment as process, see Lester G. Seligman, *Recruiting Political Elites* (New York: General Learning Press, 1971).

Chapter 2

CONTINUITIES IN RECRUITMENT THEORY AND RESEARCH: TOWARD A NEW MODEL

DWAINE MARVICK

University of California

Almost every term in the lexicon of political recruitment terminology is ambiguous in ways that are understandable but troublesome. Terms like opportunity, career, eligibility, apprenticeship, risk, sponsorship are usually made workably clear in the research context when they are invoked, because there is an operational definition which fits the concept to the data requiring analysis. Such terms are also familiar to those participating in recruitment contexts, who are reasonably clear about what is meant because there are usually practical alternatives referred to by them, which are at issue in some pending decision. Taken out of context, however, recruitment terms tend to be allusive and unclear.[1]

Recruitment is a process by which individuals are inducted into active political roles. Critical links between society and polity are said to result—personified links. Are all active roles critical? Does every warm body filling an active role turn it necessarily into a "personified link?"

The study of political recruitment is in an important sense equivalent to the study of political performance—or governance—itself. Starting from different points, both approaches move toward a common set of problems. Political recruitment study is an empty and futile exercise if it merely asks "who governs?" instead of asking how governance is shaped by the skills, contacts and values of those who participate. By the same token, political performance research is bloodless and unreal if it seeks to understand how decisions are made, policies revised, coalitions formed, or institutions run without systematic attention to the abilities, interdependencies, and sensitivities of those who are the participants.[2]

In other words, political recruitment is the study of politics with a special eye to how the participants got there, where they came from and by what paths, and hence what ideas and skills and contacts they acquired or discarded on the way. Its payoff as a mode of inquiry comes when it helps the observer to anticipate what viewpoints are likely to be introduced into a political context by virtue of the presence of politial actors with particular kinds of credentials.

Career considerations are not the whole of any explanation for political performances turned in by individuals or by groups. However, they are a valuable corrective for a common illusion: that "rational" deliberation and "situational determinants" are the only controlling factors most of the time. Often the professional scholar's aim is to learn what the political choices look like to the participants. To grasp what they face as problems, it is first necessary to give weight to the sociohistorical forces which intrude implacably—war, famine, community tension, population changes, crime, inflation, and so forth. These forces are said to mold the agenda of political and governmental discussion as well as action. It is possible to analyze a policy problem in these terms, and to conclude that any rational participant, once apprised of the alternatives and their consequences, would be virtually certain to behave in a similar way.

It is in the concessions made to "style" and "temperament" that room is found in such a rational-situational analysis for the kinds of sensitivities and capacities that recruitment analysis seeks to explain generically. Such concessions are common enough. Leaders can be slow or pompous, impulsive, angry, prone to hedge their moves on one front by countermoves elsewhere, or they can often vacillate. Sometimes these idiosyncracies of lethargy or temperament, of rearing or physical makeup, are held to cause significant and definable distortions in official actions. More commonly they are used to illustrate the presence of imponderables which have caused an otherwise cogent explanation to be wrong. They constitute a kind of excuse-box in case events take unexpected turns.[3]

In taking stock of political recruitment research, one can observe three rather different emphases used by modern investigators. First, a structural component has seemed essential. Schlesinger and Seligman, among their major contributions, have each stressed the notion of a "political opportunity structure"—that is, a changing roster of impending and/or potential vacancies in a relatively stable apparatus of political positions and roles.[4] Linked to this has been a notion of "risk"—the cost of losing. Attention has turned to consideration of what the ingredients are that make an "effective opportunity" rather than a merely formal one. In the electoral contexts in which these studies have been made, the stage is set by a formal impending contest for office. It is assumed, too, that some self-promoting efforts to enter the fray will occur. What else is looked for are factors that will help one to decide how "serious" each contender is, either in the risk he is willing to take in order to win, or in the threat he poses to the victory chances of other aspirants. Such considerations have been noted as these: the status placed in jeopardy, the cause that may be slowed or undermined, the financial support ready to be expended, the organizational sponsorship that can be claimed and even preempted so another cannot have it, the media access to be competed for, the programmatic goals to be championed or opposed. These are some of the complexities in the "risk" that is keyed to an electorate's hiring-and-firing decisions.

To Schlesinger, the notion of an opportunity structure is keyed to vacancies in public office. Using biographical data, he has shown how opportunity rates for any given group of offices can be computed, and how comparisons can be made between different countries as well as between different groups of offices within the same country.[5] Opportunity rates are turnover rates for any given public-office set. If elections occur only every four years and a twelve-year span is used to correct for short-term fluctuations, the proportion of new men defines the rate. If cooptation is the method and if it takes place fairly often at unscheduled intervals, again by averaging over a longer time-span a suitable computation of the opportunity rate can be obtained. Schlesinger examined national public offices filled by competitive elections. However, there is no reason why the map of a polity's political opportunity structure for any period of time, and including local as well as national openings, party positions as well as public posts, nonelective as well as elective jobs, and whether for fixed terms or indefinite terms, should not be drawn on whatever scale or level of detail is wanted. Additionally, for each party or "sponsoring organization," a separate map could readily be made, showing the extent and locus of each party's success as a sponsor of office seekers. In one of his more general formulations, Schlesinger links the opportunity structure idea to his key concern—ambition theory. "The number of offices of significance and the frequency with which they become available to new men define for the ambitious their sense of chances for advancement."[6] For his purposes, the connection is critical, though perhaps overstated. Again, however, there is nothing about the opportunity concept that makes it only significant to the ambitious. As Schlesinger shows, a genuine cross-polity comparison is possible, one able to identify the number and strength of parties that, by straightforward tests, can be said to provide realistic routes to significant office.

For Seligman, political opportunity is a phrase referring to all those who can and want to seek political roles. Eligibility for any given office is indexed by a person's status in the opportunity structure. This is a strikingly different usage from Schlesinger's.[7] "Those with the resources, abilities and motivations for political activity who are not barred by law from political participation have effective opportunity," Seligman holds. Political opportunities expand or contract with changes in the *supply* of eligibles and changes in the *demand* for people to fill political roles. If nonpolitical roles in life become relatively less attractive than political ones, the supply of political eligibles will increase. If the scope of the public sector expands, the demand for aspirants is also heightened. The dynamics of the marketplace apply to the political labor market.[8]

The difficulty about using the concept of opportunity structure as Seligman does is made clear when one turns to the task of giving it an operational definition. It refers to a wide range of different factors, some very much in flux and others very stable, some due to public policies, some to personal efforts, some to cultural rigidities. The sense of "structure" is lost. Thus, he notes that the determinants of political opportunity are not only a person's birth chances but also his or her access to education and wealth or other avenues of social mobility and political advancement. Eligibles for any given role are "those with appropriate resources and skill who are socialized, motivated, and certified" to fill such a role.[9] The term thus also includes political resources as well as social credentials. Group sponsorship, financial support, mass media access, programmatic goals: At some point, the researcher must measure these factors in order to rate the *effective opportunity* available to a political aspirant. Political parties are constituent elements of the opportunity structure, since they legitimize and sponsor candidates, mobilize voters, socialize career aspirants, and cushion defeat. The phrase identifies a research agenda for students of polical recruitment, and it suggests an analytical strategy familiar to economists. But it loses the very quality of operational clarity that Schlesinger's quite different usage possesses.

Some further difficulties are suggested by noting the difference between roles and positions. To be *selected* by any formal mechanism implies that one has acquired a status of consciously agreed-upon organizational significance—a *position*. By contrast, to play an active *role* in some organized process implies only a *self-activated* performance, perhaps constrained by what other participants expect, but largely optional in content. If one person does not play the role, it may happen that for long periods no one does so. Alternatively, a lot of other people may do so. It is clear, however, that such a role is not a position that needs to be filled in order to control and direct institutional resources in an approved manner.

A second distinction is useful, between a single, isolated, or *discrete* opportunity, on the one hand, and a *sequence* of opportunities, on the other hand. The formality of the opportunity—whether it is to play roles or to fill positions—is probably linked in practice to the kind of sponsoring mechanisms involved. Thus, a discrete opportunity can perhaps be exploited successfully with only makeshift and temporary arrangements for joint effort. To sustain a significant career of office-holding, on the other hand, would seem to call for continuing organizational support. *Career* opportunities, as contrasted with *ad hoc* chances to play optional roles or even to achieve formal positions, will probably tend in politics as elsewhere to be sponsored by organizations; factions or cliques may be instrumental in starting a career, or cutting it short, but rarely can they sustain one.

Political careers are sponsored by organizationally controlled venture capital, so to speak. Parties control the high-risk thresholds that distinguish one kind of career from another—a local career, a legislative career, a party functionary's career. For various reasons, those who act for the party select from a rather limited eligible-aspirant pool, and thus "invest" party capital in the chosen individual. The importance of a given career is significantly measured by how much the sponsoring group has invested in it—both at launch times and for minor job shifts as well as changes in orbit. From this, it follows that a *career in orbit* is treated differently from a *career in transit* between orbits. Once those who control the jobs and roles available at a given organizational node, in a given institutional setting, or at a given geographic locale have taken an eligible aspirant seriously enough to invest organizational resources by sponsoring him in a formal way, he is probably certified for at least a modest career *in the same orbit*, subject of course to the sponsoring organization's continued ability to find jobs or roles that will support him. To put the same person in transit to a different career orbit, however, takes venture capital—party organizational resources more difficult to control and more jealously husbanded.[10]

Using the structural approach, the expectation is fostered that a political opportunity structure will be found in any given domain, its positions and roles for the most part filled and unavailable, especially to outsiders. A small subset of effective opportunities typically can be discerned, in part by noting the impending formality of institutionalized elections whose outcome depends on mass-preference patterns, in part by noting the open or closed character of competition for the offices in question. If a wide open field contend for electoral support, the pattern of risks—financial, programmatic, organizational, and personal—for each contender is a function of the *field* against him. Some candidates divert support from a front runner and change the risks significantly for others but not for themselves; some candidates need the exposure, the experience, the electoral calesthenics; and even though they expend considerable resources only to lose, they and their backers may view the problem as a long-term investment rather than a demonstrable loss. While difficult to pin down, the notion of "risk" is a provocative one to use in appraising a contested-election situation.[11]

The very quality that gives clarity to the opportunity structure/political risk scheme is its great weakness, however. It crystallizes one's conception of the recruitment process, which is by the accounts of participants actually fluid and ambiguous. It fosters the illusion of a honeycomb of posts and roles, and of opportunities and risks as properties that attach to discrete situations, whenever office-holding vacancies occur or can realistically be brought about by effectively marshalled campaign efforts. In this approach, the preliminaries leading to the formal election-day choice tend to be viewed as events that are divided into clear-cut stages. Stages are of course useful to the analyst, providing they are really present in the process under study and are not conceptual figments of the analyst's imagination. They are useful because they culminate. Typically, a stage starts rather inclusively, goes through a narrowing process, and then reaches a final sequence of events. Thus delineated, each stage can rather handily be studied: Who makes the recruitment choice? By what criteria? By what sponsoring mechanisms is the choice narrowed? Seligman distinguishes four such mechanisms: self-promotion, agency, cooptation, and conscription.[12]

Immediately prior to the popular election comes the multi-party campaign process in which each sponsoring group touts the claims of its standard bearers. Before the campaign begins, in turn, a candidate-selection process within each party must occur. This sometimes entails a similar winnowing of aspirants, each under some sponsoring aegis, each with certain assets that make him formidable and/or attractive, each with some drawbacks, each faced by a degree of ambiguity about who else will be chosen by other parties. The risk factor is a dynamic calculation, in short, based upon each contender's "effective presence" in the nomination process itself coupled with his "potential presence" in the subsequent election campaign.[13] But only "serious eligibles" are effective contenders in a nomination process, it is argued, however open in formal terms the lists may be. Logically, prior to the candidate-selection and popular-election stages, there must come a credential-certification stage. From among the eligible aspirants who are in various forms of apprenticeship, some individuals come to be "taken seriously" while others do not. This emergent stage is the least satisfactory part of the multi-stage structural model. It has a distressing tendency not to narrow in scope, and not to culminate in any definitive event sequence.[14]

As used here, political recruitment occurs in the organized, geographically delimited and institutionalized contexts of party affairs and/or public affairs. It includes recruitment into the ranks of a "constituted body" of government—a legislature or council or other policy-making group—or to fill governmental leadership positions functionally linked to such conciliar units, or to staff the organizational apparatus of each political party or auxiliary organization which functions as a linkage mechanism between polity and society.

If a political opportunity structure is a changing roster of impending and/or potential vacancies in organizational positions and public offices, and if risk is the cost of losing a formally staged contest either for candidacy nomination or official election, the question of incentives and motivations becomes a crucial one. It is the second major emphasis found in recruitment studies. Jacob, Wilson, and Eldersveld, in their quite different ways, have put special stress on the motivational wellsprings that shape the recruitment processes of politics. Jacob, in his work on initial recruitment into elective office, formulates a model in which persons with self-selecting propensities (e.g., for power, prestige, and/or public attention) are found to occupy strategic nonpolitical status positions that channel their ambitions toward the conventionally useful skills, permit a range of social contacts, facilitate efforts to obtain financial backing and group support, and make feasible a persistent if low-keyed search for office-holding opportunities. These same appropriately motivated persons, if their search for power, prestige, and attention had been channeled differently, could just as readily have entered a profession, business, or commercial vocation. The "brokerage positions" they did occupy, however, put them on the availability-threshold for public office-seeking ventures.[15]

Affiliation needs, achievement needs, power needs: These and similar personality parameters are not only seen as motivating people. Equally important, those who lead organizations can cater selectively to those needs. Clark and Wilson have argued that three optional modes are in practice available as "incentive systems" that organizational leaders can control—incentive systems that are specialized to provide organizational participants mainly with solidary, purposive, or material gratifications, but only in modes that emphasize one of the three while tending to drive out the alternatives.[16] Thus, the kind of gratifications dispensed by the organizational incentive system of one kind of political party—the machine—created a professionalized perspective that was interest-conscious, policy accommodationist, and organizationally success-minded. Quite different was the "amateur" perspective in voluntary politics, nurtured by the gratifications peculiarly available to voluntary club participants: a perspective that was principle-conscious, issue-sensitive, and programmatically success-minded, and which was molded and harnessed by an organizational incentive system that routinely dispensed opportunities for purposive gratification—through discussion of policies, championing of causes, and clarification of issues.

Eldersveld has been especially sensitive to the difficulties hidden by such neat equations. It is extraordinarily difficult to get evidence that convincingly shows that a material incentive system fosters a professional politician's outlook or that a purposive incentive system dovetails and nurtures a political amateur's point of view. Eldersveld's analysis of the motivational diversity of party organizational personnel at several echelons in the rival parties of Detroit has been a useful cautionary tale. It is especially difficult to argue persuasively that each kind of incentive system tends to drive out the alternatives when one considers the ubiquitous importance of solidary gratifications in sustaining participation through "thick and thin"—not only for idealistic enthusiasts who nevertheless admit to enjoying the fun and excitement of campaign work, but also for machine politicians comfortable in the friendship of their clubhouse circle.[17]

It seems likely that incentives are time- and place-bound, that motivations for participating in political life are neither blind nor persistent, but instead are selectively invoked by an individual, depending on what his own experience in a given organizational setting tells him are the kinds of gratifications one can expect. If he feels that material rewards are out of the question, in any immediate sense, he may lose interest. Or he may cultivate a "faithful servant" posture in hopes of future material reward. Alternatively, he may find himself enjoying a set of solidary gratifications arising out of the social contacts, excitement, and companionship he finds with organizational colleagues. Finally, he may find that, while he pursues a living elsewhere and has lots of close friends apart from politics, he relishes the pleasure of being a zealous and selfless champion of some transcendent cause—country, party, program, ideology, or whatever. In short, the same person may have more than one set of motives, and more than one social context in which to seek gratification.[18]

As a third approach, Eulau, Prewitt, Huntington, and Dahl are among those who have stressed the need for measuring the systemic effects traceable to political recruitment practices.[19] What kinds of leaders and cadres are produced by particular grooming and advancement methods, in terms of their capacity and willingness to secure a particular kind of polity? It is when recruitment is viewed from this perspective—as more than a set of career opportunities for which resources must be husbanded and ultimately risked, and as more than a set of personal motivations imperfectly catered to and given gratification by the incentive systems of party organizations and public service in exchange for a more or less competent job done—that it is necessary to examine the sponsoring criteria used and the grooming arrangements made routinely in a political system's recruitment process.

Parties sometimes sponsor candidates solely as a reward for long years of organizational service: grooming sometimes consists only of learning a bag of political tricks. As organized groups, however, political parties acquire their legitimacy by virtue of the public purposes they ostensibly serve. As a result, not uncommonly party leaders are prompted to assess potential candidates in terms of their ability, training, and merit as individuals appropriate to fill the job available. In quite a different mode but with equally important systemic effects, moreover, party leaders often size up aspirants for organizational sponsorship by asking what social and community interests such aspirants can evoke, and hence what utility they probably have as embodiments of human resources needed to accomplish the tasks of the job in question.[20]

A basic question about any system of public order is how smoothly it provides career opportunities to each successive generation. In formerly colonial lands like India, the agitational elite, whose political skills and beliefs often were acquired in conspiratorial circles, in crowd situations, and in prisons, had inherited the modern apparatus of nationhood and power while still young in years. As a group, however, its members typically lacked the educational credentials and executive skills called for when governmental agencies are charged with responsibility for programs of rapid modernization and social transformation. Subsequent generations typically have felt themselves better prepared and have found themselves at odds with the generation ahead of them on the political career ladders.[21]

Everywhere it seems that political recruitment is a system-maintenance process that is only partly institutionalized. The trade of politics is largely learned through an apprenticeship system. The career perspectives of each generation are molded both by new priorities placed on skills and knowledge to meet changing functional needs and by the performance examples, good and bad, of men ahead of them on the political ladder. Typically, even at early stages in their careers, tomorrow's leaders are being screened for capacities their elders never had to possess. Somehow they must be schooled to handle well the kinds of complex problems that current incumbents fumble. Tomorrow's tasks of political decision-making have to be met and can only be met successfully by somehow acquiring an awareness and sensitivity that amount to a new style and new standards of responsible conduct when in office.[22]

However the political system is defined, recruitment to its posts inevitably draws upon people from various subcultures where early political socialization lessons were learned. By giving apprentice personnel a closeup view of the political world, it trains them in necessary skills and furnishes them with political sensitivities and cognitive maps. Probably the primordial perspectives acquired early in life remain operative in later years, being overlaid by values, attitudes and conduct patterns considered appropriate to one's career aspirations—that is, to what one wants to make of one's life. It is an open question how important those early experiences are, in coloring one's later political judgment or sharpening one's political sensitivities. Inferences are sometimes uncritically made that imply a person's subsequent career experiences have only minor weight in shaping his fundamental adult views and conduct, so important are the prototypic attitudes formed in childhood. Yet little is yet known systematically about the political socialization of leaders, either about their childhoods or the adult apprenticeship years they underwent. An individual's life path through the communal and corporate infrastructure of his society never ceases, in one sense, to be an apprenticeship, one that equips him with crucial skills and typical attitudes as well as with material resources and organization sponsors—all of which are necessary as credentials at subsequent major career thresholds. Especially in poorly developed nations that lack political consensus and have only weak infrastructures, perhaps roughly equal importance should attach to early political socialization, on the one hand, and to later adult experiences, on the other, as factors determining the viability of the political order.[23]

Political recruitment is a process, found in all systems, by which the policy shaping personnel of government and the cadres of ancillary political structures are groomed and selected. As a learning process, it is preceded by *citizen socialization,* on which it builds, and even more immediately, by *activist socialization,* which is cadre-supervised but seldom explicitly taught and which takes place largely during mobilization phases of a nation's political life. In turn, it is augmented by the specialized norms, practices, and skills of *leadership socialization,* learned in a never-ending sequence of apprenticeship roles, and preoccupied with the institutional practices and organizational arrangements found in the career orbits in which leaders aspire to make their way.

To keep the term political recruitment within useful limits, it seems advisable to exclude most political activists and most government bureaucrats by introducing the qualifier—"policy-shaping"—to identify those organizational and governmental personnel who are necessarily part of a political recruitment system. It seems appropriate to exclude many of those who are periodically active in political parties and other ancillary political organizations. Typically they are not screened nor explicitly apprenticed, nor does the organization have much of an investment in their continued participation and advancement. They are not in any clear sense a part of the political cadre.[24]

It is possible, of course, to identify sequences and episodes in a nation's history when elements of the state bureaucracy have taken over significant parts of the policy-making reins of government, just as it is possible to find predictably recurrent and consciously created circumstances under which large numbers of the self-activated rank and file membership of parties, movements, and interest groups do exercise decisive weight in determining what their own organizational cadres can do and must do, how they are to be chosen and deployed, and how they are to serve policy makers. These, however, are the limiting cases that help to delineate the political recruitment process of modern states realistically.[25]

Political recruitment refers to a varied set of institutional processes by which political jobs beyond the citizenship level and beyond the activist rank-and-file participants in campaigns and organizational life are filled. Patterns of incumbency in these political offices and positions are called "careers." Subjectively, career perspectives are moving vantage points from which men in politics appraise their duties and opportunities, whether they treat public life as a calling or as a vocation, or both.

Mosca, Pareto, and Michels each explored the stultifying implications of incumbency.[26] Modernity features the proliferation of organizational jobs and nonhereditary elites to fill them, into every field of endeavor. The ascriptive credentials of birth increasingly must be validated by achievements through merit. Nor is elitehood readily transferred from a specialized field into public policy-making processes. To negotiate, legitimize, and implement plans involving collective communitywide efforts calls for distinctively political skills; to gain them requires extended political grooming.

Everywhere, public life becomes possible for poor men only with the development and institutionalization of politics as a vocation, in the sense of livelihood, as Max Weber insisted. In most parts of the modernizing world, a successful political career has become an occupational possibility even if one starts from disadvantaged social or communal status, through a combination of merit, luck, tactics, sponsorship, and perseverance. Politics as a mission is also a possiblitlity for the would-be leader. However, men often enter politics for reasons only remotely linked to public purposes or shared ideals, and they are not easily turned away from it. The attitude of modern civility is cultivated widely; it is a view that expects personal career calculations and concern for the commonweal to exist uneasily but simultaneously in the perspectives of fellow citizens.[27]

Men are born with certain life chances, by virtue of their social circumstances and personal endowments, and the availability of avenues of social mobility. In elite "mission" studies, the major dimensions of analysis are those that deal with social origins, activation patterns, and the changing kinds of political jobs available in the polity. In virtually all the new states of Asia and Africa, political recruitment patterns since independence have shifted significantly, both in terms of class and educational levels and in terms of urban-rural and center-hinterland derivations. Always these shifts have been downward and out—that is, in directions that broaden and diversify the pool of eligibles and the roster of aspirants.[28]

By contrast, in studies of organizational personnel selection in politics, analysis has centered on the effects of grooming, on differential career commitments, and on the selective screening criteria by which institutions safeguard their key roles from being held by misfits. While elite recruitment studies tend to assume almost random selection from the eligibility pool, work on organizational recruitment more often assumes that those selected will not be a cross-section sample from the social pool of eligibles, nor even from the roster of political career aspirants.[29]

Empirical investigations of organizational recruitment processes typically call for these steps. First specify the range of positions and roles. Identify the incumbents. Consider the formal and informal screening arrangements used to fill vacancies and to evaluate apprentices. Then compare the fit between what is wanted functionally and what is obtained. Organizations do not regularly get what they want by way of manpower. Nor, for that matter, do organizations in politics necessarily seek what, functionally speaking, they need. Many key positions are already filled; incumbency is a brake on any updating of an organization's functional rationality. In general, institutional manpower studies suggest that the correspondence between functional role structures and organizational position rosters in the political process is rarely good. It is risky to treat a job incumbent as a functional role incumbent.[30] Organizational charts are useful but inconclusive. Performance norms and leadership objectives tend to be set by the incumbent himself, interacting with close associates. Depending upon organizational routines and momentum, resources may or may not be free to be reallocated toward newly defined goals. Political culture also can dictate important differences in what a political job entails; positions that are equivalent in form, in norms of performance, and in resources commanded may call for a distinctive style in one milieu but not in another.[31]

Formal recruitment processes in politics are typically organizational threshold processes—that is, they involve getting manpower from an extramural roster of aspirants. Formal title to the political office and some control over institutional resources keyed to the office are conveyed to the new incumbent at the time of formal investiture, as when a legislator takes his seat or when a new party chieftain is installed. But formal election seldom bestows a distinctive and pervasive influence within the organization. Instead, such influence comes when one can show special prowess, rally a following, claim inside knowledge, or otherwise be treated as a serious presence by colleagues.

> In the extreme sense of hiring and firing personnel, the formal processes can override the informal ones; extramural controls can prevail over intramural ones. In the ordinary course of political business, however, the intramural screening and reception system for the neophyte legislator, official, or party functionary is a more searching and more unnerving process than any formal, or extramural, hurdle. Moreover, apart from official prerogatives that come with formal induction, the influence wielded inside a political organization is largely determined by the intramural role patterns that a member finds himself conforming to, or—more rarely— carving out for himself.[32]

Recruitment theories and models have thus far tended to be formulated with specific data configurations or documentary materials keyed to particular institutional arrangements, times, and places in mind. Because of this ad hoc quality, they are not readily applicable either later or elsewhere. Few recruitment studies have drawn systematically on a quantitative data base. Most of the elite-mission genre have been content to note marked shifts over time in social origins, the enlargement of career opportunities, or striking changes in training and grooming practices.[33] On the other hand, much of the institutional-composition genre has tried to characterize the kinds of careers sponsored and shaped by ideological movements, interest groups, mechine bosses, kingmakers, or party bureaucrats. Typically a combination of personal observation and historical documentation has seemed adequate to support the conclusions reached.[34]

Models of political recruitment have been largely tailored to fit the data obtainable. Conceptual frameworks often seem to have been fashioned to display research findings obtained by inquiries remarkable for their pragmatic design. It is quite understandable that these studies have been undertaken with a practical eye on what was feasible and with a willingness to seize unanticipated research opportunities when they arose. Field research on sensitive questions where one must depend on participating informants is always imperfect and frustrating. The results have often been provocative, but the slowly emerging consensus about terminology is not yet matched by impressive bodies of evidence. A few pioneering inquiries have been very influential—Eulau's work on career patterns, Schlesinger's opportunity structure concept, Seligman's political risk formulation, Clark and Wilson's incentive system options, Prewitt's preapprenticeship approach, Jacob's motivational parameters—and the result has been a de facto definition of the research field.[35]

Certain conclusions result from a stock-taking exercise. Most contributions have been unselfconsciously culture-bound. Most sample frames have been locale-or institution-specific; few have been politywide with any demonstrable claim to representativeness. Most of those whose career paths have been studied are people working in the same milieu, seeking a similar office, or participating at a certain stage of the overall process. Structural features in the immediate political environment have typically delimited the scope of the research efforts undertaken.[36]

It seems likely that more systematically gathered evidence will tend to disclose more complexities and subtleties in actual recruitment practices than is commonly appreciated now. Career opportunities are probably more agglutinated, more commingled and more presumptively closed to outsiders than the opportunity-structure schema tends to suggest is the case. Opportunities in politics are almost inevitably characterized by some elements of cooptation. Aspirants for political careers cross an unmarked threshold when and only when they are "taken seriously" for a given job by those already in command of some of the political resources needed to secure it. Consider the following scenario. A neophyte political activist is mobilized for campaign work, partly by his own predispositions to do so but partly by the awareness of others that he is so minded and is a likely prospect. Even at this early stage and certainly at subsequent stages when and if some party cadreman assigns him certain tasks, trains him in particular routines, explains how scheduling decisions are made, helps or hinders him in any apprenticeship aspect of his work, the most salient fact in the daily life drama of becoming organizationally involved is not the self-activating effort of the person himself. Rather it is the fact of being "taken seriously" by those in a position to help or hinder his fledgling career steps.

Probably the first basic threshold of a sustained political career comes when a person is allowed to become (invited in some cases, but the term is too strong for many) an accepted part of the cadre roster that controls and stabilizes the work of a semi-autonomous segment of any extended political apparatus. It seems likely that a considerable gulf is maintained between the small group of outpost cadres in a given locality and the larger ranks of occasionally mobilized workers in that locality. The informal circle of party cadremen typically coopts its new members—and on occasion squeezes out its reject personnel—without any formal decision-making event. Often it may be a simple case of someone proving to be useful and reliable and gradually being taken for granted.

The model here proposed is one that anticipates some mutual adjustment and matter-of-fact accommodation by the custodial group of cadres who run things at any given node in an extended political apparatus. Confronted by a new participant in the affairs of their domain, they learn how to live with him. If for any reason the newcomer is thought to be worth taking seriously, the custodial group may be expected to work toward a stable solution. If the newcomer leaves, the problem solves itself. If he is welcomed into the inner circle and coopted by the custodial group, a stable solution presumably results. In many instances, it is likely that neither of these clear-cut patterns will apply. Instead, a stable situation emerges as all participants come to take the outsider's presence for granted, as they come to rely upon him in recurrent ways, and as they discover that a reciprocal pattern of accommodation is not hard to sustain.

Two features of this model deserve note. First, it emphasizes the idea of mutual adjustment and accommodation as a spontaneous process through which a newcomer becomes a familiar part of the scene, the longer he remains. Second, it postulates that every node or segment in an extended political apparatus is run by a semi-autonomous circle of custodial cadres. A stratarchic image of party is conveyed by such a scheme; a multi-nuclear concept of party is also suggested. Neither the question of organizational cohesion and ideological distance which concerned Eldersveld in his explorations of stratarchic practics, nor the preoccupation with office-seeking ambition that Schlesinger sustained while he examined the potentialities of loosely-knit multi-nuclear party organizations is in point here. Rather, what is stressed is the likelihood that, at every level of an extended party apparatus—and between different institutional contexts at the same level as well—the de facto custodial group who run affairs in their particular node will find it convenient to adjust to outsiders—that is, to newcomers who have some claim in credentials or support for seeking to participate in organizational affairs at that nodal point, and who are thus taken seriously in a minimal degree.

NOTES

1. Major sources in this section include Kenneth Prewitt, *The Recruitment of Political Leaders* (1970); Samuel J. Eldersveld, *Political Parties: A Behavioral Analysis* (1964); Joseph A. Schlesinger, *Ambition and Politics* (1966); Dwaine Marvick, "Political Recruitment and Careers," *International Encyclopedia of the Social Sciences* (1968); Samuel Huntington, *Political Order in Changing Societies* (1969); and Lewis Edinger, ed., *Political Leadership in Industrialized Societies* (1967).

2. For an exemplary study of the results possible when attention is given to both aspects, see the full-scale report on their Bay Area Councilman Project by Heinz Eulau and Kenneth Prewitt, *Labyrinths of Democracy: Adaptations, Linkages, Representation and Policies in Urban Politics* (1973).

3. An impressive but heavily intuitive demonstration of the persistent importance of character and style is David Barber's study of state legislators, *The Lawmakers: Recruitment and Adaptation to Legislative Life* (1965). More explicitly concerned with recruitment mechanisms and adjustment processes and extraordinarily rich in empirical details about career turning points culled from lengthy interviews with state legislators is another basic study, John Wahlke, Heinz Eulau, William Buchanan, and Leroy Ferguson, *The Legislative System* (1962).

4. Schlesinger, op. cit., and "Political Careers and Party Leadership," in Edinger, op. cit.; Lester Seligman, "Political Parties and the Recruitment of Political Leaders," in Edinger, op. cit.; "Party structure and political recruitment," American Political Science Review (March 1961), and Seligman, *Recruiting Political Elites* (1971).

5. Schlesinger, "Political Careers and Party Leadership," in Edinger, op. cit.

6. Ibid., pp. 269-270.

7. Ibid., passim.

8. Seligman, op. cit., p. 4.

9. Ibid.

10. See the study of differential recruitment practices in contemporary Chicago by Leo Snowiss, "Congressional recruitment and representation," American Political Science Review (September 1966).

11. For empirical work that is relevant, consult Gordon S. Black, "A theory of political ambition: career choices and the role of structural incentives," American Political Science Review (March 1972).

12. Seligman, in Edinger, op. cit., pp. 321-323.

13. Seligman is aware of this. He writes as follows: "Neither the attributes of the individual nor the character of the selection process alone determines who is chosen; the relationship among candidates, sponsors, and selection is reciprocal." *Recruiting Political Elites,* p. 4.

14. A different conception of career convergence is developed in Heinz Eulau and John D. Sprague, *Lawyers in Politics: A Study in Professional Convergence* (1964).

15. Herbert Jacob, "Initial recruitment of elected officials in the United States: a model," Journal of Politics 24 (1962), 703 ff.

16. Peter B. Clark and James Q. Wilson, "Incentive systems: a theory of organizations," Administrative Science Quarterly 6 (September 1961), 219-266.

17. Eldersveld, op. cit.

18. For empirical work on this point, consult Dwaine Marvick, "The Middlemen of Politics," in William Crotty, ed., *Approaches to the Study of Party Organization* (1968).

19. In addition to the previously cited work of these authors, consult Zbigniew Brzezinski and Samuel Huntington, "Cincinnatus and the apparatchik," World Politics (October 1963). For a rigorous empirical exercise, see Kenneth Prewitt, "Political ambitions, volunteerism, and electoral accountability," American Political Science Review (March 1970).

20. Eldersveld's treatment of this basic complication in recruitment analysis is especially impressive because it is keyed to the empirical patterns disclosed in his Detroit investigation of party activists and citizens, op. cit., Part II.

21. See Harold D. Lasswell's still challenging "Agenda for the Study of Political Elites," in Dwaine Marvick, ed., *Political Decision Makers: Recruitment and Performance* (1961). Also consult Suzanne Keller, *Beyond the Ruling Class* (1963), and P. Thoenes, *The Elite in the Welfare State* (1966 translation).

22. See Donald Matthews, *U.S. Senators and Their World* (1960); Everett Ladd, *Negro Political Leadership in the South* (1966); and Morris Janowitz, *The Professional Soldier* (1960) for full-scale studies of the apprenticeship component in political leadership.

23. An impressive and provocative analysis of adult resocialization is set forth for the contemporary Venezuelan elites in Frank Bonilla, *The Failure of Elites* (1970).

24. This usage is slowly emerging; Prewitt's discussion of the convenience of reserving the notion of appreticeship and the phenomenon of recruitment proper to these stages in the larger political mobilization and induction process which come after people have already entered the "active political stratum" is part of the trend.

25. Austin Ranney's careful study of *Pathways to Parliament* (1965) illuminates these aspects in the modern British case.

26. Gaetano Mosca, *The Ruling Class* (1939 translation); Roberto Michels, *Political Parties* (1962 edition). The paperback edition, issued in 1966 as the "First Free Press Paperback Edition," includes an introduction by S.M. Lipset.

27. Consult Edward Shils, "Demagogues and Cadres in the Political Development of the New States," "Ideology and Civility," and other essays in his volume, *The Intellectuals and the Powers* (1972).

28. See the extensive treatment in Keller, op. cit.

29. Consult Rupert Wilkinson, "Political leadership and the late Victorian public school," British Journal of Sociology (1962); Morris Janowitz, *The Military in the Political Development of New Nations* (1963); and Henry Valen, "The Recruitment of Parliamentary Nominees in Norway," *Scandinavian Political Studies* (1966), for inquiries sensitive to these considerations.

30. For consideration of what factors those making recruitment selections have in mind, see A.L. Hunt and R.E. Pendley, "Community gatekeepers: an examination of political recruiters," *Midwest Journal of Political Science* (August 1972); and Dean Mann, "The selection of federal political executives," American Political Science Review (March 1964).

31. A model of insightful scholarly study of this point is Glendon Schubert, "Judges and Political Leadership," in Edinger, op. cit.

32. Cf. Joseph Bensman and Arthur Vidich, "Power cliques in bureaucratic society," Social Research (Winter 1962); Frank Bonilla, "Action in Power Roles," Chapter 7 of his *Failure of Elites* (1970); and Michael Crozier, "Human relations at the management level in a bureaucratic system," Human Organization (Summer 1961) for studies of intramural screening practice.

33. Keller, op. cit., summarized the basic literature.

34. See Lewis Edinger, "Political science and political biography," Journal of Politics (May and August 1964), for a systematic discussion of documentary source materials.

35. The seminal work is Max Weber, "Politics as a Vocation" in Hans Gerth and C. Wright Mills, eds., *From Max Weber: Essays in Sociology* (1946).

36. In one sense, this is an inescapable concomitant of any serious quantitative inquiry, since no serious sampling of relevant evidence can be undertaken before delimiting the sample universe and providing a structural frame that makes it finite.

Chapter 3

ASPIRING AND ESTABLISHED POLITICIANS:
THE STRUCTURE OF VALUE SYSTEMS AND ROLE PROFILES

MOSHE M. CZUDNOWSKI
Northern Illinois University

This chapter reports some of the findings of an exploratory research on the structure of value-systems and role projections and perceptions of politicians at different levels of active involvement. The study was exploratory in two major respects: (1) Introducing a line of analysis which had not been previously applied in the study of political elites and for which little theoretical guidance and no empirical evidence were availble, the study did not attempt to test a set of specific hypotheses. The purpose of the study, therefore, was to explore whether the structure of value systems and role images were areas in which theoretically interesting distinctions could be made between different types of political elites. (2) The observations were derived from a "sample" which was practically exhaustive of territorially defined subsets of populations of political actors (candidates from an Illinois district for the delegation to the 1972 Democratic National Convention, and the 1972 congressional incumbents and challengers from Illinois), but it was not a representative sample of the total 1972 population of Democratic National Convention delegates, of congressional incumbents and congressional challengers. Although some tests of statistical significance have been applied in the analysis of the data and will be reported here, this paper is intended to describe an attempt to formulate some theoretical questions rather than to convey a set of acceptable answers.

Author's Note: An earlier version of this paper was presented at the Ninth World Congress of the International Political Science Association in 1973. I wish to thank the Center for Governmental Studies, Northern Illinois University, for financial and administrative assistance in the research project reported in this paper, and my research assistant Mr. Viktor Hofstetter for his dedication to this project.

The interest in the structure of value systems and the structure of role images of politicians which led to this study originated in three different though not entirely unrelated problem areas in political and sociopsychological research. The most far-reaching of these problem areas reflects a fundamental issue in theories of elite-recruitment: After one has accounted for the differential impact of social origin, pre-adult and adult socialization, for the syndrome of variables associated with occupations (status, income, skills, proximity to governmental processes, availability, value-orientation), and for the structural constraints of constituencies, party systems, and party organizations, how does one explain that within the categories of individuals who "qualify" as potential candidates, only a few will seek political office, and how can one identify the characteristics which distinguish them from the many others who never sought and will never seek a political career? Instead of concluding that this was a matter of accidental and therefore unpredictable events, some political scientists have hypothesized that differences in personality structure would explain a large proportion of politically oriented behavior. Following Lasswell's early attempt to describe a modal political personality, psychology-oriented studies have sought evidence for a motivational syndrome characteristic only of political activists, office-seekers or office-holders.

Although intuitively appealing, this hypothesis is not well supported by convincing and conclusive evidence. In addition to serious methodological shortcomings, these studies display sufficient motivational variability to suggest that in the present state of the discipline, it is probably safe to assume that there are several personality needs (status, power, achievement, adulation, acceptance, nurturance, etc.) which politicians share with the members of other social elites.[1] It seems that additional variables have to be drawn into the analysis in order to explain why some individuals will seek satisfaction in politics and others in a military, business, or professional career.

In the research reported in this chapter, I have hypothesized that the structure of value-systems is one such set of additional variables which (when combined with other individual-level variables) could perhaps yield a better insight into the characteristics of the orientational profiles of politicians. In an earlier study, it was suggested that the conceptual framework, the measuring instruments, and the findings of occupational sociology are not entirely irrelevant to this line of approach.[2] For example, a reinterpretation of Rosenberg's data on value orientations and occupational choice revealed that college students who expressed a desire to choose a career in government displayed only a moderate preference in their orientations toward all four value-complexes examined in Rosenberg's study (people-oriented values, security, extrinsic rewards, and self-expression-oriented values), whereas students who had chosen other careers expressed high preferences for one set of values and low preferences for another.[3] This lack of strong preferences for any of the four value-complexes was interpreted as a possible indicator of the flexibility inherent in the generalist orientation of a political or governmental career—i.e., the ability to move with relative ease from one type of values to another. Rokeach's recent theorizing and research on the structure and stability of belief systems provide a new line of approach to the study of the sociopsychological differences between different types of politicians, between politicians and other elites and politicians and non-elites.[4]

The second problem area from which this study originated concerns the structure of value systems. Some definitions of terms are required to clarify the dimensions of "structure" which will be dealt with in this study. Rokeach defines *values* as "enduring beliefs that a specific mode of conduct or end-state of existence is personally and socially preferable to alternative modes of conduct or end-states of existence. Once a value is internalized, it becomes, consciously or unconsciously, a standard or criterion for guiding action, for developing and maintaining attitudes toward relevant objects and situations, for justifying one's own and others' actions and attitudes . . . and for comparing self with others."[5] Thus defined, values fall under the category of "existential beliefs" which are relatively "central" (i.e., have "more implications and consequences for other beliefs"); they are not necessarily shared with all other members of one's environment, but neither are they psychologically incontrovertible (i.e., impervious to persuasion or argument by others). To the extent that they are authority beliefs (e.g., which authorities are we to trust and distrust in seeking information about the world?), they are typically controvertible. Yet, as enduring internalized beliefs about modes of conduct and preferable end-states, values are more resistant to change than less central beliefs, such as attitudes, which are organizations of several beliefs focused on specific objects or situations.

A *value-system* is a hierarchical rank-ordering of values along a continuum of importance.[6] There are systems of instrumental values (modes of conduct) and systems of terminal values (end-states). The concept of a value-system does not imply that behavior will always be congruent with all of a person's values; a value-system is a set of rules for making choices and resolving conflicts when a situation activates two or more values in conflict with one another. Values can also be inconsistent with some attitudes. Rokeach posits that changes in value-systems occur when psychologically upsetting inconsistencies are revealed between values (especially terminal values) or between values and attitudes. Consistency is thus defined as consistency with self-esteem rather than with logic or reality, although these different criteria are not mutually exclusive. They may indeed overlap and lead to the same change in values. One pair of terminal values has often been considered as reflecting inconsistencies in its logical, social and political implications: equality and freedom. Rokeach has demonstrated the centrality of the relative ranking of each of these values in a person's value-system—i.e., its consequences for other beliefs, attitudes, and behavior.[7]

With this conceptual framework in mind, the student of political elites would be inclined to explore whether or not the rankings of values in a person's value-system are affected by a self/other dimension: If a value ranks very high as a preferred end-state for society, does the politician also rank it high as a preferred end-state for himself? It is likely that within the culturally determined configuration of value-systems, individuals will differ in their self-oriented ranking of specific values according to the predominance of one rather than another psychological need, or the person's evaluation of his position, relative to that of others, in terms of opportunities for achieving the preferred end-state. Would the same determinants of evaluation apply to the ranking of the value on the individual's other-directed scale of values? For example, would a relatively affluent liberal who ranks the economic well-being of underprivileged groups as an important political goal and economic well-being as an important societal value also rank it as an important personal value? Obviously, if he values his own well-being very highly and feels that it might be threatened, he will engage in behavior intended to protect it; yet, this may be inconsistent with behavior intended to improve the well-being of others (e.g., opposing an increase in taxation to finance a public welfare program). When other-directed values imply a threat to a self-directed value (e.g., when it involves scarce resources), can we not expect behavior inconsistent with the value-system?

These considerations are particularly relevant in the case of political elites. Active political involvement is always predicated on the espousal of a set of political goals, and these goals reflect a certain segment on a scale of society-oriented values. Yet, active political involvement is also determined by personal motivations (i.e., an orientation toward personal goals which reflect a segment of a self-oriented scale of values). If a value scale can be interpreted as either self- or other-oriented, an assessment of differences in the rank ordering between self- and other-oriented scales will require separate measurements. However, the use of a separate measurement instrument for self-oriented value rankings raises a methodological problem. Since active political involvement requires both private and public (self- and other-directed) goal orientations, but a political actor's private goals are inconsequential and possibly even dysfunctional for his efforts to draw support and promote his public goal achievement, private goal orientations and the value rankings they reflect are not likely to be overtly professed. We may therefore expect the ordinal rankings in an instrument for the measurement of self-oriented interpretations of values to distort the real ordering of preferences of politicians.

One way of detecting these distortions is a comparison with the rankings made by control groups of non-elites and nonpolitical elites; another way is a comparison with the politician's own ranking of the same items on a scale of other-directed interpretations. The latter procedure would be predicated on the hypothesis that the greater the *inverse* rank-order correlation between an item on the self- and on the other-directed instrument, the greater the probability that the "inconsistency" in the response (i.e., in test-situation behavior) does not reflect an inconsistency in the respondent's value system.

These methodological considerations are not devoid of substantive interest. If, for example, there is considerable agreement between political actors of different persuasions and with different commitments to a political career on the inverse rank ordering of values on self-directed and other-directed scales, this can be interpreted as a reflection of common cultural constraints; if, however, there are differences in these rankings between types of political actors, such differences may reflect "situational" determinants of value orientations, and the values with respect to which these differences occur may be indicative of patterns of incentives or patterns of strategies and image projection in recruitment or role performance. Rokeach has consistently argued that attitudes consist of beliefs about objects combined with beliefs about situations—i.e., beliefs about objects-in-situations. "Situation" must be interpreted, however, as referring not only to the object, but to the belief-holder.

Another problem related to the structure of value systems is the degree of correspondence between the importance attached to a value defined in general and abstract terms and that assigned to an operationalization of the abstract value in terms of political goals. The importance attached to political goals can be compared, in turn, with that assigned to specific political issues which are spatiotemporally defined examples of generalized political goals. Thus "freedom from fear" would be a personal terminal value which can be interpreted as self- or other-directed, "law-and-order" would be a corresponding generalized political goal and "stricter penalties for drug pushers" would be a specific issue exemplifying the "law-and-order" goal. Do politicians perceive these different levels of conceptualization as representing the same value-dimension and are their value-systems consistent across levels of conceptualization? Does the consistency of value systems across levels of generalization vary according to types of actors and political involvement?

The study of belief and value systems across types of political actors and political involvement constitutes the third problem area from which this research originated. One of the most frequently encountered typologies in the study of political elites is based on differences in incentives between "professionals" and "amateurs."[8] The amateur finds intrinsic rewards in politics: the determination of public policies on the basis of principles—as opposed to the professional's extrinsic rewards of power, income, status, or the fun of the game. The professional conceives politics in terms of winning an election or in terms of party interests, which usually involves making compromises and appeals to special interests; the amateur conceives politics in terms of substantive or procedural issues. During the last decade, the syndrome of amateur-orientations has been amply documented in the United States.[9] Wolfinger rightly points out, however, that idealistic reformers are a recurring feature in American politics.[10] Neither is it a typically American phenomenon, since "nonacquisitive" or "post-bourgeois" values have been characteristic of a generation raised in the relative affluence of the post-World War II era in Western Europe.[11] More important in the context of the present discussion is the fact that the amateur-syndrome is more strongly associated with perceived norms of party organization and procedure than with specific issue dimensions.[12] Furthermore, when a "reformer" faces a pluralistic environment, it is his commitment to a continuous political career which will determine whether and to what extent he will abandon the uncompromising posture of the amateur.

The preceding observation suggests that it is perhaps useful to hypothesize that the structure of both instrumental and terminal value systems differs not only across ideological positions, but also across stages in the development of a political career. Using the Weberian criteria of continuous involvement and full-time activity as measures of professionalization in politics, it is possible to consider different levels and types of political roles, which reflect differect commitments to professionalization, as involving different contexts and vantage grounds which affect the structure of belief and value systems. Thus, one may wish to inquire whether the "occasional" activist, the "continuous" part-time party worker or city councillor, the challenger in a congressional election who is willing to accept a full-time commitment but structures his world view from the perspective of the "aspiring candidate," and the incumbent full-time office holder will display differences in the structure and consistency of their value systems.

Studies of the orientational profiles of political actors have too often been limited to sets of participants at a particular level of office or type and extent of involvement. Cross-level comparisons have been rare exceptions,[13] and comparing the findings of separate case studies of political actors at different levels of office or involvement implies secondary analyses of data generated for theoretical purposes which do not always overlap and with research instruments which are not always comparable. One type of political actors—the unsuccessful challengers—has been greatly neglected in empirical elite studies and only recently have several studies provided some information on the sociopsychological and political profiles of winning and losing "opposition candidates."[14]

This study has attempted to apply its theoretical questions and research instruments to politicans at three levels of involvement and commitment. A comparative analysis of some of its findings, as well as a comparison with some data on non-politicians generated for Rokeach's studies of belief systems, will be reported in this paper.

THE RESEARCH INSTRUMENT AND THE DATA SET

Personal interviews were conducted prior to the 1972 Illinois primary elections with the twenty-five candidates for the National Democratic Convention from a

Northern Illinois district, and in the fall of the same year, prior to the November 1972 elections, with forty-one of the forty-five congressional candidates from Illinois, including nineteen incumbents and twenty-two challengers. The interviews followed a loosely structured schedule covering personal and political biographies, recruitment patterns, incentives, and career perspectives. The interviews also included four value inventories and a list of items from which the respondents were asked to construct the role profile they thought they were projecting or intended to project, as well as the perceived role profile of "politicians in general." The value inventories and the role profile items were randomly distributed on separate cards.

The lists of *Personal Instrumental Values* (PIV) and *Personal Terminal Values* (PTV) consisted of eleven items each, selected from Rokeach's lists of eighteen instrumental and eighteen terminal values:

Personal Instrumental Values	Personal Terminal Values
Ambition	Economic Security
Imagination	Social Recognition
Independence	Self-Respect
Logical Thinking	Freedom from Fear
Self-Control	Equal Chance at Life
Courage	Active Challenging Life
Tolerance	Friendship
Helpfulness	Self-Reliance
Honesty	Freedom from Constraint
Sympathy	Rising Standard of Living
Responsibility	Personal Achievement

No assumption was made about a structural consistency between instrumental and terminal values, and the choice of items on the two lists reflects this statement.

The *Terminal Political Values* (TPV) were operationalizations of the items included in the PTV list, and the list of *Political Issues* (PI) consisted of one specific example for each item on the TPV list drawn from the 1972 campaign issues. Below are listed the PTV, TPV, and PI inventories in the order determined by the PTV list and in accordance with the hypothesized correspondence of items at different levels of conceptualization.

Personal Terminal Values	Terminal Political Values
Economic Security	Stable Economy
Social Recognition	Strong Nation
Self-Respect	National Dignity
Freedom from Fear	Law and Order
Equal Chance at Life	Civil Rights
Active Challenging Life	Political Competition

Friendship	Political Loyalty
Self-Reliance	Private Enterprise
Freedom from Constraint	Self-Government
Rising Standard of Living	Growing Economy
Personal Achievement	Social & Technological Progress

Political Issues

Full Employment
Defense Expenditure
Fulfilling Treat Commitments
Dangerous Drugs Control
Equal Rights for Women
Open Presidential Conventions
Political Campaign Funding
Abolition of Wage and Price Controls
Local Control of Schools
Increased Exports
Mass Transit (Programs in Illinois)

The respondents were asked to rank these items 1 through 11 from what they considered the most important to the least important item. They were directed to interpret the PTV values as self-oriented and the TPV and PI lists as representing societal values. The lists were presented separately at different stages of the interview. The role profile inventory consisted of the following nine items:

Responsiveness to all the interests in the constituency
Uses a "commonsense" approach to problems
Stands up to political convictions on issues
A trustworthy man
Social prominence
Experienced in an important policy area
"Represents people like me"
Career of public service
Willingness to compromise in order to get things done

The list was presented twice. The first time the respondents were asked to use it for the construction of their role self-image by listing the items in the perceived order of importance. The procedure was repeated at a later stage of the interview for the construction of the perceived role profile of "politicians in general." It was assumed that the respondents would interpret "politicians in general" as meaning their opponents in the congressional race, or at least a profile from which they could dissociate themselves if they so desired. The role profile of "politicians in general" could thus serve as a frame of reference for the assessment of the *distinctiveness* of self-assigned role profiles and of the differences between self-images and the perception of these images by other political actors.

The inventory of items for the construction of role profiles also reflects an attempt to measure the internal consistency of self-assigned images. The nine items of this list included four pairs of somewhat conflicting attributes and one noncontroversial and highly valued item: "a trustworthy man." The four pairs of somewhat conflicting attributes are as follows:

Responsiveness to *all* interests in the constituency	"Represents people like *me*"
Stands up to political convictions on issues	Willingness to compromise in order to get things done
Uses a "commonsense" approach to problems	Experienced in an important policy area
Social prominence	Career of *public* service

To believe the folklore of politics, one would have to hypothesize that politicians would *not* perceive these pairs of items as consisting of somewhat conflicting statements, since they would tend to project an image capable of eliciting the support of different voters with many different perceptions of the most desirable image of a candidate. Similarly, opposition candidates would be likelier to project a more "purist" and therefore more consistent image than incumbents. The extent to which the data support these popular stereotypes will be discussed in the following section.

Needless to say, the nine items of the role profile scale do not exhaust the dimensions on which politicians tend to construct the images they project or perceive. These would include ideological postures and specific issue stands. However, such ideological postures and issue stands have not been included in the instrument for two reasons: (1) They would have required a far more elaborate instrument in an already lengthy interview schedule, and (2) some information is already available on ideological differences among and between elites, whereas the present study attempted to investigate only the relatively unexplored dimensions of the variability of role profiles according to "political status" (or type of involvement) which transcends the specific constituency-, party-, and issue-determined characteristics of political profiles.

Three types of data will be reported here: (1) the structure of each of the four value systems across three categories of elites, and a comparison with non-elites for the first two value scales, (2) the cross-value-systems consistency (rank-order correlations) for each of the three categories of politicians, and (3) projected and perceived role profiles.

In order to control for party affiliation, the congressional candidates have been subdivided into four groups: Democratic Incumbents (D/I), Democratic Challengers (D/C), Republican Incumbents (R/I), and Republican Challengers (R/C). This has further reduced the number of cases in each cell, increasing the homogeneity of each category at the cost of statistical significance. The four groups displayed a fairly equal homogeneity with respect to all four scales of values. The coefficient of concordance (Kendall) varied between .235 and .396 for the Personal Instrumental Value scale, .286 and .426 for the Terminal Political Value scale, .401 and .535 for the Political Issues scale, and .406 and .635 for the Personal Terminal Value scale. Thus, *homogeneity was lowest for the instrumental values and highest for the personal terminal values.* Levels of statistical significance have been indicated for all measurements, and although in this type of study a more liberal interpretation of levels of significance can be justified, only the most acceptable findings will be discussed.[15]

SELECTED FINDINGS

Personal Instrumental Values

Of the four lists of values from which the respondents were asked to construct rank-order scales in terms of importance, the PIV list is the most universalistic. It does not imply any reference to social or political values and represents a set of criteria which can be validly used for comparisons across sociopolitical cultures and subcultures. It is an instrument for assessing differences in nonpolitical value commitments between types of political actors or between elites and non-elites. Table 3.1 presents the rank ordering of mean PIV item scores for all congressional candidates, for the Democratic Convention candidates, and for a sample of voters.

TABLE 3.1
PERSONAL INSTRUMENTAL VALUES
Rank Orders of Mean Scores

	All Congressional Candidates	Democratic Convention Candidates	Voters*
	(N = 39)	(N = 25)	(N· = 1233)
Ambition	11	11	2
Imagination	6	2	11
Independence	2	5	9
Logical Thinking	5	4	10
Self-Control	7.5	9	8
Courage	3	7.5	5
Tolerance	9	6	4
Helpfulness	7.5	7.5	6
Honesty	1	1	1
Sympathy	10	10	7
Responsibility	4	3	3

* Rank orders adjusted from data presented in Rokeach, 1971:32.

There is complete agreement between voters and all types of politicians about the first rank assigned to *honesty*[16] and extreme disagreement on the ranking of *ambition*. The inverse rank ordering of ambition in the value systems of politicians and those of the average citizen is a reflection of the dysfunctionality of overtly expressing *personal* needs and value preference for politicians, who are identified according to their *public* goal-orientations. What is perhaps surprising in this value ranking of ambition by politicians is what one may consider either the naiveté or the cynicism of professing a lack of ambition. Ambition has been found to be not only the second most important, but also the most *stable* instrumental value (with a test-retest reliability of .70 at three to seven weeks' interval).[17] Is it possible that politicians have come to accept the images they want to project as reality?

While politicians and voters differ in the relative importance they attach to a value, there is also considerable disagreement between the part-time activist and the full-time professional politician. In the latter comparison, there is a greater probability that we are dealing with a measure of differences associated with degrees of involvement in the subculture of politics. This applies to *imagination* and *logical thinking*, which are the *two lowest-ranking* values for the sample of voters, rank second and fourth for the convention candidates, and are at the mid-scale point for congress members and their challengers. In this respect, the "occasional" or part-time activist is further removed from the average citizen, and therefore less "representative" than the full-time politician or his challenger. Finally, congressional candidates place more emphasis on *independence* and less emphasis on *tolerance* than the average citizen, whereas the activist takes a mid-scale position on both values. The generalized value-profile of the politician, as it appears from this comparison of instrumental values, differs from that of the voter in the following respects:

(a) refusal to admit the importance of ambition,
(b) greater importance attached to independence, imagination, and logical thinking, and
(c) less importance assigned to tolerance.

There is complete agreement on the importance of honesty and only minor differences in the ranking of other values.

Distinguishing between established and aspiring congressional candidates and controlling for party affiliation, we obtain the measures displayed in Table 3.2. Commenting first on the rank-order correlation for the entire value-system between subgroups of respondents, we note that the highest correlation (.854) at the highest level of significance (.001) is that between the value systems of Democratic and Republican incumbents. The lowest rank-order correlation is that between the challengers of the two parties (.543; $p<.10$). Thus, in the case of incumbency, the similarity of "political status" reduces the differential "impact" of party affiliation on the structure of instrumental value systems,

TABLE 3.2

PERSONAL INSTRUMENTAL VALUES	Ranks of Means				Means and Stand. Deviations				Differences of Means			
	D/I	D/C	R/I	R/C	D/I N=8	D/C N=10	R/I N=9	R/C N=12	Demo. D/I-D/C	Repub. R/I-R/C	Incum. D/I-R/I	Chall. D/C-R/C
Ambition	11	10	10	11	10.13 1.25	8.10 2.60	7.89 2.42	9.42 2.68	2.03++	-1.53+++	2.24+	-1.32
Imagination	6	3	8.5	7.5	6.25 3.41	4.30 2.63	7.78 2.68	6.17 3.38	1.95+++	1.61	-1.53	-1.87+++
Independence	3	2	4	5	3.75 1.91	3.90 2.77	5.11 2.85	5.42 2.28	-.15	-.31	-1.36	-1.52+++
Logical Thinking	5	4.5	5.5	7.5	5.75 2.82	5.50 3.03	6.56 2.88	6.17 3.19	.25	.39	-.81	-.67
Self-Control	7	8	5.5	9	6.38 3.50	6.60 3.47	6.56 2.96	6.25 2.45	-.23	.31	-.18	.35
Courage	1	4.5	2	6	3.38 2.00	5.50 3.57	3.44 2.01	5.92 3.03	-2.13+++	-2.47+	-.07	-.42
Tolerance	10	9	7	4	7.50 1.93	8.00 2.16	6.89 2.47	5.00 2.95	-.50	1.89+++	.61	3.00*
Helpfulness	9	7	8.5	3	7.38 2.26	6.30 2.31	7.78 1.79	4.92 3.03	1.08	2.86+	-.40	1.38
Honesty	2	1	1	1	3.50 3.02	2.70 2.00	1.56 0.73	2.83 2.89	.80	1.28	1.94++	-.13
Sympathy	8	11	11	10	6.63 2.50	8.30 2.83	8.33 2.69	8.42 1.93	-1.68	-.08	-1.71+++	-.12
Responsibility	4	6	3	2	5.38 3.78	6.10 2.47	3.67 2.45	4.42 2.28	-.73	-.75	1.71	1.68+++

Rank-Order Correlations Between Ranks of Means, Spearman's Rho: D/I-D/C, .802***, Democrats; R/I-R/C, .652+, Republicans; D/I-R/I, .854***, Incumbents; D/C-R/C, .543++, Challengers. *** p<.001, ** .01, * .02, + .05, ++ .1, +++ .2.

whereas in the group of challengers, party affiliation is a strongly differentiating factor despite the similarity of "political status." These findings are congruent with the hypothesis of in-role socialization for the incumbents, and with the elementary observation that the aspiring challenger will emphasize a posture which differentiates him from the incumbent and that, therefore, we ought to find greater interparty differences among challengers. Perhaps the distinction between safe seats and marginal seats could provide some further information on the degree of homogeneity of incumbents' value systems, but given the small number of cases, this further distinction has not been included in the analysis reported in this section. One should also note that the type of correlational analysis used in this chapter does not provide any indication of causal links; are differences and similarities "consequences" of political status, or is there a self-selection process which results in this distribution of value systems between types of political actors? Any attempt to answer such questions would require measurements of value stability and change.

Reverting to the findings, we note the far greater internal homogeneity of value systems among Democratic incumbents and challengers (.802, $p<.01$) than among their Republican counterparts (.652, $p<.05$). This could perhaps account for the greater similarity in political *styles* among the Democrats.[18] An examination of the structure of personal terminal value systems will reveal that in terms of preferred end-states, the Republicans are a more homogeneous group.

The difference-of-means test for individual values on the PIV list points at only a few significant differences. The single most interesting finding is the consistent difference between challengers and incumbents of both parties in the ranking of *courage*. One would hypothesize that courage is a more important value for challengers than for incumbents, yet the reverse seems to be the case, with differences significant at the .05 level for Republicans and .01 level for Democrats. Why do incumbents value courage more highly than challengers? A possible answer can be sought in the structure of role profiles. Whereas both Democratic and Republican incumbents rank the item "stands up to political convictions on issues" *first* in their political self-images and fairly low on the scale for "politicians in general," both groups of challengers rank this item at a mid-scale point in their self-images and at the very end of the scale for "politicians in general." It is possible that, for the incumbents, courage is associated with "standing up to convictions on issues" and that they believe they are standing up to their convictions in role performance or at least wish to project this image. Challengers cannot adduce evidence for courage in role performance and may have interpreted courage as referring to the electoral context where they did not wish to project it as an important indicator of risk. What seems to be beyond doubt, though not very helpful in this matter, is the fact that the challengers do not share at all the belief that "politicians in general" stand up to convictions on issues.

Two other values for which significant differences were found are *tolerance* and *helpfulness*, which Republican challengers value considerably higher than both Republican incumbents (p<.05) and Democratic challengers (p<.02). Democratic incumbents and challengers place a lower value on *responsibility* than their Republican counterparts, but the statistical significance of these differences is low (p<.20).

Including the Democratic Convention candidates in the comparison, we find that the structure of their instrumental value systems correlates *significantly higher* with that of the Democratic *challengers* (.807, p<.01) than with that of the Democratic incumbents (.589, p<.10)(see Table 3.3). Since this pattern occurs in three of the four value scales, it may be indicative of a rank ordering of types of political actors in terms of the structural similarity of their value systems. These are also types of actors which represent increasing levels of involvement and commitment to continuous and full-time political activity: the part-time activist (convention delegates), the aspiring politician (congressional challengers) and the established politician (incumbent congressmembers). This rank ordering in terms of value system similarity does not hold true for the list of Personal Terminal Values (PTV), because all Democratic subgroups display a very similar value structure. Thus (Democratic) part-time activists differ considerably from incumbents but much less from challengers, as far as instrumental values,

TABLE 3.3
RANK-ORDER AND DIFFERENCES OF MEANS
Congressional Candidates (Democrats)
and Candidates for Delegates

PERSONAL INSTRUMENTAL VALUES	Rank-Order			Differences of Means		
	D/I	D/C	Deleg.	D/I D/C	D/I Deleg.	D/C Deleg.
Ambition	11	10	11	2.03++	2.13++	.10
Imagination	6	3	2	1.95+++	1.33	- .62
Independence	3	2	5	- .15	-1.97++	-1.82+++
Logical Thinking	5	4.5	4	.25	.11	- .14
Self-Control	7	8	9	- .23	- .98	- .76
Courage	1	4.5	7.5	-2.13+++	3.22*	-1.10
Tolerance	10	9	6	- .50	1.46+++	1.96++
Helpfulness	9	7	7.5	1.08	.78	- .30
Honesty	2	1	1	.80	.94	.14
Sympathy	8	11	10	-1.68	- .85	.82
Responsibility	4	6	3	- .73	.10	.82

Rank-Order Correlations		*	p<.001
Spearman's Rho		**	.01
D/I—D/C	.802**	***	.02
D/I—Deleg.	.589++	+	.05
D/C—Deleg.	.807**	++	.1
		+++	.2

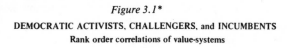

Figure 3.1*

DEMOCRATIC ACTIVISTS, CHALLENGERS, and INCUMBENTS

Rank order correlations of value-systems

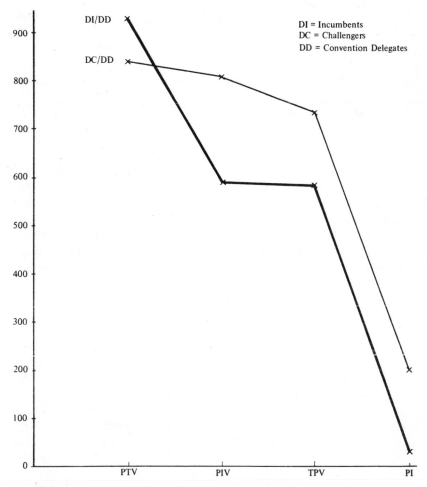

DI/DD

DC/DD

DI = Incumbents
DC = Challengers
DD = Convention Delegates

900
800
700
600
500
400
300
200
100
0

PTV   PIV   TPV   PI

* The connecting lines in Figures 3.1–3.4 have been added for visual clarity only.

political terminal values and political issues are concerned; there is, however, little difference among the personal terminal values of all three groups. These relationships are presented in Figure 3.1 and can be summarized as follows:

(a) all three types of Democratic politicians share—in addition to party affiliation—a common structure of Personal Terminal Values (PTV);

(b) each type represents a different structure of orientations toward modes of conduct (PIV);

(c) each type represents a different structure of orientations toward Terminal Political Values (TPV); and

(d) the strongest dissimilarity is revealed in the ranking of Political Issues (PI).

Can these findings be interpreted as indicating that a party will attract political activists with very similar personal terminal value systems across levels of involvement, but these actors will have different orientations toward modes of conduct according to their position on the scale of involvement or career commitment and that, furthermore, there will be disagreement between actors in different positions on the relative importance of specific political values and even greater disagreement on issues?

Personal Terminal Values

As Tables 3.4 and 3.5 indicate, there are very few differences in the structure of the PTV systems among incumbents, challengers, and convention candidates. Statistically significant differences are found for three values only: (1) the higher value placed by Republican incumbents on "active challenging life" and (2) their lower valuation of "social recognition" in comparison with both Republican challengers and Democratic incumbents; (3) the difference among Democratic incumbents, challengers, and convention candidates in their valuations of "personal achievement." A comparison of all groups of politicians with the sample of voters reveals, however, *two inverse rank orderings* (Table 3.6): Voters rank (family) security first, whereas for all categories of politicians (economic) security ranks ninth on a scale of eleven items; furthermore, politicians rank "active challenging life" second, whereas for voters, it is the last item on the scale.

The low ranking of economic security on the value scale of politicians is another example of the distortion caused by the cultural constraints placed on the expression of private motivations by politicians. It also exemplifies the need for a sharper distinction between relatively short-term goals and end-state values. Unless he is the candidate of a political "machine," the American politician tends to be an independent political entrepreneur. The independence of political entrepreneurship is predicated on the ability to raise funds and involves an assumption of personal financial independence. The independent entrepreneur is therefore economically secure and although a political campaign and even office-holding may involve a financial sacrifice, the very act of candidacy is an acknowledgement of the higher value assigned to the expected rewards of political office compared to the possibility of a financial sacrifice. Since economic security is very frequently a prerequisite of "availability" for political office, the politician is unlikely to profess a great concern for personal economic

TABLE 3.4

PERSONAL TERMINAL VALUES	Ranks of Means				Means and Stand. Deviations				Differences of Means			
	D/I	D/C	R/I	R/C	D/I N=8	D/C N=10	R/I N=9	R/C N=12	Democ. D/I-D/C	Repub. R/I-R/C	Incum. D/I-R/I	Chall. D/C-R/C
Economic Security	11	9	10	9.5	9.63 1.19	7.80 3.39	9.00 1.41	7.92 2.94	1.83+++	1.08	.63	− .12
Social Recognition	9	11	11	9.5	8.00 3.16	9.60 1.51	10.22 1.39	7.92 2.75	−1.60+++	2.31+	−2.22++	1.68++
Self-Respect	1	1	2	1	2.50 1.41	3.30 2.11	2.89 1.62	3.00 2.09	− .80	− .11	− .39	.30
Freedom from Fear	7	8	8	8	6.00 2.88	6.30 2.98	6.67 2.45	6.93 3.03	− .30	− .25	− .67	− .62
Equal Chance at Life	4	5	7	5	5.13 3.14	5.10 3.21	6.22 2.05	5.75 1.92	.03	.47	−1.10	− .65
Active Challenging Life	2	2	1	2	3.50 2.56	3.40 2.36	1.33 0.50	3.67 2.81	.10	−2.33+	2.17+	− .27
Friendship	6	6	4.5	7	5.75 3.06	6.10 2.86	5.44 2.07	6.17 3.38	− .35	− .72	.31	− .07
Self-Reliance	5	4	3	3	5.37 1.68	4.70 2.79	4.44 1.51	4.00 2.37	.68	.44	.93	.70
Freedom from Constraint	3	7	4.5	4	4.38 2.93	6.20 2.44	5.44 3.36	5.17 2.89	−1.83++	.28	−1.07	1.03
Rising Standard of Living	10	10	9	11	8.88 2.36	9.10 1.60	8.89 1.36	9.33 1.78	− .23	− .44	− .01	− .23
Personal Achievement	8	3	6	6	6.88 2.36	4.40 1.60	5.89 1.36	5.83 1.78	2.48+	.06	.99	−1.43

Rank-Order Correlations Between Ranks of Means, Spearman's Rho: D/I–D/C, .763**, Democrats; R/I–R/C, .913***, Republicans; D/I–R/I, .861***, Incumbents; D/C–R/C, .893***, Challengers. ***p<.001, **.01, *.02, + .05, ++ .1, +++ .2.

TABLE 3.5
RANK-ORDER AND DIFFERENCES OF MEANS
FOR THE CONGRESSIONAL DEMOCRATIC CANDIDATES
AND THE CANDIDATES FOR DELEGATES

PERSONAL TERMINAL VALUES	Rank-Order			Mean-Differences		
	D/I	D/C	Deleg.	D/I D/C	D/I Deleg.	D/C Deleg.
Economic Security	11	9	9	1.83^{+++}	1.91^{+}	.08
Social Recognition	9	11	11	-1.60^{+++}	-1.00	.60
Self-Respect	1	1	1	- .80	- .18	.62
Freedom from Fear	7	8	8	- .30	- .76	- .46
Equal Chance at Life	4	5	6	.03	.05	.02
Active Challeng- ing Life	2	2	2	.10	- .34	- .48
Friendship	6	6	4.5	- .35	.91	1.26
Self-Reliance	5	4	4.5	.68	.53	- .14
Freedom from Constraint	3	7	3	-1.83^{++}	- .30	1.52^{+++}
Rising Standard of Living	10	10	10	- .23	.12	.34
Personal Achievement	8	3	7	2.48^{+}	.48	-2.00^{+}

Rank-Order Correlations	D/I—D/C	.764**	$^{+}$	$p<.05$	*	$p<.001$
Spearman's Rho	D/I—Deleg.	.925*	$^{++}$	.10	**	.01
	D/C—Deleg.	.839**	$^{+++}$	.20		

TABLE 3.6
TERMINAL PERSONAL VALUES
Rank orders of mean scores

	All Congressional Candidates (N = 39)	Convention Candidates (N = 25)	Voters* (N = 1233)
Economic Security**	9	9	1
Social Recognition	10	11	10
Self-Respect	1	1	3
Freedom from Fear	8	8	not given
Equal Chance at Life**	5	6	5
Active Challenging Life	2	2	11
Friendship	7	4.5	8.5
Self-Reliance	3	4.5	not given
Freedom from Constraint	4	3	2
Rising Standard of Living**	11	10	8.5
Personal Achievement**	6	7	6

* Adjusted rank orders, based on data reported in Rokeach 1971: 31.
** Closest approximation of equivalence in item description between instruments used for sample of voters and sample of politicians.

security, especially if it could be interpreted as a reluctance to incur a financial sacrifice. He therefore interprets economic security as a goal (i.e., some desirable *future* state of affairs) rather than a value and assigns it a very low rank on his professed scale of personal values. He will not deny, however, that economic security is a highly preferred value in the value systems *of others*, as demonstrated by the high priority given to this item on the value scale of the voter sample (if such a demonstration were needed at all). Recognizing this fact, the politician ascribes a very high priority to the other-directed interpretation of economic security on the TPV scale—i.e., "stable economy"—which ranks second on the eleven-item scale for both established and aspiring politicians.

"Active challenging life" ranks second in the personal terminal value systems of all groups of politicians, but is the very last value on Rokeach's eighteen-item inventory for voters. Since there is no social norm compelling the politician to profess a preference for an "active challenging life," one must conclude that the single most discriminating item which distinguishes between the value system of political elites and non-elites is the propensity to seek an active challenging life. This propensity is sometimes equated with "risk-taking behavior," an achievement drive or need for "self-actualization," and it is possible that an "active challenging life" is merely a socially acceptable substitute designation for any of these terms. Yet, the "challenge" of a political career does not necessarily imply a risk and unless he is an "advertiser" (in the sense Barber has used this term in his analysis of recruitment motivation),[19] the losing candidate will have "achieved" only the experience of an unsuccessful campaign. The "challenge" is probably a reward per se, typical of all entrepreneurial roles, and politicians who are not entrepreneurs (e.g., the candidates "appointed" by the hierarchical organizations of European mass-parties) are likely to be motivated by a different aspect of *participation* per se, if they do not also seek other personal rewards in a political career.

Personal Terminal Values, Terminal Political Values, and Political Issues

An item-by-item comparison of the lists of Personal and Political Terminal Values indicates that the TPV items are "translations" of the self-oriented value interpretations on the PTV inventory into sociopolitical formulations. There were, of course, a number of different ways in which these "translations" could be formulated. The TPV items used were chosen by a panel of judges as the closest approximation of a "translation" that would convey to a group of Illinois politicians in 1972 the meanings these items were intended to reflect. For example, it was preferred to use a politically controversial but conceptually unambiguous item if a politically neutral formulation would have made the item appear irrelevant to a politician engaged in an election campaign. The respondents were informed, each time they were

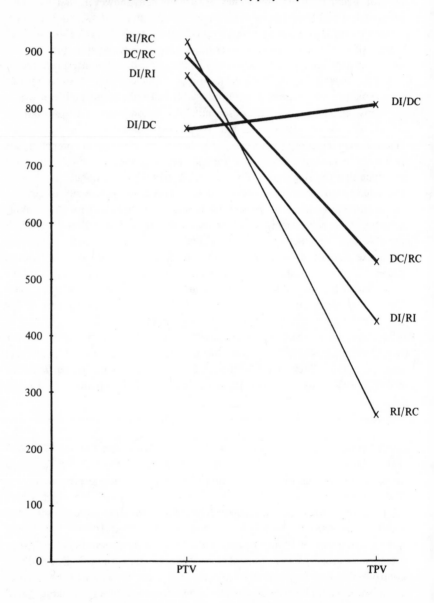

Figure 3.2

PERSONAL TERMINAL VALUES and POLITICAL TERMINAL VALUES

Between-group rank order correlations, by party and political status

Figure 3.3

PERSONAL TERMINAL VALUES and POLITICAL TERMINAL VALUES
Rank order correlations between incumbents and challengers of opposite parties

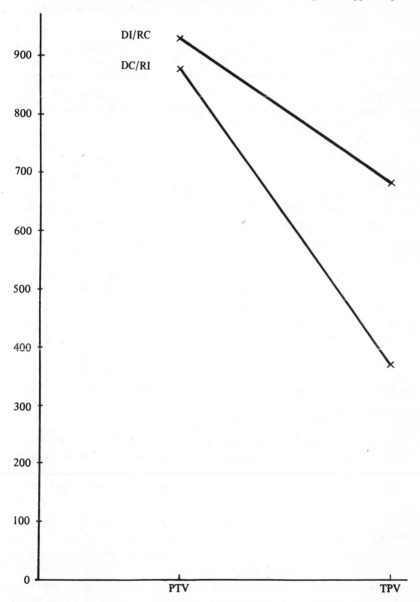

asked to rank-order one of the value lists, that we were interested in their perception of the importance of the issue-area and *not* in whether they supported or opposed a particular issue-stand, since we already knew what positions they had taken. A similar explanation was given for the rank ordering of issues, adding that the PI list was not considered exhaustive of all relevant issues in the 1972 campaign.

Figure 3.2 is a graphical representation of the between-group rank order correlations of PTV and TPV value systems. It reflects the substantial transformation of a group of relatively like-minded individuals (with between-group rank-order correlations ranging from .763 to .913) into a heterogeneous set of four contrasting groups ranging in the (dis)similarity of their value systems from a rank-order correlation of .263 to .809.

The correlations shown in Figure 3.2 refer to groups sharing either party affiliation or incumbent/challenger status; thus, no pair of individuals—one from each group in a pair—would face each other in an electoral contest. When groups were defined in terms of contrasting status on both the party affiliation and incumbent/challenger dichotomies—i.e., when Democratic challengers were compared to Republican incumbents and Republican challengers to Democratic incumbents, a very similar pattern of change became apparent (Figure 3.3).

It is extremely unlikely that our choices of TPV items have consistently contradicted the intended correspondence between the PTV and TPV values and that the respondents, while consistent with their own PTV scale, have detected our inconsistencies in varying degrees depending on their own party affiliation and incumbent/challenger status. Even if this implausible interpretation were correct, it would still prove that it was legitimate to hypothesize that incumbents and challengers, within and across parties, have different perceptions of the relative importance of political values and issue areas grouped in two different and—according to this implausible interpretation—inversely related lists of items.

Correlations based on ordinal scales are not very precise measures, but they are "somewhat analogous to product-moment correlations."[20] Let us consider, however, only the general configuration of the findings, which points at an *inverse* correlation between self-oriented and socially oriented interpretations of values. This is also apparent from Table 3.7, where the correlations between rankings on the value scales and the issue-list are calculated *across value-systems within groups*.

For all groups, the PTV-TPV correlation is *negative*, being lowest among Democratic incumbents and highest among their Republican counterparts. Democratic Convention candidates displayed again a greater similarity with their party's challengers than with the incumbent Democrats. Table 3.7 also indicates

TABLE 3.7
PERSONAL TERMINAL VALUES, TERMINAL POLITICAL VALUES
AND POLITICAL ISSUES
Rank order correlations by party/status groups

	PTV–TPV	PTV–PI	TPV–PI
Democratic Incumbents	–.036	–.555	.382
Democratic Challengers	–.245	–.627	.027
Democratic Convention Candidates	–.275	–.207	.809
Republican Incumbents	–.352	–.707	.614
Republican Challengers	–.257	–.639	.655

that there is a considerably stronger negative correlation between the rank ordering of Political Terminal Values and that of Political Issues (with the exception of the convention candidates). Thus, the ranking of political issues within each group of congressional candidates is *more* consistent with the Personal Terminal Values scale than is the ranking of the Terminal Political Values, but it is *more consistent in its inverse relationship* to the PTV scale.

The correlation between TPV and PI rankings is indicated in the last column of Table 3.7. All correlations are *positive,* ranging from an insignificant .027 for Democratic challengers to .809 ($p < .01$) for the Democratic Convention candidates. We find, therefore, that the convention candidates—i.e., the *part-time activists*—*are the most consistent group* in their translation of the structure of political values into a ranking of political issues. This seems to indicate that the absence of a commitment to "professional" political roles is correlated with a greater consistency between value systems and the perception of issues, a finding consistent with the observations made in studies of "amateurs."

Let us consider how the politicians aspiring to full-time political office—i.e., those from whom we wish to distinguish the part-time activists—compare with the established politicians in their perceptions of political values and issues. Figure 3.3 has shown that at the TPV level, the correlation between values systems of Democratic challengers and Republican incumbents had dropped to .364, and that between Republican challengers and Democratic incumbents to .684. Figure 3.4 indicates that at the level of Political Issues, the DC/RI and RC/DI correlations are considerably higher—. 721 and .814, respectively. The data show that this is a consequence of the fact that Democratic challengers and incumbents (DC/DI) became increasingly dissimilar, whereas the differences between Republican

Figure 3.4

TERMINAL POLITICAL VALUES and POLITICAL ISSUES

Incumbents and challengers, within and between
status groups rank order correlations across parties

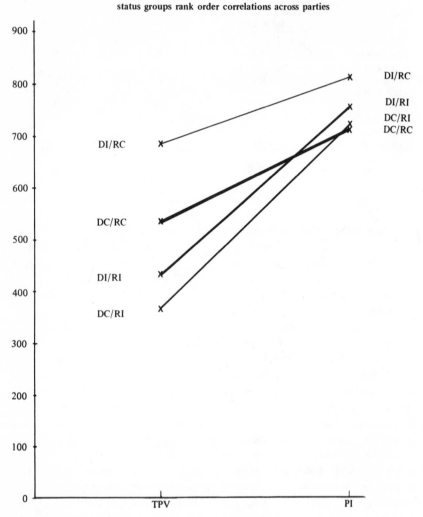

challengers and incumbents (RC/RI) tended to disappear. Stated otherwise:
although Democrats and Republicans differ considerably in the structure of their
value systems, Democratic challengers and Republican incumbents, or Republican
challengers and Democratic incumbents, display very similar perceptions of the
relative importance of campaign issues.

Let us summarize these findings and suggest a model to which one could refer in order to probe more deeply into the relationships between degrees of involvement or commitment to a political career, party affiliation, and consistency of value scales.

(1) Political elites, at all levels of involvement, share a fairly similar set of Personal Terminal Values. They differ from the population of voters primarily in their (professed) extremely low valuation of economic security and in their extremely high valuation of an active challenging life.

(2)(a) In terms of Personal Instrumental Values, political elites share with the voters a very high valuation of honesty, and display an extreme reluctance to acknowledge the importance of ambition, which is highly valued by the voters.

(2)(b) All elite groups value imagination, independence, and logical thinking considerably higher than voters, but differ among themselves in this respect.

(2)(c) Full-time office holders and office seekers place a higher value on courage and a lower value on tolerance than part-time activists.

(2)(d) The differences in Personal Instrumental Values between categories of politicians reflect different personal and political styles associated with levels of active involvement within an elite with fairly similar Personal Terminal Values.

(3)(a) At the level of Terminal Political Values, the value systems of part-time activists differ from those of office holders and office seekers, but there is greater similarity between activists and aspiring politicians than between activists and established politicians.

(3)(b) The fairly homogeneous group of politicians, in terms of Personal Terminal Values, becomes a set of contrasting groups at the level of political value systems, with both party and incumbent/challenger status as intervening variables.

(4)(a) The difference between part-time activists and both office seekers and office holders is considerably greater in their perceptions of the importance of issues than in the structure of their political value systems, but the difference between activists and challengers is smaller than that between activists and incumbents.

(4)(b) All correlations between Personal Terminal Values and perceptions of the relative importance of issues are negative.

(4)(c) Office holders and office seekers are more consistent in their inverse valuation of Personal Terminal Values and Political Terminal Values. In this respect, they differ from the part-time activists.

(4)(d) All correlations between terminal political value systems and the perception of issues are positive, with party affiliation as the major intervening variable among office holders and office seekers. Part-time activists, however, are considerably more consistent than the incumbents and challengers of their party.

(4)(e) Differences between incumbents and challengers of opposite parties, which were observed at the level of political value systems, tend to disappear at the level of political issue perceptions.

We thus find that personal values which are more likely to be associated with differences in *personality structure* (ambition, active challenging life) are effectively discriminating criteria between non-elites and all groups of political elites, while other personal instrumental values (independence, imagination, logical thinking, tolerance) tend to discriminate, though less effectively, between individuals with different involvements in or commitments to a political career and, in turn, between the latter and non-elites.

Personal terminal values which are likely to be determined to a great extent by formal and informal *socialization* do not tend to distinguish between different types of politicians (at least within the political culture to which this study refers). In the political value systems, *parties* seem to be the most discriminating variable: While Democratic incumbents and challengers have very similar value systems, their Republican counterparts differ considerably. At the issue perception level, this relationship is reversed, presumably because incumbents and challengers of opposite parties have very similar perceptions of the relative importance of issues. Thus, at the issue level, *incumbent/challenger/activist status* seems to be more strongly associated with changes in the cross-system structure of values, with activists displaying the highest consistency across value systems. This model is presented here by listing the observed dependent variables associated with each hypothesized major determinant:

Major Hypothesized Determinants

	Personality structure	Socialization	Party	Involvement/ Commitment
Observed Dependent Variables	Recruitment Style	Personal terminal values	Political terminal values	Issue perception
	Involvement/ Commitment			

TABLE 3.8
ROLE PROFILES—SELF IMAGES
MEAN SCORES, STANDARD DEVIATIONS AND RANK ORDERS

	Total N = 39	Rank	Democrat Incumbent N = 8		Democrat Challenger N = 10		Republican Incumbent N = 9		Republican Challenger N = 12	
Responsiveness to all the interests in the constituency	3.03 2.10	2	3.14 1.95	3	2.50 2.07	2	4.00 2.35	4	2.67 2.02	2
Uses a "common sense" approach to problems	3.50 1.27	3	3.86 1.77	4	3.40 2.12	3	3.11 2.03	3	3.67 1.37	3
Stands up to political convictions on issues	3.55 2.14	4	2.29 1.38	1.5	4.30 2.67	4	2.33 1.50	1	4.58 1.73	4
A trustworthy man	2.47 1.48	1	2.29 1.49	1.5	2.30 1.06	1	2.67 1.23	2	2.58 2.02	1
Social prominence	8.53 1.01	9	8.86 0.38	9	8.50 0.97	9	8.78 0.67	9	8.17 1.40	9
Experienced in an important policy area	5.05 2.01	5	4.43 0.54	5	6.20 1.93	6	4.56 1.67	5	4.83 2.59	5
"Represents people like me."	6.11 1.98	6	6.71 1.38	7	5.40 2.17	5	6.56 1.24	6.5	6.00 2.52	6
Career of public service	6.45 1.62	7	6.43 1.62	6	6.60 1.57	8	6.56 1.88	6.5	6.25 1.66	7.5
Willingness to compromise in order to get things done	6.53 1.83	8	7.00 1.73	8	6.40 1.65	7	6.67 1.80	8	6.25 21.8	7.5

TABLE 3.9
ROLE PROFILES—POLITICIANS IN GENERAL
MEAN SCORES, STANDARD DEVIATIONS AND RANK ORDERS

	Total N = 39		Democrat Incumbent N = 8		Democrat Challenger N = 10		Republican Incumbent N = 9		Republican Challenger N = 12	
	Mean/SD	Rank	Mean/SD	Rank	Mean/SD	Rank	Mean/SD	Rank	Mean/SD	Rank
Responsiveness to all the interests in the constituency	3.51 / 0.37	1	3.13 / 3.04	1	4.60 / 2.50	5	3.11 / 2.21	1	3.17 / 1.64	1
Uses a "common sense" approach to problems	4.90 / 1.92	4.5	4.63 / 1.60	4	5.40 / 1.90	6	4.67 / 2.40	3.5	4.83 / 1.89	3.5
Stands up to political convictions on issues	5.80 / 2.76	8	5.13 / 3.00	6	6.90 / 2.42	9	5.00 / 3.16	5	5.92 / 2.58	8
A trustworthy man	4.05 / 2.32	2	3.50 / 1.60	2	3.90 / 2.23	3	3.67 / 2.18	2	4.83 / 2.89	3.5
Social prominence	6.87 / 2.64	9	7.75 / 2.19	9	6.60 / 2.63	8	7.56 / 2.40	9	6.00 / 3.05	9
Experienced in an important policy area	4.90 / 2.25	4.5	5.00 / 2.14	5	4.20 / 1.55	4	5.33 / 2.50	6.5	5.08 / 2.71	5
"Represents people like me."	5.56 / 2.42	7	4.38 / 2.20	3	6.50 / 2.17	7	5.67 / 2.24	8	5.50 / 2.78	6
Career of public service	4.21 / 2.33	3	5.75 / 2.49	7.5	2.70 / 2.11	1	4.67 / 1.80	3.5	4.08 / 2.19	2
Willingness to compromise in order to get things done	5.10 / 2.71	6	5.75 / 2.77	7.5	3.80 / 2.53	2	5.33 / 2.74	6.5	5.58 / 2.78	7

Candidate Role Profiles

The findings reported in this subsection provide further support for the statement made in the preceding summary with respect to the impact of incumbent/challenger status on the beliefs related to the immediately relevant and contextually defined position of the candidate. Political status is as important as party affiliation, if not more so, in determining the role profile the candidate wishes to project and his perception of the manner in which his role profile differs from what he considers to be the role profile of "politicians in general."

Role profiles have been defined in this study as consisting of a specific rank ordering, in terms of perceived importance, of a list of nine items combining personal attributes and political postures. Tables 3.8 and 3.9 present the mean scores, standard deviations, and rank orderings of these items for self- and other-oriented profiles, by party affiliation and political status. The literature on candidate profiles has focused primarily on images of personal attributes and issue stands of candidates, as perceived by the voters, whereas self-profiles of politicians have been explored predominantly in terms of issue stands or the functional typology developed in *The Legislative System*.[21] The items included in the role profile inventory used in this study do not completely overlap with any of these perspectives; they were intended to provide summarizing measures on four different dimensions: (1) consistency of projected self-images; (2) distinctiveness of self-images; (3) interparty differences; and (4) interstatus differences. In reporting the findings, the same sequence of dimensions will be followed.

Consistency of projected self-profile. The data presented in Table 3.8 suggest that either the folklore of politics does not refer to congress's members and congressional candidates or that at least two of our four pairs of items have been ranked at a considerable distance from each other on the self-profile scale by pure chance. It is likely that the item "social prominence" was so intensively rejected by all respondents that it was not perceived as differing considerably from "a career of public service" which was also rejected, but less intensively. Table 3.10 presents the mean scores and rank orderings grouped in pairs of contrasting items. Since the "neutral" item ("a trustworthy man") ranked first in all groups (and second only for the incumbent Republicans) and "social prominence" ranked last in all groups, the span left for the remaining items ranges between two and eight.

The single most convincing evidence of within-scale consistency in self-profiles is the high ranking of "stands up to convictions" and the low ranking of "willingness to compromise." The Democratic challengers have the most consistent perception of what they wish to dissociate themselves from in terms of these items: in their description of the role profile of politicians in general "standing up to convictions" ranks *last* and "willingness to compromise" ranks second—i.e., the two conflicting items are still perceived as such, *but their rank*

TABLE 3.10
CANDIDATE SELF PROFILE STRUCTURE
Mean scores and rank orders, for pairs of contrasting items,
by party affiliation and political status

	DI	DC	RI	RC
Stands up to political convictions on issues	2.29 (1.5)	4.30 (4)	2.33 (1)	4.58 (4)
Willingness to compromise	7.00 (8)	6.40 (7)	6.67 (8)	6.25 (7.5)
Responsiveness to all interests	3.14 (3)	2.50 (2)	4.00 (4)	2.67 (2)
Represents people like me	6.71 (7)	5.40 (5)	6.56 (6.5)	6.00 (6)
Uses a commonsense approach	3.86 (4)	3.40 (3)	3.11 (3)	3.67 (3)
Experienced in an important policy area	4.43 (5)	6.20 (6)	4.56 (5)	4.83 (5)

ordering has been reversed. For the remaining groups, "politicians in general" project an image according to which neither item in this pair is valued very highly.

Distinctiveness of self-image. The discussion of the preceding pair of items has shown that self-profiles and perceptions of "politicians in general" differ considerably in terms of both the ranking, and the implied consistency, of "standing up to convictions" and "willingness to compromise." It is not surprising that candidates wish to project a self-image of political intransigence or courage and that they describe "others" as not projecting this attribute very strongly. Another item on which self- and other-oriented images differ considerably is "career of public service." One would expect incumbents to project a self-image of experienced public servants, yet this item ranks low in the projected self-image of both challengers and incumbents. Challengers perceive "others" (presumably their incumbent opponents) as ranking "career of public service" very high (which they do not) and incumbents rank this item somewhat higher for "others" than for themselves. Only Democratic challengers rank "responsiveness to all interests" on the profile of "politicians in general" considerably lower than on their self-profiles; all other groups believe they are themselves less responsive to all interests than are "politicians in general." As a result of these differences, there is a somewhat higher overall rank-order correlation between self-profile and profile of "politicians in general" for both groups of incumbents (RI : rho = .659; DI: rho = .642) than for the Republican challengers (.550). The greatest distinctiveness of self-image is displayed by the Democratic challengers; their self-profiles do not correlate at all with their perceptions of the profiles of "politicians in general."

It is again not surprising that incumbents see themselves much closer to their image of "politicians in general" than do challengers, but when combined with the great similarity of self-profiles across party affiliation and political status this finding reflects the fact that although politicians do not tend to project different images of themselves, they differ considerably in the manner in which they view the structure of the self-other relationship, and this view obviously varies according to the vantage ground on which the individual is situated. Thus political status (incumbent/challenger) plays as important a role as party affiliation, if not more so, in structuring the individual's perception of the environment, as far as political role profiles are concerned. Since all incumbents had also been, at some time, challengers (although they may not always have had to face an incumbent), one must conclude that winning an election and in-role socialization bring about a considerable transformation in the manner in which politicians view themselves in relation to other politicians. We shall find additional evidence for the importance of political status when we compare incumbents and challengers of opposite parties.

Interparty and interstatus comparisons. Table 3.11 indicates the rank-order correlations between the various groups for self-profile and profile of "politicians in general." Self-profiles are highly similar across parties and political status, and only the DC/RI comparison shows a somewhat lower coefficient of rank order correlation. One should note, however, on Table 3.8 that challengers of both parties rank "stands up to convictions" much lower, and "reponsiveness to all interests" somewhat higher than the incumbents of their respective parties. For profiles of "politicians in general," Democratic challengers display a completely different structure than Democratic incumbents. No such disparity occurs in the Republican Party. Since the self-other profile similarity is high for incumbents, but low for challengers, it is perhaps the difference between the profile Democratic challengers ascribe to their opponents—i.e., Republican incumbents—and the other-directed profile of Democratic incumbents which can explain

TABLE 3.11
BETWEEN GROUP RANK ORDER CORRELATIONS OF PROFILES
by party affiliation and political status

	Self profiles	Politicians in general
DI/DC	.845	-.004
RI/RC	.870	.833
DI/RI	.975	.620
DC/RC	.979	.562
DI/RC	.900	.600
DC/RI	.796	.384

the change in the DI/DC correlation. This interpretation is congruent with the finding that the DC/RI correlation is considerably lower than the correlation between the other-directed profiles of Democratic and Republican challengers (DC/RC).

With a larger "sample" it would have been possible to control for incumbent/challenger status in order to measure the differential impact of the expected outcome of the election. The competitiveness of the party system in a given district has always been considered a major variable in the analysis of recruitment, motivations, party organization, and candidate orientations. Congressional seats, however, have not been very competitive; furthermore, estimates of the competitiveness of a seat in any given election, which go beyond past voting records in their attempts to assess the "strength" of a candidate, are subject to various interpretations. Thus, a seat may be considered "safe" according to the *Congressional Quarterly Election Reports,* but is considered "competitive" by the incumbent congressman or his challenger. More frequently, however, "a Congressman hears most often from those who agree with him." [22] The present data set provides a clear answer only with regard to those candidates who were considered "sure losers" according to the *Congressional Quarterly Reports:* for these candidates, the correlation between the profiles of self and other was an *insignificant* –.138. For "competitive" seats the correlation was .650, which comes very close to the correlation found for both Democratic and Republican incumbents.

IN LIEU OF CONCLUSION

This research has used personality-determined sociopsychological and political variables in an attempt to explore differences among activists, aspiring, and established politicians, as well as differences among all three types of politically involved individuals and a cross-sectional sample of voters. The statistically significant and perhaps acceptable findings point at some differences between the politically involved and non-involved members of society, at the negative correlation between personal and political terminal values and at the inverse relationship between cross-value-system consistency and degree of commitment to a political career. Furthermore, perceptions of the relative importance of issues and of the distinctiveness of political role self-images seem to be determined, to a great extent, by contextual configurations of variables such as incumbent/challenger status or the perceived closeness of a political contest. With the possible exception of the structure of value systems across levels of imputation, and the consistency of candidate self-profiles, the findings of this study have been in line with the beliefs, hypotheses, and otherwise defined non-documented statements, as well as some of the documented evidence, concerning the personal, social and political orientations of political elites. In addition to its findings, however, this chapter was intended to suggest that it might be useful to distinguish, in the formulation of our questions about politicians, between the more and the less stable determinants of their behavior in the subculture of politics and that this distinction might help bring together the separate findings based on theories of recruitment, professionalization, and role performance in politics.

NOTES

1. For recent reviews of this literature, see Fred I. Greenstein, "Political Psychology: A Pluralistic Universe," in Jeanne N. Knutson, ed., *The Handbook of Political Psychology* (San Francisco: Jossey-Bass, 1973), pp. 438-469; also Fred I. Greenstein, "Personality and Politics," and Moshe M. Czudnowski, "Political Recruitment," in Fred I. Greenstein and Nelson W. Polsby, eds., *Handbook of Political Science*, Vol. 2 (Reading, Mass.: Addison-Wesley, 1975), 1-92, 155-242.

2. See Moshe M. Czudnowski, "Toward a New Research Strategy for the Comparative Study of Political Recruitment" (presented to the Eighth World Congress of the International Political Science Association, 1970), 19-20.

3. Morris Rosenberg, *Occupations and Values* (New York: Free Press, 1957), 22-24.

4. Milton Rokeach, *Beliefs, Attitudes and Values* (San Francisco: Jossey-Bass, 1968); "The Measurement of Values and Value Systems," in Gilbert Abcarian and John W. Soule, eds., *Social Psychology and Political Behavior, Problems and Prospects* (Columbus, Ohio: Charles E. Merrill, 1971).

5. Rokeach, *Beliefs*, 160.

6. Ibid., 161.

7. Ibid., 168-178.

8. See James Q. Wilson, *The Amateur Democrat* (Chicago: University of Chicago Press, 1962).

9. See Robert S. Hirschfield, Bert E. Swanson and Blanche D. Blank, "A profile of political activists in Manhattan," Western Political Quarterly 15 (1962), 489-506; Nelson W. Polsby and Aaron B. Wildavsky, *Presidential Elections* (New York: Charles Scribner, 1971); John W. Soule and James W. Clarke, "Amateurs and professionals: a study of delegates to the 1968 Democratic National Convention," American Political Science Review 64 (1970), 888-898.

10. Raymond E. Wolfinger, "Why political machines have not withered away and other revisionist thoughts," Journal of Politics 34 (1972), 365-398.

11. See Ronald Inglehardt, "The silent revolution in Europe: intergenerational change in post-industrial societies," American Political Science Review 65 (1971), 991-1017.

12. Richard C. Hofstetter, "The amateur politician: a problem in construct validation," Midwest Journal of Political Science 15 (1971), 31-56.

13. See Warren E. Miller and Donald Stokes, "Constituency influence in Congress," American Political Science Review 57 (1963), 45-56; Herbert McClosky, Paul J. Hoffman and Rosemary O'Hara, "Issue conflict and consensus among party leaders and followers," American Political Science Review 54 (1960), 406-429; Samuel J. Eldersveld, *Political Parties: A Behavioral Analysis* (Chicago: Rand McNally, 1964); Allan Kornberg and Norman Thomas, "The political socialization of national legislative elites in the United States and Canada," Journal of Politics 27 (1965), 761-775; Norman R. Luttbeg, "The structure of beliefs among leaders and the public," Public Opinion Quarterly 32 (1968), 398-409; G.R. Boynton, Samuel C. Patterson, and Ronald C. Hedlund, "The missing link in legislative politics: attentive constituents," Journal of Politics 31 (1969), 700-721.

14. See John W. Kingdon, *Candidates for Office* (New York: Random House, 1966); David A. Leuthold, *Electioneering in a Democracy: Campaigns for Congress* (New York: John Wiley, 1968);

Robert J. Huckshorn and Robert C. Spencer, *The Politics of Defeat* (Amherst: University of Massachusetts Press, 1971); Jeff Fishel, *Party and Opposition* (New York: David McKay, 1973).

15. Gudmund Iversen, "Social sciences and statistics," World Politics 25 (1972), 145-154.

16. As mentioned in the introductory section of this paper, no guidance can be sought from previous findings in different settings. Among the studies of candidate self-images, Grawitz's interviews with forty-four candidates to the French legislature in the Lyon area in 1958 included an instrument for the ranking of seven attributes comprising nonpolitical and political instrumental values: honesty, dedication, "character," intelligence, knowledge of voters' demands, general political information and eloquence. The only item common to this French study and the research reported in this paper is "honesty" and both studies report identical findings for this item. In the French study, twenty-two of thirty-four respondents (the number of responses in Grawitz's study varies from item to item) ranked honesty first (with a mean score of 1.64), followed by "character (2.89), dedication (2.90), and intelligence (3.32). See Madeleine Grawitz, "La psychologie des candidats," Cahiers de la Fondation Nationale des Sciences Politiques 109 (1960), 195-217.

17. See Rokeach, "The Measurement," 25.

18. See Leo M. Snowiss, "Congressional recruitment and representation," American Political Science Review 60 (1966), 627-639.

19. See James D. Barber, *The Lawmakers* (New Haven: Yale University Press, 1965).

20. Hubert M. Blalock, *Social Statistics* (New York: McGraw-Hill, 1960), 317.

21. John C. Wahlke, Heinz Eulau, William Buchanan and Leroy C. Ferguson, *The Legislative System* (New York: John Wiley, 1962).

22. Lewis A. Dexter, *The Sociology and Politics of Congress* (Chicago: Rand McNally, 1969), 159.

Chapter 4

PARTISANSHIP IN THE RECRUITMENT AND PERFORMANCE OF AMERICAN STATE LEGISLATORS

CHONG LIM KIM, JUSTIN GREEN,
and SAMUEL C. PATTERSON

University of Iowa

Central to the success of a political party is its ability to recruit candidates capable of winning elections. Unless a party recruits a group of viable candidates and wins a majority of public offices, it cannot expect to attain power and implement its policy goals. Political parties engage actively in the recruitment process not only to win elections with their candidates but also to influence policy outcomes through those who win offices. Therefore, the capacity of a party to identify and encourage candidates potentially loyal to the party is essential to its success and survival.

The role of parties in recruitment has been extensively studied. However, recent empirical studies of legislative recruitment have for the most part focused upon the factors which determine an individual's chance of selection. Typical of this approach are the studies of legislators' social background characteristics, their personality traits, their political ambitions, their socialization, and the opportunity structures within which their careers unfold.[1] In many of these studies, recruitment has been treated as the dependent variable to be explained by one or a combination of the factors cited above. By comparison, the study of the *consequences* of recruitment has been relatively rare until now.[2] Do the social

Authors' Note: We are grateful to Professors Lester G. Seligman, Malcolm E. Jewell, and Moshe M. Czudnowski for their helpful comments and suggestions.

and career background characteristics of legislators make any difference in terms of their attitudes and behavior? Do differences in recruitment experiences affect the functional and decisional outputs of a legislative system? In fact, existing studies of legislators' background characteristics assume that differential recruitment determines the attitudes and behaviors of legislators and, thereby, affects the performance of the legislative system.[3]

The nexus between the commitment of political parties in legislative constituencies to the recruitment of legislators on the one hand, and on the other the partisan attitudes and loyal party voting of elected legislators, has been observed by several students of Congress and the state legislatures. In his study of the recruitment of congressmen in Cook County, Illinois, Snowiss observed that:

> The study of recruitment and the study of representation are complementary. Knowledge of representative institutions gives direction to analyses of recruitment; in turn, knowledge of factors affecting recruitment may explain much about the behavior of legislative bodies.[4]

He demonstrated that, especially among Chicago Democrats, loyalist partisan attitudes and predispositions to legislative party cohesiveness were very profoundly rooted in the party organizational matrix of the constituency. Kingdon's analysis of congressional voting decisions in the Ninety-First Congress does not take into consideration the extent of a role for the party organizations in the recruitment of congressmen. However, he did find exceptionally high agreement between congressmen's attitudes on policy issues and their perceptions of the attitudes of their constituents, and he implies that congressional decisions are, in the main, consistent with constituents' wishes and desires. This consistency occurs in large part because of the recruitment process: "If one starts to explain variance in legislative voting, the mechanism that probably explains the most variance is the recruitment process which brought a man of one set of attitudes to the Congress rather than another."[5]

Olson's research on the reciprocal relationships between the congressman and his district underscores the decentralized character of the American parties. Studying a sample of congressmen and their districts, Olson showed that legislators are much more active and involved in constituency party activities when they are elected from districts where there is a high reliance on party organization in nominations and elections than are those congressmen who did not rely on their party for their recruitment. His analysis demonstrated the vagaries of local party organizational constraints upon congressmen, including the limited interest on the part of local party leaderships in non-local congressional activities and issues. Olson points to the contrast between the United States and Great Britain in the relevance of constituency party recruitment of legislators to party cohesion in the legislative assembly, a contrast which has been elaborated in the research of Ranney.[6] In addition, Olson argues that "the American state legislator and county and city officials are probably more closely involved with their local extragovernmental parties than is the congressman.''[7] What research there is on this question for state legislators indicates a strong connection between constituency party recruitment and legislative party loyalty. Sorauf's study of candidates for the Pennsylvania legislature in 1958 clearly indicated that "protestations of fealty to the party came from those candidates who were the product of strong party organizations," and that "the degree of loyalty the candidate gives the party is greater among those from strong party organizations and from parties active in the preprimary and primary recruitment chores.''[8]

In this study of American state legislators, we will examine the effects of differential recruitment. Our main focus is on the consequences, rather than the determinants, of legislative recruitment. More specifically, our study is divided into four sections: (1) a characterization of the role of parties in recruitment, (2) an examination of the partisan effects of differential recruitment, (3) an analysis of behavioral consequences of recruitment through a roll-call study, and (4) a discussion of the theoretical implications of the findings. We draw upon five sets of interview data collected in Iowa, California, New Jersey, Ohio, and Tennessee. In 1967, Patterson and his associates conducted an interview survey with members of the Iowa General Assembly.[9] The data for other states are derived from the well-known four-state legislative study.[10] These data sets contain many comparable items and, in particular, similar questions pertaining to recruitment experiences and partisan attitudes. To relate differential recruitment to behavior we rely on the roll-call data collected in Iowa.[11]

PARTIES AND RECRUITMENT: A TYPOLOGY

The recruitment of candidates for elective office is generally considered as one of the principal functions of American parties.[12] However, the role of parties in recruitment varies considerably from state to state. In the state of New Jersey, sixty-nine percent of the state legislators were initially drafted for candidacy by their parties. Among Iowa legislators, fifty-six percent indicated contact by county party chairmen about running for the legislature.[13] In Tennessee and California, only seventeen and twenty percent were similarly drafted by the party. The extent to which parties are active in recruitment seems to vary in different states, and such variations also seem to be related to the degree of statewide partisan competition. In highly competitive states like New Jersey and Ohio, party organizations played an active role in candidate recruitment. In less competitive states, the role of parties in recruitment was relatively small.

Political parties are directly involved in the recruitment of candidates. One motivating force for such involvement in recruitment is desire of party leaders to exercise control over policy outcomes. Therefore, it is essential for the party to identify and instigate candidates who are both attractive to the electorate and loyal to the party programs, and to extend to them its sponsorship in the form of financial or organizational support. Seligman suggested two main types of party sponsorship: conscription and cooptation.[14] Conscripted candidates decide to run primarily because of their loyalty to the party. They recognize that their party needs a candidate and make themselves available when the party calls for their service. Yet, in another respect, their candidacy may be considered as a reward given by their party for their long-standing loyalty and contributions. In either case, their loyalty to the party and dependence upon it for political advancement are uppermost.

Coopted candidates, although similar to the conscripted ones in the sense that they are also drafted by the party, are individuals who have established their reputations independently of the party. Because of their personal achievements or illustrious careers outside politics they command a great deal of respect in the community. Despite the fact that these individuals are not active in partisan organizations, a party often persuades them to run in order to enhance the visibility of its ticket. These two types of candidates may in effect serve somewhat different objectives of the party. While the coopted candidates may increase a party's chance of winning elections by lending their names and prestige, the conscripted candidates may ensure tighter party control over policies. Because the coopted candidates may feel that their personal achievements and their community standing help the party more than the party helps them, they are not likely to see themselves as much beholden to the party for the opportunity to serve in office, as do the conscripted. On the other hand, those drafted by the party for their loyalty and service to it—namely, the conscripted candidates, are the most effective agents through whom the party can implement its policy goals.

Implicit in the above discussion are two important variables of legislative recruitment: the role of party and the partisan record of candidates. The recruitment process is an interplay between an aspirant for office and a sponsor such as a political party.[15] The two recruitment variables that we have outlined relate to the key actors involved in recruitment: the party and the candidate. On the basis of these two variables, we have constructed a typology of legislative recruitment. As indicated in Table 4.1, candidates fall into four distinct types in terms of their recruitment experiences: party agent, coopted candidate, careerist, and entrepreneur. These four types represent different patterns of interplay between the party and the candidate at the initial recruitment stage. Table 4.1 also indicates the total number of legislators in each recruitment type from the combined data for the five states in this analysis.

TABLE 4.1
TYPES OF RECRUITMENT: FIVE STATE DATA

Partisan Record	Role of Party	
	Drafted	Self-Starter
Active	Party Agent N = 86	Careerist N = 155
Inactive	Coopted N = 55	Entrepreneur N = 101

The Party Agent

If a party has any ambition to influence policy outcomes, it needs to recruit the type of candidates whom we have called "the party agent." Typically, two major characteristics define a party agent. First, the instigation of a party is a critical factor in the decision to run. What distinguishes him from other types of candidates is the fact that he is "drafted" by a party. Second, a party agent is an active party member whose loyalty has been tested over a long period of time. Subsequently, his loyal service to the party is recognized and rewarded with a nomination to public office. When elected, a party agent will faithfully implement the policies of the party.

The party agents show distinctive social and career characteristics when compared to the rest of candidates. The available profile data presented in Table 4.2 show that the party agents are generally older than other candidates. Also, they are more likely to be employed in occupations of the brokerage type such as the real estate business, insurance, stock brokerage, banking, and law practice. Moreover, the typical party agent is a man who has strong local ties. He has spent most of his life in the area, has served the district many times in office, and has no further ambition beyond the state legislature. Because of his unswerving loyalty to the party and his deep sense of local ties, the party agent provides the basic material from which a party can build a strong local political organization.

The Coopted Candidate

Political parties often adopt a strategy of recruiting candidates outside their ranks in order to win elections. Although the coopted candidate has not distinguished himself in partisan activities, he is a man of considerable prominence and personal achievement. Therefore, a party which recruits him as a candidate hopes to increase the luster of its ticket and to enhance its chance of election victory. As compared to other types of candidates, the coopted candidates are relatively younger. Although they are highly successful in their occupations and

TABLE 4.2
SOCIAL PROFILES OF VARIOUS TYPES OF CANDIDATES IN NEW JERSEY, OHIO,
TENNESSEE, CALIFORNIA, AND IOWA
(in percentages)

Profiles	Party Agents (N = 86)	Others (N = 311)	Coopted Candidates (N = 55)	Others (N = 342)	Careerists (N = 155)	Others (N = 242)	Entrepreneurs (N = 101)	Others (N = 296)
Age: % over 40 years	78	67	66	70	67	71	68	70
Occupation: % engaged in brokerage jobs[a]	59	50	38	56	57	51	51	53
Occupation: % lawyer	54	53	38	55	57	50	52	53
Ambition: % aspiring to higher office	35	46	34	46	53	39	43	44
Length of residence: % spending 50 percent of their life in district[b]	77	69	76	75	75	80	85	76
Incumbent status: % incumbent	78	51	78	54	69	71	56	60

[a]The brokerage occupations include those in the real estate business, insurance, banking, and law practice. For lack of comparable data, Iowa legislators are not included in these computations.

[b]For the lack of comparable data, Iowa legislators are not included in these computations.

are locally prominent figures through their active participation in civic or other community activities of a nonpartisan sort, they do not seem to have combined politics with their careers until they were drafted by the parties. In this respect, the coopted candidates are different from the party agents, who tend to be drawn predominantly from the "brokerage" occupations. Many of the coopted candidates were born in the area or at least spent a significant part of their lives there. Moreover, they have strengthened such local ties through their repeated service in the state legislature. We see yet another facet of their local orientations in their political ambition. A majority of the coopted candidates (66%) in our data expressed limited ambition: They seemed quite willing to serve their districts for several terms, but they did not aspire to offices higher than the state legislature. Not only are the coopted candidates part of a party's strategy for winning elections, but also their recruitment represents a major method by which local, nonpartisan notables are brought into the fold of party politics.

The Careerist

The candidates whom we have called "careerists" are, first of all, self-starters. Political parties or interest groups do not play a critical role in their initial decision to seek office. Nor do they enjoy the benefits of party sponsorship as is the case for party agents or coopted candidates. The single factor which appears to characterize careerists best is the level of their political ambition. They approach politics with a serious career commitment. Their decision to run is not one made on the spur of the moment, but is an important part of their carefully considered, long-term career plans. To the careerists, the state legislature tends to be a stepping stone toward higher office. In this respect, careerists are quite a different breed of political animal than the majority of politicians on the state legislative level.[16] Because a careerist has political ambition and probably a carefully worked-out career strategy geared to his political advancement, his style of action in office may be distinguishable from that of other candidates.

The Entrepreneur

Candidates in our fourth category are called "entrepreneurs." These candidates appear, in comparison to other types of candidates, to be singularly interested in the instrumental value of political activity. They declare their candidacy and serve in office insofar as they feel such activities help promote their private careers. Like Barber's "advertisers," our entrepreneurs probably participate in election campaigns in order to gain publicity.[17] If elected, they will serve in office only as long as they perceive that their political involvement brings significant benefits to their private occupations. Two main characteristics define an entrepreneur: He lacks extensive experience in partisan activities, and he does not have the support of his party when he decides to run. Lacking two very important advantages for winning an election—namely, that of party sponsorship and political skills learned through partisan activities, the entrepreneur nevertheless decides to run and subsequently wins an office. However, he is markedly less inclined to serve in the legislature for several terms than other types of candidates. The proportion of veteran legislators among entrepreneurs was the smallest (56%) among the four categories of candidates, which suggests that the primary objective of entrepreneurs' political involvement is to quickly maximize the benefits that accrue to them from their participation in the election campaign or from their service in office. Once this objective is satisfied, they tend to withdraw promptly to their private lives.

The four categories of candidates represent, in effect, different kinds of interplay between office-seekers and political parties as recruiting agents. Also, the four categories indicate important differences in the recruitment experiences of individual candidates. As stated earlier, a key assumption underlying many studies of legislative recruitment is that differential recruitment has implications for the attitudes and behavior of elected officials. In the analysis that follows, we will examine the validity of this assumption. We will consider first whether or not different types of recruitment are related to the partisan attitudes of legislators, and then proceed to analyze the effects of such differential recruitment on roll-call behavior.

RECRUITMENT AND PARTISAN ATTITUDES

In all but two American states, legislators are selected in partisan elections. When successful candidates move on to the state capitols, political parties become salient reference groups for their behavior. Although very high levels of party cohesion are rarely achieved in American legislatures, and levels of party cohesion vary considerably from one state legislature to another, the parties in the legislature still remain a powerful determinant of legislative behavior.[18] How do the newly elected legislators adapt to legislative life? What sort of attitudes do they develop toward the role of the party in the legislature? Do they show different partisan attitudes as they feel indebted in varying degrees to the activities of their parties during the campaign?

Part of the reason why parties are active in candidate recruitment is to secure party discipline and unity among their legislative members. The following is Sorauf's description of this relationship:

> State legislators are far more dependent on the local and state party for nomination and election than are the members of Congress. And what the local party hath given, it may take away. . . . In some states the parties control the election of state legislators to such an extent that these positions approach an "elective patronage," which the party awards to loyal toilers in its organizational ranks.[19]

One intended effect of a party's control over nominations and elections is, therefore, to foster party loyalty and support among its legislative members. This reasoning leads us to expect that, ceteris paribus, those legislators whose nomination and election are directly influenced by the local party and who are therefore most beholden to it, are likely to show stronger partisan attitudes than others elected without the benefit of party support.[20]

In order to determine whether different types of recruitment are associated with different degrees of partisan attitudes, we have constructed an index of partisanship employing four questionnaire items included both in the four-state study and in the Iowa survey. This index ranges from a score of zero to a score of one; the greater the score, the greater the degree of partisanship.[21] A score of 1.0 would mean in this case that a legislator has given pro-party responses to all the questions; a score of 0.0 would indicate that he has failed to report even a single pro-party response.

Although the differences are not markedly striking for all legislators in the five states, the four recruitment types do show the expected variations in partisan commitment. In Table 4.3, we report the mean partisanship score for each of the recruitment types. The party agents recorded the highest mean partisanship score, indicating that those legislators drafted by their parties for their loyalty do indeed exhibit the strongest partisan attitudes. The least partisan legislators were, as we expected, those whom we have called entrepreneurs. Their candidacy was not instigated by the party in their decision to run, nor were they very active in the local party organizations before they became legislators. Consequently, they did not feel closely tied to party programs and policies and were much less beholden to the party for the opportunity to serve in office than legislators who were drafted by the party. This fact seems to account for the relatively low partisan commitment of the entrepreneurs.

TABLE 4.3
MEAN PARTISANSHIP SCORES FOR DIFFERENT TYPES OF RECRUITMENT:
FIVE STATE DATA

Types of Recruitment	All states	Individual States				
		Iowa	New Jersey	Ohio	California	Tennessee
Party agents	.506	.343	.616	.565	.461	.438
Coopted candidates	.460	.367	.500	.607	.222	.429
Careerists	.429	.296	.700	.560	.500	.375
Entrepreneurs	.427	.276	.500	.550	.238	.506
All members	.451	.301	.582	.564	.384	.451
Number of cases	397	122	64	119	58	34

The coopted candidates and careerists fall between party agents and entrepreneurs in terms of their levels of partisan commitment. Because coopted candidates are persuaded to run by the party, although primarily for their prominence in the community rather than for their party loyalty, they may still feel to some degree indebted to the party when they later serve in the legislature. The coopted candidates indeed showed the second highest mean partisanship score, which is not surprising in view of the fact that parties played a critical role in their initial decision to seek office. Both careerists and entrepreneurs are self-starters in the sense that they contest in elections without the benefit of party sponsorship. Yet, in some other respects, they are quite different from one another. The careerists were active in the local party organizations before they were elected and had ambitions for political advancement. Moreover, they recognized the importance of the party as a vehicle through which they could best promote their political careers. The opposite was true of the entrepreneurs. They did not have extensive experience in partisan activities, nor did they have a progressive ambition in politics. Their primary political motive appears to have been to help their private occupations. As soon as they attained this goal, they tended to dissociate themselves from further political involvement. In light of such differences, it is understandable that the careerists would have stronger partisan attitudes than the entrepreneurs, not because they are obligated to the party for nomination and election but because they need its future support in order to realize their political ambitions. Although careerists and entrepreneurs did not differ substantially on the index of partisanship, the partisan attitudes of careerists indicated a pro-party response to an agree-disagree item: "If a bill is important for his party's record, a member should vote with his party even if it costs some support in his district." Among the entrepreneurs, only fifty-one percent gave similar replies. Likewise, when asked to respond to another item, "The two parties should take clear-cut, opposing stands on more of the important state issues in order to encourage party responsibility," forty percent of the careerists agreed with the statement, compared with thirty-one percent of the entrepreneurs. The careerists indicated consistently more favorable attitudes toward the role of party than the entrepreneurs did.[22] In summary, party agents showed the highest degree of partisan commitment, followed next by coopted candidates, careerists, and entrepreneurs, in that order.

The extent to which political parties play an active role in candidate recruitment varies from state to state, depending upon the structure of its party competition. Such state-by-state variations might also have implications for the consequences of recruitment. In some states, the effects of differential recruitment could be quite visible in terms of partisan attitudes. In others, recruitment variables may not exert as great an influence on the partisan attitudes of legislators. Do recruitment variables affect the partisan attitudes of legislators in some states to a greater degree? Drawing upon our five-state data, we array in Table 4.3 the mean partisanship scores for different recruitment types by states.

The analysis of partisanship exhibited by legislators shows considerable fluctuation across both states and recruitment types. New Jersey and Ohio legislators are the most partisan, and Iowa legislators the least partisan; legislators from California and Tennessee fall between. As Wahlke, Eulau, Buchanan, and Ferguson have shown, in the late 1950s New Jersey and Ohio were highly competitive states, a condition reflected in the fact that legislators in these two states, in contrast to those in California or Tennessee, showed a high cognitive orientation to party, a strong affective orientation to party, and a very positive evaluation of party influence.[23] California and Tennessee represent states which, while different in many important respects, share a tradition of bifactional rivalry in the dominant party.[24] Iowa, a state with many small towns and small cities, has not experienced the kind of partisan cleavage more characteristic of states with major urban centers, and local party organization, while playing an important part in legislative recruitment, has not been relatively strong in campaign support for candidates.[25]

State political cultures bring forth variations from state to state in the levels of partisanship to be found within different recruitment types, and some of the interstate variations are not easy to interpret. In general, legislators who were conscripted by their parties indicate higher levels of partisanship than those who were self-starters. In every state except Tennessee, party agents showed more partisanship than entrepreneurs. At a minimum, it seems possible to assert that, despite important differences in the socioeconomic conditions of these five states and in their party systems, party agents, active in and recruited by their parties, exhibited relatively high levels of partisanship in their attitudes. Party agents indicate a high degree of partisanship in the most partisanly competitive states—New Jersey and Ohio.

Insofar as coopted candidates are concerned, they actually show even stronger partisan commitments than party agents in Ohio and Iowa. However, they also showed the lowest level of support for their parties in California and New Jersey. On the one hand, one might argue that the coopted candidates will manifest strong partisan attitudes because they, like party agents, are drafted by the party for legislative positions. On the other hand, one might also argue that because coopted candidates lend their names and personal reputations to the party ticket, they are likely to take positions on legislative issues independent of their party's line.

Either of these two arguments can be partially supported, depending upon which state we look at. However, this is not the real answer to our basic question: Why do coopted candidates become the most partisan group in some states while they become the least partisan legislators in other states? Although it is an extremely important question, we can only speculate here because of the limited amount of evidence available to us. So far, we have considered only recruitment variables as potential determinants of partisan attitudes. However, there are many variables other than recruitment experiences which may also operate on the partisan attitude of legislators. Not only is an average legislator subject to pressures from the local party, but also to pressures from the state party, the party in the executive, the legislative party, or the national party. In addition, he is also susceptible to the demands of his constituents and organized interest groups. The way in which these variables intermesh may vary from state to state. In some states, these variables may be mutually reinforcing in the direction of strong partisan politics. In some other states, the meshing of these variables is such that legislators do not need to behave in an overtly partisan manner. Such variation in the state legislative environment may account for the different partisan adaptations that we discovered among the coopted candidates.

The extent to which careerists develop partisan attachments after they move into legislative positions again varies a great deal from state to state. The careerists in New Jersey and California exhibited the strongest partisan attitudes of all legislators, while their counterparts in Ohio, Iowa, and Tennessee indicated the lowest or next to the lowest level of support for their party. What might account for such differences in the partisan orientation of the careerists? Speculatively, the presence or absence of strong party machines in a state seems to be an important factor which influences career strategies of ambitious legislators. In states where party machines are strong, a careerist will recognize that he cannot realize his ambition unless he works through the party organizations. Consequently, he will seek the party's support for his career by becoming a very partisan legislative member. This may explain in part why some careerists exhibit even stronger partisan attitudes than party agents, despite the fact that they are not beholden to the party through both stages of nomination and election. Among the five states, New Jersey had the strongest, best-functioning party machines in both parties. In the southern counties, it was the Republican Party machine firmly based in Atlantic City which dominated state politics. The best-known Democratic machine was that of Frank Hague in Hudson County.[26] Ambitious politicians of both parties had to take account of such realities of machine politics in the state. Therefore, it is not surprising at all that the careerists in New Jersey turned out to be one of the staunchest partisan groups.

Despite the fact that the partisan attitudes of careerists varied a great deal from state to state, they nevertheless showed consistently stronger partisan attitudes than did the entrepreneurs in all states but Tennessee. Here again, what appears to push the careerists closer to the party lines is their ambition for political advancement. While entrepreneurs do not intend to stay long in the state assemblies, let alone harbor aspirations to higher offices, careerists are trying to make a career out of politics. Given such a marked difference in their political ambition, it is not difficult to understand why the careerists tend to be more partisan than are the entrepreneurs.

The least partisan group were those legislators whom we have characterized as entrepreneurs. Their mean partisan scores were the smallest in Iowa, New Jersey, Ohio, and California. In Tennessee, however, the entrepreneurs surprisingly recorded the highest score on our partisan index. The case of Tennessee should be interpreted with caution, for the partisan scores were computed there from a limited number of cases. Moreover, there were too few cases of entrepreneurs in Tennessee to make the index score very meaningful. At any rate, it seems clear that, among all legislators, the entrepreneurs show the weakest partisan orientations. If one considers the lack of a party's instigation and support at the time when entrepreneurs seek nomination, and if one also considers the main reason for their political involvement, which is to help promote their personal occupation through politics, it is not surprising that they should be a group of legislators least attached to their parties.

Overall, the evidence indicates that recruitment variables do indeed have an impact upon partisan attitudes of legislators. The party agent, the coopted candidate, the careerist, and the entrepreneur, each of whom represents a different type of recruitment, showed varying levels of partisan orientations after they were elected to the legislature. Although differential recruitment may not be the only variable salient to the legislator's partisan orientation, it nevertheless seems to be a major factor in the formulation of partisan attitudes.

RECRUITMENT, PARTISAN ATTITUDES, AND DISTRICT RECRUITMENT MILIEUX

Some of the ambiguities in the pattern of partisanship scores reflected in the state-by-state presentation in Table 4.3 may be clarified if district characteristics are taken into account. It is likely that constituency milieux will have a bearing upon legislators' partisan attitudes when they have experienced their political careers in districts typical of their own party. Accordingly, we have roughly categorized districts in the five states into those which are typical and nontypical for the legislators' parties, considering typical districts to be the urban Democratic and rural Republican ones, and nontypical districts the rural Democratic and urban Republican ones. In Table 4.4, we show mean partisanship scores for each recruitment type under conditions of district typicality in each state we have analyzed. In general, it can be seen that legislators from districts typical of their party are more partisan than those from nontypical districts in Iowa, California, and Tennessee. However, in the states which are highly competitive politically, New Jersey and Ohio, the legislators from nontypical districts are, in fact *more partisan* in their attitudes than those from typical districts. Moreover, considerable unexpected variations in partisan attitudes for recruitment types remain even when legislators in each state are classified according to district typicality.

Nevertheless, in Iowa, California, and Tennessee, patterns of partisanship

TABLE 4.4
PARTISANSHIP SCORES FOR RECRUITMENT TYPES OF DISTRICT TYPICALITY
IN IOWA, NEW JERSEY, OHIO, CALIFORNIA, AND TENNESSEE

Types of Recruitment	State and District Typicality									
	Iowa		New Jersey		Ohio		California		Tennessee	
	Typical	Non-typical	Typical	Non-typical	Typical	Non-typical	Typical	Non-typical	Typical	Non-typical
Party agents	.402	.200	.556	.661	.333	.606	.546	.333	.563	.313
Coopted candidates	.126	[a]	.396	.569	[a]	.615	.111	.278	.417	.444
Careerists	.310	.238	.833	.643	.469	.618	.535	.448	.500	.250
Entrepreneurs	.254	.333	.438	.625	.442	.598	.292	.198	.440	.583
All members	.301	.256	.522	.671	.461	.561	.365	.270	.366	.312

[a] Too few cases for a meaningful mean.

among recruitment types are clarified to some extent for legislators elected in districts typical of their parties. The differences in partisan attitudes between party agents and entrepreneurs is greater for legislators from typical districts than in the states as a whole. However, coopted candidates from typical districts in Iowa and California are relatively much lower in partisanship than we expected. In these districts, next to party agents, the most partisan legislators are the careerists. In New Jersey and Ohio, the careerists constitute the most partisan group of all the recruitment types in the typical districts, which suggests that in highly politicized environments, where presumably party and constituency forces are mutually reinforcing, the active self-starter comes to express stronger partisan attitudes than those with other recruitment experiences. Finally, it is clear from Table 4.4 that the complexity of the recruitment process for American legislators precludes simple explanation, but that nevertheless party activity in this process has some marked effects upon the partisan attitudes of legislators. These degrees of partisanship may vary between the parties, but our data preclude further analysis because of the small number of cases available for this purpose.

The variations in partisan attitudes among states do suggest the effects of political competitiveness upon such attitudes, and competitiveness may affect recruitment patterns within both typical and nontypical constituencies. For the legislators in New Jersey, Ohio, California, and Tennessee, we have calculated mean partisanship scores by extent of political competitiveness in legislative districts (see Table 4.5). In both one-party and competitive districts, party agents indicate the strongest partisan attitudes. And, once again, careerists prove to be the next most partisan group. However, in districts only moderately competitive, careerists are by far the most partisan legislators. It appears that political parties recruit the most partisan legislators in milieux which they either fully dominate or in which they must compete briskly. In semi-competitive constituencies, the most partisan legislators are those self-motivated politicians who engage actively in constituency party leadership.

TABLE 4.5
PARTISANSHIP SCORES FOR RECRUITMENT TYPES BY
DISTRICT COMPETITIVENESS*

Types of Recruitment	District Competitiveness		
	One-party	Semi-Competitive	Competitive
Party agents	.580	.488	.567
Coopted candidates	.517	.451	.397
Careerists	.544	.625	.511
Entrepreneurs	.517	.465	.431
All members	.420	.467	.442

* Iowa legislators are not included in this table.

TYPES OF RECRUITMENT AND ROLL CALL BEHAVIOR:
THE CASE OF IOWA

Legislators with different recruitment experiences exhibited divergent partisan orientations, indicating that differential recruitment has important attitudinal consequences. Does recruitment experience entail behavioral consequences, too? The answer to this question becomes crucial if we are going to argue that differential recruitment affects the decisional and functional outcomes of a legislative system, for it is largely through the individual actions of legislators—such as roll call votes—that major policy decisions are made in the legislative body.

In the 1967 session of the Iowa legislature, 345 nonunanimous roll calls occurred in the House and 359 in the Senate.[27] Among these, 175 cases in the House could be designated as party votes. By party votes, we refer to significant roll call votes in which a majority of the members of one party vote against a majority of the members of the other. In the Senate, we found 180 cases of roll calls that could be classified as party votes. Using all roll calls defined as party votes, we have computed the percentage of the time that a legislator voted with his party in order to obtain a measure of conformity to the party position. In Table 4.6, we summarize such roll call data by type of recruitment.

Party agents voted most frequently with their party in the Iowa legislature. They voted with their party more than forty-seven percent of the time, indicating that the party agents were a very partisan group, not only in terms of their attitudes but also in terms of their roll call behavior. Those who exhibited the least party loyalty were the coopted candidates. Only about thirty-five percent of the time did they vote with their own party. Despite the fact that both party agents and coopted candidates were initially drafted by parties, they behaved quite differently on the

TABLE 4.6
TYPES OF RECRUITMENT AND SUPPORT FOR THE
PARTY ON ROLL CALLS IN IOWA
(In percentages)

Types of Recruitment	All Legislators	Republicans	Democrats
Party agents	47.4	51.9	36.5
Coopted candidates	35.2	42.0	*
Careerists	40.6	49.8	22.5
Entrepreneurs	43.5	47.4	36.2
Number of Cases	122	82	40

* Not enough cases for computation.

floor. This clearly suggests that the kind of role that a party plays in a candidate's recruitment alone does not explain his partisan activity when he serves as a legislator. It is not enough to know whether or not one was drafted by his party, but we must also know why his party came to him and asked him to run. Those legislators who were asked to run because of their reputations in the community tended to be considerably less partisan in their roll call behavior than other legislators drafted for reason of their long-standing party loyalty.

Among the self-starters, the entrepreneurs acted in a slightly more partisan manner than did the careerists. The entrepreneurs conformed to their party's position about forty-four percent of the time, which compares somewhat favorably with forty-one percent for the careerists. The data revealed much more when we scrutinized the partisan behavior of the self-starters within each party. In the Republican Party, the careerists were one of the most partisan groups, voting almost fifty percent of the time with the party. However, the careerists in the Democratic Party proved to be the least partisan group—they voted with their party only twenty-three percent of the time. Why did the careerists of the two parties make such strikingly different partisan adaptations? The answer seems to lie in the degree of saliency of party organizations and their utility as career channels for political advancement. As we noted earlier, the careerists are likely to be strongly partisan under certain conditions. Where the local party organizations are strong and effective, ambitious politicians as a career strategy will gravitate toward the party and develop highly partisan attitudes. Conversely, where party organizations are weak the careerists will concentrate their time and energies elsewhere to realize their ambitions rather than through partisan activities. Under such conditions, the careerists would become the least partisan group.

Throughout most of its history, Iowa has had a one-party-dominant party system. For the most part, the Republican Party has controlled the governorship and both houses of the state legislature. Only in recent years have some major changes in the partisan complexion taken place. For instance, in 1965 the Democrats won the governorship and a majority of seats in both houses.[28] Since then, the party system in Iowa may be best described as a competitive two-party system, with each of the two parties having a good chance of winning a majority. Thus, the Democratic Party is a relative newcomer in Iowa as compared to the long-established Republican Party. This difference has important implications for those individuals who have political ambitions. Because the long-established Republicans have stronger and more effective local organizations, the careerists in the Republican Party more than their counterparts in the less highly organized Democratic Party will endeavor to move up the political ladder through the party. Consequently, we would expect to find quite different partisan adaptations between the Republican and Democratic careerists. Indeed, the roll call data indicate that the Republicans voted markedly more frequently with their party than did the Democrats.

Many studies of roll call behavior have shown that the tendency of legislators to vote with their parties varies with the type of issues involved.[29] These highly partisan issues consist of three general types: (1) those involving the prestige and programs of the governor, (2) those pertaining to the socioeconomic interests of the state or districts, and (3) those affecting party organizations and structure such as election and registration laws, apportionment, patronage, and elections of the Speaker and other officers. Depending upon the type of issues that legislators face, those with different recruitment experiences are likely to conform in varying degrees to their party lines. It takes little imagination to see that different patterns of recruitment—i.e., party agent, coopted candidate, careerist, and entrepreneur —imply that different tangents of obligations and expectations exist for legislators, and therefore make them vulnerable to varying sources of pressure. Moreover, because legislators have different political ambitions they are also likely to vote on the floor of the legislature according to different expectations and with different constituencies in mind. Such considerations suggest that legislators will act differently even on those key partisan issues, depending upon how they were initially recruited.

The roll calls which produced the highest party cohesion in the Iowa state assembly were those relating to party organizations and structure (see Table 4.7).[30] On such issues, the legislators voted with their parties almost eighty-four percent of the time. Another type of issue which resulted in strong partisan alignments pertains to socioeconomic concerns including health, education, wages, welfare services, tax, public works, and all kinds of labor legislation. The legislators conformed to their party lines seventy-seven percent of the time when they voted on socioeconomic issues.[31] Of the three types of issues, the governor's bills and programs elicited the least partisan action. Members of the Iowa legislature voted with their parties over such issues only sixty-nine percent of the time.[32]

TABLE 4.7

TYPES OF RECRUITMENT AND THE INCIDENCE OF PARTY VOTES ON
CERTAIN TYPES OF ISSUES IN IOWA

(In percentages)

Types of Recruitment	Types of Issues		
	Governor's program	Socioeconomic	Party
Party agents	69.1	66.8	85.0
Coopted candidates	70.9	78.6	82.2
Careerists	69.0	80.6	83.7
Entrepreneurs	67.2	74.8	84.0
All members	68.7	77.3	83.8

The legislators voted quite similarly on the governor's bills and on the issues relating to the special interests of parties, regardless of their differences in recruitment. For example, the entrepreneurs followed their party lines least frequently in roll calls on bills from the governor's program, voting with their parties sixty-seven percent of the time. However, this figure is not significantly smaller than that for the coopted candidates (71%), who recorded the highest party voting on the governor's bills. Similarly, there was also little variation in the roll calls on the party issues. The legislators aligned themselves along the partisan line eighty-two to eighty-five percent of the time when they voted on such issues.

However, voting on the socioeconomic issues sharply differentiated members of the Iowa state assembly. On the one hand, the careerists exhibited party loyalty almost eighty-one percent of the time on such issues, indicating the highest incidence of party voting among all groups. On the other hand, the party agents displayed the lowest party support—sixty-seven percent. The coopted candidates and entrepreneurs supported their parties seventy-nine and seventy-five percent of the time, respectively. What is particularly interesting here is the marked difference between the careerists and the party agents. Why is it that those legislators who were initially recruited by the party for their loyalty conformed considerably less to party lines than did the careerists who were little beholden to the party through the stages of nomination and election? The presence or absence of a progressive ambition and the character of issues involved seem to be the two main explanatory factors here. The socioeconomic issues are normally of broad public concern because they involve such basic matters as wage legislation, unemployment compensation, social services and the like, all of which by their nature can directly affect the daily life of individual voters.[33] In contrast, the party issues typically include those bills which have direct or indirect implications for the relative advantages or disadvantages of parties. Although decisions on these issues can enhance or jeopardize the relative position of one party vis-a-vis another party and therefore, are vitally important matters to party leaders and party activists, they are of little interest to the majority of the electorate. Now consider how an ambitious politician like a careerist might act upon issues of broad public concern, such as the socioeconomic issues. Careerists intend to seek reelection, and some of them aspire to higher office. They are therefore likely to be most concerned with those issues which will enhance their electoral support—i.e., the socioeconomic issues. Moreover, ambitious politicians can demonstrate their party loyalty through their voting on such issues, and thereby can obtain their party's support for their future careers. The socioeconomic issues are, in effect, one strategic area of action for the careerists. It is in this area in which they can consolidate or even broaden their constituency support and acquire the vitally important party sponsorship—two very essential requisites for political advancement.

The socioeconomic issues are less salient to the party agents, who neither aspire to higher offices nor have strong incentives to broaden their constituency support. The party agents are themselves the local party leaders or at least the most active elements in the local party organizations. Therefore, they are likely to be more keenly interested in the issues relating to the special interests of parties. In fact, the data in Table 4.7 show that the party agents voted with their parties more frequently than any other groups on the so-called "party issues." However, they also conformed least to their party position on socioeconomic issues, suggesting that there is little need for the party agents to please the electorate as long as they can depend on solid electoral support from their party organizations. Thus, ambition and issues interact in such a way to produce different partisan adaptations among legislative members.

The analysis of party voting in Iowa by legislators reflecting different types of recruitment in terms of the typicality of their districts provides a further useful refinement of the analysis. In Table 4.8, this kind of analysis is arrayed. Partisanship among legislators from districts typical of their parties is about as high for socioeconomic issues as for legislative party issues, and party voting is somewhat higher on the part of typical-district legislators on legislation in the governor's program than it is for legislators from atypical districts. Although among recruitment types from typical districts, levels of party voting do not vary substantially on the governor's program or on party issues, careerists in Iowa exhibit considerably greater party voting on socioeconomic issues than other legislators. Among legislators from typical districts, entrepreneurs are lowest in party voting on the governor's program and on legislative party issues, but those from atypical districts are consistently the most loyal to their parties for all three sets of issues. The lowest level of party voting is provided by the party agents from

TABLE 4.8

PARTY VOTING IN THE IOWA LEGISLATURE FOR RECRUITMENT TYPES BY
TYPES OF ISSUES AND DISTRICT TYPICALITY
(In percentages)

Types of Recruitment	Types of Issues and District Typicality					
	Governor's Program		Socioeconomic		Party	
	Typical	Nontypical	Typical	Nontypical	Typical	Nontypical
Party agents	70.6	65.7	73.6	50.5	84.8	85.6
Coopted candidates	70.9	a	78.6	a	82.2	a
Careerists	69.8	65.4	83.7	67.2	84.3	81.0
Entrepreneurs	66.9	68.1	77.4	67.7	82.0	89.6
All members	69.4	66.2	80.9	64.1	83.8	84.2

a Too few cases for a meaningful mean.

districts atyical of their parties, where party survival may depend upon partisans developing a record in legislative voting more like that of their political opponents than like that of their own party colleagues.

The analysis of roll call behavior in the Iowa state assembly offers some evidence for the conclusion that differential recruitment affects the partisan behavior of the legislators. Party agents, coopted candidates, careerists, and entrepreneurs conformed to their party lines in varying degrees when they voted on significant roll calls. Moreover, the extent to which the legislators voted along their party lines varied over different types of issues. The "party issues" elicited the most partisan voting patterns, followed by socioeconomic issues and the governor's program. The effects of differential recruitment were sharply reflected in the roll call votes on socioeconomic issues. The careerists voted in the most partisan manner over such issues, probably because of their ambitions for political advancement and their desire to obtain the party's sponsorship for their future careers. On the other hand, the party agents voted with their parties most frequently on the party issues and least frequently on the socioeconomic issues, because of their activist status within the party and their primary reliance for electoral support on their party organizations.

CONCLUSION

We have tried to thread our way through a body of data for American legislators which could contribute to our understanding of the bearing of their recruitment experiences upon their behavior as partisan politicians. We began our analysis with a simple two-dimensional typology, and we were able to show some empirical reality for that typology in the general corpus of legislators we examined. At the same time, our analysis revealed to us the complexity of linkages between recruitment and partisan political attitudes and behavior. We attempted to clarify these linkages by making our observations in different kinds of constituency milieux, believing that both the recruitment environment and the partisan terrain could affect partisan attitudes and behavior.

The results of the analyses we have performed lead us to believe that, in general, party recruitment activities do have a considerable tendency to produce legislators who are more partisan in their attitudes. Party agents generally do exhibit more partisan attitudes than other legislators. At the same time, our analysis indicates that partisan recruitment and partisan attitudes are not very well converted into party voting behavior in the legislature. The cohesiveness of legislative parties in their roll call voting seems to depend more upon the structure of constituencies, so that partisan voting homogeneity appears more to be brought about by the reinforcing factor of constituency typicality than by recruitment experience.

Wahlke, Eulau and associates found that the very real ideological differences

between Democratic and Republican legislators were not significantly transformed into party role behavior. They concluded that

> the role of "party man" is a highly ambiguous one. It is not the same from one state or
> party to another. The line between a "party man" and an "independent" or a
> "maverick" is a tenuous one. On the whole, the role of "party man" tends to be
> defined in terms of minimal activities—e.g., roll call voting—in response to party
> cues. In spite of the fact that ideological differences among party members appear to
> be much sharper than are such differences among average citizens, there is little
> correspondence between ideological attitude and party role.[34]

Our analysis suggests that active party members who are recruited by their party to
legislative candidacy generally are the most partisan legislators. But this linkage
between party recruitment and partisan attitude does not appear to carry over very
sharply in legislative party voting behavior. In party voting, except for the most
blatant of party legislative issues, cohesion of partisans seems to reflect the
character of their constituencies more sharply than their recruitment experience. It
must be noted that our findings with respect to party voting are limited to Iowa, a
state without particularly strong statewide party organization.

Jewell has pointed out that because

> the districting systems in many states have maximized Democratic representation
> from urban centers and Republican representation from rural areas . . . there is a clear
> difference between constituencies—and consequently the interests—represented by
> Republican and Democratic legislators. Because a party represents relatively
> homogeneous constituencies, the legislators in that party find that they can go along
> with the party's position on issues without damaging or ignoring the needs and desires
> of their constituencies.

He further argues that the answer to the question of why "rank-and-file legislators
follow party leadership, participate in caucuses, and accept party cues in
committee" is that "such behavior is most likely to occur when the legislators see
little conflict between party and constituency, because they represent similar
constituencies."[35] In our Iowa analysis, it seems clear that differences between
typical and atypical districts have a greater bearing upon levels of party voting than
do differences between recruitment experiences for the legislators.

Partisan differentiation in the United States displays an agonizing variety and
complexity. We have tried to bring some order to the explanation of legislative
partisanship by showing linkages between party recruitment and partisan
attitudes. But party voting cohesion in American states probably is not, and
certainly not in Iowa, a marked result of partisan recruitment experience. In their
formal decision-making behavior, American legislators do not convert their
ideological differences, fairly sharply defined as between the parties, into party
roles or party voting. Neither do they convert their recruitment experiences into
party voting through more partisan attitudes. This evident gap between ideology,

party recruitment, and partisan attitudes, on the one hand, and party roles and party voting cohesion, on the other, reflects the strong tie of the American legislator to his constituency, and the overriding impact of the parties in the constituencies in diminishing the effect of recruitment experience on legislative party voting.

NOTES

1. The literature is vast. Studies representative of such approaches include: Frank J. Sorauf, *Party and Representation: Legislative Politics in Pennsylvania* (New York, 1963); Donald R. Matthews, *U.S. Senators and Their World* (Chapel Hill, N.C., 1960); Victor S. Hjelm and Joseph P. Pisciotte, "Profiles and careers of Colorado state legislators," *Western Political Quarterly* 21 (December 1968), 698-722; Heinz Eulau and David Koff, "Occupational mobility and political career," *Western Political Quarterly* 15 (September 1962), 507-521; Joseph A. Schlesinger, *Ambition and Politics* (Chicago: Rand McNally, 1966); Kenneth Prewitt and William Nowlin, "Political ambitions and the behavior of incumbent politicans," *Western Political Quarterly* 22 (June 1969), 298-308; John W. Soule, "Future political ambitions and the behavior of incumbent state legislators," *Midwest Journal of Political Science* 13 (August 1969), 443-447; Gordon S. Black, "A theory of political ambition: career choices and the role of structural incentives," *American Political Science Review* 66 (March 1972), 144-159; Charles G. Bell and Charles M. Price, "Pre-legislative sources of representational roles," *Midwest Journal of Political Science* 13 (May 1969), 254-270; John Wahlke, Heinz Eulau, William Buchanan, and Leroy Ferguson, *The Legislative System* (New York: John Wiley, 1962), pp. 69-134; Allan Kornberg and Norman Thomas, "The political socialization of national legislative elites in the United States and Canada," *Journal of Politics* 27 (November 1965), 761-774; John B. McConaughy, "Certain personality factors of state legislators in South Carolina," *American Political Science Review* 44 (December 1950), 897-903; and Rufus Browning, "The interaction of personality and political system in decisions to run for office," *Journal of Social Issues* 24 (1968), 93-110.

2. A few existing studies of the consequences of legislative recruitment include: James D. Barber, *The Lawmakers: Recruitment and Adaptation to Legislative Life* (New Haven: Yale University Press, 1965); Donald D. Searing, "Comparative study of elite socialization," *Comparative Political Studies* 1 (January 1969), 471-500; Chong Lim Kim, "Attitudinal effects of legislative recruitment," *Comparative Politics* 6 (October 1974) and also his "Political attitudes of defeated candidates in an American state election," *American Political Science Review* 65 (September 1970), 879-887; and Leo M. Snowiss, "Congressional recruitment and representation," *American Political Science Review* 60 (September 1966).

3. Malcolm E. Jewell and Samuel C. Patterson, *The Legislative Process in the United States* (New York: Random House, 1966), 529.

4. Leo M. Snowiss, "Congressional recruitment and representation," op. cit., 627.

5. John W. Kingdon, *Congressmen's Voting Decisions* (New York: Harper & Row, 1973), 46.

6. David M. Olson, "The Congressman and the Congressional District Party," in William E. Wright (ed.) *A Comparative Study of Party Organization* (Columbus, Ohio: Charles E. Merrill, 1971), 487-507. Austin Ranney contrasts British and American processes of candidate recruitment in "Candidate Selection and Party Cohesion in Britain and the United States," in William J. Crotty (ed.) *Approaches to the Study of Party Organization* (Boston: Allyn & Bacon, 1968), 139-157. He analyzes the constituency recruitment basis of parliamentary party cohesion in *Pathways to Parliament: Candidate Selection in Britain* (London: Macmillan, 1965).

7. Olson, "The Congressman and the congressional district party," op. cit., 506.

8. Frank J. Sorauf, *Party and Representation: Legislative Politics in Pennsylvania* (New York: Atherton, 1963), 131-132.

9. The Iowa Legislative Research Project was supported by grants and other research assistance from the National Science Foundation, the Social Science Research Council, the Research Department of the Des Moines *Register and Tribune,* the University of Iowa Graduate College and Computer Center, and the Laboratory for Political Research, Department of Political Science, University of Iowa. The principal investigators for this project were Samuel C. Patterson, G. Robert Boynton, and Ronald D. Hedlund.

10. Wahlke et al., op. cit.

11. Although it would have been preferable to have tested the various hypotheses with roll call data from more than one state, the necessary data are apparently unavailable. A reasonably thorough search of archives most likely to possess roll call data for the legislators interviewed as part of the four-state study failed to unearth usable material.

12. Leon D. Epstein, *Political Parties in Western Democracies* (New York: Praeger, 1967), 11; Frank Sorauf, *Party Politics in America* (Boston: Little, Brown, 1972), 18; and Joseph A. Schlesinger, "Political party organization," in James G. March (ed.) *Handbook of Organizations* (Chicago: Rand McNally, 1965), 767.

13. Samuel C. Patterson and G. R. Boynton, "Legislative recruitment in a civic culture," *Social Science Quarterly* 50 (September 1969), 257.

14. Lester G. Seligman, "Political recruitment and party structure," *American Political Science Review* 55 (March 1961) 77-86.

15. Lester G. Seligman, Chong Lim Kim, Michael R. King, and Roland Smith, *Patterns of Recruitment: A State Chooses Its Lawmakers* (Chicago: Rand McNally, 1974).

16. The four-state study has concluded: "Only relatively few (state legislators) indicated political aspirations beyond the state legislature. In fact, of course, even fewer are likely to move on to other governmental positions. One gets the impression that though they are in politics, the bulk of these state politicians do not expect to live *off* or *for* politics. Their legislative career appears to be only a temporary episode in their total life space, to be cherished while it occurs, but an episode, even if protracted, nevertheless." Wahlke, Eulau et al., *Legislative System,* op. cit., 134. For a similar observation, see also, Lester G. Seligman, et al., *Patterns of Recruitment,* op. cit., 194-196.

17. Barber, op. cit., 67-115.

18. Sorauf, *Party Politics in America,* op. cit., 356.

19. Ibid., p. 346.

20. Seligman et al., chapter 2.

21. The four items were asked in essentially the same form in the two studies. The following quotations are from the four-state study; question references are to the instrument reproduced in Wahlke et al., op. cit., 492-504. These are all five-point agree/disagree statements. 1. If a bill is important for his party's record, a member should vote with his party even if it costs him some support, in his district (q. 39f). 2. The two parties should take clear-cut, opposing stands on more of the important state issues in order to encourage party responsibility (q. 39k). 3. It's just as important to be on guard against ideas put out by people of one's own party as against ideas put out by people in the opposite party (q. 39p). 4. The best interests of the people would be better served if legislators were elected without party labels (q. 39w). The partisanship score was obtained by summing the number of "pro-party" responses to these items, and then dividing by the number of items to which the legislator responded. Thus, failure to answer does not operate to reduce the partisanship score.

22. Using the questionnaire numbers from note 21, the full distribution of pro-party responses by recruitment types is as follows:

	Recruitment Types			
	Party Agent	Coopted	Careerist	Entrepreneur
39k.	37.7	24.0	39.5	31.5
39p.	13.4	14.3	64.5	51.4
39w.	80.0	86.3	23.5	85.3

23. Wahlke et al., op. cit., 351-359.

24. See William Goodman, *Inherited Domain: Political Parties in Tennessee* (Knoxville: University of Tennessee, Bureau of Public Administration, 1954), 30-48; William Buchanan, *Legislative Partisanship: The Deviant Case of California* (Berkeley and Los Angeles: University of California Press, 1963), 108-122; Joel M. Fisher, Charles M. Price, and Charles G. Bell, *The Legislative Process in California* (Washington, D.C.: American Political Science Association, 1973), 81-102.

25. Harlan Hahn, *Urban-Rural Conflict: The Politics of Change* (Beverly Hills, Calif. Sage Publications, 1971), 173-217.

26. Wahlke et al., 40-68.

27. All roll call data obtained from the *Journal* of the appropriate chamber.

28. Ronald D. Hedlund and Charles W. Wiggins, "Legislative Politics in Iowa," in Samuel C. Patterson (ed.) *Midwest Legislative Politics* (Iowa City: Institute of Public Affairs, University of Iowa, 1967), 7-36.

29. Jewell and Patterson, op. cit. 443-444.

30. The "party issue" roll calls relate specifically to the operation and organization of the political party system. Most of the roll calls in this category during the 1967 assembly dealt with legislative reapportionment.

31. This category is primarily a residual group composed of those roll calls on issues such as welfare, taxation, and the like that were *not* related to the governor's program.

32. Governor Harold Hughes delivered his inaugural address to a joint session of the assembly on January 12, 1967. As is the custom with most executives, he took advantage of the occasion to set before the legislature his plans for the term then beginning. The address is published in the *Senate Journal* for 1967, pp. 57-72. Hughes directed his comments to programs in at least ten areas, including economic development, governmental reorganization, tax reform, and education. In each case, the governor requested specific legislation from the Assembly; the roll calls on these measures constitute the "Governor's Program" group.

33. Jewell and Patterson, op. cit. 431.

34. Wahlke et al., op. cit., 376.

35. Malcolm E. Jewell, *The State Legislature* (New York: Random House, 1969), 112-114.

Chapter 5

CHANGES IN THE AMERICAN EXECUTIVE ELITE, 1930-1970

KENNETH PREWITT and
WILLIAM McALLISTER
University of Chicago

Political recruitment is an ongoing political process. Individuals are constantly preparing themselves for or are being brought into top political positions: Aspirants use apprentice roles to demonstrate their suitability for more prestigious posts; the already established use sponsorship to nurture careers of their favorites; fortune puts a few lucky ones in the right spot at the right moment. While some are climbing, others are moving aside or even descending. Room at the top occurs as death, weariness, and political failure usher an older elite out of office.

Political recruitment has been defined as the "processes through which individuals or groups of individuals are inducted into active political roles."[1] We accept this as a starting point, but want to push the definition away from a focus on the development of political careers and toward an analysis of the character and composition of a ruling group.[2] To study political recruitment is to study how a ruling group is being reproduced, yet transformed, through time. The mixture of "reproduction" and "transformation" produced by the recruitment processes is an index of how the polity is adjusting and responding to social, economic, and technological changes.

The study reported here seeks to identify aspects of the political recruitment process which might be transforming a ruling group over time. The characteristics of the ruling group singled out for attention include standard demographic traits as

Authors' Note: Support for data collection was provided by a grant from the Division of the Social Sciences, University of Chicago. Manuscript preparation was provided by the National Opinion Research Center. We want to thank Kristi Andersen and Robert Pearson for their suggestions.

well as the skill composition of the ruling group. Because similar data are normally used to demonstrate that top political leaders are selected from a narrow social stratum, it is perhaps worth emphasizing that this is *not* our concern. Biographical data are here being used to inquire into the political recruitment process, not to report once again on the social origins of political leaders.

The "ruling group" selected for attention is the elite of federal executives in the United States; we refer to cabinet and high subcabinet positions and to top posts in important regulatory agencies and independent commissions as the executive elite. The time period covered is four decades, from the administration of Herbert Hoover to the administration of Richard Nixon. The biographical data collected are used to describe changes in the executive elite across this time period.

To study the executive elite is to do more than simply describe the ruling group which happens to be in charge of the executive branch, though this perhaps is sufficient reason for the study. But such a study also probes the larger issue of what kind of governing coalition has been put together by the President. We are accustomed to thinking about how presidential candidates build electoral coalitions—how they adopt positions designed to attract financial and voter support from critical regional, occupational, ethnic, and racial groups and from major issue constituencies. But we have given much less attention to governing coalitions. As Huntington has observed, what counts in governing is the President's "ability to mobilize support from the leaders of key institutions in society and government. He has to constitute a broad governing coalition of strategically located supporters who can furnish him with the information, talent, expertise, manpower, publicity, arguments, and political support which he needs to develop a program, to embody it in legislation, and to see it effectively implemented.[3]

There is more to a presidential governing coalition than the executive elite. It might include dependable congressional leaders, perhaps some state governors and big city mayors, and actors outside government, such as media elites, interest group leaders, and depending on the content of the presidential program, some mixture of corporate and labor leaders. But if the governing coalition is broader than what we have defined as the executive elite, this ruling group is clearly central to the coalition. We have collected data on persons responsible for establishing and maintaining the governing coalition; it is the set of persons who link the Oval Office to the constituencies which must be "brought along" if the presidential program is to succeed. In describing the attributes and skills of the executive elite, we are indirectly characterizing central features of the governing coalitions which successive presidents have created.

POLITICAL RECRUITMENT AND DEMOCRATIC THEORY

Democratic theory assumes a necessary link between elections and electoral activity, on the one hand, and elite recruitment and governing, on the other. Who the leaders are, how they are selected and removed, and the manner in which they govern is in democratic theory related to how the preferences of the population are aggregated through periodic elections. That this assumption rests near if not at the core of democratic theory hardly needs iteration. What celebrant of American democracy has not in one fashion or another propounded it?

The assumption that elections and governing are strongly related has not been, however, an easy assumption to investigate empirically. In this chapter, we attempt to bring the theorized relationship into empirical focus by concentrating on whether the presidential *governing* coalition systematically varies with the President's *electoral* coalition, the latter being indexed by which political party controls the White House.

Though the elite studied is an appointed elite, it is appointed at the direction of and by the authority of an elected President. Every four years, the American electorate in choosing a president also elects an executive elite. In terms of democratic theory, the inevitable question to ask is whether the party affiliation of the President has identifiable consequences for the skills and characteristics recruited into executive elite positions? In language adopted from Huntington, will the key traits of the central actors in the governing coalition vary with the electoral coalition responsible for putting the administration in power? Huntington himself is not so sure; he writes that "the governing coalition need have little relation to the electoral coalition."[4] If such a finding emerges from our data, we will need to reexamine a core assumption in democratic theory.

Research Design

In order to maximize the number of party shifts which occurred in our time period, we collected data from four pairs of time points, each pair representing a party shift. Table 5.1 summarizes the design by showing the years for which data were collected and the party shifts for each pair of data points.[5]

We have said that the broad research question asks whether the electoral activity of the national electorate has a systematic relationship to the character and composition of the executive elite. It is tempting to bring specificity to this very general question, such specificity as would be suggested by identifying the concrete changes in the elite which are expected to follow from any given party shift. No such specificity is forthcoming. Data limitations impose modesty on our claims. The available data cannot, for example, speak at all to the interests and demands which are represented in any given governing coalition. All that we can offer is a view of the broad contours of the recruitment process and ask whether they vary in

TABLE 5.1

Years in Which Executive Elite Data Collected	National Administrations	Direction of Party Shift
1930 & 1934-1936 [a]	Hoover to Roosevelt	Republican to Democrat
1950 & 1954	Truman to Eisenhower	Democrat to Republican
1958 & 1962	Eisenhower to Kennedy	Republican to Democrat
1966 & 1970	Johnson to Nixon	Democrat to Republican

[a] A two-year period was used here in order to include data from the New Deal agencies begun after 1934. The appendix to this chapter provides numbers for each administration and detailed information on positional and personnel identification.

interpretable ways with changes in party administration. Though the study is guided by a theoretical assumption drawn from democratic theory, in design and data presentation the study is modestly descriptive.

The variables on which information has been collected fall into two rough classifications: social attributes and governing skills. The social attributes measured—religion, region, and educational background—will help us understand whether the recruitment pool from which the executive elite are chosen varies from one party to the other, or varies across the time period studied. The governing skills are indexed by type of education and career background represented in the executive elite. Again we will want to take note of variations which follow from party shifts and pay close attention as well to over-time trends.

If social attributes and governing skills regularly vary by party, then there is reason to infer a systematic relationship between electoral coalitions and governing coalitions. If, however, attributes and skills either do not vary or vary independently of party control, then there is reason to doubt this relationship.

Religion

Religion has frequently served as a barometer of the rise and decline of different forces in politics. Dahl, for example, makes much of the hold which establishment religions, especially the New England Congregationalists, had on New Haven politics. The rise of the ex-plebes in New Haven is in part indicated by the number of Catholics found in public service positions.[6] Baltzell similarly focuses on religion in charting the downfall of the nineteenth-century political establishment. He gives particular emphasis to the New Deal era, when "Catholics and Jews were brought into the higher levels of government as never before: of the 214 Federal judges appointed by Harding, Coolidge, and Hoover combined, only eight were Catholic and eight were Jewish; of the 196 Roosevelt appointments, fifty-one were Catholic and eight were Jewish."[7]

TABLE 5.2
PERCENTAGE OF RELIGIOUS PREFERENCE FOR THOSE REPORTING
RELIGION IN EACH ADMINISTRATION

Religion	Herbert C Hoover	Franklin D. Roosevelt	Harry S. Truman	Dwight D. Eisenhower-I	Dwight D. Eisenhower-II	John F. Kennedy	Lyndon B. Johnson	Richard M. Nixon
N	30	47	47	42	49	35	40	45
"Establishment" Protestant	83	47	34	50	45	31	40	33
Non-Protestant:								
Catholic	3	19	21	5	10	29	25	20
Jewish	0	4	2	7	2	6	8	4
Index Protestant advantage	+80	+24	+11	+38	+33	−4	+7	+9

Table 5.2 records the percentage of the executive elite reporting their religion who were "establishment Protestants" (Episcopalians, Presbyterians, and Congregationalists) and who were Catholic and Jewish. The bottom line presents an index of Protestant advantage, with a plus figure indicating a greater number of Protestants and a negative figure a greater number of Catholics and Jews.

Two things stand out. First, there are sharp shifts associated with party fortunes, especially in the earlier period. The first transition from a Republican to a Democratic administration shows a drop of fifty-six percent in the Protestant advantage, while the subsequent transition from a Democratic to a Republican administration causes the Protestant advantage to increase twenty-seven percent. Looked at another way, Catholics and Jews gain twenty percent with the Democrat Roosevelt in power, decline under Eisenhower's White House tenure, but come back when Kennedy is President.

Second, superimposed on the abrupt shifts associated with changes in administration is a gradual trend which establishes something fairly close to parity between the Protestant and non-Protestant groups by the time we are in the post-Kennedy period. Indeed, this trend seems to be crystallized around the time of Kennedy, for it persists through the administrations of Protestant-Democrat Johnson and Protestant-Republican Nixon.[8] In this context, we should note that although the index of Protestant advantage for the Truman administration is similar to that of the last two administrations, what is important is that this does not remain low when the Republicans come into power. In contrast, a sharp rise in the index does not occur when a similar change in administrations occurs between 1966 and 1970.

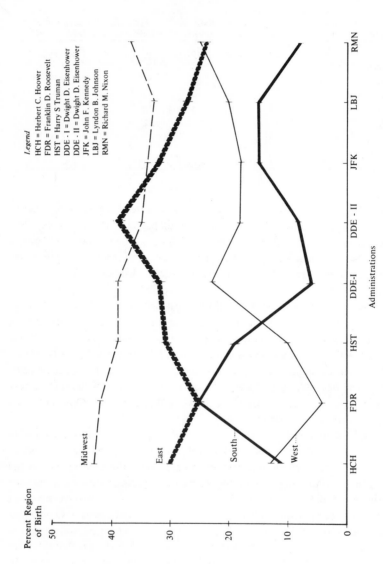

Figure 5.1 – REGION OF BIRTH FOR EACH ADMINISTRATION

Region of Birth

In terms of our argument, the birth region of elites is not intrinsically interesting, except for the possibility that it indexes whether there is in fact an "Eastern establishment" and whether the persistence of a geographically rooted establishment has wavered over time. Figure 5.1 presents the percentage of the executive elite born in the East, the South, the Midwest, and the West.

Two things stand out. There is some fluctuation depending on the party which controls the White House: Under Democratic control, the access of Southern-born increases; under Republican control, the access of Westerners increases. Yet these variations are not particularly strong and are less interesting than the second finding which emerges from the graph.

Over the four decades, there is a gradual decline in Midwestern and Eastern presence and a corresponding increase in the proportion of Westerners among the executive elite. The Midwest contributed forty-three percent in 1930, and had declined to thirty-three percent during Johnson's administration, with a slight increase again under the Republican administration of Nixon. The percentage of those born in the East fluctuates more but has declined steadily since 1956. The West has advanced at the expense of the East and Midwest, going from thirteen percent in Hoover's term to twenty-five percent in the Nixon administration (both are Republicans with Western roots). The advance of the West is clearest when comparing 1930 with 1970. The Midwestern advantage over the West has been reduced from thirty percent to eleven percent; the Eastern advantage over the West, seventeen percent in 1930, has been completely eliminated by 1970.

Other than making the obvious point that the shift of birth region of the executive elite parallels the general population shifts in the United States during the years in which virtually the entire elite studied was born, 1870-1940, there is not much of substantive importance about Figure 5.1. Still, it is worth noting that the basic pattern is similar to that discovered for religion: trend lines superimposed over party-associated fluctuations.

Educational Background

Table 5.3 reports the standard finding in recruitment studies: a very high percentage of political elites are from the college-educated stratum in society. In the earlier decades, there is some shifting between party administrations. There is a sharp drop in the number of college-educated when the Roosevelt administration replaces the Hoover administration and an increase of twelve percent when Eisenhower takes over from Truman. This party argument is tempered, however, by the fact that the percentage of college graduates goes up eleven percent from Roosevelt to Truman—both Democratic administrations. The latter administrations show little of this fluctuating. Table 5.3 does not reveal marked changes

TABLE 5.3
PERCENTAGE OF COLLEGE GRADUATES
IN EACH ADMINISTRATION

Administration	%	N
Herbert C. Hoover	83	54
Franklin D. Roosevelt	67	81
Harry S. Truman	78	78
Dwight D. Eisenhower-I	90	72
Dwight D. Eisenhower-II	88	92
John F. Kennedy	96	96
Lyndon B. Johnson	94	100
Richard M. Nixon	89	107

associated with party shifts so much as it reveals a gradual trend over the four decades. The college degree has increasingly become a requisite for joining the executive elite.

Of more theoretical interest is information about the kinds of educational institutions which feed the executive elite. Changes in the types of schools attended by the elite can indicate alternation in the relationship between the class structure and political recruitment. Different kinds of schools have historically selected their student bodies from different social strata, with the established prestige schools (e.g., the Ivy League universities), generally drawing from upper social strata; the newer prestige schools (e.g., quality state universities) and the nonprestige schools (local and sectarian colleges) tending to draw from the professional and middle classes. Although this distinction has been breaking down under the pressure of post-World War II political events and educational needs, most of the elite in our sample attended college before there occurred substantial changes in the class selectivity of prestige universities. Figure 5.2 shows the proportion of college educated persons in each administration who attended established prestige, newer prestige, or nonprestige undergraduate colleges (see the Appendix for coding conventions).

We find two patterns. First, as with other traits, there are some identifiable party differences. Republican administrations, more than the Democratic, recruit from the established prestige schools.[9] Republicans average thirty-six percent from this category; Democrats, twenty-six percent. The sharp drop in recruitment from the old-line prestige schools during the Truman administration is the strongest case of the party effect, but across the decades there is a tendency for graduates of the established prestige colleges to be more numerous in Republican administrations than in the Democratic administrations which preceded them.

The second pattern in Figure 5.2 plays a variation on a familiar theme: the more recent administrations look quite different from those before them, and the change cuts across party lines. This is dramatically seen by focusing on the

Republican administrations which are the end points of the study. During the Hoover administration, twelve percent more of the executive elite came from the established prestige colleges (39%) than from the newer prestige schools (27%). Forty years later, under Republican Nixon, the advantage had dramatically reversed. The newer prestige schools contributed seventeen percent more of the executive elite (44%), than the established prestige schools (27%). The shift to a comparative advantage of the newer prestige schools occurs with the Kennedy administration, and then persists through the following Democratic and Republican administrations. This institutionalization of a pattern around the Kennedy years was observed also in connection with religion.

Our comments about Figure 5.2 emphasize the shift in the recruitment significance of the older and the newer prestige schools. In part, this is no doubt a result of the increasing number of what we have called newer prestige schools. More than that, however, it indicates change in the linkage between American universities and national political recruitment—i.e., more, rather than fewer, institutions control the route to top political office.

Figure 5.3 gives added weight to this conclusion. There we present the type of graduate school attended by the elite in each of the eight administrations. The overall pattern is very similar to what we observed about the source of the undergraduate degree.

At the beginning of the period, advanced degree holders from established prestige universities outnumbered their colleagues from newer prestige universities by eighteen percent, thirty-nine, and twenty-one percent, respectively. This gap is not altered with the election of Roosevelt, is closed under Truman, re-establishes itself in the Republican administrations of Eisenhower, but then closes again under Kennedy and remains relatively closed in the administrations of both Johnson and Nixon. Though in the case of graduate degrees, the newer prestige schools gain more at the expense of the nonprestige schools than at the expense of the established universities, the general pattern is the same as elsewhere. That is, the data show some party fluctuations, but, more importantly, they demonstrate a break in past patterns at the time of the Kennedy administration, and the establishment of new patterns which continue through Republican Nixon.

Summary

The evidence so far presented provides clues about changes in the social attributes of our ruling group, the executive elite, and about changes in the recruitment processes which supply the executive. Three summary observations can be made.

    (1) There are short-term fluctuations in recruitment criteria and recruit-
        ment processes which are related to the political party in power. Particular

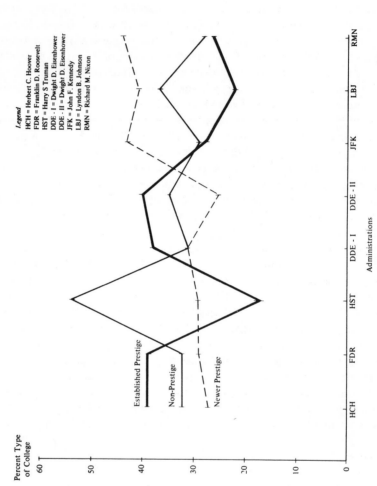

Figure 5.2 – TYPE OF UNDERGRADUATE COLLEGE FOR EACH ADMINISTRATION

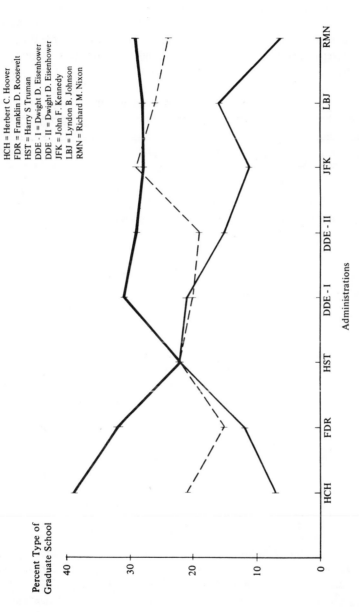

Percent Type of
Graduate School

Legend

HCH = Herbert C. Hoover
FDR = Franklin D. Roosevelt
HST = Harry S Truman
DDE - I = Dwight D. Eisenhower
DDE - II = Dwight D. Eisenhower
JFK = John F. Kennedy
LBJ = Lyndon B. Johnson
RMN = Richard M. Nixon

Administrations

Figure 5.3 – TYPE OF GRADUATE SCHOOL FOR EACH ADMINISTRATION

social attributes or recruitment sources can vary between Democratic and Republican administrations.

(2) Some trends are sufficiently strong to be noted across the four decades and seem to have a momentum occasioned by factors outside the party system. There is no clear indication that either Democratic or Republican control of the executive somehow establishes a new set of recruitment criteria.

(3) Insofar as the different trend lines share a common trait, it is the tendency for the 1960s to be a break point. This is the point at which Catholic parity with Protestants is established, and it is the point at which recruits from the newer prestige colleges and universities gain a hold on elite positions equal to that long held by the established institutions.

Bearing these summary comments in mind, we turn next to a consideration of our second characteristic of an elite—its skill composition.

ELITE SKILLS AND RECRUITMENT

Political sociologists have long been interested in the range of skills recruited into top leadership. Mosca saw in the skills of ruling classes the clue as to whether they were rising or falling in power. He writes that ruling classes decline "when they cease to find scope for the capacities through which they rose to power" or "when their talents and the services they render lose in importance in the social environment in which they live."[10] The implicit functionalism in this argument has been made explicit by latter-day theorists such as Keller:

> Strategic elites move into ascendency when their functions do likewise. . . . The rank order of elites, therefore, is generally determined by the types of problems confronting a society, priority accorded to these, and the functional and moral solutions proposed to solve them.[11]

Lasswell has applied the term "skill revolution" to describe those historical periods during which the skill characteristics of the ruling group undergo substantial transformation.[12] It is Lasswell's notion which is most relevant to the present essay, for our research task is to see whether the skills recruited into the executive elite vary depending upon the political party in power. Certainly one might expect that the election of Roosevelt and the formation of his New Deal program, altering as it did the relationship between the federal government and the economic sector of society, would have led to a transformation in the skills of those charged with governing. There is much speculative writing to this effect. Furthermore, it is reasonable to expect that the replacement of Sundquist's

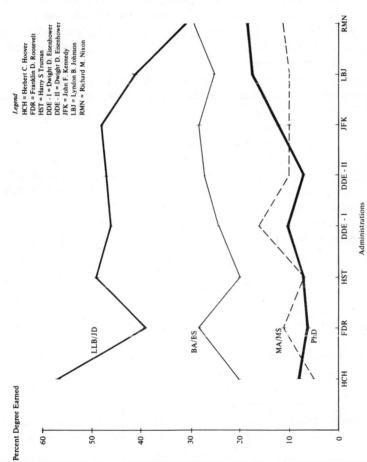

Percent Degree Earned

Legend
HCH = Herbert C. Hoover
FDR = Franklin D. Roosevelt
HST = Harry S Truman
DDE - I = Dwight D. Eisenhower
DDE - II = Dwight D. Eisenhower
JFK = John F. Kennedy
LBJ = Lyndon B. Johnson
RMN = Richard M. Nixon

LLB/JD

BA/ES

MA/MS

PhD

Administrations

Figure 5.4 – HIGHEST DEGREE EARNED FOR COLLEGE GRADUATES IN EACH ADMINISTRATION "non-activist" White House Republicans by the "activist" Democrats in the 1960s would be cause for fluctuations in the skill composition of the executive elite.[13] A similar replacement of nonactivist Republicans by activist Democrats presumably occurs in 1932, and might result in important shifts in skill traits.

Of course, the difficulty with this working hypothesis is in the specification of skills. The Mosca-Lasswellian notions are more theoretically fertile than empirically testable, at least with the type of historical data easily available. It is necessary to stretch a few indicators pretty far in order to get any empirical handle at all on the skills of the elite.

The initial indicator used in this study is the kind of education represented in each administration. If, as Lasswell writes, "Skill is a teachable and learnable operation," then for a highly educated elite skill acquisition presumably starts with their type of formal education.

Figure 5.4 shows the kind of skill education characterizing each administration as measured by the highest degree earned. Several things of importance are revealed in the graph. First, the 1932 election did bring about a sharp change in the skills of the executive elite. Thirty-nine percent of those in FDR's first administration held law degrees, a drop of eighteen percent from the Hoover administration. This roughly corresponds with a combined thirteen percent gain in those receiving Bachelors or Masters—degrees of lesser skill.

However, this party pattern is not sustained. With Truman's administration, the proportion earning only B.A.s or M.A.s returns to the levels of the Hoover administration. While the number holding law degrees does not reach earlier heights, there is a leveling off at approximately fifty percent which continues for several succeeding administrations. The sharp change in "skills" associated with FDR turns out to be a temporary phenomonon.

More dramatic in Figure 5.4 is the declining proportion of lawyers which occurs in the Johnson and Nixon administrations. Beginning in the early 1960s, elites with doctorates gain at the expense of those trained in law. Table 5.4 establishes the point clearly by presenting the ratios of those with law degrees to those with Ph.Ds. In 1930, there were seven times as many lawyers as Ph.Ds. In Eisenhower's second term, the ratio is still 7.00. But by 1970, under the third Republican President of the era studied, there is less than two lawyers for every Ph.D.

Insofar as type of degree earned indexes skills, Figure 5.4 and Table 5.4 demonstrate some sort of skill transformation. The skill of law, which has generally been seen as integrally linked to governing, is being replaced by a different sort of expertise which might well be the hallmark of a new ruling group. This transformation apparently is immune to variations in party control of the White House.

We have constructed a second index of skill called "career space," which emphasizes the career background rather than the educational background of the

TABLE 5.4
RATIO OF LAW DEGREES TO Ph.D. DEGREES
IN EACH ADMINISTRATION

Administration	Ratio	Law Degree/ Ph.D. Degree N
Herbert C. Hoover	7.00	28/4
Franklin D. Roosevelt	6.25	25/4
Harry S. Truman	7.20	36/5
Dwight D. Eisenhower-I	4.42	31/7
Dwight D. Eisenhower-II	7.00	42/6
John F. Kennedy	4.09	45/11
Lyndon B. Johnson	2.41	41/17
Richard M. Nixon	1.73	33/19

elites. By its nature, this second indicator is contaminated by the first, for the type of degree earned influences the career pursued. While we admit that the present methodology is of the rough and ready sort, we use such data as are available to illuminate what can be illuminated about the skill composition of the executive elite.

In the context of our argument, the assumption is that different careers foster different skills so that the career backgrounds represented among the elite provide clues as to the skills represented among the elite. If there have been party shifts in the recruitment of particular skills over the forty-year period, this should appear in the career data.

We begin with a description of how individual careers were coded. We divided each person's career, as it was originally reported in *Who's Who,* into three parts. The primary criterion for this partitioning was time spent in a particular sector of society. The notion of societal sectors relates to the institutional configurations of society which develop certain skills. The most important sectors we use are law, elected government (federal, state, or local), appointed government (federal, state, or local), business, and education (almost always university-level). Every person, then, has three careers or three career parts, each of which is described in terms of sectors. An easy example of this is someone who spent eight years in private law practice, twelve as a university administrator, and then five in an appointed state government job before advancing to the position included in this study. (The executive elite post is not counted as a career part.) The first part of this person's career would be coded for the law sector, the next for the education sector, and the final part for the appointed government sector. Of course, not everyone fits as nicely into such a scheme as this example, but it was more fruitful in categorizing career data than alternative methods (see the Appendix for more detail).

The measure important to the analysis is "career space." Every administration has N number of persons. As was just described, the careers of each of these persons have been divided into three career parts. To find out the total number of career parts in any administration, we would multiply N by 3. This number would be the total career space of an administration and would provide a base by which to assess careers in each of the five major sectors as a percentage of all careers combined. For example, in the Roosevelt administration N = 81, so that the total number of careers is N x 3 or 243—i.e., the Roosevelt administration has a career space of 243. Suppose we wanted to find out how much of this career space was occupied by, say, the law sector. We would sum the number of careers in law in each of the three career parts and divide by career space. For the Roosevelt administration this would be 29 + 19 + 10/243 or twenty-four percent. We can then say that almost one-quarter of the career space in F.D.R.'s administration was law. Our purpose is to bring the three career parts together so that it will be possible to characterize an entire administration in terms of the skill sectors which formed its personnel.

Because the most significant contribution of career space will be in what it says about the movement of particular skill groups into the top positions, it would be useful to view the sectors as fostering four different skill groups. The first, lawyers, could be characterized as a "specialized-general" skill group: specialists in that they are experts in one field, but generalists in that this one field extends everywhere. The result of this is that lawyers seem to have become all-purpose professional handymen who can fill any position. The next skill group is composed of those in elected government, accomplished in the techniques of popular politics and its emphasis on party and constituent responsibilities. The third group is people whose careers were in appointed government and business, both of which are characterized by administrative-bureaucratic knowledge. Through learning by experience, each of these sectors skills its personnel in the establishing and running of bureaucratic structures.[14] Last are the educators—the Ph.D.s—with the most specialized skill of the four groups. These perhaps are the new experts and technicians which many theorists have viewed as the new elites of the postindustrial era. If there are shifts in skill recruitment, these changes should be reflected in the career space these groups occupy.

All of these theoretical speculations and mathematical calculations are given life in Table 5.5. Ignoring the "other" category (for reasons cited in the table), two patterns seem apparent. First, the law, appointed government, and business sectors appear to fluctuate roughly by party. For the most part, law and business occupy more career space in the Republican administrations than they do in the Democratic. The reverse of this is true for the appointed government sector. (Actually, this is less the case with the law sector than with the other two—and this will be taken up shortly—but for the moment the description is sufficient.) Second, elected government and education seem not to react to changes in party. In part, it would appear that the two parties do draw differentially from the skill sectors.

TABLE 5.5
CAREER SPACE OF EACH ADMINISTRATION OCCUPIED
BY THE FIVE MAJOR SECTORS (in percentages)

Administration	Law	Elected Government	Appointed Government	Business	Education	Other[a]	Total	N
Herbert C. Hoover	33	17	21	14	08	07	100%	152
Franklin D. Roosevelt	24	12	17	23	08	16	100%	243
Harry S. Truman	12	17	35	17	06	13	100%	224
Dwight D. Eisenhower-I	20	14	19	28	12	07	100%	216
Dwight D. Eisenhower-II	17	15	22	27	08	11	100%	276
John F. Kennedy	12	10	36	17	15	10	100%	288
Lyndon B. Johnson	12	07	38	14	15	14	100%	300
Richard M. Nixon	14	12	25	22	12	15	100%	321

[a] Other is an amalgamation of various sectors which were not sufficiently populated for all eight administrations to warrant separate inclusion in this table. These sectors consist mainly of the media and the military, followed by agriculture, labor, and miscellaneous. Such a conglomeration makes it difficult to speak substantively of this category.

This argument, however, cannot be left as it stands. Law, as a proportion of the total career space, is nowhere near as high under Republican Nixon as under Republican Hoover. Further, if party does not explain the fluctuations in education and elected government, what does? While appointed government and business seem most to reflect party shifts, business in Hoover and both sectors in Roosevelt look like their respective opposite parties in the rest of the table. An explanation outside Democratic-Republican party politics must be found. The search begins by focusing on the appointed government and business sectors.

Aside from the fact that these two sectors seem to fluctuate most as Democrats replace Republicans (and vice versa), and the fact that they share the same administrative-bureaucratic skill, there is another reason for considering these sectors together. Beginning at least with the industrial development of the United States, an increasing percentage of the top federal officeholders have been drawn from appointed government and business. C. Wright Mills, in his chapter on the political directorate in *The Power Elite,* documents this trend away from leaders with backgrounds of public election to persons with appointed government and business careers. He writes that in the period from 1933 to 1953, sixty-two percent of the higher politicians in the federal executive "were appointed to all or most of their political jobs before reaching top position." Later he notes that "since the Civil War, the typical member of the political elite has spent more years working outside of politics than in it."[15] Combining all eight administrations in this study, appointed government is twenty-seven percent and business is twenty percent of the total career space, while elected government is only thirteen percent.

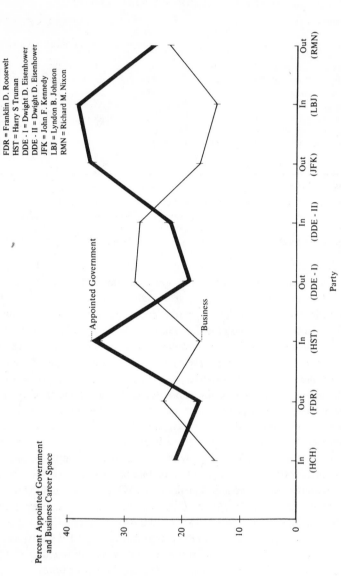

Figure 5.5 – APPOINTED GOVERNMENT AND BUSINESS CAREER SPACE FOR PARTIES IN OR OUT OF (COMING INTO) POWER

Clearly, any shifting of these two sectors is very telling for a general statement about changes in the executive elite.

A final reason for considering these sectors in tandem is that they fluctuate in relation to one another. Whenever appointed government declines, business increases—often at similar rates. This sequential rising and falling is plotted in Figure 5.5. The picture appears to show that the Republican administrations recruit people from business, while the Democratic administrations draw on appointed government personnel. But if this is so, how can the patterns for the first two administrations be explained? As noted before, each of these fits the lines of the opposite party. An explanation is at hand in the critiques of C. Wright Mills that came from Daniel Bell and Talcott Parsons. Bell summarizes the argument: "In 1952, since the Republican Party had been out of top office for twenty years and would have fewer persons who had a career in government, they would bring in a high proportion of outsiders."[16] Paraphrasing this in terms of skill groups, one would say that the "in" party recruits from government because it has dominated that sector for some time and therefore has its own in-house pool to draw on; the "out" party, coming into power, recruits from the other major source of bureaucratic personnel—business.

If this hypothesis is taken to Figure 5.5, it fits rather well. Hoover is at the end of an era of Republican dominance and so should draw more heavily from appointed government than business. Though the percentage difference is slight, this is indeed the case. Exactly the opposite situation should prevail for Roosevelt. Once again, the hypothesis holds, excusing slightness of percentage difference. Except for the deviant cases of Eisenhower's second administration and of Kennedy's administration, this pattern persists through the rest of the graph. The question exists, however, of why these two administrations do not fit the model but are instead the reverse of what "in" and "out" parties should be.

The argument might be that the two administrations of Republican rule were simply too short a period for an "in" party to gain sufficient control of government to develop an in-party, bureaucratically skilled personnel pool. It would have been virtually impossible for the Republicans in six years to reverse the skill sources of the parties that had been built up over twenty years. If this was the case, then, when the Democrats came into power there would have been no great need to look beyond the government for those with administrative skills. Apparently this was so, for Schlesinger writes: "In the end, the Kennedy administration kept most of the career people, including some on the sub-cabinet level."[17] It would seem fair to argue that this would not have been the case if these were in-party personnel. Lastly, returning to Figure 5.5, we can see that although the percentages for Nixon do not precisely fit the hypothesis, the drastic change from the Johnson years is sufficient to support the argument.

There is one other set of data we ought to consider in order to document further the in-party/out-party differences in the recruitment of personnel with administrative-bureaucratic skills. This is the relationship between the appointed government sector and the business sector for the final part of each individual's career. There are two reasons for doing this. First, personnel for elite positions are almost always chosen from near-elites. It is quite rare for a system of recruitment as institutionally based as the federal executive to ignore the hierarchical nature of such a base. Second, this set of data can be considered as a final check on the utility of the career space measure. Simply put, if this new measure showed different results from before, we would be forced to reconsider our argument, for the immediate sources of selection would not be what the over-time measure of career space more generally indicated they would be. Table 5.6 presents the data. The percentages represent the proportion of people who were in either appointed government or business in the last part of their careers. The data show in slightly more dramatic fashion what we have already seen: The "in" party relies more on those already in government and less on business for bureaucratic skill than the "out" party. The mean index of appointed government advantage vis-à-vis the business sector is thirty-one percent for the "in" party and only ten percent for the "out" party. As we saw before, the data from Eisenhower's

TABLE 5.6
PERCENTAGE OF EACH ADMINISTRATION IN APPOINTED GOVERNMENT
AND BUSINESS IN THE THIRD CAREER PART

Administration	In-Party (already in power)		
	Appointed Government	Business	Index of Appointed Government Advantage
Herbert C. Hoover (N = 54)	28	9	+ 19
Harry S. Truman (N = 78)	58	9	+ 49
Dwight D. Eisenhower-II (N = 92)	35	21	+ 14
Lyndon B. Johnson (N = 100)	54	11	+ 43
		Mean Index	+ 31
	Out-Party (coming into power)		
Franklin D. Roosevelt (N = 81)	30	20	+ 10
Dwight D. Eisenhower-I (N = 72)	29	22	+ 7
John F. Kennedy (N = 96)	38	14	+ 24
Richard M. Nixon (N = 107)	24	23	+ 1
		Mean Index	+ 10

second administration and from Kennedy's term in office do not fit the model, for the reasons already cited. If we calculate a mean index excluding these deviant administrations, the in-party index rises to forty percent while the "out" party drops to six percent.[18]

The more general point implied by all these data is that the relative presence of administrative-managerial skills in the executive elite has remained constant over the four decades. But if the same skill has been called upon, it has been recruited from different sources depending on which party controlled the White House and whether or not that party had been in control of the White House.

If, then, administrative-managerial skills have neither gained nor declined substantially during the period, what about other skills? Table 5.7 summarizes the relative contribution of the legal sector and the educational sector to the career space of the various administrations. The pattern is unmistakable and repeats what we saw in connection with degree earned. The legal sector is declining in significance, and the prime beneficiary is the educational sector. A twenty-five percent law advantage under Hoover is actually reversed under Kennedy and Johnson and is not recaptured under Nixon. There is no party variation at work here. Instead, there is a trend line which covers the entire period and which is most notably established in the 1960s, as has been true of several other trend lines examined.

If our string of assumptions is sound—career = skill, and career space of an administration = skill composition of an elite—then Table 5.7 provides strong evidence of a skill revolution, or, perhaps skill "evolution." Yet this transformation has not been in response to variable party control. We would have to look outside the party system for an explanation of this skill evolution.

One might argue that the decades studied witness the transformation of the federal government from one primarily concerned with regulation to one primarily concerned with fiscal management, economic planning, and social service. Whereas regulation calls for the talents of lawyers, the federal government's obligations taken on in the post war period require a range of much more specialized skills—hence, the gradual replacement of lawyers with (we presume)

TABLE 5.7
PERCENTAGE OF CAREER SPACE FOR LAW AND EDUCATION
IN EACH ADMINISTRATION

Career Space	Administrations							
	Herbert C. Hoover	Franklin D. Roosevelt	Harry S. Truman	Dwight D. Eisenhower-I	Dwight D. Eisenhower-II	John F. Kennedy	Lyndon B. Johnson	Richard M. Nixon
Law	33	24	12	20	17	12	12	14
Education	8	8	6	12	8	15	15	12
Law Advantage	+25	+16	+6	+8	+9	-3	-3	+2
N	(152)	(243)	(224)	(216)	(276)	(288)	(300)	(321)

more specialized Ph.D. skills. Although this argument is attractive, it is not testable with the data available. In this essay, we simply note the possibility of this particular functional thesis and will return to it in a subsequent report with additional data.

Conclusion

Our time frame has included forty years of American political history during which the executive branch of government has come under tremendous pressure to provide new services and programs in the society. Earlier we introduced the notion of "governing coalition," a phrase borrowed from Huntington. In developing this idea, Huntington writes that since the New Deal electoral coalitions have not been an important factor in the formation of governing coalitions.[19]

How do our data, drawn from exactly this time period, bear on the relationship between electoral coalitions (what a presidential candidate puts together to win the presidency), and governing coalitions (what a president puts together in order to implement his programs)? We infer that the closer the fit between executive elite attributes and changes in party administrations, the stronger the relationship between electoral coalition and governing coalition. This is only an inference, but it is suggestive enough to merit consideration. We assume that a change from Republican to Democratic control of the White House, or vice versa, implies that the electoral coalition which puts a new administration in power differs from the electoral coalition which had placed the outgoing administration in power. Moreover, we assume that if the attributes and skills of the executive elite are substantially altered from one administration to another, then such alterations represent an attempt to construct a governing coalition which resembles or reflects the electoral coalition. If, however, variations (or trend lines) in the attributes of the executive elite show no relationship with changes in party control, we are tempted to conclude with Huntington that constructing an electoral coalition and constructing a governing coalition are independent political processes.

We can now look again at the data. Two overall findings emerge. First, there are short-term fluctuations in certain social attributes of the executive elite which can be attributed to the particular political party in power. The religious composition of the executive elite and the type of educational institutions which supply its recruits are examples of Democratic-Republican party variation. Other short-term fluctuations can be traced to whether a given administration is of a party which has been in control of the executive branch for a long or short period of time. Notable in this regard is whether the party recruits managerial-administrative elites from the business world or from the government itself.

There is a second finding, however, which qualifies the first, and this is that there are various secular trends running through the period studied. More precisely, the earlier decades indicate a tendency for elite attributes to fluctuate with political party control while the later decades show little such shifting. Inferentially, these findings indicate that, in the earlier period, electoral coalitions as expressed through party victories did influence the attribute and skill composition of the governing coalition (or, at least, an important part of it—the executive elite). In the later years, however, there are trend-line changes in elite characteristics which do not result from political party fluctuation. Inferentially, we can conclude that there is a growing distance between electoral coalitions and governing coalitions. Over the forty years studied, the bases a presidential candidate needs to touch in order to win election are progressively unrelated to the bases a president needs to govern.

It is no accident that our data show this distancing of electoral from governing coalitions to have begun in the 1960s. Specialists in voting behavior and political party organization have identified a series of trends which aggregate into a picture of party decay and decomposition. There has been a sharp drop in party identification, a decline in party voting coupled with an increase in ticket-splitting, a decline in partisan consistency from one election to the next, and a surge of "issue-voting." As guides for voter behavior and as electoral organizations, parties have declined in importance. The tumultuous sixties recorded as well the difficulties party leaders faced in even controlling their most central task, the nomination and election of candidates to elected office. Challenges to incumbent presidents, splinter groups, issue-candidates, media campaigns, and now publicly financed campaigns call into question the viability of political parties as re-cruiting organizations. While much too early to pronounce the "end of the political party system," as some commentators have done, it is not too early to incorporate notions of party decomposition into our theories of American politics. This said, we simply point out that the lack of a relationship between executive elite attributes and changes in party control gain meaning in the context of party decomposition.

It is tempting to push such speculations one additional step. If not different electoral coalitions, what is at the root of the particular cluster of attributes and skills which characterize the governing elite? The data reveal two broad patterns: (1) a regional, religious, and probably social class broadening of the recruitment base; and (2) a skill evolution which appears to give greater weight to technical, more specialized skills. Because there is no necessary connection between these two broad patterns (there could be a skill change without broadening the recruitment base demographically, and there could be a broadened base without altering the skill composition), we are free to suggest unrelated explanations.

It is commonplace to observe that political life in the United States has become nationalized during the last half-century. National bureaucracies, national interest groups, national media attention, national problems, and national programs to solve the problems are the common fare of American political life. This nationalization of political life has increased the number of actors with a stake in the who and what of the federal government, especially the who and what of the White House. For the White House to take account of the many national actors with their claims on federal resources it has been necessary to construct governing coalitions ever more broadly: a Secretary of the Interior from the western states, a Secretary of Labor from the union movement, a Secretary of Commerce acceptable to business interests, meaningful posts for blacks, for ethnics, for women. "Demographic and group interest arithmetic" in constructing governing coalitions is not new to American politics. New are the stakes, which are immense, and the number of different actors speaking for national constituencies. It is in the context of the nationalization of politics that we can make sense of the broadened recruitment base into the executive elite.

The second finding, a skill evolution which is relatively independent of party and electoral politics, can be placed in a different context. It will be remembered that the skill transformation revealed in our data, as well as changes in certain social attributes of the executive elite, are particularly accelerated beginning in the early sixties.

Our suggestion is that a new generation came to power at that time. It was a generation which was born in the twentieth rather than in the nineteenth century, and which matured politically during and after rather than before the New Deal. This generation was ushered into power by the Kennedy victory, but it remained in government through Johnson and Nixon. This is a generation whose societal outlooks and career skills separate it in important respects from the elite it replaced. The executive elite drawn from this new generation accepts that government will play a managerial, perhaps even a planning, role in the economy. Moreover, they run a government which must necessarily become intimately involved in the economic and social welfare of society. The economic collapse of the thirties and the co-ordination needs of World War II caused the development of new governmental structures and responsibilities. Eventually a "new elite" fitted to the new structures came to power. What is instructive, however, is the lag time between the establishment of these structures and the existence of an elite which has the perspective to accept the new structures and the skills to use them. This lag time may help us to understand certain problems of governance, such as the capacity of government to respond to changing agendas.

NOTES

1. Moshe M. Czudnowski, "Political Recruitment," in Fred I. Greenstein and Nelson W. Polsby, ed., *Handbook of Political Science*, Vol. 2 (Reading, Mass.: Addison-Wesley, 1975), 155.

2. Czudnowski, for instance, continues his explication of political recruitment asserting that "recruitment studies investigate the *development* of political careers." Loc. cit., italics in original. It is this emphasis which we reject. Our study does not focus on individual careers; it concentrates on the character and composition of an entire ruling group.

3. Samuel P. Huntington, "The democratic distempter," Public Interest No. 41 (Fall, 1975), 27.

4. Ibid.

5. Readers may wonder why the long time gap in our data between Roosevelt's first administration and Truman. The data were initially collected to examine the relationship between "critical elections" and "elite circulation," and the choice of data points was guided by a requirement to compare critical with noncritical elections under varying conditions of party control. This explains as well why two time points from Eisenhower had to be used. The data do, however, serve present purposes. We are able to compare two different shifts from Republican to Democratic administrations, and two different shifts in the opposite direction. For an analysis of critical elections and elite circulation, see W. T. McAllister, "Some of the President's Men," M.A. thesis, University of Chicago.

6. Robert A. Dahl, *Who Governs?* (New Haven: Yale University Press, 1961), 38-42, 153-155.

7. E. Digby Baltzell, *The Protestant Establishment* (New York: Vintage, 1966), 231.

8. Kennedy's Catholicism is no doubt responsible for the slight advantage which Catholics have in his administration. But more than this personal presidential trait appears to be at work, as is attested to by the near parity which persists through the next two administrations.

9. Established prestige colleges include the Ivy League schools plus places like Amherst, Williams, Johns Hopkins and the University of Chicago. New prestige contains those schools which began to gain in recognition in the 1930s and especially since World War II. These include the major state universities as well as large private universities such as Boston University and Stanford University. The small, prestigious liberal arts colleges that dot the American educational scene are also included among new prestige schools. Examples of these are Coe, Grinnell, and Reed. These are a small percentage of this category. Nonprestige schools are those that fit in neither of the other categories. A more detailed description of this variable can be found in the Appendix.

10. Gaetano Mosca, *The Ruling Class* (New York: McGraw-Hill, 1939), 65-66.

11. Suzanne Keller, *Beyond the Ruling Class* (New York: Random House, 1963), 125-126.

12. The concept of "skill revolution" is developed by Harold Lasswell in his chapter on "Skill Politics and Skill Revolution," in *The Analysis of Political Behavior* (New York: Oxford University Press, 1948), 133-145.

13. James Sundquist, *Politics and Policy* (Washington, D.C.: Brookings Institution, 1968).

14. When Weber begins describing the characteristics of bureaucracy, he explicitly draws on the modern government and business as the two instances where bureaucracy has developed. See H. H. Gerth and C. Wright Mills, eds., *From Max Weber: Essays in Sociology* (New York: Oxford University Press, 1958), 196-204.

15. C. Wright Mills, *The Power Elite* (New York: Oxford University Press, 1956), 226-231.

16. Daniel Bell, "The Power Elite Reconsidered," in G. William Domhoff and Hoyt B. Ballard, *C. Wright Mills and the Power Elite* (Boston: Beacon, 1968). Talcott Parsons' similar critique is found in this same volume in an article entitled "The Distribution of Power in America," 76.

17. Arthur M. Schlesinger, Jr., *A Thousand Days* (Boston: Houghton Mifflin, 1965), 147.

18. The Truman and Johnson figures are inflated because of special conditions associated with the time at which they originally took office.

19. Huntington, op. cit. 27. He writes, for example, that "once he is elected President, the President's electoral coalition has, in a sense, served its purpose. The day after his election the size of his majority is almost—if not entirely—irrelevant to his ability to govern the country."

APPENDIX TO CHAPTER 5

Positional Identification

For the administrations of Roosevelt through Nixon the top executive posts were considered to be those identified as such by the *Government Organization Manual*. In this study, all of the departments and agencies listed in the manual for the year studied were used, with the exception of one or two independent commissions which were determined to be of little national policy import—e.g., those governing the Smithsonian Institute or the District of Columbia.

To identify the elite posts in Hoover's administration was not as simple, since the manual did not exist in 1930. What we used was the list of "principal officers" enumerated in *The Hoover Policies* by Ray Lyman Wilbur and Arthur M. Hyde (pp. 537-540). This identified as the most important positions the top cabinet posts plus the four or five independent agencies then in existence.

With the exception of the Hoover administration, the attempt was made to keep constant the number and level of the posts identified in each department or agency. The purpose of this was to prevent a false picture of an administration caused by an oversampling of one or several departments or by a sampling of noncomparative posts. Such sampling might have reflected the recruitment lines of particular departments rather than of an entire administration.

The divergence of Hoover from this scheme is due to the smallness of the federal executive in 1930. There were no White House staff to speak of, no White House agencies, and only five major independent agencies. The burden of government fell almost exclusively on the cabinet. For this reason, we sampled the cabinet more heavily in this administration than the others.

Personnel Identification

In the list below, the frequency distribution of persons studied in each administration is shown. The roughly steady increase across the eight administrations is due to the continuously enlarging federal executive.

Administration	Number of Persons	Administration	Number of Persons
Hoover	54	Eisenhower II	92
Roosevelt	81	Kennedy	96
Truman	78	Johnson	100
Eisenhower I	72	Nixon	107
		Total N	680

A problem of cabinet and agency holdovers from prior administrations occurred throughout the data collection. To include holdovers might have contributed to a false impression of the presidential appointees in an administration, since they were not appointed by the President in power. To exclude them might have caused the study to miss important personnel. The problem was solved by using presidential discretion as the criterion for judgment. If the post was such that the President could have replaced the incumbent but did not, then that person was included. This would be the case for any cabinet holdovers. If the post was such that by law the President could not remove its occupant, then these holdovers were excluded. This, of course, was true for independent agencies, since most posts were for four- to seven-year terms. This method assures that all persons who were studied in each of the administrations were appointees of the President in power.

A further note should be added concerning the personnel in Eisenhower's second term and in Johnson's administration. A problem was anticipated with 1958 concerning the lack of personnel change from 1954. As much as was possible, we wanted to treat each of these administrations as distinct and not consider Eisenhower's second term as an extension of his first. On the whole, the fear turned out to be unwarranted. The intervening four years had produced much turnover. Twenty persons—twenty-two percent of the second administration—were holdovers in the same post.

A similar problem existed for the Johnson administration. The sudden death of Kennedy and the subsequent pro-Kennedy personnel pressure that surrounded Johnson led us to think that there might be too high a percentage of 1962 people still serving in 1966. As with Eisenhower, this turned out not to be the case. The percentage of holdovers is quite small (10%), and these also were in the major cabinet posts.

Souces of Data

The primary and almost exclusive source of the data is *Who's Who in America*. The only exception to the use of this was five persons in the Nixon administration. For these, *Who's Who in the East* was used.

Creation of Variables

College/Graduate School Prestige. The construction of these two variables hinged on two issues: how to define a school's prestigiousness, and how to account for possible changes in this prestigiousness over the forty years studied.

The first issue was resolved by using a two-step method of evaluation. Initially, schools were dichotomized into prestige and nonprestige using a scheme that was employed by Kenneth Prewitt and Robert W. Pearson in "The Plateau: Toward a Theory of Elite Recruitment" (unpublished manuscript). Their list of prestige schools correlated very highly (gamma—.93) with a prestige ranking developed by the National Opinion Research Center in a 1961 study of college seniors. This method revolved around scoring several variables which were used to form a school quality index. Not all the schools in the current study were among the colleges categorized by NORC. To fill this gap, we relied on the ranking done by James Cass and Max Birnbaum in their *Comparative Guide to American Colleges*.

While the question of characterizing schools as prestigious or nonprestigious appears to be resolved, some schools which are prestigious now were not so forty to eighty years ago—the educational range for most of the people in this study. The resolution of this dilemma lay in the development of three categories which slotted schools according to when their prestige came about: established prestige, newer prestige, and nonprestige. Established prestige schools are those which, by the time of Hoover's administration, were usually recognized as the leading universities in the nation. By name, these are the rather obvious Ivy League and Seven Sister colleges, as well as places like Johns Hopkins, Amherst, and the University of Chicago. Newer prestige schools are those which have attained national recognition from the thirties to the present. These are mainly the big state universities, large private schools, and a smattering of small liberal arts colleges. The final group are those whose non-prestigiousness has remained constant from Hoover to Nixon.

Career Space. As we note in the text, each person was coded for three career parts. The precise coding procedure rests on a mixture of two criteria: (a) length of time spent in a particular sector, and (b) importance of a sector for advancement to future executive posts. Why length of time was used is self-evident—i.e., this is in fact the definition of a career part. Length of time does not necessarily mean the same number of years in each part for every person. The total career time of any individual before he or she enters the executive leadership can vary greatly. Some people have been out of college only ten to fifteen years before becoming part of the national leadership, while others have had careers of forty years or more.

The second criterion was employed because in the course of coding it became increasingly obvious that there were some people, mostly lawyers, but some businessmen and educators, who worked with government agencies and personnel for what appeared by their biographical data to be short periods of time, but whose eventual executive positions seem to have been made possible by this earlier government contact. This criterion allows us to capture those persons whose time in the government sector would not seem to warrant a government coding, but whose career at some point became importantly entangled with government.

There is one exception to much of what has been said concerning the original career coding. For all of the Hoover administration and for a quarter of the Roosevelt administration, no biographical data on length of time in a particular job was collected. The absence of such data is due to various time constraints which made it impossible to correct this oversight. However, a look at these career data will show that this is not as great a problem as it might seem: (a) sixty percent of Hoover's administration, for whom this problem cropped up, had only one career throughout his or her life—obviously these were no coding problem; (b) the bulk of the remainder for each administration had three careers, so these persons also presented no problems. For the last group, people with two careers, it was not possible without dates to decide on the middle career part of length of time and so our best educated guess was used. The percentage of people in this category was minuscule for both administrations.

Finally, there might be some slippage between career space as a theoretical measure of skills carried into an administration and the actual skills which formed an administration. We do not mean to say by this measure that someone who was in one sector his or her entire career actually had three times as much skill as someone who was in that sector for one part of her or his career. To avoid this problem, it would have been necessary to give an equal weight to a three-sector career as to a single sector career. This, we felt, would have been a more inaccurate measure than the one we developed and would have done damage to the concept of career space.

Chapter 6

RECRUITMENT PATTERNS OF CAMPAIGN ACTIVITIES IN INDIA: LEGISLATIVE CANDIDATES, PUBLIC NOTABLES, AND THE ORGANIZATIONAL PERSONNEL OF RIVAL PARTIES

DWAINE MARVICK

In this chapter, data are examined which clarify some of the ways in which modern India is recruiting and deploying its middle layers of political personnel —specifically, the organizational personnel of rival parties, the candidates for state and national legislative posts, and the public notables who are influential on village, block, and district self-government councils. The data come from a thousand interviews, taken with a representative sample of those who in 1967 were active either in polling station outposts or at translocal coordination points on the occasion of India's fourth free and seriously contested national election.[1]

As the world's largest electoral democracy, India provides a distinctive research opportunity—a setting markedly different in geographic scope, cultural diversity, socioeconomic backwardness, and political complexity from any American or European cases heretofore available for systematic quantitative study. The Indian National Election project, while its primary focus was on the campaign weeks just preceding the 1967 elections, gathered a wealth of detail from all activist informants about earlier phases of India's political recruitment processes—about the social and cultural background factors that circumscribe and make predictable each person's political life chances before he ever enters politics, about the childhood socialization patterns, motivational incentives, and facilitating circumstances that prompted people in different ways to work actively in election politics, and about the screening practices and selection criteria used in their party when deciding what kind of legislative candidates to sponsor.[2]

To use these data for an examination of Indian recruitment patterns requires attention at the outset to an interconnected set of *substantive questions* about India's talent pool of leaders and its future as a viable democracy and the *methodological constraints* imposed by the parameters of our sample design and the nature of survey responses. After these matters have been clarified, attention will turn to a range of findings—from geographic, social, and cultural differentials in India's political pool, through generational and occupational changes in the patterns of political activation, to consideration of the attitudinal and behavioral correlates of persons with different career orbits and different records of office-seeking success and failure.

THE VOCATION OF POLITICS IN INDIA

Modern India is a complex political system in which to study political recruitment patterns. Led from the center, run by the intermediate levels, its impact penetrating even remote villages, the modern polity is led by career politicians who are committed to the dual task of modernizing the nation and preserving India's culture and style of life. Participatory democracy is encouraged, even if it means harder tasks for India's leaders. The growth of opportunities to make a vocation of politics is fostered by the same ethos.[3]

By 1967, India's party system found Congress occupying the middle ground, surrounded by gadfly opposition parties on every side. As the party with historic mission to lead India and as the party of Gandhi and Nehru, Congress had become the "party of consensus"—the only truly national party both in its demonstrated popular support and in its organized scope and governing presence. A few other parties had been able to create the kind of extended coordinating machinery needed to function on a national scale, or at least on a regional one. Even the largest of these, however, functioned chiefly as "parties of pressure" bearing on Congress, parties whose activists and supporters functioned by agitating to raise the dissonance level with Congress, helping their collaborators within Congress and trying to hamper the plans of uncooperative factions therein.[4]

Modern India is a new state in an old society. The political survival of representative government along lines copied from the West has never been easily taken for granted. As much as any other condition, the goals of modernization depend upon citizen participation and communitywide enlistment of personnel. The vocation of politics is a full-time career for many. Political parties are not exclusively or even primarily electoral apparatuses. As Rajni Kothari has written:

Much of the party system functions through the government; the government party itself spreads its network through the leverage that the structure of patronage and development resources provides; the dissident factions aim at acquiring positions in this resource structure; and opposition parties and protest movements make demands on the same structure.[5]

Even before 1967, Congress had become a catch-all party—more of a framework for collaboration than a discrete political machine. During the independence movement years, Congress had sponsored a far-flung apparatus that gave it a foothold at many levels. While the district-level party committee was seen as the key organizational node, Gandhi had also stressed the importance of mobilization agencies in special sectors, such as in labor, youth, the tribal people, women, the untouchables. Local political elites were recruited as part of the common action program. Congress came to include all streams of ideological thought. Dissent came to be expected; a high tolerance of ambiguity was an organizational norm.

It could be argued persuasively in 1967 that the years of in-fighting and factionalism within Congress had crippled it seriously, making it impossible for Congress to continue as in the past to perform a consensus-nourishing role. Alternatively, it could be held that much of the factionalism was healthy, if not essential, and that otherwise the careerist mentality of party bureaucrats would face no challenges.

Congress was so vast and fragmented an apparatus that internal conflict, tension management, bargaining, and arbitration were constant features. A political apprenticeship in this environment gave skills and contacts that were distinctive; it also shaped one's sensitivities and values. At all levels, a complex variety of social and political mechanisms was operating—factional groups, caste associations, specialized clientele groups, tribal and locality-based party fragments—all pressing upon both government circles and Congress leaders for recognition, ventilation of complaints and help.[6] The strength of Congress came not only from its organization, which enabled it to mobilize the people at large, collaborate with various sector elites, and recruit its own leadership cadre, but also from its dominant role in the governing processes at all levels.

In India, there are many levels of elected bodies—not only the national and state legislatures, but the structural scaffold of local self-government councils championed by Nehru through which national planning objectives are translated into the practical considerations of elected politicians asked to secure public cooperation in the unending tasks of resource mobilization, and under whose guidance the appointed government officials are expected to work. Kothari has described the emergence of "non-officials" whose political skills and effective power are exercised at locality and district levels in the interstices of the *panachayati raj* self-government system:

Politicians in the Congress—and gradually in other parties as well—are beginning to realize the potentialities of the new institutions. They often prefer positions in *panchayat samitis* and *zilla parishads*, or in associated organizations . . . to being elected to the state legislature. . . . Known in the Indian political vocabulary as the "non-officials," these politicians are playing an increasing role in bridging the gap between local society and political authority.[7]

The basic feature of Indian politics that must be kept in mind is the extent to which government anchors and nourishes the party system. An elaborate patronage network, controlled and directed at the district and locality levels of political life, has come to surround the implementation states of government programs of development. New jobs are available. Loans and benefits are to be distributed. Institutions dealing with credit and with scarce materials can be controlled. New posts of authority and prestige are established. Patterns of influence and corruption become well defined. The proliferation of India's machinery for democratic governance means the enlargement of opportunities to pursue politics as a vocation.

In 1967, Congress was a working reality, a party concerned with the endless tasks of governing not only in the national and state capitals but in the panchayati raj system at district and local levels. No other political party had so good a performance record: of grooming and deploying a vast army of skilled and knowledgeable party cadres, of reconciling programmatic and ideological differences within ranks, of working harmoniously with other parties and auxiliary groups, of advancing the careers of would-be leaders by underwriting the risks at successive job thresholds, of shaping the vocation of politics throughout India by controlling opportunities for ingress as well as for advancement both through electoral success and through cooptation into the pervasive processes of governance.[8]

If there was inevitably a high dissonance level within Congress, it was not clearly dysfunctional. At state and district levels, the internal group alignments tended to stabilize; Congress was the governing party, but keen rivalry often persisted between its ministerial and organizational wings. In some cases, the organizational faction functioned as an opposition group so effectively that it dislodged the governmental faction from power. Opposition party leaders made calculated efforts to shift the balance of dominant dissident factional strength within Congress. At the same time, ideological and personality differences continued to split the opposition camp; in many constituencies where the combined forces in opposition might have prevailed, they were unable to work together in order to mount a sustained and formidable election campaign against Congress.[9]

The political recruitment problems that beset modern India are not hard to identify: the pervasive presence in the processes of governance of those with parochial concerns and segmental loyalties; the emphasis on practical solutions, opportunistic strategies, and nonideologically constrained thinking which is the daily catechism for neophyte participants and apprentice cadres; and the overcrowding of the vocation of politics itself, by the presence of more aspirants who want to use politics for their livelihood than India can afford to support.

Since 1947, massive efforts to carry out ambitious programs of modernization and development have been made throughout the country. Especially at local and district levels, implementation of these development programs has significantly enlarged the opportunities and occasions for active political participation. As a result, opportunities for political careers have proliferated. Much of the in-service training acquired during the early years of a political apprenticeship in these contexts has been skill in bargaining, in coalition-building, in fashioning ad hoc solutions. The great variation in social settings and problem-clusters continuously prompts those who put a premium on results to follow opportunistic strategies.

Nor is it only the implementation stages of political development programs that have enlarged the opportunities and fired the desire for lifelong careers in politics. Ironically, the very success India has had with electoral democracy has similar effects. Electoral democracy supports an inescapable functional redundancy in the form of duplicate recruitment machinery controlled by each serious rival party. In 1967, electoral competition was serious and widespread; across the country, no single opposition party regularly was effective in its challenge to Congress. But in constituency after constituency at least one formidable rival was sponsored by an effective opposition camp. Not only did the resulting level of electoral competition vest real hiring-and-firing power in the hands of India's voters in many constituencies. It also whetted the appetites for political careers of at least two aspirants for every legislative post available. To be sure, India's political activists superintended the peaceful changes in government and legislative control throughout the subcontinent that occurred after the 1967 elections. And they continue to sustain India's experiment with participant democracy, though with mounting costs, corruption, and acrimony. In a fundamental sense, however, India's problems as well as her hopes for their solution are keyed to her political recruitment and career-grooming practices.

In approaching the Indian activist data as a basis for recruitment analysis, certain theoretical departures from usual practice are taken; each of these departures reflects the same key difficulty—how to use familiar recruitment terminology and process models when seeking to analyze a large and representative sample of a nation's political activist population, interviewed at a single point in time. Major methodological constraints apply. First, it has not been possible to deal with the recruitment process by stages neatly dovetailed together. Instead, it has been instructive to concentrate on what apprentice-experience differentials characterize the roster of those present at different nodes and organizational levels in rival party structures. The equivalence of credentials and the duplication of machinery grooming rival aspirants for the same jobs are stressed. Second, it has seemed inappropriate to think of the political opportunity structure of public offices alone, without considering the interpenetration of party- and government-officeholding patterns. This is especially necessary when the public-office careers of party personnel in many instances match those of the 1967 legislative aspirants sponsored by the same party. Third, it has seemed overly formal to think of "parties" as sponsoring candidates; rather, it has seemed important to stress how party leaders at each node control the high-risk thresholds that shape the career options available to activist men and women with different credentials.

METHODOLOGICAL CONSTRAINTS IN USING
THE 1967 INDIA ACTIVIST SURVEY

In using the India activist survey as a data base for recruitment analysis, various methodological problems with theoretical overtones arise. These relate both to the suitability of survey data for recruitment inquiries and to the use of a sample design keyed to the 1967 electoral rivalry of Congress and opposition parties as a source of evidence bearing on differential career opportunities, apprenticeship options, and sponsorship considerations.

In March and April of 1967, our interviewers—more than 200 trained men and women—completed their assignments with 1,000 campaign activists. There are limitations in using any time-specific interview data to study a longitudinal process. Nevertheless, the activist sample is a close approximation of what it was designed to be: a representative cross-section of those who were the party organizational personnel, the public notables with party ties, and the 1967 legislative candidates themselves—the activists whose participation made the state and national elections an effective and meaningful expression of political democracy.

Moreover, the activist interview schedule called upon these participating informants for retrospection about themselves as well as about the campaign weeks through which they had recently lived. We learned in full detail the history of each person's party affiliations, which *party jobs* he had ever held, at what level, and for how long. In separate question batteries, information was also gathered about the level and extent of his involvement in nine different kinds of *voluntary organizations*: cooperatives, semi-official committees, caste associations, unions, professional societies, groups concerned with education, welfare, youth, and sports. Again, the full history of his *office-seeking* efforts, successful or not, and the record of his *public office-holding* experience, at what levels and when, were systematically obtained. It is by sifting and collating this elaborate descriptive detail that the frequency of different career patterns can be charted, those that go into an orbit that is geographically or institutionally circumscribed, and those that move in transit from level to level, party to party, public to private, over the years in question.

An equally severe limitation of survey data for our purpose here is its personal nature. Recruitment practices have personal consequences, of course; they affect both the respondent's attitudes and behavior in demonstrable ways. Our interest in recruitment analysis centers, however, on the transpersonal impact of such practices. For this it has been possible to call on our informants to make generalized assessments about such impacts, based both on introspection and on their participant observation of the practices in question. Specifically, they were asked a full battery of questions about what *candidate selection criteria* were important when their party sponsored its state assembly and national legislative aspirants. Again, they were called on to assess the importance of various *motivational incentives*—purposive, solidary, and material—in explaining the campaign participation of activists like themselves. In other batteries, they were asked to rate the importance of various *campaign issues,* and the record of Congress in solving different problems. Together with background data, these are the materials with which our recruitment inquiry is chiefly concerned.

A different kind of methodological problem arises because the Indian sample design was geared to a study of the closing campaign weeks of 1967. With both a voter sample and an activist sample to juxtapose, our primary interest was in the measurement of electoral responses to competitive campaign pressures. Each type of competitive situation—Congress versus the Left, Congress unopposed, Congress versus Right and Left, Congress versus local opposition, and so forth—was proportionately included in our sample. Each type of opposition apparatus, ranging from independent candidates and a variety of local parties through Jan Sangh and Swatantra on the right to two variants of socialism and two variants of communism on the left, was represented in our sample whenever its effective strength reached a minimum level—that is, one-third of the 1967 non-Congress vote. The consequence was to secure a body of evidence from voters and activists that mirrored in proper proportions the complex and varied competitive conditions prevailing in 1967. For the activist sample, moreover, this same political complexity was achieved at three organizational levels—in the rivalry configurations found in 47 parliamentary constituencies, 94 state assembly constituencies, and 188 village and urban polling stations. In fact, of course, each PC contained an average of 8 AC, while each AC included an average of 200 PS. Hence the ratios of two polling stations in every assembly constituency, and two assembly constituencies in every parliamentary constituency are purely arbitrary ones. Any collapsing steps taken during analysis run the risk not only of concealing different patterns at the three levels, but of producing results that reflect these arbitrary sampling ratios rather than a proportionately weighted composite picture of the 1967 political activists to be found in India. Only when detailed analysis makes clear what differentials are level-specific is it therefore safe to collapse levels and use the composite results. Even then, considerable caution is called for.[10]

The method of sampling also involved the use of a positional roster, to select activists at each organizational node. It was so constructed as to include, whenever the occasion arose, dissident faction leaders as well as those in the dominant faction. While this ensured us of interviews with a representative set of dissident activists—thirty-nine persons, mostly in Congress—it also complicated analysis of the "party cadre" components at each level of the activist sample; ordinarily, these cadremen were chosen because they were considered to be the "chief campaign worker" for the legislative candidate in question, while quite the opposite was true whenever a dissident activist also was interviewed. Again, special analyses were called for, to resolve doubts about including these dissident figures by finding out empirically whether it really made any difference.

Two other points should be noted. First, these same sampling problems about the proper ratios to maintain in combining organizational levels or pooling responses from differently placed persons at the same level have led us to use rather complex contingency tables. Various other data-reduction techniques that involve post-correlational matrix manipulations—factor analysis, cluster methods, and regression work—have been used extensively in exploring the structural properties of the Indian data. For the lines of inquiry here pursued, they conceal too much of the variance to be useful. Cross-tabulations that differentiate findings by levels, roles, and partisan sectors or camps convey a clearer picture. Second, virtually all percentage differences of any magnitude— say, twelve to fifteen points—sufficiently great to stand out in the tables or to be commented on in the text have presumptive validity for India in 1967. The estimated sampling error at the ninety-five percent confidence level for the sample as a whole is 3.2 points; for the smaller populations that make up the levels and roles and rival camps comprised by the composite whole, it is typically a figure between five and seven points in the 60:40 binomial percentage distribution range, with Ns of 200 to 300.

Table 6.1 provides a party-by-party breakdown of the Indian activist sample. At the same time, it gives a breakdown by sector—right, left, or other—within the opposition camp. Certain features deserve brief comment, since they reflect the political realities of Indian party strengths and weaknesses in 1967.

Not unexpectedly, there is a clear tendency for campaign activists working for independent candidates and local parties to be public notables rather than organizational personnel. By our sampling method, Congress is represented in a

TABLE 6.1
INDIAN ACTIVIST SAMPLE COMPONENTS
CAMPAIGN ROLES, ORGANIZATIONAL LEVELS, AND PARTY SECTORS

	Congress Party	Opposition Parties	Opposition Sector Breakdown				Opposition Party Frequency Count						
			Right				Swantantra Jan Sanch Communists Socialists Independents Local Party						
				Left									
					Other								
ROSTER	%	%	%	%	%	Cases	(C a s e s)						
Candidates													
Parliamentary	23	27	40	23	37:100	35	9	5	3	5	4	9	
Assembly	77	73	33	39	27:100	92	13	17	13	23	13	13	
	100	100											
Cases	(106)	(127)											
Notables													
Translocal	50	31	26	22	52:100	23	3	3	2	3	9	3	
Local	50	69	12	18	70:100	50	2	4	2	7	31	4	
	100	100											
Cases	(157)	(73)											
Workers													
PC Apparatus	18	15	46	27	27:100	40	10	8	6	5	5	6	
AC Apparatus	39	38	38	36	26:100	99	16	21	9	27	12	14	
PS Apparatus	43	47	31	41	28:100	124	23	17	18	32	13	21	
	100	100											
Cases	(274)	(263)											
SUMMARY													
Translocal	63	62	36	33	31:100	289	51	54	33	63	43	45	
Local	37	38	26	34	40:100	174	25	21	20	39	44	25	
	100	100											
Cases	(537)	(463)											

full range of electoral circumstances, where it was overwhelmingly dominant, where it had a narrow edge, where it was marginally weak, and where it was clearly no match for the opposition. The parties making up the opposition camp, on the other hand, were only sampled in contexts where they qualified as relatively effective "serious rivals" of Congress—i.e., they were able to get at least one-third of the non-Congress votes cast. In this sense, they competed against each other for inclusion in our activist sample. Systematically, our opposition thus excludes cases of activists campaigning in areas hopelessly lost to their party. Only by assuming that Congress was everywhere at least as formidable as the minimum test used in selecting opposition parties can it be held that our sample truly matches Congress and its "effective opposition" in 1967. Put another way, each opposition party apparatus was explicitly required to meet the test of campaign effectiveness in order to be included in our sample frame; no such explicit test was required in order to include the corresponding Congress Party unit.

More than sixty percent of the local notables and nearly eighty percent of those at translocal levels—*zilla parished* chairmen and *block pramuhk* heads—are Congress activists. Especially at the local level, most of the rest are unaffiliated with rightist or leftist parties also, and are classified in the "other" sector. This reflects the political realities of the sampled localities rather than any bias or convenience in our sampling techniques. Notables were included because we were convinced that they played significant facilitative roles in the 1967 national and state electoral campaigns. Their inclusion complicates the composition of the Congress roster, but it does so by mirroring operative complexities in Indian politics rather than leaving them out because they are not matched by similar proportions when we look at opposition ranks.

In summary, two differentials cause the right-left-other ratios within the "effective opposition" to be slightly different for each campaign-activity level—the intrusion of independents and local parties, on the one hand, and the greater efforts by parties of the right to win national legislative seats while parties of the left were a little more likely to be formidable in state assembly races. Both these factors reflect the political realities of Indian parties in 1967. In similar ways, slight distortions are introduced into the Congress "side" of our activist sample, first by including the Congress apparatus wherever we encountered it, without a test for how ineffectual it may have been in a particular locale, and second by including not only party organizational personnel but public notables with party connections, most of whom were tied to Congress at least in the localities sampled.

PRE-APPRENTICESHIP DIFFERENTIALS

Since independence, India has attempted a massive implementation of ambitious nationwide development policies. In a land where the caste rigidities of folk culture and the inertia of primitive rural economic practices lock people from birth into much the same "life chances" as their parents had, these centrally sponsored but locally executed programs have meant that an expanding universe of new roles and even new careers was being created.[11] The plans themselves called for enlargement of educational resources; the public philosophy for their implementation called for active citizen participation in the continuing processes of governance at locality and district levels as well as voluntary effort periodically to be undertaken in India's demonstrably competitive electoral arenas. For a quarter century, millions have been tutored and trained in modern civics and encouraged to practice participatory democracy, at the same time that the cultural and economic realities of Mother India seemed to change very slowly.

The first patterns of political recruitment disclosed by our activist sample can be characterized as pre-apprenticeship patterns. Following the useful convention suggested by Prewitt, the term "apprenticeship" (and at times the notion of "recruitment proper" as distinguished from the larger generic process) are reserved for the grooming and in-house screening that occurs after a largely self-selected and happenstantially mobilized portion of a nation's adult citizenry have somehow been mobilized into what has come to be called "the active political stratum."[12] American and European studies have tended to characterize this induction from a pre-active status into organized political life as necessarily open, with only haphazard control exercised by those already active, if the interstitial processes of democratic pluralism are functioning as the conceptual model stipulates. In the Bay Area study, Prewitt found it so; Table 6.2 reports similar patterns for the Indian activists: "It appears that penetrating the active stratum is more a result of youthful political exposure, chance factors, or personal desire than permission from the already established."[13]

Caste

The systematic quantitative analysis of caste differentials in political behavior is now well under way, with important recent contributions.[14] Here our concern is with a single, negatively phrased question: Does caste operate in the political induction stages in ways that virtually exclude the majority groups from effective participation? While the expected social stratification bias in

TABLE 6.2

PRE-APPRENTICESHIP DIFFERENTIALS AMONG INDIAN ACTIVISTS (in percentages)

	CANDIDATES		NOTABLES		APPARATUS		CADRES SUMMARY TOTALS		
	PC	AC	T	L	PC	AC	PS	Translocal	Local
CASTE, % dominant									
Congress:	42	44	80	54	66	61	58	60	56
Opposition:	51	53	78	64	65	64	54	60	57
INCOME, % 500 rup/mon									
Congress:	68	32	43	25	37	39	14	40	18
Opposition:	38	28	26	23	28	25	7	28	11
EDUCATION Congress									
Grammar	4	10	22	64	11	19	51	15	56
High School	8	32	41	27	38	45	36	40	33
Some College	88	58	37	9	51	36	13	45	11
	100	100	100	100	100	100	100	100	100
Cases	(35)	(92)	(23)	(50)	(40)	(99)	(124)	(289)	(174)
ENTRY POINT OCCUPATION									
Congress									
Agriculture	15	31	58	90	31	35	64	38	74
Commerce	5	10	15	6	12	22	21	15	15
Prof/Student	80	59	27	4	57	43	15	47	11
	100	100	100	100	100	100	100	100	100
Opposition									
Agriculture	23	35	71	79	14	28	59	31	64
Commerce	8	17	10	15	19	24	16	18	16
Prof/Student	69	48	19	6	67	48	25	51	20
	100	100	100	100	100	100	100	100	100
POLITICALLY ACTIVE PARENTS									
Congress	44	39	26	10	45	28	17	34	14
Opposition	31	37	18	10	45	29	17	34	14

favor of relatively advantaged groups is found, it clearly is *not* a major factor precluding entry into the active political stratum from any caste category. Consider the evidence from the two interlocked samples of the Indian project (see Table 6.3). While not quite thirty percent of the citizen sample could claim membership in one of the "advantaged caste" categories—Brahmins, non-agricultural upper castes, and dominant castes, as conventionally defined—these same caste groupings account for nearly sixty percent of the activist sample. The skewing is readily apparent, but it is not strikingly at odds with the ratios found in other polities. As numerous scholars have argued, under present conditions, "caste retains only a diminished saliency for partisan politics even when it retains considerable vigor in the non-partisan representation of community interests."[15] Nevertheless, certain differentials are disclosed. Candidates for national and state legislative seats were somewhat less likely than the apparatus cadres helping them to mount constituencywide campaigns to possess the credentials of an advantaged caste category; translocal notables—the "non-officials" whose importance in nonelectoral politics Rajni Kothari has emphasized—are sharply skewed the other way (see Table 6.2). About eighty percent of these 101 activists in our sample—Congress and opposition ranks alike—could claim the kind of advantaged-caste credentials that fewer than three in ten ordinary citizens possessed. For the rest, it would seem that good caste credentials are desiderata—not conclusive but presumptive—for ready induction into India's active stratum.

Income

The significance of current income differentials within the activist sample is at most tangential to an analysis of the induction-stage pluses and minuses that can be inferred. Clearly a relatively better income may reflect the result of being

TABLE 6.3
CASTE SAMPLE OF CITIZENS AND ACTIVISTS

	Brahmins	Nonagr. upper c.	Domin. castes	Sched. castes	Backwd. castes	Muslims	Others	NA
Citizen Sample (N = 1,971)	% 6.1	% 6.4	% 15.2	% 17.9	% 37.5	% 10.8	% 3.7	% 2.4:100
Activist Sample (N = 1,000)	18.4	15.7	24.9	7.7	25.2	6.8	1.0	0.3:100

politically active and influential rather than being a mark of birth or a sign of achievements made in a prepolitical career. Again, however, the negative side is worth considering. Consider the differentials disclosed by the Indian citizen and activist samples (see Table 6.4).

Nearly half the citizens earned under 100 rupees a month in 1967, three times as large a proportion as the impoverished element in the activist sample. At the opposite extreme, twenty-seven percent of the activists reported incomes above 500, a level of affluence attained by three percent of the citizens—a ninefold differential. In considering the attractiveness of careers in politics, material rewards cannot be discounted.

Still, as Table 6.2 discloses, only a third of the Congress activists and a fifth of those in opposition camps qualified as earning 500 rupees a month—considerably less purchasing power than $100 would bestow. Moreover, polling station workers on both sides of the political fence were noticeably poorer than their translocal fellow activists. At all levels and in all roles, Congress activists enjoyed an income edge over their opposite numbers. The lesson seems twofold. A career in politics must seem both attractive in material terms to many, and at the same time not so exclusive to be unthinkable. At the same time, it can probably be assumed that those who started life with some degree of affluence or were able to acquire money in their prepolitical work found it easier to enter the active stratum than did fellow citizens who started from less-favored circumstances.

Education

When educational attainments are next examined, the patterns are more sharply differentiated, both between ordinary citizens and political activists and within the politically active stratum by role and level. In India as elsewhere, getting an education requires a combination of talent, self-discipline, and help

TABLE 6.4
INCOME OF CITIZENS AND ACTIVISTS

	Under 50 rupees a month %	To 100 rupees a month %	To 200 rupees a month %	To 500 rupees a month %	Over 500 rupees a month %	
Citizen sample (N = 1,971)	27	32	25	13	3	:100
Activist sample (N = 1,000)	6	10	19	38	27	:100
Differentials:	5-fold	3-fold	even	3-fold	9-fold	

from others. The extraordinary expansion of primary schools in India since independence is slowly beginning to change the economic and social patterns of village life; as in European peasant communities, market-oriented agricultural-ists, artisans, food processors, and rural-service vendors are creating a more differentiated world. No factor is more pervasive and demonstrably important than education in bringing these changes about. Yet half the Indians in our 1967 citizen sample were illiterate and another third had never reached high school. Only six percent had any college experience (see Table 6.5).

For the illiterate, the likelihood of entering the active political stratum was roughly one chance in twenty-five. But even a modest education would bring one to par; slightly more than one-third of the citizens had only grammar school credentials, and slightly less than one-third of the activists could make the same claim. Getting to high school sharply raised the possibilities of becoming active politically, judging from the sample proportions in 1967. For that small fraction of India's citizens able to acquire some college education, the presumption that a politically active role is readily available is not hard to make. More than a third of our activist sample possessed such credentials.

Looking back at Table 6.2, it is clear that the more formal education one had, in India in 1967, the farther one could predictably expect to go—in opposition camps as well as in Congress. Level for level, candidates are likely to be better educated than their campaign associates. It is worth emphasizing, at the same time, that more than half of those public notables and campaign workers active at the local level—in villages and urban neighborhoods—have *no* high school credentials. Yet politically significant roles were open to them at least at grass-roots levels of party work. What is equally clear from the evidence, of course, is the marked advantage that educational credentials provide if one aims for a *career in transit* upward to translocal levels of public and/or party life rather than a *career in orbit* at the local level.

TABLE 6.5
EDUCATION OF CITIZENS AND ACTIVISTS

	Illiterate	Grammar School	High School Only	Some College	Total
	%	%	%	%	%
Citizen sample (N = 1,971)	49	35	10	6	100
Activist sample (N = 1,000)	2	30	33	35	100
Differential:	25-fold	even	3-fold	6-fold	

Entry-point Occupation

Next let us consider the significance of the occupational status held by Indian activists at the time they first became politically active. That is what is here meant by "entry-point occupation." Given a certain self-activating propensity, whether from the kind of political socialization in one's childhood or from personality need-dispositions for power, prestige, and/or publicity, it has been cogently argued that the individuals who actually enter the realm of active politics instead of merely being in a social stratum that would make political induction relatively easy are persons found to occupy strategic nonpolitical occupational roles and status positions. These "brokerage positions," as Jacob called them,[16] impart politically useful skills, permit a range of social contacts, facilitate efforts to gain financial backing and group support, and make feasible a persistent if low-keyed search for an entry point into politics, if not an office-holding opportunity.

For our purposes, a simple three-way classification of entry-point occupations is sufficient, distinguishing those who were farmers from those in commerce and also from those engaged in a profession or studying to do so. Table 6.2 displays the incidence differentials, by roles, levels, and partisan camps. Only about one in six activists at the PC level had been a farmer when he entered politics; at the AC level, about one in three had been; at the PS level, four out of five. Conversely, of those at the local level only a tenth were professional men when they first began—or even students preparing for professional careers—while at the translocal echelons of both Congress and opposition, half to three-quarters *began* with professional occupational goals in life.

Were we to assume that virtually all who are activated begin their work in politics at the grass-roots level, these data would pose explanatory problems. Either activists do start at the grass-roots, in which case there is a substantial selectivity linked to occupational and educational credentials when it comes to rising to a higher organizational plane of activity, or the assumption is only true in part. If the latter is so, it implies that an extraordinary level of lateral entry at higher levels into India's active political world has been taking place, again with the side-door entrants tending to make it only if their occupational and educational warranties are high.

Others have emphasized the affinities between "free professions" like law, journalism, and the like and the vocation of politics. These data highlight the other story, showing how sharply circumscribed are the career opportunities in Indian politics for a fledgling activist whose occupation of farming immobilizes him and whose limited educational attainments ill-equip him to understand political developments that are not close to home and face-to-face encounters.

Parental Examples

In a Los Angeles study of campaign activists in 1956, we found evidence pointing to the effects of the politicized family and politically active parents on the subsequent pattern of active participation manifested by children so reared. Especially was this so among those who formed the reliable nucleus of activists whose efforts sustained a voluntary party apparatus in campaign after campaign, "maintaining the continuity of talent and skill, experience and conviction, essential at this level of a democratic political order."[17]

While only six percent in the Indian citizen sample reported their fathers to have had a strong interest in politics, plus another ten percent whose fathers were somewhat interested, quite a different picture emerged when those in the activist sample were asked not simply about parental interest but whether any family member had ever provided an example of being active in a party or political movement. Overall, one-fourth of the Indian activists recalled such a model. The differences between local and translocal proportions are noteworthy. While one in six outpost personnel came from family backgrounds featuring activist adults, at translocal levels the ratio was nearly twice as high. Evidently parents who exemplify active citizenship by their own adult behavior are creating the kind of home environment rich in meaningful references to political events and symbols which politicizes many of the children while still young and which helps to explain why in their own adult years they move into the active political stratum.

GENERATIONAL DIFFERENTIALS AMONG INDIAN ACTIVISTS

The pre-apprenticeship differentials disclosed by the foregoing analysis point to the presence in India of the same stratification and mobility mechanisms that in other societies also have been shown to bias entry into the politically active stratum in predictable and systematic ways. In any time and place, it seems likely that such mechanisms operate; inquiry turns on how steep the success ladder is and how sharp the contrasts in life chances are, not on the more elementary point that systematic biases persist. Generational differences have a more historical focus.

India's history as an autonomous polity dates from 1947. Those in our survey whose political lives began during the years of struggle for independence were likely to be over fifty in 1967. At least twenty-five years had passed since they first became politicized; at least sixteen years of active participation in Indian electoral democracy were apt to be on their records. At the other extreme, anyone under thirty-five was unlikely to remember the independence struggle with any clarity; if the first stirrings of political interest which they recall took place within the last fifteen years and if their own records of active participation were confined to the years since 1963, they came to politics in India after the formative years were over for the nation.

Presumably the study of political recruitment includes analysis of just these kinds of generational differences. But when does a generation begin? What age bracket does it include? The climax points in a nation's history suggest a partial answer. Consider the summary data from the Indian activist sample shown in Table 6.6. It was readily apparent that the grass-roots level of polling-station party work in 1967 was largely carried out by post-independence-period inductees. Only one in five had been politically alert, much less politically active, in those historic years. At the assembly constituency coordination level of party life also fully a third lacked firsthand sensitivity to independence-relevant issues and problems. They, too, had come to feel involved with political events in India only after the new polity was a functioning reality. Quite different, however, was the PC-level picture. Here nearly a majority possessed at least a quarter-century of political involvement. Inevitably their assessment of issues and problems in 1967 would be shaped by their memories of independence-stage politics; they had been old enough and alert enough to grasp the meaning of the subcontinent's partition firsthand.

When a somewhat different question is posed—namely, how many years since the informant first became active in party politics—our time perspective is still further foreshortened. One in five had served no more than five years. Only a third had been active more than fifteen. The summary data suggest certain apprenticeship complications; the tutorial workload for polling-station cadres is twice as heavy as for their translocal counterparts (Table 6.7). Learning political campaign methods is not especially difficult. Novices may lack skills, contacts, and knowhow, but these are deficiencies only briefly. Given even a few years' experience, those who are activists probably reach a "plateau of competence." How quickly a neophyte learns the channels and practices of organizational life no doubt varies from person to person. Typically the adjustment period need not be long. When too many come at the same time, it is the organizational cadres who must cope. The term "cadre" includes all those who provide the skeleton staff of an organization, those who must socialize, train, and assign additional members as needed. In addition to their tutorial functions, cadres also are commonly expected to perform various managerial functions: staging, coordinating, planning, research, and liaison work.

If a party apparatus, or some semi-autonomous echelon or salient thereof, is faced by an influx of inexperienced personnel, the burden of training and guidance falls unavoidably on the small nucleus of journeymen cadres available. Complications of this kind need to be studied by students of

TABLE 6.6
YEARS SINCE FIRST POLITICIZED
(by organizational echelon)

	Parliamentary Constituencywide Level	Assembly Constituencywide Level	Polling Station Level
	%	%	%
More than 25 years	45	31	21
16 to 25 years	33	34	31
No more than 15 years	22	35	48
	100	100	100

TABLE 6.7
YEARS SINCE FIRST POLITICALLY ACTIVATED
(by organizational echelon)

	Parliamentary Constituencywide Level	Assembly Constituencywide Level	Polling Station Level
	%	%	%
More than 15 years ago	43	34	20
6 to 15 years ago	45	53	54
No more than 5 years ago	12	13	26
	100	100	100

recruitment processes. Survey methods are ill-suited, and case studies will be needed. In general, when too many newcomers need tutelage, in politics as elsewhere, two developments probably occur: One, the cadres become more jealous of their time and more selective in choosing whom to help; and two, a considerable fraction of the newcomers are thrown onto their own resources. They learn by trial and error, and by peer assistance; they feel consciously self-educated, and they feel a sense of cohort solidarity. Both effects seem likely to create and to sharpen lines of generational cleavage within organizational ranks, especially if different levels and segments of the apparatus are heavily staffed by activists with a distinctive generational perspective.

In light of these indications that generational differences in political sensitivity and experience may tend to coincide with where people work in the kind of extensive political apparatus that is a modern party, and that our Indian

TABLE 6.8

PARTICIPATION IN INDEPENDENCE MOVEMENT

"In selecting party candidates in your party,
how important is participation in the
independence movement?"

	Parliamentary Constituencywide Level	Assembly Constituencywide Level	Polling Station Level
	%	%	%
Very important	24	29	48
Somewhat important	33	29	21
Hardly important	43	42	31
	100	100	100

data suggest that these kinds of organizational tensions and strains are present there, consider several attitudinal cross-tabulations. At one point, each of our participating informants was asked an extended battery of questions about the criteria used in his party when selecting its state and national legislative candidates. One specific question concerned the independence movement (see Table 6.8). Overall, only thirty-five percent stressed the fact of independence-movement participation as very important, when selecting a legislative candidate in 1967. What is more interesting, however, is that nearly half the polling station activists—most of whom were too young to have experienced the movement years—felt that it was an operative criterion important to those who chose party nominees. In contrast, activists at the translocal levels are noticeably inclined to deemphasize this consideration. Presumably those at higher echelons have more influence as well as greater knowledge about how the candidate-selection process works; grass-roots personnel are more likely to be speculating on the basis of little knowledge and little influence. It reflects, however, the extent to which those in the outposts of India's parties in 1967 tended to assume that party nominees were screened and chosen by higher-echelon colleagues whose preoccupations were those of an earlier generation.

Analysis of the candidate-selection criteria information gathered in the Indian survey discloses substantial consensus on many points. Almost seventy-five percent stressed the importance of "recognition for work done in the area"; half felt that "status within the party organization" was a major consideration. Forty-five percent believed candidates were chosen because of "connections with important leaders"; another forty percent stressed the importance of having the "backing of special groups in the constituency." On none of these counts were differences in emphasis noticeably keyed to organizational echelon. On one count—"the candidate's own ability"—substantially more affirmation came from grass-roots personnel than from those at higher levels. In all party sectors from left to right, five out of six local activists stressed ability. Translocal activists, on the same count, affirmed its importance only about two-thirds of the time.

Combining the various open-ended responses to disclose more generalized differences is a complex undertaking. Two measures were created, in no sense mutually exclusive. One tallies the kind of response that speaks of special group support, of sponsorship by powerful individuals, or of qualities that especially appeal to certain publics. It is a complex of considerations, all of which stress *extrinsic connections*. Quite different is the other, which registers concern with the candidate's *intrinsic qualities*: with abilities, leadership capabilities, honesty, and character. It is instructive to consider separately the scores on these two measures registered by local and translocal activists of Congress and the opposition. In doing so, analysis is first made of the apparatus cadres in our sample; thereafter, it is noteworthy that the same patterns are disclosed by analysis of the public notables whom we interviewed. In both Congress and opposition camps, for public notables as well as for the apparatus cadres, at the *grass-roots levels* the emphasis is roughly twice as often placed on the intrinsic qualities of leadership style than on the connective considerations of what groups and persons support or oppose a potential candidate. In one sense, it is an individualistic bias that is preferred—in favor of merit and autonomy in one's leaders. In another sense, it is probably a naive and untutored preference—unconcerned with coalition-building, with group interests, with institutionalized prerogatives (Table 6.9).

Looking at the response patterns by *translocal personnel,* a more complicated picture is found. In both Congress and opposition ranks, appreciation is greater for the importance of extrinsic connections as appropriate selection criteria. This is especially true in the more bureaucratized structure of Congress, where it is also true that a considerable reduction occurs in the emphasis given to intrinsic leadership qualities. What occurs at translocal levels among Indian opposition party activists is more affirmative; the level of affirmation given by them to intrinsic considerations is just as high as their simultaneous stress on connective considerations, and it is almost as high as the vote registered for ability and leadership by their fellow-activists at polling station levels.

TABLE 6.9
CONCERN WITH EXTRINSIC CONNECTIONS AND INTRINSIC QUALITIES
AS CRITERIA USED IN CANDIDATE SELECTION PROCESSES
(cells register percent emphasizing factor)

| | CONGRESS | | OPPOSITION | |
	Translocal	Local	Translocal	Local
APPARATUS CADRES	%	%	%	%
Stress extrinsic connections	63	38	53	37
Stress intrinsic qualities	41	68	59	65
PUBLIC NOTABLES				
Stress extrinsic connections	76	32	61	38
Stress intrinsic qualities	41	70	65	76

CAREERS IN ORBIT AND CAREERS IN TRANSIT

Whether generational modalities rooted in India's tumultuous and brief history as a modern electoral democracy coincide with the division of labor between those whose contributions to party life are made in outpost villages and urban wards and those who work at the coordination nodes of constituencywide efforts made by modern parties in India is a question only touched upon by our survey data in limited ways. To be differently placed in the party apparatus, however, clearly did mean that one was likely to have a quite different view of the considerations taken into account by party leaders when selecting legislative candidates. Those whose participation orbits were local stressed intrinsic qualities and downgraded resource mobilization; those active at translocal levels gave considerably greater emphasis to the extrinsic connections a candidate needed. Among opposition cadres and notables, this was not offset by any diminuation of emphasis on individualistic qualities of leadership; among Congress personnel, it was offset by such a downgrading of style considerations (Table 6.10).

Since the activist sample consists of 1,000 cases, the matrix cell-frequencies are conveniently expressed as proportions. As can be seen, careers in public life are less common and more likely to be locality-bound than careers in party organizational life. Nearly half had never held public office (470); within this same category, somewhat more than half had served as party officials.

TABLE 6.10
PATTERNS OF PARTY OFFICE HOLDING AND PUBLIC OFFICE HOLDING
AMONG INDIAN ACTIVISTS
(actual frequencies)

PARTY OFFICE HOLDING	PUBLIC OFFICE HOLDING				
	Never Held	Only Local Public Offices	Only Translocal Offices	Both Local and Translocal	TOTAL
Never Held	226 [a]	115 [c]	21 [e]	16	378
Only Local Party Offices	126 [b]	85 [d]	9	17	237
Only Translocal Offices	61 [e]	51 [e]	63 [e]	24	199
Both Local & Translocal	57 [e]	49 [e]	43	37	186
TOTAL	470	300	136	94	1000

Legend: In creating the "orbit" typology, level of campaign work in 1967 is also considered along with office-holding experience. These reclassifications result:
[a] includes 82 classed as Translocalists because of 1967 campaign role
[b] includes 77 classed as Dualists because of 1967 translocal role
[c] includes 38 classed as Dualists because of 1967 translocal role
[d] includes 35 classed as Dualists because of 1967 translocal role
[e] scattered cases deleted from "orbit" typology because of 1967 downward shift to local activist role only. A total of 39 cases is so handled.

Conversely, about two-fifths of the activist sample had never held party office (378), and within that category only two-fifths had public office-holding records.

The career orbit typology which is derived from these data permits us to examine some of the distinctive credentials and contributions made to Indian politics by three contrasting types. *Localists* are not only people found to be working in the 1967 campaign at grass-roots levels of the party apparatus; they are people who have *never* been active at a translocal level, either in public or party jobs. (Only ten percent of the polling station activists were excluded by this test; these thirty-nine activists are of special interest for us, but they are not further examined here.) These localists are the outpost personnel who are indispensable to partisan mobilization plans in a country like India. They carry the message into lukewarm or even hostile quarters. They personalize the standardized party appeals that come from headquarters. Inevitably, too, they add their own evaluations of political events and impending choices, by word or gesture, and they represent the outside world to fellow villagers living in illiteracy, poverty, rural immobility, personal pessimism, and an associational vacuum.

In 1967, the other two types were all activists at translocal levels of the campaign. By the test of where they had previously held formal party or public office, they were divided into *Dualists* or *Translocalists*. Those who have *never* worked at a village or urban neighborhood level, either in party or public affairs, are here called Translocalists. Their entry-points into the active political stratum were atypical; their apprenticeships gave them some familiarity with political practices at intermediate and higher echelons of India's processes of governance, but no firsthand sensitivity to the grass-roots difficulties which inevitably occur. Dualists, on the other hand, have had just such apprentice-ships. Although the category includes men of varied style, social credentials, and political convictions, the dualists are by virtue of their own job experience in politics persons who play bridging roles. Because their careers have crossed orbits—are careers in transit, as we say—they do constitute "personalized links" between society and polity in a special sense. As a category, they have been closer to the cutting edges of politically instigated social and economic change. They have also found the resources to pursue distinctive, high-risk career paths.

Consider the social credentials with which these three types entered the active political stratum. What educational qualifications did they have? What occupation were they pursuing at the time of political entry? The answers are predictable. Most Localists had only limited educational credentials; by lopsided majorities, they were farmers when they took their first political steps. At the other extreme, most Translocalists had been to college; by full majorities, most were in professional occupations or preparing for professional life at the time of their first ventures into Indian politics. Predictably, Dualists occupied a middle ground; both their educations and their entry-point occupations were mixed and varied. The majority had succeeded in reaching translocal political orbits after starting at the grass-roots without benefit of college and without the hallmarks of professional men (Table 6.11).

There are various ways of measuring the extent to which a cadreman is an asset, politically speaking. At best, they only provide a rough basis for assessment. Still, whether an activist is a full-time worker is a relevant clue to his importance in the apparatus: Only one in five Localists gave full-time efforts to his party in 1967, while Dualists were twice as likely to have done so. Translocalists within the dominant apparatus of Congress were most likely of all to have been full-time workers while those in opposition-party ranks were significantly less so: Forty percent compared with thirty-one percent. One explanation could be the larger availability of paid employment either in public or party posts to those in the governing party entourage.

A second measure of the organizational mileage secured from an activist is the extent to which he performs diverse liaison functions, discussing with fellow activists at different levels in the organizational apparatus all manner of problems. In politics, those with long experience tend to be skeptical about the utility of the printed word or the group conference; they put trust in personal contacts and individual messengers instead. In the Indian activist sample,

TABLE 6.11
SOCIAL CREDENTIALS OF CAREER ORBIT TYPES

	CONGRESS			OPPOSITION		
	Local-ists	Dual-ists	Transloc-alists	Local-ists	Dual-ists	Transloc-alists
	%	%	%	%	%	%
Education						
Grammar school	61	19	7	57	25	12
High school	30	40	33	30	30	28
Some college	9	41	60	13	45	60
	100	100	100	100	100	100
Cases	(172)	(228)	(110)	(159)	(182)	(105)
Entry-point						
Occupation						
Agriculture	77	42	28	65	36	22
Commerce	12	17	11	16	19	17
Prof. & preprof.	11	41	61	19	45	61
	100	100	100	100	100	100
Cases	(157)	(210)	(95)	(138)	(170)	(92)

Localists scored least impressively on a liaison index based on self-descriptions of the frequency with which they talked about political matters with other activists, including those at other organizational levels. Understandably, those at the translocal campaign level nearly half the time rated themselves high on the liaison index. Evidently Dualists and Translocalists engage with roughly equal frequency in some kinds of intramural communication; our data do not enable us to probe more closely.

A third measure asks what kind of office-seeking history, successful or not, different types of political activists possess (Table 6.12). Not only does such a measure reflect some ambition and intiative in most cases; it also indicates the kinds of publics—local or constituencywide, familiar or mass, homogeneous or diverse—whose responsiveness (or lack of it) to particular political appeals and issues those who have sought public office worry about. The measures we use are two: One for local office-seeking, the other for legislative office-seeking. Each measure distinguishes those who have always, sometimes, and never lost in their efforts. Translocalists only rarely had even tried for local elected office, and even so they had rather often failed considering how likely victory every time was to those Localists and Dualists who ventured to compete. Although from forty to fifty percent of these latter types had never sought local public office, it is surprising how infrequently a record of both losing and winning is found among the rest. Evidently, for most aspirants even if affiliated with an opposition party, the task of gaining local office is not very risky and is not a truly competitive threshold. Most of those who tried, including as many

TABLE 6.12
PERFORMANCE RECORDS OF CAREER ORBIT TYPES

	CONGRESS			OPPOSITION		
	Local-ists	Dual-ists	Transloc-ialists	Local-ists	Dual-ists	Transloc-alists
	%	%	%	%	%	%
Fulltime worker	19	39	49	17	40	31
Frequently perform liaison functions	28	42	50	34	52	49
Local Public Office Seeking						
Never sought	39	40	82	56	47	82
Always lost	2	2	4	6	4	4
Always won	53	53	13	32	41	13
Both won and lost	6	5	1	6	8	1
	100	100	100	100	100	100
Cases	(174)	(228)	(126)	(159)	(183)	(106)
Legislative Office Seeking						
Never sought	98	55	41	99	46	46
Always lost	2	14	11	1	26	20
Always won	0	17	27	0	10	19
Both won and lost	0	14	21	0	18	15
	100	100	100	100	100	100
Participation in Voluntary Groups						
Members of None	43	14	25	55	27	39
Cooperatives	45	61	55	33	40	33
Education Groups	24	58	56	14	40	30
Welfare organizns	10	45	36	9	28	26
Youth organizns	13	34	31	13	28	28
Semi-official committees	6	39	29	5	27	17
Recreational gps	17	35	22	13	31	18
Busin.-Prof. gps	6	27	22	9	24	12
Caste associations	16	24	15	8	23	18

Dualists who subsequently went on to translocal work as Localists who remained at the grass-roots level throughout their careers, always won.

As for legislative office-seeking records, Localists are simply out of the picture while roughly similar proportions of the Dualists and Translocalists in our sample had never sought either state assembly or national parliamentary office. About half in each group, whether Congress or opposition activists, had made at least one try, however. In both camps, Dualists were discernibly more likely always to have lost such attempts while Translocalists more frequently had records of always winning. The proportions are not large, but they suggest the relatively easier career pathways traveled by Translocalists. One possible explanation is that social credentials—education and occupation—open doors to political opportunity for Translocalists, while Dualists more painstakingly establish their eligibility by a grass-roots political apprenticeship period.

Such a proposition is borne out by a careful study of a fourth kind of activist performance measure—the extent to which active participation in voluntary associations is part of their record. Not surprisingly, only about half of our Localists belonged to any such groups. For the rest, Dualists were clearly more likely to have such activities as part of their scheduled lives than were Translocalists. Moreover, this pattern of participation in group affairs is at least slightly greater among Dualists *in each of eight* particular kinds of voluntary organization—a replication that holds (with one tie) for all the opposition cases as well as for Congress.

In modern India, the growth of party structures and auxiliary organizations has not yet penetrated to all the peripheral localities where the bulk of citizens live. But modernizing plans are being implemented by associational efforts in a multitude of ways. Opportunities for political participation beyond voting and talking about public affairs continue to expand. The organizational scaffolding of leadership positions and cadre roles has vastly enlarged the possibility for careers in public life. At the same time that larger numbers of political jobs are being created, the avenues of access to them are complex and changing. By examining the notion of "career orbits" and including the special case of Dualists whose records are those of "careers in transit" between local and translocal centers of governance, we have tried to identify some of the actual career patterns apprenticeship sequences, and political risk-bearing practices disclosed in the Indian activist survey. As such, then, this inquiry has been an empirical case study, testing the methodological constraints, conceptual ambiguities, and substantive questions about democracy and political survival that need to be clarified and understood if the intellectual gains hoped for through more systematic political recruitment analyses are to be realized, in the study of India or of any modern polity.

NOTES

1. The 1967 India National Election project is a collaborative one. The senior investigators are Samuel J. Eldersveld, University of Michigan, Dwaine Marvick, University of California, and Rajni Kothari, Director of the Center for the Study of Developing Societies, in New Delhi. Support for the project came from funds administered by the two American universities and from the Center itself, whose personnel carried out the field work and coding process under the direction of Bashiruddin Ahmed.

2. A full discussion of the data basis is given in a 1973 UCLA doctoral dissertation, Douglas K.

Madsen. *The Sense of Political Efficacy in India: An Exploration in Political Psychology* (University Microfilms, 1973). Chapter 2 makes clear how various data-gathering and data-processing difficulties were handled. Analyses are provided which establish the representativeness of the data. See also the November 1970 issue of Asian Survey, "Elections and party politics in India: a symposium," which contains five articles based on the India data.

3. Major source materials include Rajni Kothari, *Politics in India* (1970), Lloyd I. Rudolph and Susanne H. Rudolph, *The Modernity of Tradition: Political Development in India* (1967), Myron Weiner, *Party Politics in India* (1957) and his sequel volume, *Party Building in a New Nation: The Indian National Congress* (1967), and George Rosen, *Democracy and Economic Change in India* (1967).

4. Rajni Kothari, "The Congress 'system' in India," Asian Survey (December 1964). Some emendations in the theoretical model have been suggested. See Paul R. Brass, "Coalition politics in North India," American Political Science Review (December 1968). Also W. H. Morris-Jones, "From monopoly to competition in India's politics," Asian Review (November 1967).

5. Kothari, *Politics in India,* 164.

6. See the essays in Myron Weiner, ed., *State Politics in India* (1968); Mary C. Carras, *The Dynamics of Indian Political Factions* (1972); and Sidney Verba, B. Ahmed, and A. Bhatt, *Caste, Race and Politics* (1971).

7. Kothari, op. cit., 135-136.

8. Ibid., 126-128.

9. Ibid., 160.

10. The concern of Heinz Eulau and Kenneth Prewitt in *Labyrinths of Democracy* (1973), with the basic question of "levels of analysis," is closely related to this point.

11. See M. C. Carras, op. cit., B. S. Cohn, *India: The Social Anthropology of a Nation* (1971).

12. Kenneth Prewitt, *The Recruitment of Political Leaders* (1970), especially chapter 3.

13. Ibid., 105.

14. Verba et al., op. cit.; Andre Bateille, *Caste, Class and Power: Changing Patterns of Stratification in a Tanjori Village* (1971); and B. Ahmed, "Caste and electoral politics," Asian Survey (November 1970).

15. Ahmed, op. cit., 981.

16. Herbert Jacob, "Initial recruitment of elected officials in the United States," Journal of Politics 24 (1962), 703.

17. Dwaine Marvick and Charles R. Nixon, "Recruitment Contrasts in Rival Campaign Groups," in Dwaine Marvick, ed., *Political Decision Makers: Recruitment and Performance* (1961).

Appendix A.   GENERATIONAL DIFFERENTIALS AMONG INDIAN ACTIVISTS (in percentages)

| | | CANDIDATES | | NOTABLES | | APPARATUS | | CADRES | SUMMARY TOTALS | |
		PC	AC	T	L	PC	AC	PS	Translocal	Local
AGE										
CONGRESS	Up to 40	25	31	24	33	13	32	38	27	36
	41 to 50	29	39	40	35	45	32	37	36	36
	51 plus	46	30	36	32	42	36	25	37	28
		100	100	100	100	100	100	100	100	100
OPPOSITION	Up to 40	31	45	39	34	38	49	54	43	48
	41 to 50	32	38	44	38	27	34	28	35	31
	51 plus	37	17	17	28	35	17	18	22	21
		100	100	100	100	100	100	100	100	100
YEARS SINCE FIRST POLITICIZED										
CONGRESS	Up to 15 yrs	29	32	29	52	11	26	43	26	46
	16 to 25 yrs	21	32	30	20	41	35	33	33	28
	26 plus yrs	50	36	41	28	48	39	24	41	26
		100	100	100	100	100	100	100	100	100
OPPOSITION	Up to 15 yrs	26	45	48	47	27	39	51	38	50
	16 to 25 yrs	40	25	30	35	27	42	38	34	36
	26 plus yrs	34	30	22	18	46	19	11	28	14
		100	100	100	100	100	100	100	100	100
YEARS SINCE FIRST ACTIVATED										
CONGRESS	Up to 5 yrs	9	11	12	24	4	8	23	17	29
	6 to 15 yrs	52	37	55	56	40	54	52	54	54
	16 plus yrs	39	52	33	20	56	38	25	29	17
		100	100	100	100	100	100	100	100	100
OPPOSITION	Up to 5 yrs	27	18	19	15	10	15	33	9	24
	6 to 15 yrs	44	53	48	70	56	60	50	48	54
	16 plus yrs	29	29	33	15	34	25	17	43	22
		100	100	100	100	100	100	100	100	100

Appendix B. PARTICIPATION DIFFERENTIALS AMONG INDIAN ACTIVISTS (in percentages)

	CANDIDATES		NOTABLES		APPARATUS			CADRES SUMMARY TOTALS	
	PC	AC	T	L	PC	AC	PC	Translocal	Local
FULL TIME WORKER: Congress	45	50	41	17	64	26	21	42	20
Opposition	43	51	23	11	32	25	18	37	17
HIGH COMMUNICATOR: Congress	33	56	40	28	51	38	30	44	29
Opposition	59	54	23	41	50	51	37	51	38
HEAVY MASS MEDIA USER: Congress	46	46	53	23	55	44	28	48	26
Opposition	49	54	48	18	63	48	24	52	22
HIGHER ECHELON FIGURE IN VOLUNTARY GROUP: Congress	92	62	56	5	83	46	13	61	10
Opposition	66	44	39	8	45	32	13	42	11
ACTIVE IN COOPERATIVES: Congress	58	52	65	51	62	56	44	58	47
Opposition	40	37	39	38	32	39	36	38	37
ACTIVE IN CASTE ASSOC.: Congress	25	26	20	17	17	23	17	22	17
Opposition	26	21	13	2	25	20	11	21	9
ACTIVE IN EDUCATIONAL MOVEMENT ACTIVITIES: Congress	58	56	59	27	55	56	27	57	27
Opposition	43	37	43	16	40	31	14	37	14
ACTIVE IN SOCIAL WELFARE ORGANIZATIONS: Congress	54	38	40	9	53	43	15	43	13
Opposition	29	26	35	6	30	25	10	27	9
ACTIVE IN YOUTH GROUPS: Congress	42	37	23	13	45	31	13	33	13
Opposition	29	30	17	8	27	28	16	27	14
ACTIVE IN TRADE UNIONS: Congress	33	30	14	2	30	23	6	24	4
Opposition	37	27	9	6	27	25	13	26	11
ACTIVE IN BUSINESS OR PROFESSIONAL GROUPS: Congress	29	17	18	6	43	27	8	25	8
Opposition	14	18	13	10	32	19	11	20	11
ACTIVE ON SEMI-OFFICIAL COMMITTEES Congress	42	33	31	6	43	37	10	34	9
Opposition	31	24	26	6	20	21	6	23	6

Chapter 7

PARTY, ACCOUNTABILITY AND THE RECRUITMENT OF MUNICIPAL COUNCILMEN IN THE NETHERLANDS

GALEN A. IRWIN

University of Leiden

How "from the many are chosen the few" is Prewitt's formulation of the problem of political recruitment.[1] Included in his work on city councilmen in the San Francisco Bay area is information on "the social bias in leadership selection" and on the careers of councilmen from "entry into the active stratum" and "apprenticeship," to plans for the future. One of the most significant aspects of the recruitment studies of Prewitt is that he has not stopped with the presentation of extensive recruitment data, but that the process of recruitment has been related to other aspects of the political system. Alone and with Heinz Eulau, he has studied the recruitment pattern of these local councillors and its impact on electoral accountability.[2] Elements such as "frequency of appointment to office," "rates of incumbent eviction," "volunteerism," "perceived electoral sanctions," and "political ambitions" are analysed with regard to the degree to which one can say that the system works to hold councilmen accountable and make them responsible.

The picture which seems to emerge is a recruitment process which allows local elites to perpetuate themselves in office and in which accountability is left to the conscience and sense of civic obligation of the individual council members.

Author's Note: More than the usual amount of thanks are due to Professors Hans Daalder of Leiden University and Robert L. Morlan of the University of Redlands. Both were involved in the discussions which began this work and were available for advice as the project developed. The final product is mine, however, and they bear no responsibility for its contents. Appreciation is also due to the Netherlands Institute for Advanced Study (Wassenaar) at which I was a fellow at the time this research was begun.

These were found in the Bay Area to behave as "volunteers," entering and leaving the council with little attention to the elections which placed them there. This is not to say that individual consciences and senses of duty may not be productive of responsive, if not responsible, government. This may indeed be the case, but is not the issue, since few theorists of democracy seem satisfied with enlightened oligarchies. The important questions which arise are how widespread this phenomenon may be, and whether there is something in the recruitment process of the Bay Area which helps to produce this situation. Or, stated alternatively, is there something lacking in the Bay Area system which allows this situation to occur? A possible clue may be found in the political organization of the Bay Area communities.

The most striking and unique feature of Bay Area politics is the nonpartisanship required by California law. Thus nowhere in Prewitt's presentation do political parties play a role. This does not necessarily mean that the political parties are totally inactive in council politics, but that this activity is at most indirect. "Party activists may campaign for council candidates, they may appear before the council to petition their causes, and they may even recruit for partisan elections from among the more attractive and successful councilmen." But parties do not directly compete for city offices, nor are council members identified as representatives of political parties. Moreover, Prewitt states that "party activity itself is not a frequent route into the particular stratum from which councilmen come."[3]One cannot generalize from the Bay Area pattern before trying to determine whether the absence of political parties is not at least partially responsible for the lack of accountability which was found. Eulau and Prewitt have implied that this may be the case in stating that "often electoral accountability is promoted by the presence of a competitive party system."[4]

An attempt will be made to replicate partially the Bay Area studies of recruitment and accountability, however in a quite different political setting. The data to be presented were collected in another country (The Netherlands) with a different political system and with a different political culture. More importantly, political parties play an important role in local politics in the Netherlands, in contrast to the nonpartisanship of the Bay Area. Czudnowski has drawn attention to the fact that Prewitt was laying down "an entire agenda for future recruitment studies. . . . Is recruitment from informal groups of friends characteristic only of non-partisan government? Is it a consequence of the size of the constituency?"[5] These and other questions will be dealt with in light of the Dutch data. In some respects, and especially with regard to the questions of responsibility and accountability, the great dissimilarities between the two political systems make replication quite difficult. The "theory of accountability" will be seen to be particularly American in nature, and difficult to adapt to the Dutch situation. Comparisons with Bay Area data become less replication and more an instrument for understanding the recruitment of Dutch councilmen. In this regard we have concentrated on explaining the Dutch recruitment patterns and their effects rather than in trying to make additional comparisons with partisan settings in other parts of the United States.

THE RESEARCH SETTINGS

Even though the nine counties of the San Francisco Bay Area form only a portion of California, the physical area is not substantially smaller than that of the entire country of the Netherlands. Within this territory live approximately four million persons as opposed to the thirteen million Dutchmen. Nevertheless, the Bay Area may be more typically urban and suburban as these four million are centered in San Francisco and its surroundings, while the outlying areas are mountainous and less densely inhabited.

Although the overall population density in the Netherlands is high, careful planning has left areas of green between the cities and towns. The City Council Research Project in the Bay Area conducted interviews with all of the council members in each of the ninety municipalities in the nine counties. In the Netherlands there are somewhat less than 900 municipalities so that even if direct replication had been the aim, interviews with all 11,000 council members would have been impossible. The needs of the political participation study—out of which the current study arose—dictated that interviews be held in those communities in which interviews with a sample of the voting population had been held. The seventy-nine municipalities which fell in the sample and in which interviews were held do not comprise a random sample of Dutch communities. However, they are distributed across all the provinces, all degrees of urbanization, and varying political make-up. The political party affiliation of the respondents reflects reasonably well that of all council members.[6]

Rather than interview all the members of councils in these seventy-nine municipalities, four were chosen from each community. This was done even though the size of the councils varies from seven to forty-five members. These four included two commissioners (selected from within the council for administrative duties as described in the subsequent section) and two regular councilmen. (Mayors of all except the very largest communities were also interviewed, but as these are appointed by the national government they are not included in the study.) The commissioners and council members were selected by a procedure which would insure a spread across the important political divisions within the community, diversity being considered more important than a strictly random sample.

LOCAL GOVERNMENT IN THE NETHERLANDS

The form of local government in the Netherlands is specified in national law (Gemeentewet). At the head of the local government is the council, varying in size from seven to forty-five members according to the population of the municipality. As the head of the local government, this council has administrative responsibilities as well as the usual representative, legislative functions. Since not all of the members can be continually involved with administration of city matters, a committee is chosen from among the members which together with the mayor carries out the daily administration of the city. These commissioners (or aldermen, as the Dutch term "wethouder" is some-times translated) have traditionally not been chosen by a majority party or a majority coalition, but are apportioned proportionally to the strength of the parties on the council. This reflects the idea that it is the council which is formally responsible and that the commissioners are merely entrusted with day-to-day responsibilities. There are currently groups and parties which would prefer to make the committee of commissioners more similar to a local cabinet, that is chosen by a majority to carry out a specific program. This, they feel, would make alternatives clearer and more real for the voter. However, at present such a program committee is a rare exception and most committees are chosen to be as reflective as possible of the council. Although the commissioners may divide up the policy areas of local administration (each taking responsibility for one or more department), they form a collegial body and make collective decisions.[7] Mayors of Dutch cities are formally appointed by the Crown, which in a constitutional monarchy means the national government. Each is appointed for a period of six years with provisions for renewal. Being a mayor is a possible career position and it is not unusual for an individual to move from one city to another. A portion of the duties of the mayor consists of heading the local fire and police departments (except in smaller communities in which the latter are provided by national units) and in performing certain activities for the national government (e.g. issuing passports). For the rest, the mayor serves as chairman and member of the committee of commissioners, which is known as the Committee of Mayor and Commissioners (College van Burgemeester en Wethouders). (He chairs council meetings, but is not a member and has only an advisory vote.)[8]

The city council is elected by means of proportional representation.[9] The groups participating in Dutch local elections may be divided into three groups. The first and most obvious are the local divisions of the national political parties. The participation of the national parties is quite varied, but all have some local divisions which take part in local elections. Second, the local divisions may combine forces to submit a single list for the municipal elections. The most frequent of these combinations are among the parties of the left and among the religious parties. For the left there may be any variation among the four parties: PSP, PPR, PvdA, and D'66. The ARP and CHU may combine to present a common protestant list or join with the KVP in a Christian Democratic list. (The full name of each party is given in Table 7.1).[10]

Of particular interest are groups which have no national ties, but are composed of individuals with no or unspecified national connections. These are lumped together under the heading of "local lists," but two sorts may be distinguished. In the southern portion of the country, separate local lists may be submitted by groups who for national elections would work together within the Catholic Peoples Party (KVP). For the remainder, little is known about possible national affiliations of those individuals appearing on the list. Unfortunately, no extensive research has been done on these local lists, so that little is known about their composition or why and how they get organized. From known examples, one can merely make some guesses about the nature of these lists. Some are organized by individuals who feel that the basis for the party structure at the national level is not appropriate for local politics. Social and interest divisions may not be comparable, and local groups should reflect the local divisions. Thus a common name for such groups is "Community Interest Party," and it is possible to find in a group persons with widely divergent national party affiliations. Other groups represent local conflicts within national parties which are buried when national interests and elections are involved. This must be a frequent cause for factionalism in one party dominant areas. Finally, other groups may come about due to personal or group conflicts and rivalries. One or more villages which make up the municipality may submit lists as a demand for separate representation. Prominent individuals may head a list built around themselves. Disgruntled citizens may submit a list in order to draw attention to their position. This certainly does not exhaust the possibilities.

What is most interesting about these local lists is their generally loose structure. They seldom have permanent organizations and virtually never have a mass membership. As such, they tend to resemble somewhat the nonpartisan situation of California. This resemblance is not complete since the Dutch ballot provides for lists of candidates rather than election of individuals. And even though one does not sit on the city council under a national party label, he is well aware that others either in his own or other communities do. Yet the lists must occupy an intermediate position between the non-party, non-group situation in California and the organized party structure of other groups in the Netherlands. If political party is really important in terms of recruitment and accountability, then those who represent the national parties should differ from those elected from local lists. Furthermore, patterns for the lists should deviate in the direction of the nonpartisan California patterns if we are to attribute any overall differences to the existence and importance of parties rather than merely to possible national differences in cultural norms of behavior. Comparisons of the local lists with national party lists play an important part in the discussion to follow.

Table 7.1 compares the party affiliation of the respondents in our survey with that of all Dutch councilmen. The sample appears to be representative of the general distribution, despite the fact it was not selected by random sampling procedures. Briefly stated, one notes that fifty-four percent of the sample are affiliated with national parties, nineteen percent are affiliated with national parties but have joined with other parties in a local coalition, and twenty-seven percent represent local lists which have no national organization.

TABLE 7.1

DISTRIBUTION OF DUTCH COUNCIL MEMBERS BY PARTY

	Percentage of all Dutch Council Members [a]	Percentage of Council members in sample
(KVP) Catholic Peoples Party	18.3	9.5
(ARP) Anti-Revolutionary Party	9.8	4.6
(CHU) Christian Historical Party	9.3	5.9
(SGP) Political Calvinist Party	3.1	1.6
(PCG or CGP) Christian Combinations		14.8
Total Religious	40.5	36.4
(PvdA) Socialist (or Labour) Party	17.0	14.4
(PPR) Radical Political Party	.8	—
(PSP) Pacifist Socialist Party	.6	.3
(D'66) Democrats '66	2.5	2.9
(PAK's) Left Combinations		4.6
Total Left	20.9	22.2
(VVD) People's Party for Freedom and Democracy[b]	8.8	10.8
(DS'70) Democrats-Socialists '70	c	.6
(GPV) Calvinist Political League	.5	.6
(BP) Peasant Party	.2	.3
(CPN) Communist Party of the Netherlands	1.7	1.0
(Binding Rechts) Right League	.2	.3
Local Lists	27.2	27.2

[a] These percentages are based on the figures of the Central Bureau of Statistics. The Bureau lists those serving for combined lists according to their basic party label.
[b] Hereafter referred to as the Liberal Party.
[c] Included under "Local Lists."

THE DATA

The Dutch study of local councilmen was not designed primarily as a replication of the City Council Research Project, but formed part of a larger study of political participation. The needs and demands of the participation project prevailed, even though they led to some difficulties of replication which have been mentioned above. In order to obtain the best possible combination of the two projects, advice was sought from Eulau and Prewitt[11] concerning whether and which items from the City Council Project might usefully be included. From this cooperation emerged most of the items included in this article.

In the City Council Research Project questions were formulated to obtain information concerning the individual respondent. In later analysis it was often found that the council, rather than the individual, formed a more appropriate unit of analysis. This led to a time-consuming recoding of questionnaires. For this reason, and because only a portion of the Dutch councilmen were to be interviewed, it was decided to treat these directly as informants. Thus in many cases the respondent was not asked to express his individual opinion but to report on some aspect of his party or the council on which he served. For example, one will not find information on what qualities the respondent felt to be important for nomination to the council or what qualities made him a good choice as council candidate, but his report of the criteria his party deemed important in making up the list. This strategy was only partially satisfactory, since apparently it was rather difficult for the respondents to make such reports. With only their own experience in the party or on the council, it was perhaps difficult to know what was "a lot," "seldom," "very important," or any of the other comparisons they were asked to make. As a result, there is often considerable disagreement among individuals presumably reporting on the same situation. With such disagreement one wonders if the personal opinion has not dominated the reporting element. To be on the safe side, we decided not to lump the responses together by council, but to utilize the individual responses either as personal opinions or as reports with a clear personal tint.

Some Background Comparisons

Some comparisons of the social background characteristics of the respondents in the two studies give some indication of the general comparability of the data. Moreover, this leads us into more substantive areas as one can learn something about the types of individuals produced by the recruitment process.

We may begin with the sex biases in recruitment. In the Dutch sample ninety-two percent of the respondents were male as compared to ninety-five percent in the Bay Area sample. Despite some notable exceptions in the Netherlands, politics remains a predominantly male activity.

Prewitt found that "a man's occupation, wealth, and education affect whether he becomes a member of the politically active stratum and whether he is likely to hold political office." The median level of education in the Bay Area communities was a high school degree, while for the council members it was a college degree. Median income for the population was $7,920 compared to $14,907 for the council members.[12] The Netherlands is no exception to this general pattern. Table 7.2 shows that half the respondents of our mass survey reported only basic or elementary education as compared to only one in seven of the councilmen. At the other extreme four out of ten councilmen have an education beyond secondary school, something achieved by only one in fourteen in the mass survey. In terms of income, the median income for those reporting in the mass survey (more than 20% refused to answer the question) was 944 guilders per month. The median for the council members was 1947 guilders per month. Although only the roughest of comparisons can be made, it would appear that in relation to their constituencies the Bay Area and Dutch councilmen are rather similar. In addition to these indicators of social and economic advantage we can compare the Dutch and Bay Area council members on three additional relevant variables. Eulau and Prewitt report that "councilmen in the Bay region are predominantly middle-aged, usually coming to the council while in their forties or around fifty years of age. The turnover rate of city council positions is relatively high, with only a few members staying in office for more than

TABLE 7.2

COMPARISON OF EDUCATION AND INCOME FROM MASS PARTICIPATION SURVEY AND COUNCILMEN SURVEY (in percentages)

	Mass Survey	Councilmen
Education		
Basic or Elementary	50	14
Lower Technical, some secondary	31	30
Secondary	11	14
Beyond Secondary	7	42
	99	100
Income (guilders/month)		
less than 500	7	2
500—800	31	3
800—1200	34	16
1200—2000	21	30
more than 2000	7	49
	100	100

three or four terms," and "most of the councilmen are not natives of their present city or county. Most, however, are California or West Coast natives."[13] Comparable information for the Dutch group of council members is given in Table 7.3.

In terms of age, the two groups do not seem to diverge greatly. The presentation of the Bay Area data makes direct comparisons impossible, but the general pattern seems to be similar. Although the median age for commissioners is somewhat higher than for regular council members (54 years versus 48 years), neither figure is far removed from the median age of fifty years reported for the Bay Area.

TABLE 7.3

AGE, GEOGRAPHICAL MOBILITY AND LENGTH OF SERVICE COMPARISONS
OF DUTCH AND BAY AREA COUNCIL MEMBERS[a]

CURRENT AGE			
	Dutch		*Bay Area*
Years	Commissioners	Councilmen	
Under 40	8%	19%	
40–49	29	38	
50–60	33	31	Median around 50 years[b]
Over 60	29	12	
	99%	100%	

BIRTHPLACE			
Dutch		*Bay Area*	
Same Province	68%	Same City or County	28%
Other Province	32	California or West Coast	38
	100%	Non-West Coast	34
			100%

LENGTH OF SERVICE			
	Dutch		*Bay Area*
Years	Commissioners	Councilmen	Years
1–4	14%	56%	2 or less	29%
5–8	17	19	3–5	38
9–12	17	15	6–8	16
13–16	17	6	9 or more	17
More than 16	35	4		
	100%	100%		100%

[a] Data from Figure A-1, Eulau and Prewitt, *Labyrinths of Democracy, op cit.* p. 627
[b] Data not available due to mistake in the data source.

The Dutch councilmen do appear to have been somewhat less geographically mobile than their Bay Area colleagues. Approximately two-thirds serve on a council in the province in which they were born, as compared to less than one-third of the Bay Area members who serve in the same city or county. Only if the entire West Coast is included does the Bay Area figure exceed that for the Netherlands. For the Dutch group, the median years of residence in the community in which they serve is thirty-five for commissioners and twenty-seven for regular councilmembers.

RECRUITMENT BY POLITICAL PARTY

Prewitt's description of candidate recruitment for city council positions appears to be strikingly similar to that of a self-perpetuating elite. Sitting council members are active members of various local organizations. Through such organizations, they become acquainted with individuals of similar standing. As councilmen, they appoint members to various municipal boards (especially the planning commission, but also the library board, etc.). Through acquaintance with those appointed, their abilities, and their attitudes, councilmen are able to select potential successors. These are then encouraged to run for the council, or are actually appointed to the council when vacancies occur.

We do not have directly comparable information concerning Dutch council members. Instead, respondents were asked if there were qualities important in putting together the list of candidates of their group. In Table 7.4 these qualities have been ordered according to the percentage of respondents which reported the quality to be important.

As was to be expected, activity in the party stands out. Four out of every five respondents report that party activity is important as a consideration for

TABLE 7.4

QUALITIES IMPORTANT IN NOMINATIONS, BY PERCENTAGE
REPORTING QUALITY TO BE IMPORTANT

Being active in party	82
Being well known locally	81
Holding positions in organizations	63
Having knowledge of national problems	46
Having been involved in local governmental activity (advisory board, etc.)	43
Holding important positions in business	35
Having lived long in the community	32
Being known by the incumbent councilmen	28

candidacy. This certainly substantiates one's supposition concerning the importance of party in the recruitment process, and reinforces the very basic distinction from a nonpartisan system. In the nonpartisan system of the Bay Area, party activity had not been a pathway to city council membership, but in the partisan system of the Netherlands it is a virtual necessity. Even those who represent local lists rather than national parties feel that party activity is important when the group is considering its list of candidates, although the percentage is somewhat lower. Of course, a different interpretation of the responses is also possible. It may be that for such groups the emphasis is upon party activity in general, on political experience as a criterion rather than activity on behalf of the particular local group. Or it may be that only those who had been active in forming the group or keeping it functioning are placed on the list.

In addition to the local lists the percentage reporting party activity as "important" is somewhat lower for more conservative parties, and in the suburbs. However, the differences are never more than ten percent. For more conservative parties the emphasis may not be on party workers, but on community leaders outside the party, especially in the business sector. The suburbs have a more fluid population and may be willing to take advantage of the talent of those newly arriving in the community. These are merely hypotheses; and even if substantiated, they would account for only a small portion of the variance. Other possibilities might be that parties with more representatives on the council can look outside the party for outstanding individuals who may not have been party workers, while relying simultaneously upon the fact that the bulk of council members from the party will have considerable party experience. On the other hand, it is possible that the smaller parties cannot afford to place a high premium upon party service, since they must seek candidates with other attractive qualities in order to garner enough votes to gain a place on the council. These hypotheses cannot be tested with the available data. We must be content with the finding that party is indeed the most important factor in the nomination of candidates.

The second most frequently mentioned quality is how well the individual is known in the community. One is not active in local activity without gaining a certain local reputation. For the Netherlands, the situation is not dissimilar from that elsewhere; those who have been active in political parties and in local politics become well known. The commissioner who has served for twenty years may be an important vote-getter for the party. This emphasis on local reputation is surely meant to apply primarily to those at the top of the lists—i.e., those who are likely to be elected. Parties often deem it important to present a complete or nearly complete list (i.e., equal to the number of seats to be filled plus 5, with a maximum of 20) and may fill out their lists with lesser known individuals. Some of these are possibly being groomed for future elections; others may be rewarded for party service.[14] The frequency of responses in this category indicates that in a partisan system it is not only service to the party that is important, and that candidates are also expected to have achieved a certain reputation within the community.

Mentioned less often than party activity and local reputation but nevertheless by two-thirds of the respondents is "holding positions in organizations," the quality most comparable to the most important road to candidacy in the Bay Area. Although there is thus heavy emphasis on organizational experience in both cases, one must question whether the types of organization considered are the same for the Netherlands as for the Bay Area. The examples given by Prewitt of such organizational activity included PTA committees, service club officer, church leadership, Chamber of Commerce position, etc. Such organizations are generally removed from direct involvement in political activity, although the last mentioned might be seen as an interest group which would be so involved. The situation in the Dutch parties is quite different. It is likely that the respondents here are referring more directly to economic and social interest group activity, rather than volunteer and recreational organizations which might only occasionally be concerned with local political activity.

One of the results of a system of proportional representation is that parties make a clear attempt to provide representation for various interests. Persons who have been active and have held positions in local divisions of national interest groups provide excellent links between the interests and the party. They allow the party to point out to the voter that his interests are represented within the party. This type of internal proportionality or appointment is especially important for the religious parties, and the Catholic People's Party in particular. Catholics and Protestants come in all sorts—rich, poor, self-employed, etc.—and are held together in the party by their religious beliefs. Parties on the left and right pull on them as being more directly related to their economic interests. It is therefore in the direct interest of the party to make clear to the potential voter that these interests are also being protected by the party, and that defection is not necessary. Selection of individuals clearly identified with such interests makes this evident.

To show more clearly how this system works, one may take the list of candidates presented in the election brochure of the Catholic Party in the author's village. The candidates were advertised as follows:

(1) Works for the post office. Local chairman of Catholic Labor Union. Spiritual father and founder of the Organization for Youth Recreation.
(2) Owner of book and office supply store. Knowledgeable of problems of the retailer.
(3) Retired general. Member of Parliament. Provides connection with Parliament and national government.

(4) Local chairman of farm organization. Knows the problems of the farmers.
(5) Experienced in statistics and journalism. Science editor for a publisher. Represents the newcomers in town.
(6) Showroom manager of tile business. Local chairman of labor union.
(7) Barber and cigar store owner. Has held leadership positions in various local organizations (e.g., ice skating club).
(8) Manager of a bulb company. Local chairman of labor union.
(9) Dairy farmer. Executive in farm organization.
(10) Foreman in a cement factory. Considerable experience in various local organizations.

There is here an obvious attempt to provide a wide representation of interests within this list of candidates. Business representatives, retailers, bulb growers, workers, self-employed, intellectuals, and newcomers are included. Only candidates 7 and 10 on the list (both with no chance of election) would seem to come from less economically and socially oriented groups which were important in the Bay Area. [15] Such a wide selection and clear designation of interest groups is not uncommon for the religious parties in the Netherlands. Although the emphasis may be slightly different for the secular parties, a comparable system of apportionment among relevant subgroups is often used.

The two final factors mentioned by Prewitt—apprenticeship in local government and acquaintance with incumbent councilmen—are far less important in the Dutch case. Only forty-three percent mention "work in local governmental activity" as important, and twenty-eight percent "being known by the incumbent councilmen." Part of the difference for the first factor may lie in the structure of local government in the Netherlands whch provides fewer citizen boards. The activities of planning and library boards are carried out directly as a council or municipal bureaucracy responsibility. With fewer opportunities for these types of service it is not surprising that they are mentioned less frequently. As for the final item, given the emphasis on party and organizational activity and upon reputation, no place remains for the kind of "cronyism" which appears to be common in the Bay Area. Knowing the incumbent council members may make cooperation within the council easier, but it need only seldom play a role in nomination of candidates.

Qualities for Candidates and Local Lists

We have suggested that the specifically local lists which have no relation to the national parties may bear some resemblance to the nonpartisan situation of the Bay Area. If this is truly the case, then one should expect to find differences in emphasis in the qualities stressed in the nomination of candidates for the nationally affiliated and local lists, with the latter displaying greater similarity with the pattern in the Bay Area. In Table 7.5, the percentage considering a quality to be important is reported for these local lists and for groupings of national parties (left, religious, right).

The indication in the expected direction are at best modest. The percentage reporting emphasis on party is lower among those representing local lists than those from left or religious parties, but slightly higher than the percentage for national right parties. On the other hand, the members of lists attribute more importance to "being well known locally" and "achievement in business," but again this is shared with the right. Being known by incumbent councilmen is apparently somewhat more important, but this is also found in the religious parties. More emphasis is given by the lists to length of residence in the community, but this may be due partially to the size of the community—i.e., smaller communities place greater emphasis on residency and lists occur more frequently in smaller communities. As a general pattern one may say that the lists emphasize qualities which resemble those stressed in the nonpartisan situation, but individual qualities may also be important for other types of parties.

Election

Candidacy is the next to last step in the recruitment process. The last step is election. At least that is the way the theory goes. Prewitt was somewhat surprised to discover that this was not always the practice in the Bay Area. Any system of elected representation is always faced with the problem of replacing

TABLE 7.5
QUALITIES STRESSED IN CANDIDATE NOMINATIONS BY LOCAL LISTS
AND NATIONAL PARTIES [a]

	National left parties N = 53	National religious parties N = 69	National right parties N = 34	Local lists N = 80
Being active in party	85%	84%	74%	77%
Being well known locally	73	90	74	85
Holding positions in organizations	52	69	71	77
Having knowledge of national problems	45	46	33	49
Having been involved in local government activity	58	41	38	38
Holding important positions in business	15	35	40	43
Having lived long in community	13	36	29	44
Being known by sitting councilmen	19	32	23	35

[a] Members from combined lists have been excluded.

those who drop out between elections. For more important offices a new election is sometimes held prior to the next scheduled official election. But this is far too costly a procedure for all elective posts and other procedures for replacement have been devised. In the Bay Area the incumbent council members may appoint a successor to fill the unexpired term of a retired member and almost a quarter of the council members in the Bay Area were recruited in this manner. This is indeed an unusual procedure for systems which place high value on elections as a legitimizing process. Nevertheless replacement by appointment remains one of the anomalies of democratic systems to which little thought is given as long as the system seems to be functioning reasonably well. There is, however, the obvious possibility that a council will attempt to use this power to preclude entry of certain individuals or types of individuals and to determine its own successors. Prewitt discovered that for the Bay Area this was more than just a possibility, and that there were very clear cases in which the council used a type of apprenticeship system clearly designed to give the apprentice all advantage over other candidates.

In some areas and for some offices this appointment strategy is a dismal failure. Governors who allow themselves to be appointed Senator and friends of governors appointed to fill out unexpired terms often find it tough going at subsequent elections. At the local level in the Bay Area this does not seem to be the case, as voters do not appear to bear any particular recrimination toward the appointed individuals. When running as incumbents, equal percentages were successful among those appointed between elections as among those who had entered the council by election. The percentage in both cases was a rather high 80%, and in general, Prewitt found that most cities were quite willing to reelect incumbent councilmen.[16]

Concern with reelection, however, gets ahead of the theory, as the electoral situation for the proportional election system of the Netherlands is quite different. Each party presents more candidates than it can possibly hope to have elected. Despite the relative stability of the number of votes received, one can always hope that there will be a sudden swing to the party. Thus one would always want to present more candidates than the number of seats presently held on the council. Most parties will therefore present more candidates than can possibly hope to be elected. Candidates are even referred to as "electable" and "nonelectable." These nonelectable candidates are important for a number of reasons.

It may be important for a party to balance its ticket with regard to various interests. More important interests and factions are given high places on the list and insured representation on the elected body. Lesser interests are given recognition in the form of candidates, even though these may have little chance of election. Extremely popular individuals may occasionally be placed on the list to attempt to secure votes for the party, even though it is known that an individual will be unwilling to serve if elected. Of considerable psychological importance to the parties and perhaps to the voters is the idea that a full list should be presented. Despite the fact that only a few may be elected, the party does not wish to give the impression that it is too small to fill up a list.

Some individuals are placed on the list as a recognition of service to the party and as an indication to voters that these are "coming men" in the party. As those higher on the list drop out, the latter will move into positions of more importance. In fact, a substantial number of the respondents in the Dutch survey indicated that they were not chosen to the council the first time they were on the list. Slightly more than thirty percent indicated they had been candidates in previous elections. Prewitt does not provide any figures for how many individuals were candidates prior to their election, but judging from the general tone of his report, one would not guess the figure to be high. Where the emphasis is on recruitment through party, individual candidates will often have been active for long periods of time within the party and thus identified with its goals and ideals. For the Netherlands, almost one in three will have been a candidate before he is eventually elected.

Finally, surplus candidates on the list for election are important for succession. As in the Bay Area, there is no provision in the Netherlands for a by-election when an elected member is unable to complete his term. However, rather than relying upon the remaining members to appoint a successor, the replacement process is clear. Replacement is made by the party of the lost member according to the order of candidates on the original election list. This insures that the newcomer will resemble the old member at least in terms of party preference and insures the voter that some continuity will be preserved. As the emphasis in the system is upon the party rather than the individual, succession is provided by and within the party. There is, of course, little to be gained by resigning a few months before election, as incumbency is of little or no advantage in the ensuing election. On the other hand, a member who feels the position is too demanding may resign knowing that a member of his own party will replace him. The percentage of the Dutch respondents who entered the council between elections is somewhat lower than the percentage of Bay Area councilmen who were appointed to office. Eighteen percent reported such between-election entry as opposed to the twenty-four percent for appointed councilmen in the Bay Area. (Such figures must surely vary depending on the time elapsed between the previous election and the date of the research.)

RECRUITMENT AND ELECTORAL ACCOUNTABILITY

Czudnowski has suggested that the question of responsibility and responsiveness might be better researched in a partisan than in a nonpartisan system.[17]

In the following sections we shall examine the available data in attempting to determine what role "party" and recruitment by party may have in producing responsible and responsive council members in the Netherlands. We begin by examining the applicability of the "theory of accountability" to the Dutch situation. After a discussion of representational roles, presentation of data begins again with the perceptions of local officials concerning the important responsibilities of a city councilman. This is followed by more specific questions dealing directly with the relationships between voters and councilmembers, and finally the triangle is completed with the element missing in the nonpartisan system, namely the relationship between the council member and his party.

The Theory of Accountability

In examining the implications of the modes of recruitment in the Bay Area, Prewitt tested the "theory of electoral accountability." Here is Prewitt's summary of this theory:

> The elaboration, especially where grounded in empirical studies, has established (1) that the public, being largely apathetic about political matters and in any case ill-informed regarding public issues, cannot provide the necessary and sufficient conditions for the maintenance of democratic procedures; (2) that a liberal political and social elite are committed to the preservation of democratic forms, at least more committed than the average citizen; therefore, (3) what maintains the democratic tradition is not extensive public participation in political policy-making, but, instead, competition among elites whose behaviour is regulated by periodic review procedures. Competition among elites and review by citizens of political leaders are provided by elections. Thus elections hold political leaders accountable to non-leaders.[18]

Prewitt is most concerned about the third point, and goes on to show that elections can have only a minimal influence upon the councilmen of the Bay Area in holding them "accountable." But nowhere in this formulation is party (which has just been shown to be so important in the Dutch context) mentioned as a factor.

Yet the "theory of electoral accountability" at least implicitly postulates a two-party system. If elites are really to "compete," then there must be something to "win." In a system of majority rule, this means obtaining such a majority—something done more easily if there are two opposing groups. Similarly, if citizens are to "review" the elites by means of elections, then they must be able to cast out one elite by voting for another. Such ideas are more difficult to hold when the elites are more numerous and the chance of "winning" rather small. Thus assumptions concerning the nature and number of elites do not fit well in the Netherlands, where only two "competing elites" would be a rarity. Fewer than three percent of the municipalities have an electoral choice from only two lists. On the average, the voters in a municipality have between five and six lists from which to choose, and the city councils are generally composed of representatives from several parties.[19] Even in those communities in which one party or list might have a majority, the voters would not have a clear alternative if they wished to discard the dominant group. Indeed a theory of electoral accountability can never fit very well a system of proportional representation, since one can never eliminate the opposition by obtaining a majority; one merely reduces its numbers. Moreover, where the party controls the lists of candidates and determines the order of the candidates on these lists, the voters have hardly any possiblity of directly discarding a set of elites. The presence of ideological parties and differences in the social bases of parties between the Netherlands and the United States indicate that the relationships between parties and supporters must also be different. The social lines distinguishing between the Democratic and Republican parties are far less clear than those characteristic of Dutch parties (at least for the older, more extablished parties). Parties developed out of politically relevant social cleavages and membership and support reflect these cleavages. Thus a Protestant voting for the Catholic People's Party would be a rare exception as would be a Catholic voting for the Anti-Revolutionary Party or the Christian-Historicals. Although the elites of the Socialist Party include many academics and intellectuals and thereby differ less than might be expected from the Liberal Party, the social background of their fathers and grandfathers, their work experience, their orientation and their electoral basis are quite different. Similarly, the smaller religious parties and the Communist Party are very clearly aligned with particular segments of the population. Only some of the newer parties (D'66, PPR, DS'70) are not so clearly identified, a fact which may partially account for their difficulty in attracting a consistent following. Although it is not impossible to defect from one's social group and vote for another party, these strong ties do have an inhibiting effect. If one wishes to oust a member of the elected elite, he would do better to work within the party than to cast his vote elsewhere.

Finally, as far as the Netherlands is concerned, a pattern of cooperating rather than competing elites has developed. Lijphart has called this "the politics of accommodation."[20] The agreement to share rather than conquer is seen at the local level in the recruitment of commissioners. Traditionally, the various commissioners have not been apportioned to a majority coalition, but distributed across all parties in the council on a proportional basis. Here the pattern of recruitment weakens the principle of accountability through elections. Electoral shifts might alter the proportions, but there is no possibility of replacing one group with another. Attempts are now being made by some parties to alter this selection procedure in accordance with a system of electoral accountability but this imposes severe strains on the system.

In summary, the theory of accountability cannot be applied directly to the Dutch situation. This does not mean that Dutch council members are not responsible or responsive, nor does it mean that elections are unimportant in keeping the council members attuned to the wishes of the public—i.e., holding them accountable. What it does mean is that one must look beyond the simple fact of election in dealing with the forces playing on the councilman. In particular, we must look for the missing factor in the "theory of accountability"—i.e., the political party, and for the general norms and role conceptions within which council members work.

Conceptions of Representative Roles

In the San Francisco Bay Area, candidates emerge from the community in a variety of ways. They may present themselves, they may be encouraged by others, they may be asked to run, or they may even be appointed and run later. In any case, except for appointment, the link between the office holder and the electorate is direct. He is chosen by the electorate on his merits and responsible to the electorate for his deeds. Since he is chosen by "all the people," his responsibility is to "all the people," and it is perhaps not surprising to find that a large majority do not see the position as a political one. Instead, council membership is a "citizen duty" in much the same manner as Chamber of Commerce, PTA, and the other activities which were so important in recruiting the councilmen. Prewitt has argued that this

> norm of volunteerism can serve to undermine an already weakened election system. Although the volunteer in office, especially if relatively indifferent to staying there, may be a devoted public servant as he defines the role, he is unlikely to be constantly sensitive to voter preferences. His political thinking has been formed by a series of experiences which minimize for him the importance of mass electorates.[21]

There is, of course, a voluntary element in council service in the Netherlands, since it is a service for which one receives very little remuneration. But, as we have seen, the importance of partisan activity means that virtually by definition, council service is a "political" activity. No one may be elected without being part of a list which is most often in the form of a political party. Even if an individual is chosen from a local list, he must be aware that other councilmen, either in his own community or in another, are there as representatives of national political parties. For those who are elected from these national parties, the political nature of the position must be even more obvious. Even if local conflicts are not seen as part of national ones, the identification of the local council member with a national party in itself emphasizes the "political" nature of the position. However, in discussing candidate selection, we have only shown that persons presented as candidates by the parties may be identified with these parties. Nothing has been said about accountability and responsibility of the members once they have been duly elected. How do they perceive their roles as councilmen—as delegates of the party who nominated them, or as trustees of all the people? To whom do they feel responsible, the party or the voters? Who is to hold them accountable? And how? These are questions which are not only of interest and importance for our consideration of party and recruitment, but actually have become live issues in Dutch municipal election campaigns.

Four Representational Roles. Accountability and responsibility are closely related to one's conception of his function as a councillor. In particular the councillor's conception of his representative role should give an indication as to whom and by whom he might be held accountable. For present purposes it is important to distinguish four possible representation roles.

Where representatives are elected by the inhabitants of a specified geographical subdivision (as in the single member district system or election at large) the question of who is to be represented is not difficult to answer. Whether or not the representative is identified according to party affiliation, he is the representative of all the people in his district. The concept of role is important insofar as the representative feels that his constituents should dictate the stand which he will take ("citizen delegate") or that he should be guided by his own knowledge and conscience in determining what is the best for the people of his district ("citizen trustee"). In much of the writing on representative roles, the place of party is hardly considered. At most it would seem to be a guide, either in determining what the majority of the citizens wished or in helping the trustee to establish his position. The nature of the recruitment and electoral process in the Bay Area might lead one to expect a trustee role perception on the part of those councilmen. A delegate role perception would be the exception and would depend upon norms developed by an individual councilman.

Where in turn representatives are elected by proportional representation, the place of party becomes central. After all, there is no geographical subgroup of individuals which the representative is to represent. Instead, many representatives represent the entire geographical area according to the number of votes cast for the party. A representative may not be elected by anywhere near a majority of the citizens, but by a small proportion thereof. Does he represent only this proportion or all the citizens? If he is to adopt a delegate perception, is he delegated by his party's voters or by the entire electorate? And if he is still to represent all the people, how does the party fit in? The introduction of political parties into the political process brings with it the question of a triangular relationship between representatives, voters and party. In certain respects the legal structure has run behind actual practice. No mention of parties is made in the Dutch Constitution and until recently no recognition was given to parties in the electoral law. The importance of parties in the nomination and election process has finally been given legal status by listing party names on the ballot above the lists of candidates, rather than merely numbering the lists. Still the status of councilmen as representatives of parties is not acknowledged by the law which states, "The members shall vote without commands from or consultation with those who nominate them."[22] Yet few would really argue that the representatives should not consult with other party members or that the party should not try to convince a wavering representative to vote the party position. Instead, the law reflects a view which, in the early history of modern parties, has been expressed by many representatives who disagreed with the position of their party. Duverger summarizes it as follows: "Democracy requires that (parliamentary) representatives should take precedence over party leaders and the members of the electorate over the members of the party, since the electors constitute a larger group than the party members who are moreover included in it."[23] According to this role definition (which might be called the "party trustee") the representative is launched by the party, and can be expected to conform to his conception of party positions and principles, but is accountable to the voters at large.

There remains a final model in which the representative is responsible directly to the party, and which we may call the "party delegate" model. As noted above, the degree of independence achieved by parliamentary representatives or the degree to which the party can dictate the actions of its representatives in parliament is a question of long standing. Michels observed in 1915: "In view of their greater competence in various questions, the socialist parliamentary groups consider themselves superior even to the congresses, which are in theory the supreme courts of the party, and they claim an effective autonomy."[24] In a more disapproving tone, Duverger continues the above quote: "In practice the opposite often takes place: in many parties there can be seen a tendency of party leaders to give orders to the parliamentary representatives in the name of militant members."

These writings deal with national representatives and national parties, but the question of the degree of accountability of municipal councilmen to the local party has recently been raised in the Netherlands. In fact, the Labour Party has adopted the position that councilmen should be subject to recall by the local party if they fail to carry out the party program. In a recent issue of the party journal, Van den Bergh and Janssens have defended this position, and it may be useful to summarize their argument here.[25]

They argue that the party does not ask the voters for "trust" in its candidates, but for support of its program. This program is brought about after consultation with the grass roots; i.e., organized as well as unorganized voters are heard through action groups, neighborhood committees, hearings, letters, ombudsman teams, etc. The party promises to the voters that its candidates will carry out the program which is presented. The voters must be able to depend on the party to do all that is possible to realize the program. If it is the party which is to be held responsible for its program, then it must have the means to insure that its elected representatives remain true to that program. There must be some means beyond merely trusting that this will be the case. Some means must be available whereby representatives who lose the trust of the party or who act in opposition to the party position can be disavowed by the party. Preferably there should be the possibility to force such representatives to resign. It is unacceptable that there be a gap between the party and its representatives to the extent that party members are no longer able to accept such representatives as fellow party members. If such a gap does somehow exist, it is the representative and not the party which must give way.

Perceptions of Functions of Council Members

There were several questions in the municipal councillor questionnaire which can provide us with some information related to these four representational roles. Moreover perceptions of representational roles are likely to shed some light on the question of the possible role of parties in producing responsible and accountable council members. In an effort to obtain as wide as possible a range of council functions and roles, an open-ended question was asked: "What do you think is the primary role of a member of the city council?"[26] Up to four responses per member were coded. Table 7.6 lists all categories mentioned by at least ten percent of the sample as one of the four responses. Thus any individual member may be included in more than one category.

Serving the best interests of the entire community is by far the most important function perceived by a majority of councilmen. This is 23% more than the second most frequently mentioned category and several times more than any other representational role. These answers seem indicative of a "citizen trustee" role perception. Whatever the validity of this interpretation, it seems that the goal toward which supporters of a party-delegate model are

TABLE 7.6
PERCEPTIONS OF THE ROLE OF A MEMBER OF THE CITY COUNCIL
(in percentages)

Serve the best interests of the population	52
Accept responsibility for municipal administration	29
Check the mayor and commissioners	20
Maintain contact with the population	13
Represent citizens on basis of party program	12
Represent social groups or specific interests	12

striving will require considerable changes in the way councilmen perceive their roles. Only twelve percent mentioned anything related to a party program and many of these answers refer more to the so-called "party trustee" role than to the "party delegate" role. Before turning to more specific information on these questions, some explanation is needed for the remaining responses in Table 7.6.

The second most frequent response concerning the function of a member of the city council does not deal directly with representation. Almost thirty percent mentioned something related to the administration of the city government. This may be a consequence of the fact that the council selects the commissioners who together with the appointed mayor carry out the day-to-day business of the municipality. This Board of Mayor and Commissioners is not responsible to the council in the same way a Cabinet is responsible to the Parliament. The traditional system of appointing the commissioners according to the strength of the parties rather than trying to form a majority coalition means that there is no way to distinguish between governmental and opposition parties at the local level. Commissioners may be dismissed, but this is usually on an individual basis. Hence the administrative role perception of their function. The fact that the mayor and the commissioners are engaged in expediting the daily business of the city while the council meets only at specified times, means that it is the Board of Mayor and the Commissioners who take the initiative in many matters. They have immediate access to the information generated by the local bureaucracy and are probably the first to become aware of many problems. Although the commissioners are members of the council, it is probably correct to consider the remaining council members as a control group or a counterweight to these leaders. Almost a quarter of the respondents mention this as a role of the council member.

A corollary of the proposal of the Socialist Party that council members should be responsible to the party and committed to the party program is that the method of selecting commissioners should also be changed. As mentioned, at present the commissioners are selected from all the parties according to their relative strength. No coalition is made, no joint program is discussed. Both policy making and administration are the responsibility of the entire council, not merely of the commissioners. In such a system there is no way for the voters to show their approval or disapproval of the manner in which the commissioners carry out their daily duties. Moreover, as a consequence of the selection procedure, no party is able to carry out its program without dealing and consulting with the other parties. "Program boards," as they are called, have been proposed by the Socialist Party. In such a system, a majority party or coalition of parties would gain all the commissioner positions. Having control over all these positions, it could proceed to carry out its program. If the voters disapproved, they could vote for other parties at the next election. However they chose to vote, the voters would have much clearer choices. We shall not attempt to further explore this problem here. Some information on how our respondents view the proposed change is presented by Morlan.[27] The issue is mentioned here only to clarify why so many of the respondents conceive their roles in terms of administration and checks on the mayor and the commissioners. Since answers to this open-ended question do not tell us much about the relation between the member, his party, and the voters, we must search for additional information. This may be done by viewing how the respondents related to the public and how they felt about reelection.

INCUMBENCY AND REELECTION

In the Bay Area study councilmen thought of themselves as volunteers and were not particularly concerned about reelection. They did not feel that one should let elections influence decisions on issues. Instead, they felt that they should act independently in making their decisions. When their period of community service was concluded, they were happy to step aside for others. Furthermore, the voters of the Bay Area communities enhanced these feelings by generally returning those incumbents who sought reelection. Prewitt concludes: "Men enter and leave office not at the whim of the electorate, but according to self-defined schedules."[28] We can now examine the Dutch councilmen and try to determine whether the existence of partisan connections alters this pattern.

Voting with the Majority and Concern with Elections

No data are presented by Prewitt on whether council members vote in accordance with the opinions of the majority of citizens, and on whether they believe that elections should have an influence upon decisions. But he does present a series of responses to the question whether it was "easy or difficult to go against the majority preferences when choosing community policies." The quotations indicate that the councilmen did not find this difficult and did not believe they should find it difficult. Prewitt concluded: "It is very clear that councilmen infrequently refer to elections and, when they do, it often is in a manner which directly contradicts the premises of a theory of electoral accountability."[29] This was, of course, the set of responses which led him to be concerned with the theory of accountability. The data which are presented on a community basis indicate that in about half the communities the "council votes with perceived majority public opinion" and in slightly less than half the "council reflects concern with next election."[30]

In the Dutch study each respondent was asked, "Has it ever occurred that a definite difference of opinion appeared between what a majority of the council wanted and what the majority of the citizens apparently wanted?" Surprisingly, a majority (55%) of the respondents reported that such differences had never occurred. We have no additional evidence against which to check such responses, and therefore cannot know whether such a difference has "actually" existed in each of the communities. What we do know is that there is little unanimity in these communities concerning whether such a situation has ever existed. Morlan reports that in only eleven of the seventy-nine communities involved in the study were all of the interviewed respondents (incl. mayors) in agreement: In eight all said such a situation had never occurred and in three that it definitely had.[31] One cannot be certain that the lack of unanimity in the remaining sixty-eight communities indicates an incorrect perception on the part of some of the respondents, since differential length of tenure may give some respondents a different time perspective than others. One might excuse such differences with the argument that it is undoubtedly difficult to know just what the majority in the community really wishes. However, these same respondents would not be in complete agreement with such a statement. More than 40% answered that it was "fairly easy" or "very easy" to get to know what the inhabitants of their community desired with regard to local policies. "Knowing what the community wants" and "perceiving a difference between citizens and council" are undoubtedly rather individual perceptions based upon personal observation and incorporating personal biases and prejudices. What is important here is that more than half of the respondents have never felt themselves to be in a position in which they had to choose between the "majority will" and their own consciences.

Those who had perceived a conflict were asked what the council usually did in such cases and if they considered this appropriate behavior. Those who did not perceive any conflict were asked what the council should do if such a situation ever occurred. More than eighty percent of the first group felt that the council generally adhered to its own position rather than adopting the opinion of the majority. Whatever they thought the council did, three-fourths were in agreement with the action taken by the council. Those who have never been confronted with a choice between their own opinion and their belief concerning what the majority of the population wanted are somewhat more likely to feel that the council should adopt the citizen position. There is however, only a ten percent difference, since seventy percent feel that the council should adopt its own position. If all these questions are combined one finds that seventy-two percent of the respondents feel that the council ought to make its own decision and should not yield even if the majority of the citizens opposed it. This figure is quite similar to the seventy-three percent reported by Daalder and Rusk with regard to the members of the Dutch Parliament.[32] Their conclusion that "an overwhelming majority of Dutch members clearly embrace a Burkean concept of representation in their relation toward the electorate" could equally well apply to the Dutch councilmen.

To say that council members view themselves as "trustees" does not mean that they are unconcerned about what the voters will think. Politicans have means of avoiding such open conflicts between themselves and the citizenry. Controversial matters may simply never come to a vote. Proposals may be altered and compromises hammered out before open conflict emerges. Actions may be cast or interpreted in a different light so that conflict is submerged. Prewitt found it was not the case that "men in office anticipate the likely response of voters because the incumbents want either to retain that office or to move to a more elevated one."[33] This applies, however, to the highly personalized nonpartisan politics of the Bay Area where councilmen viewed themselves as volunteers serving for a limited time and with little ambition. Those who serve for a party or group are concerned with more than their own personal future. Even if such a councilman does not wish to run for reelection, it must be exceptional if he does not care whether his party loses at ensuing elections. The nonpartisan councilman has no one to think of but himself; the partisan councilman must think about his party. The two-way link between the people and the representatives in the nonpartisan setting becomes a triangle in the partisan setting, and the representative must consider both people and party in arriving at his decisions. Not only must he attempt to judge what the majority wants, and what the majority of his party wants, but also what is the most advantageous position for his party. In many cases it may be advantageous for the party to try to appeal to the majority or search for a majority coalition. Yet, in a political system with numerous minority parties, there may also be instances in which the party is decidedly in a minority position. When the party and the party's voters are in such a minority position it is surely going too far to ask that the representative vote with the majority. Perhaps we should have asked how he felt about voting against a majority of his party's voters. Lacking that information we may examine how much the council members feel the decisions they and their caucus make are influenced by the effect these decisions will have upon the electorate.

This involves a consideration of "anticipated reactions," and in terms of accountability may be more important than role perception (which may, of course, be important on other counts).

Prewitt provided no direct evidence on how the individual Bay Area councilmen viewed electoral considerations in making up their minds on impending policy questions. One can recalculate some figures which are presented to conclude that forty-five percent of the Bay Area councilmen are concerned with the next election.[34] If party really is a factor of importance in distinguishing between the two systems, we would expect this figure to be somewhat higher for the Netherlands. The results are presented in Table 7.7.

Although the figures are not strictly comparable, it would appear that electoral considerations are indeed of more importance to Dutch councilmen than to their colleagues in the Bay Area. Approximately two-thirds state that the party caucus considers the electoral consequences of its action. This provides at least some evidence that a theory of electoral accountability contained some validity, though not necessarily because the individual councilmen are ambitious, but because they are also concerned with the future of their party.

If such a difference between the Netherlands and the Bay Area is to be attributed to concern for the fate of the parties, one would hypothesize that representatives from the Dutch local lists would be less concerned about electoral consequences of actions than councilmen representing national parties. That this is only partially true can be seen in Table 7.8.

The respondents from local lists do have the highest percentage reporting "not important." The difference is greatest when compared to the national parties of

TABLE 7.7

ROLE OF ELECTORAL CONSIDERATIONS
IN CAUCUS DECISIONS (in percentages)

	N = 300
Electoral considerations regularly play a role	27
Electoral considerations play a role but are not the sole determinants	39
Electoral considerations seldom or never play a role	34
	100

TABLE 7.8

IMPORTANCE GIVEN TO ELECTORAL CONSEQUENCES WHEN ARRIVING
AT A DECISION IN THE PARTY CAUCUS, BY TYPE OF PARTY
(in percentages)

	National left parties N = 52	National religious parties N = 68	National right parties N = 34	Local lists N = 81
Important or somewhat important	72	62	65	61
Not important	28	38	35	39
	100	100	100	100

the left, but rather small when compared with the parties of the right and virtually nonexistent in comparison with the religious parties. This is not so surprising. The religious parties have traditionally relied upon voters who supported the party not because of specific programs, but because of religious identification. Parties of the left and right are more program oriented, with those of the left the most so.

Furthermore, since the local lists represent groups rather than individuals, there may be concern for perpetuating the group on the council. If this were indeed the case, then the group might be concerned with the electoral consequences of its action, thereby differing little from other local parties. This explanation has to be interpreted contextually, however, since the existence of the lists is related to another factor of considerable importance for this question of electoral considerations—namely, the size of the community.

As reported in Table 7.9, the largest difference in the frequency of electoral considerations occurs between the two smaller categories of municipalities (all of which have less than 10,000 inhabitants and an essentially rural character) on the one hand, and the remaining three medium to large categories on the other. Respondents from smaller municipalities are far less inclined to report that electoral considerations are important in their deliberations.

One can easily imagine that local politics in these smaller communities is quite different from "local" politics in Amsterdam, Rotterdam, or other larger communities. A "volunteer" conception of council service may be more frequent in areas where the likelihood of a voter personally knowing a council member is greater. In the cities, politics is less personalized and must be carried out through groups and organizations, thus increasing the concern with electoral consequences for the party. Besides, council service is more demanding in the cities where council members report spending considerably more time on council business. It may be harder to think of oneself as a "volunteer" when so much time and effort are involved. It is likely that the commitment in terms of

TABLE 7.9
IMPORTANCE OF ELECTORAL CONSIDERATIONS
BY SIZE OF COMMUNITY
(in percentages)

	small rural N = 87	small urban N = 35	medium cities N = 89	subur- ban N = 30	large cities N = 60
Important or somewhat important	49	57	74	90	75
Not important	51	43	27	10	25
	100	100	100	100	100

service and time has some bearing on how one views the importance of electoral considerations.

Two variables related to the individual council member's involvement in the council and its activity should shed some light on this issue. First, there is the distinction between commissioners and regular council members. The commissioners, whether by ambition or circumstances, have moved into positions of greater prestige and power within the council and within the community. In general, they have had longer tenure in office (in this sample a median tenure of thirteen years against slightly less than four years for the council members). If Schlesinger's "ambition theory of politics" is correct in claiming that "the desire for election and, more importantly, for reelection becomes the electorate's restraint upon the public officials,"[35] Then the commissioners should show greater concern for electoral consequences. Second, there is a difference in the amount of time which councilmen spend on council work, ranging from less than five hours per week to the full-time commissioners in larger cities. One would hypothesize that the more time a councilman invested in serving his party on the council, the more he would be concerned about the consequences of the actions of the party caucus upon the electorate.

These hypotheses receive some confirmation from the figures presented in Table 7.10. Among council members who spend less than five hours weekly on council matters a majority report that electoral considerations are not important to their caucus, more than twice the percentage of those spending more than twenty hours per week. These frequency distributions are in the expected direction, but since the amount of time spent is related to the size of the community one must be somewhat cautious in drawing conclusions. The difference in percentage reporting the importance of electoral considerations between commissioners and council members is not as great as for amount of time spent, but still sufficient to support the hypothesis. Commissioners are

TABLE 7.10
IMPORTANCE OF ELECTORAL CONSIDERATIONS BY POSITIONS IN
COUNCIL AND AMOUNT OF TIME SPENT ON COUNCIL BUSINESS
(in percentages)

	commissioners N = 150	council members N = 151	less than 5 hours weekly N = 46	5-10 N = 76	10-20 N = 56	more than 20 hours weekly N = 114
Somewhat important or very important	73	60	46	63	69	76
Not important	28	40	54	37	31	24
	101	100	100	100	100	100

indeed more likely to view such considerations as important when the caucus makes its decisions.

In summary, we may conclude that the electorate's anticipated reaction has some bearing on councilmen behavior in the Netherlands. Substantial proportions of the respondents in this survey felt that the electoral consequences of action were important to the caucus in reaching its decisions.

Several factors may be weakening the importance of such considerations or may make the respondent less likely to perceive their importance. The less worried the member is about the loyalty of the voters, the less he need worry about the consequences of his action. The less concerned the councilmen is about the future of his group, the less ambitious he is personally, and the less commitment he displays in terms of time spent on council business, the less likely he is to perceive the electoral consequences of action as important. For various reasons these factors converge in smaller communities and produce less concern with electoral consequences among council members.

Reelection and Reasons for Quitting

Prewitt found two aspects of reelection and retirement from the council which undermined the principle of accountability: (1) most councilmen were not ousted from office by the voters, but retired voluntarily when they felt like it; (2) when reelection was desired the electorate usually complied, as incumbents were usually returned to office. In a majority of cases, those who decided to quit did so not because they feared defeat or because they found the job frustrating or unrewarding, but as a consequence of their feeling that it was time to "give the next guy a chance."[36]

The situation in the Netherlands is somewhat different, for it is not only up to the councilman and the electorate to decide whether an incumbent will be returned. The important element of party again dominates the picture. It is the party which puts together the list of candidates and determines the order in which the candidates will be listed. Although no data are available, it seems fairly certain that the probability of leaving the party and achieving success on a new ticket is rather slim. There are well-known examples of popular councilmen who have been unable to carry voters with them when quitting a party. (There may be exceptions where local lists or personalized politics prevail.) Therefore, in looking at chances for reelection, one must look not at the percentage of incumbents who successfully sought reelection, but at the incumbents' chances of obtaining a secure position on the list. This is itself an aspect of accountability, since one's performance may be reviewed in drawing up the new list. Those who support the party delegate model argue that mid-term recall is merely an extension of the right of parties to review the candidate lists.

Achieving a Place on the List

Respondents were asked the following question: "Apart from the willingness for a renewed candidacy one can ask how great the chance is that you and *your colleagues in the caucus* can gain a safe position on the list." Table 7.11 presents the distribution of their responses.

It does not appear that councilmen believe they can perpetuate themselves in office with little concern for their position on the party list. More than half of the respondents believe that they or other members of their group would have to work hard for a secure place on the list, and even then not all of them would be successful. Little difference is found in the distribution of responses by size of the community, but some difference seems to be associated with party-type. Councilmen from local lists are highest in percentage reporting "no doubt" that they would be able to secure safe positions on the list. This is not surprising given the generally looser structure of such lists—i.e., the lack of a party apparatus, and the fact that those on the council are probably the ones drawing up the lists. Duverger has noted, for example, that cadre parties tend to make nominations by ruling committees, whereas mass parties more often make nominations by a vote of the membership.[37] Nomination by ruling committee surely leads to greater security concerning the incumbent's position on the list. Those representing parties of the right give almost as frequently a response of "no doubt" as members of local lists, but also the lowest percentage reporting "not all will be able to return." To the extent that these are also mass parties, this difference may lie more in the role which the party members accord their representatives than in the nomination procedures employed.[38]

Several questions were asked concerning possible conflicts within the party in the nominating process. Each respondent was specifically asked if in the nomination process there was conflict within the party between young and old,

TABLE 7.11

CHANCES OF GAINING A SAFE POSITION ON LIST OF CANDIDATES
(in percentages)

If we wish to be candidates we can pretty much count on a safe position on the list	48
There is a good chance that we could gain a safe position, but we must work for it	30
Not all sitting members will be able to gain a safe position even if they do everything to try to obtain it	21
	99

political factions, and old and new inhabitants in the community. An additional question was asked whether any other sort of conflict occured and if so, between whom. The percentages reporting such conflicts are shown in Table 7.12. The least amount of conflict was reported between old and new inhabitants (10%); for the other items at least twice as much conflict was reported. The more important categories of conflict mentioned were: conflicts in trying to put together a list combining various parties (mentioned 14 times), conflicts between theorists and pragmatists, workers and intellectuals, university trained and others, etc. (mentioned 13 times), and conflicts between the councilmen themselves or councilmen versus others (mentioned 12 times). Less frequently mentioned were conflicts between different villages in a municipality, religious conflicts and conflicts between socioeconomic groups. Although less than a quarter of the respondents reported any particular conflict, when combined one finds that almost one half report at least some conflict in putting together a list of candidates. That conflict can occur whatever the type of party (local or national, left, religious, or right) can be seen from the breakdown by party type in Table 7.13.

There is a slight tendency for left parties to report multiple conflicts and for right parties to report singular conflicts, but the difference is only ten percent. Knowing that there may be vigorous discussions over the composition of

TABLE 7.12
CONFLICT REPORTED IN THE NOMINATION OF CANDIDATES
(in percentages)

	N = 305
Young versus old	20
Between political factions	23
Old versus new inhabitants	10
Other	23
At least one type of conflict	49

TABLE 7.13
CONFLICT IN CANDIDATE NOMINATION BY TYPE OF PARTY
(in percentages)

	Reporting conflict
National left parties	45
National religious parties	43
National right parties	43
Local lists	49

candidate lists can hardly help but affect the behavior of the incumbent councilmen. They are likely to be aware that at least some party members are observing and evaluating their actions, and this knowledge may keep them responsive. Not all councilmen can be renominated without at least having to work for it.

Desire for Reelection

Whatever the chances of achieving a high place on the list, not all council members will wish to seek reelection. Prewitt reported that eighteen percent of the Bay Area councilmen intended to retire at the end of their present term. Twenty-nine percent planned to seek higher office, leaving fifty-three percent who would seek another term. We do not have data for Dutch councilmen on how many would seek a higher office, but the percentage is likely to be considerably smaller than the twenty-nine percent in the Bay Area. There are only three offices in the Netherlands which are subject to direct election by the voters—municipal councilman, member of the provincial legislature, and member of Parliament. Becoming a member of the provincial legislature will not always be considered a step upward. In fact, it is not certain whether moving from commissioner of a city like Amsterdam or Rotterdam to the Parliament will be considered a political promotion. Moving either to a provincial legislature or to the Parliament is also controlled by the parties and thus not something one can achieve on the basis of electoral success at the local level. Table 7.14 reports the willingness of councilmen to stand for reelection.

The percentage who are certain that they do not wish to be candidates again is higher than for the Bay Area, and if one assumes that a portion of the intermediate group ("not yet sure") will also drop out, the percentage becomes substantially higher. Breakdowns by party, function on the council, amount of

TABLE 7.14
"WHAT ARE YOUR THOUGHTS AT THIS MOMENT CONCERNING A NEW
CANDIDACY FOR A POSITION ON THE COUNCIL?"
(in percentages)

As far as I can say, I would like to be a candidate	51
I am not yet sure if I would like to be a candidate	23
I probably will not become a candidate again	25
	99

time spent on council business, and size of the community do not indicate that these are related to a decision not to seek reelection.

The reasons given by the Dutch councilmen for not returning as candidates are summarized in Table 7.15. By far the most frequently indicated personal reasons are family, age, health, etc., or interference with job. Somewhat more than one-fourth indicate that they have done their duty and it is time to "give others a chance." The remainder give more political reasons: dissatisfaction with what could be accomplished, ineffectiveness of the council or council members, or unsurmountable local problems or difficulties.

Although direct comparisons cannot be made because of reporting of multiple responses in the Bay Area data, there do appear to be differences in emphasis among those retiring from the council. Mention of "responsibility completed" or "giving others a chance" was made by a majority of the Bay Area retirees, twice as many as among the Dutch group. On the other hand, even though only one response was coded for the Dutch councilmen, a higher percentage (24% versus 13%) gave reasons relating to dissatisfaction with their job as a councilman. The Dutch also were slightly more likely to mention personal or job reasons for retiring (49% versus 42%).[39] Apparently Dutch councilmen feel more personal pressure and political frustrations than do the Bay Area councilmen, leading larger percentages to retire from council service. Along this line, for example, one finds a steady increase in the number of "personal" reasons the more time the member reports spending on council business. Further analysis is not feasible, since breakdowns of the retirees yields too few respondents in the various subcategories for reliable results.

TABLE 7.15

REASONS GIVEN BY COUNCILMEN FOR NOT SEEKING ANOTHER TERM.
(includes those definitely not seeking another term and
those "not sure," in percentages)

		N = 144
Personal Reasons	49	
Family, age, health, etc.		38
Interference with job		11
Dissatisfaction with Council Job	24	
General dissatisfaction		6
Too little effectiveness		11
Too political		2
Local problems and difficulties		5
Responsibilities Completed	28	
Give others a chance		28
	101	101

THE COUNCILMAN AND HIS PARTY

In the previous section we have seen that concern for one's chances for renomination and concern for the party's success at subsequent elections are factors which help keep the representative attuned to the wishes of the party and the voters. In this final section we turn directly to the relationship between the representative and his party. Specifically, how much independence does the council member have or should he have from the local party executive? What should he do if he disagrees with the party executive? And what should he do if he leaves his party? These questions are particularly important if one wishes to work toward a "party delegate" model of representation, which would make the council member directly and at all times accountable to the party.

The Party Executive

If the members of the city council are to be held accountable by the party, there must be some distinction between the party structure and its selected representatives. Respondents were asked to report whether their particular party or grouping had an executive which was separate from the members of the council. All of those representing a national party indicated that this was indeed the case. However, fifty-eight of the eighty-one councilmen in the sample who represent local lists indicated that no such separate executive existed. As we have stated earlier, little is known concerning these local lists and how they arise. From the responses to this question it would appear that few have any permanent organization. More or less ad hoc groups of individuals, including those who take seats on the council, become active in putting together a list of candidates. Once the list is put together any semblance of organization generally ceases. Although the friends may continue to consult informally, almost none of the groups ever hold formal meetings. It is precisely the lack of such elements as executives and party meetings which has led us to compare these lists with the nonpartisan procedures in the Bay Area. The primary difference between the nonpartisan system and the local lists in the Netherlands consists in the fact that candidates did present themselves as a group in competition with other groups. Nevertheless, it is doubtful if one can speak of a party to which the member is accountable.

The existence of a party executive is insufficient to hold council members accountable if there is no distinction between the two. Even the most carefully structured system of checking and competing organizations can be subverted by interlocking directorates. Each respondent who indicated that the party had a separate executive was asked whether this executive consisted primarily of individuals who were members of the council or primarily of nonmembers. Ninety-two percent indicated that such an executive consisted primarily of others, thereby indicating that at least a rudimentary organization exists which may serve to observe and check the behavior of the councilmen.

Party Executive and Council Members

For those representing lists for which no party executive exists, or for those for whom the council members dominate the executive, there can be no question of independence from an executive. But most of those representing national parties indicated that there exists a party executive which is separate from the council members. For these, one can examine the relationships assumed in the "party delegate" model. The pleas for such a model and the infrequent mention of party in the open-ended question concerning roles and functions of council members would indicate that council members presently operate in relative independence from their parties. This can be examined more closely by looking at responses to the question: Does the party executive try to influence the position of the caucus? If so, how often does this occur? What does the caucus do or what should it do in case of disagreement with the executive?

Among those who mentioned a separate executive, only a small majority (55%) indicated that this executive ever attempted to influence the decisions made by the caucus. Only forty-seven percent indicated that this occurred either occasionally or often.[40] (See Table 7.16.)

Whether or not the party executive has ever tried to influence the caucus, the councilman may be asked what he thinks ought to be done if a disagreement occurred between the two. Supporters of the party-delegate doctrine would clearly answer that it is the party which must prevail. ("In such a situation it is the chosen representatives who must give and not the party.")[41] This would involve a change in the opinions of the councilmen questioned in this survey. A majority (56%) hold exactly the opposite opinion, namely that the caucus

TABLE 7.16
FREQUENCY WITH WHICH PARTY EXECUTIVES ATTEMPT TO
INFLUENCE DECISIONS TAKEN BY PARTY CAUCUS
(in percentages)

	N = 304
Executive tries often to influence caucus	17
Executive tries occasionally to influence	30
Executive tries to influence, but seldom	8
Executive never tries to influence caucus	45
	100

members ought to have the final say and not the party. Equal percentages (22%) give preference to the party or feel that a compromise should be found between the party and caucus (see Table 7.17). Despite the fact that the Socialist Party has since adopted a party-delegate plan as part of its program, one finds among these respondents no more support for the dominance of party than among representatives of the religious or local lists. National parties of the right do, however, tend to favor the independence of the caucus. One should note, perhaps, that despite the negative response of most councilmen, as far as the dominance of the party executive is concerned, there is nevertheless a greater willingness to accept directions than has been observed among Members of Parliament. Daalder and Rusk report that only five percent of the MP's "granted supremacy to organs outside the parliamentary arena."[42]

TABLE 7.17
IN CASE OF CONFLICT BETWEEN PARTY EXECUTIVE AND
PARTY CAUCUS, WHO SHOULD HAVE FINAL SAY?
(in percentages)

Who should have final say?	National left parties N = 52	National religious parties N = 68	National right parties N = 34	Local lists N = 81	Total N = 235
Caucus	53	53	77	50	56
Party executive	22	21	18	25	22
Should seek compromise	25	25	6	25	22
	100	99	101	100	100

Leaving the Party

The ultimate conflict between an individual and his political party is that which might result in his quitting his party. When a member of a legislative body such as a city council quits his party, the question arises whether or not he should surrender his seat. Since the law does not directly recognize the council members as agents of political parties, such a member may retain his seat. In political systems in which the individual candidate is more important than the party (as for example in the single-member district system of the United States) it is not surprising that the individual continues in office after his break with the party. Thus the Wayne Morses and Strom Thurmonds occasionally switch parties with little difficulty. However, in a political system in which the party is more important, especially with regard to the nomination of candidates and the determination of party policy, current practice would seem to involve a contradiction: It does seem inconsistent that a legislator may leave the party to which he is indebted for his position and yet remain in office.

An overwhelming majority (85%) of the respondents agreed that a council member who left his party should then vacate his seat. As we should expect from what has been said about the difference between local lists and national parties, the representatives of these two types differ on whether the member should resign. Only seventy-one percent of those representing local lists feel that the member should resign, as opposed to eighty-nine percent of those from national parties. No substantial differences were found between positions on the council, amount of time spent on council business, or size of community. One should keep in mind, however, that this is only a statement of principle, and one cannot know what these individuals might do if they were actually confronted with such a situation themselves. An undetermined number would undoubtedly reject the proposition that the law should be changed to make vacating mandatory.

SUMMARY AND CONCLUSION

This chapter has explored some of the effects of the participation of political parties in the recruitment of Dutch municipal councilmen. Concern for the role of parties arose from some findings presented by Prewitt in his studies of the recruitment of councilmen in the nonpartisan system of the San Francisco Bay Area. In particular, such aspects as the amount of "cronyism" involved in recruitment and the lack of electoral accountability led us to ask how this might be different in the Dutch partisan system of elections. The effects of parties in the Netherlands have been tested in two ways. First, insofar as possible, direct comparisons have been made cross-nationally. Second, comparisons have been made internally by comparing council members representing organized political parties with those representing local lists. It was found that the bilateral relationship between representative and voter in a nonpartisan system becomes a triangular relationship when parties are introduced. Four representational roles were discussed depending upon whether the councilman viewed himself as a "delegate" or a "trustee" either of the party or of the voters. Responses to an open-ended question indicated that service in the interests of the community was the most frequent orientation. Only a few mentioned party or party program in their discussion of the tasks of a council member. This does not mean that parties had no impact on the council member's regard for the electorate. Dutch councilmen showed more concern for the effects of their actions on the results of subsequent elections than did the Bay Area councilmen. The argument was presented that where representatives are nominated by a party, elections may be more effective in holding them accountable to the public and attentive to public demands. Awareness of the caucus being concerned with electoral consequences was found to be greater among commissioners, among councilmen from larger cities and among those who devoted more time to council work.

Finally, the relationship between the council member and his party was examined. Despite the emphasis upon party in recruitment, parties do not seem to perform an important role in supervising the day-to-day functioning of the representatives. In some cases no independent party executive existed at all. And when such a separate executive did exist, it often made no attempt to influence the decisions taken by the caucus. Nevertheless, the party does provide a check on the council members through the role in the renomination of incumbent members. Some conflict over nominations seems to occur in about one half of the groups, and many incumbents cannot be renominated without having "to work for it." In the decision not to seek renomination, the Dutch councilmen distinguished themselves from their Bay Area counterparts: Whereas "giving others a chance" was important in the Bay Area, personal reasons dominated the responses of Dutch councilmen.

In evaluating such findings, one must always face the question of the extent to which they are generalizable and what other factors might possibly interfere with the findings which could not be controlled in the research. There is, for example, the size of the community. For the Dutch data, size was shown to have an effect upon the "importance of electoral considerations" in making decisions. In this case, the pattern for small rural communities resembled the volunteer pattern of the Bay Area. If size is important, one might wish to know what it was about the size of a community which contributed to the development of the volunteer role conception. When a community is very small it is possible that almost everyone knows everyone else, so that more formal channels of communication may be unnecessary in order to find out what the community as a whole is thinking. One could argue that this would lead to a volunteer spirit in which it did not really matter which individuals were on the council. Yet one also finds that tenure is somewhat longer in smaller communities. This indicates that more permanent local oligarchies might develop, dominating both council caucus and party. Certainly it is not always the case that small size means greater homogeneity, yet this must be considered. Perhaps a measure of homogeneity or perceived homogeneity could be developed which would be independent of size and which could be related to patterns of recruitment. Would greater homogeneity lead to greater accountability or to less concern with the opinions of the electorate?

Of related interest is the stability of the local population. A real estate agent once told the author that Americans move once every three years (on the average), but Dutchmen only once in eight. Whether or not these are the true figures, it may be that the communities considered in this study differ considerably in terms of the stability and mobility of their populations. Could stability or geographical mobility have an effect upon patterns of recruitment? Again, contradictory hypotheses can be developed. A stable community might develop recruitment patterns with a considerable turnover, high volunteer spirit, etc., as council membership is passed on to the many available candidates. Or it might lead to control by a few dominant individuals who are as stable in their positions as the stability of the population. Similarly, mobile communities might bring constant infusion of new blood into the community and into the council. Community service might be seen as a way of contributing to one's new community. On the other hand, new individuals might care little about the community, especially if they do not intend to remain there, and the local government might easily be dominated by the few who are interested and who need not be concerned with the opinions of the rest of the population. These are issues which must be considered in determining whether, and to what extent influence can be attributed to the existence of political parties.

NOTES

1. Kenneth Prewitt, *The Recruitment of Political Leaders: A Study of Citizen Politicians* (Indianapolis: Bobbs-Merrill, 1970).

2. Kenneth Prewitt, "Political ambitions, volunteerism, and electoral accountability," American Political Science Review (March 1970) 5-18; Heinz Eulau and Kenneth Prewitt, *Labyrinths of Democracy: Adaptations, Linkages, Representation and Policies in Urban Politics* (Indianapolis: Bobbs-Merrill, 1973).

3. Prewitt, *The Recruitment*, 88-89.

4. Eulau and Prewitt, op. cit., 451.

5. Moshe M. Czudnowski, American Political Science Review 67 (March 1973), 227-228.

6. Detailed information concerning the selection of the sample has been presented by the author as an appendix in Robert L. Morlan, *Gemeentepolitiek in debat: Opvattingen van burgers en bestuurders* (Alphen a/d Rijn, Samson Uitgeverij, 1974), or may be obtained directly from the author.

7. See Robert L. Morlan, "Cabinet government at the municipal level: the Dutch experience," Western Political Quarterly 17 (June 1964).

8. For information concerning attitudes toward the selection of mayors, see Robert L. Morlan, *Gemeentepolitiek in debat.*

9. In order to get on the ballot a party or group must submit signatures of 25 eligible voters (if the number of eligible voters is less than 1,200 this number is reduced to 1/50 of the eligible number). Although most voters cast their vote for the first name on the list, they may express a "preference" for any name of the list. If an individual candidate receives a sufficient number of these "preference votes" he may be elected before someone above him on the list. At the national level the incidence of preference votes is decreasing, but little is known about such voting at the local level, as the Central Bureau of Statistics keeps no such records. Presumably, the incidence of preference votes is higher, even if for no other reason than the fact that more candidates will have more friends. Election by preference votes may also be easier since mounting a campaign for such votes can be localized.

Seats are allotted proportionally with "rest seats" apportioned according to the largest average system in large cities and a variation of the largest remainder system in smaller municipalities.

According to the size of the community and the distribution of the vote, a party may need from approximately 2 to 10% of the total vote cast in order to gain representation on the council.

10. Two useful English language accounts of the Dutch party system are H. Daalder, "The Netherlands: Opposition in a Segmented Society," in R. Dahl, ed., *Political Oppositions in Western Democracies* (New Haven: Yale University Press, 1966) and P. Baehr, "The Netherlands," in Stanley Henig and John Pinder, eds., *European Political Parties* (London: George Allen & Unwin, 1969).

11. Special thanks are due to both Eulau and Prewitt for their most gracious help. The Netherlands Foundation for Pure Scientific Research (ZWO) made it possible for Prewitt to spend one month in the Netherlands discussing possible lines of analysis. Of course, neither of these scholars should in any way be held responsible for decisions taken concerning the formulation of questions in the questionnaire or the analysis presented here.

12. Prewitt, *The Recruitment,* 25-26.

13. Eulau and Prewitt, op. cit., 628.

14. One can only speculate what effect this system may have upon how well the voters know the candidates. On the other hand, repeated nominations should produce some recognition among the electorate. We have seen that being well known is an important quality in candidacy. On the other hand, the emphasis on party correspondingly deemphasizes the individual. How these factors weigh against one another in giving the voters a clear picture of whom they are dealing with is a puzzle for future research.

15. It may be of interest to note that number 6 on the list received sufficient preference votes to be elected in preference to number 5.

16. Prewitt, op. cit., 137-138.

17. Czudnowski, loc. cit.

18. Prewitt, "Political ambitions," 5.

19. For more information concerning the participation of parties in municipal elections and the composition of the municipal councils, see H. Daalder, K.L.L.M. Dittrich, R. P. van den Helm and J. Verhoef, "Gemeentepolitiek in kaart gebracht" (mimeo from Department of Political Science, University of Leiden).

20. Arend Lijphart, *The Politics of Accomodation: Pluralism and Democracy in the Netherlands* (Berkeley and Los Angeles: University of California Press, 1968).

21. Prewitt, "Political ambitions," 10.

22. For mention of this portion of the law and its importance in the 1974 municipal election campaigns, see W. Drees, "Programcolleges: democratie in geding," *NRC-Handelsblad,* May 21, 1974.

23. Maurice Duverger, *Political Parties: Their Organization and Activity in the Modern State* (New York: John Wiley, 1963), 182.

24. Robert Michels, *Political Parties,* translated by Eden and Cedar Paul, (New York; Free Press, 1962), 157. The relationship between parliamentary representatives and party is a subject of importance in treatments of political parties. See, for example, M. Y. Ostrogorski, *Democracy and the Organization of Political Parties,* (London: Macmillan, 1962), Vol. 1; R. T. McKenzie, *British Political Parties* (London: Heinemann, 1963); L. Epstein, *Political Parties in Western Democracies* (New York: Frederick A. Praeger, 1967).

25. J. van den Bergh and P.M.G.P. Janssens, "Recall' niet herroepen," Socialisme en Democratie 31 (April, 1974).

26. The Dutch word "taak" is rather difficult to translate here. Literally, it is translated as "task" or "job," but it also carries some of the connotation of "function" or "role."

27. Robert L. Morlan, *Gemeentepolitiek in debat,* Chapter II.

28. Prewitt, "Political ambitions," 10.

29. Ibid., 7.

30. Ibid., 11, Table 5.

31. Morlan, *Gemeentepolitiek in debat,* 66.

32. Hans Daalder and Jerrold G. Rusk, "Perceptions of Party in the Dutch Parliament," in Samuel C. Patterson and John C. Wahlke, eds., *Comparative Legislative Behavior* (New York: John Wiley, 1972), 161-162.

33. Prewitt, *The Recruitment,* 175-203.

34. Prewitt, "Political ambitions," 11

35. Joseph A. Schlesinger, *Ambition and Politics* (Chicago: Rand McNally, 1966).

36. Prewitt, *The Recruitment,* 176-180.

37. Maurice Duverger, op. cit., 360.

38. The Liberal Party (VVD), for example, follows rather open procedures in drawing up the lists. First a form requesting suggestions for candidates is sent to all local members. From all the names received a list is drawn up and recommendations are made by the party executive. The list of candidates is determined by a majority vote of the party members in meeting.

39. Prewitt, *The Recruitment,* 177.

40. After discussion of such matters as the party delegate model, one begins to think in terms of strong party organizations with powerful executives. Obviously, in view of the above figures, this is not always the case. Even where a separate executive is present it does not try to influence caucus decisions. This leaves open the possibility that it is the caucus on the council which is strong and the executive which is weak. This is not altogether unlikely, especially in smaller municipalities. In many communities the city commissioners are extremely important men, both in the party and the community at large. Such individuals and even council members who are not commissioners may dominate an executive of which they are not a part.

41. Van den Bergh and Janssens, op. cit. 148.

42. Daalder and Rusk, loc. cit.

Chapter 8

CRISIS RECRUITMENT AND THE POLITICAL INVOLVEMENT OF LOCAL ELITES: SOME EVIDENCE FROM ITALY AND FRANCE

SIDNEY TARROW and V. LAMONTE SMITH

Cornell University

How often has it been said that a man is the product of a generation of crisis?[1] Thucydides wrote that, during times of revolution or civil war, "reckless audacity came to be considered the courage of a loyal ally; prudent hesitation, specious cowardice; moderation was held to be a cloak for unmanliness; ability to see all sides of a question, inaptness to act on any."[2] Could a man who entered public life during similar time—however lowly his station or unexalted his motives—ever escape the influence of such an atmosphere?

Although historians and biographers can point to men whose beliefs or behavior were determined by the epochal times through which they lived, there is little proof that groups of elites in particular roles are uniformly marked by the period of their initiation into public life. In this essay, we shall study one such group in the context of contemporary Italy and France: samples of mayors

Authors' Note: The Ford and Guggenheim Foundations made this study possible by grants to support the fieldwork and parts of the analysis. The Concilium on International Studies of Yale University and the Center for International Studies at Cornell also provided resources that have helped with the analysis. We are grateful to Peter Katzenstein, Glaucio Soares, and Robert Weissberg, as well as to the editors, for comments on an earlier draft of this paper. The analysis was facilitated—and enlivened—by Barbara Lynch, at Cornell, who has our sincere thanks.

who emerged from the historical crises of Western Europe in the 1930s and 1940s—from the Popular Front and the struggle against fascism to the liberation and the restoration of democratic government between 1944 and 1948. In addition, we include a smaller group of younger, crisis-recruited mayors: Those who entered public life during the late 1950s in France and during more recent years in Italy.[3] Throughout this chapter "recruitment" has been operationally defined as reported first entry into "active political life." The first problem we shall address is how, if at all, recruitment during a period of crisis affects the patterns of political involvement of an actor in local politics many years later.

This question is not without its ambiguities. A political actor grows up in a particular family, belongs to a specific age cohort, and has an ideological formation which may mark his later political involvement in many ways, irrespective of the conditions surrounding his recruitment.[4] If we are to have any hope of explaining patterns of political involvement in a man's later political career, in addition to the systemic influences around him—such as the presence of a great historic crisis during his recruitment—we must examine individual, group, and ideological influences on his socialization to politics.[5] The second task of this report will therefore be to examine both childhood and young adult experiences within the individual's environment as well as the broader systemic context of his recruitment.[6].

In one sense, this is no more than saying that we wish to examine the accumulated influence of early and late socialization on the behavior of certain political leaders. But it is more than this: entering politics during a crisis of systemic magnitude (unlike personal, family, or strictly local crises) affects not only an individual, but an entire generational cohort as well. As such, it can remain as a reservoir of shared or consensual symbols, sources of solidarity, and roots of conflict for the entire political system. On the other hand, in countries like Italy and France, which have yet to develop ideologically neutral myths of their own past, the survival of a crisis mentality among older cohorts of leaders and voters may underpin current conflicts with older tensions and help to render their solution more difficult. Thus, the proportion of leaders recruited during years of crisis who are still in the political system, the impact of their recruitment experiences on the character of their political involvement, and the importance of their role in contemporary politics may constrain the system's capacity to routinely resolve its current problems. If each new crisis that comes along—the events of May 1968 in France, the combined economic and political crises of 1972-1974, the resurgence of fascism in Italy—is but poured into the vessels of old, then newer cohorts of leaders who arise during these periods may be unable to resist the divisions and conflicts of their elders.

Several difficulties beset an analysis of these problems and will probably obscure the links between past crisis recruitment and current political attitudes and behavior that we shall uncover. First, the men we interviewed have been active in local politics for many years: Much water has passed under the bridge since their initial entry into politics, and the character of their political involvement may have changed a great deal as a result of intervening experience. Second, two important factors limit the representativeness of the two samples: For reasons not connected with this report, they were chosen from the French and Italian provinces rather than from large cities or metropolitan areas.[7] Neither can we speak with confidence of the entire universe of leaders who entered local politics during times of crisis, because many of them have, in the interim, died, while others have moved upward in the political system or left political life altogether. Third, although our definition of years of crisis in each system was arrived at with the advice of a panel of experts, any such definition is of course largely subjective, particularly where recent years of crisis are concerned.

HISTORICAL CRISES AND POLITICAL INVOLVEMENT

Two basic models suggest themselves regarding the impact of crisis recruitment on an actor's political involvement: A subcultural and an exchange model. From the point of view of the first, if a man has entered political life during an age of national crisis, it seems plausible that he will then adapt with difficulty to the pedestrian problems of politics in more normal times.[8] Instead of resisting fascism, he must resist the pressures of the bureaucracy; rather than struggling to bring about an insurrection, he must struggle to balance a municipal budget; and in place of the solidarity of great aims shared with ideological comrades, there is the political horse-trading that infests so much of everyday politics in democratic systems. A local leader recruited during a crisis, but serving during a later period of relative calm, might find himself alienated from precisely those aspects of political life that are essential to success in local government. He might remain more committed to the political party or movement through which he entered politics and more intensively involved in a partisan subculture than in administrative life: More so, certainly, than actors who enter politics during normal times.

But a second hypothesis which emerges from an exchange model of the polity also seems worth examining.[9] The solidarities engendered by a period of historic crisis could, with time, become transformed into the exchange bases for the workaday relationships of everyday political life. More than once in history, the militants of an aggressive social or national movement have turned into an "old boy" network organized around the centers of power in the system that their struggle has helped to create. If this were the case, then crisis recruitment might have an effect precisely opposite to the one described above. Entry into politics as part of the generational cohort which earned its spurs during a period of crisis might serve as an entrée into greater administrative involvements, more affect for the game of politics, and higher satisfaction with its achievements than was the case for those who entered politics during more normal times. A generation that was revolutionary in the past sometimes preserves the rhetoric of crisis mainly as part of its ideological baggage, playing out the game of politics as a system of exchange in the interstices between militant ideological pronouncements. Indeed, so pervasive may the requirements of the game of politics become that the intense attachments of a partisan subculture may serve as a foundation for the more prosaic exchanges of political life.

Undoubtedly, both subcultural and exchange models of the polity have something to tell us about the patterns of political involvement in any political system. But so does a third model, one which links political attitudes and behavior to the larger system of institutional roles and practices in the system at large.[10] The institutional roles occupied by those who have been active in local politics for many years and the constraints surrounding these roles may compete with earlier predispositions and attachments in determining the dominant character of their political involvement. And in systems in which local institutional roles differ as radically as in Italy and France, we might expect an increasingly differentiating "institutional effect" to pervade the political involvement of local actors as they settle into such roles.

This institutional effect can be conceived as a screen through which various patterns of political socialization and recruitment are filtered to bring out either their exchange or their subcultural aspects. Where the institutions linking local government to the national state are stronger—as in France—they may integrate local decision makers into administrative roles sufficiently to suppress, or render superfluous, an earlier involvement in partisan subcultures. Where institutions are weaker—as in Italy—involvement in a party can more easily become a springboard for political exchange around which the local decision maker organizes his efforts to channel resources into the community. In other words, the institutional effect of local government roles in France would be to dampen the intensity of partisanship or exclude it from the workings of local government, while, in Italy, it could lead the local official to utilize his partisan ties to build up a network of contacts for political exchange.

But what of the special kind of political involvement in a party or movement that emerges from periods of crisis? Does this type of identification—forged in blood and glory—produce a special resistance against both integration into administrative roles and the transformation of partisanship into a medium of political exchange? As we shall see, not all of the crisis-recruited mayors retain their identification with the party or movement that brought them into politics. For others, the intense and ideological identification of the past has been transformed, through the years, for some into a vehicle of political exchange, and for others into a residual identification distinct from their administrative roles. The explanation for this erosion of partisan intensity, and for the different paths of political involvement followed by the crisis-recruited mayors in each country, can be found in part in the effects of earlier socialization experiences, and in part through the effects of involvement in local institutional roles in each political system.

The three models of the polity referred to above—the subcultural model, the exchange model, and a model of institutional constraints—will guide us as we turn, first, to the actual distribution of periods of recruitment—crisis and noncrisis—among the mayors in each sample; secondly, to their present-day patterns of political and administrative involvement, and, third, to the impact of earlier political socialization experiences on their later political roles.

Crisis-Recruited Mayors in Local Politics: Definition and Distribution

Our first problem was to arrive at a definition of the periods of modern French and Italian history that we could reasonably consider "years of crisis." Historians often define crisis periods with the eye of the omniscient observer, and, indeed, such an approach has recently been explored by students of politics, too. But it is conceivable that a political system may experience a crisis in which particular groups of individuals are not deeply involved.[11] We needed a definition of periods of crisis that would have been meaningful to a man entering politics at the time. On the other hand, a *wholly* subjective approach to the definitional problem presented other dilemmas. If our only criterion were subjective involvement in a crisis, it would be easy to define the concept so broadly as to include the initial involvement in politics of almost every future political leader.

Our response to these dilemmas was to follow a two-stage definitional procedure. First, we turned to the history texts, where there was little difficulty in isolating the *general* periods of recent French and Italian history that historians consider to be years of crisis. Several of these periods were common to both countries and, indeed, to Europe as a whole. The war years from 1914 to 1918 and from 1939 to 1945, and the crisis of parliamentary democracy between 1945 and 1948 were the most obvious of these. In addition, French historians commonly referred to the Popular Front as an era of crisis, while Italian sources tended to regard the entire period from the end of World War I to the definitive installation of fascist totalitarianism as one of substantial political tension.

In order to refine these categories further, we decided to poll twenty historians and political scientists who have worked extensively on modern French and Italian politics in order to define a particular year as one of crisis or normalcy.[12] The problems with this approach were obvious, but a reasonable amount of consensus did, in fact, emerge among our two panels of experts, allowing us to settle on the definition of the "years of crisis" in the recruitment experiences of the two samples of local elites that is found in Table 8.1.

Several features stand out about the crisis-recruited mayors in each system. First, there has obviously been a high attrition rate due to death and retirement from the crises during and after World War I. Second, still the largest proportion of the mayors—approximately forty percent in each system—entered politics during the *central* crisis period of modern European history, the 1940s, when the conflict between left and right coincided with a territorial struggle of unprecedented magnitude. Estimation is difficult, but assuming something like a normal rate of attrition, upward mobility, and death, it appears that an unusually large core of the sample remains in each country from this generation of war, resistance, and liberation.

In contrast, the *non*crisis periods of domestic politics between 1948 and the late 1950s produced a sharp decline in the recruitment of local elites, or at least in the number of mayors recruited from this period who were still in office when this study was conducted. Compared to the forty-two percent of the Italians who came from the 1939-1948 crisis period, only twenty-six percent entered politics between 1948 and 1959. And compared to the thirty-seven percent recruited from the 1940s in France, only five percent of the French mayors entered politics between 1949 and 1958. Under "normal" circumstances, one would have expected to find a larger proportion of mayors in power now who were recruited during the more recent period. The fact that the generation of war, the Resistance, and the liberation was still numerically dominant between 1969 and 1972, when our study was conducted, seems to

TABLE 8.1
CRISIS-RECRUITED MAYORS:
NUMBERS AND PERCENTAGE OF TOTAL SAMPLE

ITALY			*FRANCE*		
Period of Recruitment	N	%	Period of Recruitment	N	%
1914-1924	(3)	2.5	1914-1919	(4)	3.7
1939-1948	(51)	42.1	1934-1939	(16)	14.6
1960-1961	(14)	11.6	1940-1948	(40)	36.7
1968-1971	(4)	3.3	1958-1959	(6)	5.5
			1968	(0)	0.0
Total Crisis-recruited	(72)	59.4	Total Crisis-recruited	(66)	60.5
Total Sample	(121)[a]		Total Sample	(109)[a]	

[a] There were an additional 10 Italian and 8 French mayors whose period of recruitment could not be exactly determined.

testify to the continued importance, even in local politics, of the central crisis of each country's recent history.

Nevertheless, from the political and social composition of the crisis subsamples, we can see that a certain amount of attrition or mobility seems to have occurred from the crisis generation. The war and the Resistance were apparently times of great left-wing recruitment into French and Italian politics.[13] Yet the ideological composition of both our crisis cohorts leans slightly to the right. In Italy, nearly two-thirds of the mayors who entered politics during years of crisis are Christian Democrats or rightists, and only thirty-five percent are Communists or Socialists, probably a sign that many leftists whose political careers began after the war have now moved upward or have left politics altogether. In France, over half the crisis-recruited mayors are centrists, Gaullists, or Independent Republicans, and less than one-third are Communists or Socialists. In both countries, as Table 8.2 shows, relatively more conservatives than radicals from those who were recruited into local politics during years of crisis have remained in the local political elite, in contrast to the non-crisis-recruited group, where the balance is further to the left.

Much the same can be said for the social bases of the mayors' recruitment. In the resistance culture of each political system, there are images of strong proletarian and rural mobilization: The *capopopolo* who emerged from the Resistance as a local political militant in Italy; the peasant *maquis ard* who hid allied agents in his cellar in France. However, twenty-five years after the end of the war, there were few of these lower-class or rural militants left in the crisis-recruited group of mayors. On the contrary, as Table 8.3 reveals, if there is a social imbalance in the crisis-recruited group in each system, it is slightly weighted toward the traditional political class of teachers and liberal

TABLE 8.2
CURRENT PARTY ATTACHMENTS OF
CRISIS-RECRUITED AND NON-CRISIS-RECRUITED MAYORS
ITALY AND FRANCE (in percentages)

ITALY	Nonpartisan	PCI	PSI	PRI	DC	RIGHT
Crisis-recruited	0.0	19.7	15.5	1.4	63.4	0.0
Non-crisis-recruited	2.0	28.0	12.0	6.0	48.0	4.0

FRANCE	Nonpartisan	PCF	PSU-SFIO	RADI-CAL	CEN-TER	UDR
Crisis-recruited	4.6	18.5	13.8	12.3	18.5	32.3
Non-crisis-recruited	11.6	18.6	32.6	7.0	11.6	18.6

TABLE 8.3
PROFESSION AT TIME OF FIRST POLITICAL INVOLVEMENT,
CRISIS- AND NON-CRISIS-RECRUITED MAYORS,
ITALY AND FRANCE
(in percentages)

	Farmers	Urban and Rural Workers	Old Middle Class	New Middle Class	Teachers and Lib. Profs.	Owners Mgrs.	Coop. Syndical	Soldier P.O.W. Resistant
ITALY								
Crisis-recruited	2.8	14.1	5.6	14.1	54.9	1.4	1.4	4.2
Non-crisis-recruited	6.0	20.0	8.0	18.0	40.0	4.0	2.0	0.0
FRANCE								
Crisis-recruited	10.6	9.1	10.6	22.7	30.3	3.0	4.5	9.1
Non-crisis-recruited	25.6	20.9	9.3	11.6	30.3	2.3	0.0	0.0

professionals in Italy (with 55% of the total) and toward the new middle class of white-collar workers and public employees (with 23%) in France. Both farm owners and rural workers are *under*-represented among the crisis-recruited mayors in both systems, particularly in the latter country.

Thus, there seems to have been a certain amount of leadership renewal among the local political class in each country over the past twenty-five years. But the differences between the two samples in this respect are great, with surprisingly few of the French mayors having entered the political system around the epochal crises of 1958 and 1968, and a larger number of Italian mayors having begun their political careers during the less explosive crises of the early and late 1960s. The French mayors are, first of all, older. Table 8.4 shows that, while three-quarters of the Italian crisis-recruited mayors were born after 1920, less than thirty percent of their French counterparts are found in this age group, and, while only six percent of the Italian crisis-recruited mayors were born before 1911, over two-fifths of their French counterparts were born during this earlier period. The average age of the French mayors recruited during times of crisis was 58.5, somewhat less than the average of 63.3 of their non-crisis-recruited colleagues, but much higher than the 46.7 average age of the crisis-recruited in Italy.

What do these age differences mean? In part, they reflect a historical difference; almost fifteen percent of the French mayors entered politics during the crisis period of the Popular Front in the 1930s, a period when it would have been extremely difficult for an Italian to have entered politics and still be active today. But there is another reason as well, one which takes us into the nature of the recruitment process as it affects the individual's future political involvement. The French crisis-recruited mayors were older, on the average, than their non-crisis-recruited compatriots *when they entered* political life. As Table 8.5

TABLE 8.4
PERIOD OF BIRTH,
CRISIS- AND NON-CRISIS-RECRUITED MAYORS,
ITALY AND FRANCE

	Before 1911	1911-1920	After 1920	Total % (N)
ITALY:				
Crisis	5.6	19.5	74.9	100.0 (72)
Non-crisis	16.0	30.0	54.0	100.0 (50)
FRANCE:				
Crisis	42.4	28.8	28.8	100.0 (66)
Non-crisis	64.3	21.4	14.3	100.0 (42)

TABLE 8.5
AGE OF FIRST POLITICAL INVOLVEMENT,
CRISIS- AND NON-CRISIS-RECRUITED MAYORS,
ITALY AND FRANCE

	Before 20 years	21 to 30 years	Over 30 years	Total % (N)
ITALY:				
Crisis	33.3	53.7	13.0	100.0 (69)
Non-crisis	21.2	51.1	27.7	100.0 (47)
FRANCE:				
Crisis	25.8	24.3	49.9	100.0 (66)
Non-crisis	42.8	42.8	14.4	100.0 (42)

shows, half of them were over thirty at this time, compared with only fourteen percent of their colleagues, and only one-quarter entered politics before the age of twenty, compared with forty-two percent of their colleagues. In contrast, the Italian crisis-recruited group was more likely to have entered politics at an early age than the rest of the Italian sample. One-third of them were less than twenty at the time they entered politics, compared with twenty-one percent of the other Italians, and only thirteen percent were over thirty compared with twenty-eight percent of the rest of the Italian sample. Thus, if the French crisis-recruited group turns out to have a lower level of political involvement and activity than their Italian counterparts, it may reflect, at least in part, their greater age and more complete prior formation at the time of the crisis during which they entered public life.

Crisis and Non-Crisis Recruitment:
The Experiences Compared

Local politics has often been described as the realm of factional bickering and petty interest trading or of local drives to improve the community. In a well-documented study, Prewitt has shown that local leaders in California most frequently entered politics in connection with civic or community issues or in search of personal status or rewards, and that the vehicles of their recruitment were mainly local associational groupings.[14] For the *non*-crisis-recruited mayors interviewed in Italy and France, local issues and group memberships were also quite important in bringing them into politics for the first time. For example, when asked about the circumstances which led to their first election to the council, forty percent of these mayors in Italy and thirty-five percent in France spoke of local or community problems as the direct cause of their political recruitment and another eighteen percent in Italy and thirty-five percent in France mentioned local associations as their channel of recruitment. As one non-crisis-recruited French mayor said,

> I've always been president of something or another; the veterans, the prisoners of war. . . . I've always been pointed out by people who say, "He has the air of someone who knows how to get things done" [nonpartisan].

And according to an Italian mayor,

> Even before becoming mayor, I had been for years the president of a sport society of 800 members. After that, in 1948, I became president of the provincial section of the Federation of Sport Fishing and also of the SAT (Tridentine Alpinist Society) [DC].

The crisis-recruited mayors were far less likely to mention community problems or local associations when discussing their entry into politics. In Italy, thirty-five percent mentioned these two categories combined (68% for the non-crisis mayors) and in France forty-six percent did (70% for the non-crisis-recruited). In both countries, the crisis-recruited mayors talked mainly about massive social movements, important national or international events, and great personal tragedies in connection with their entry into public life.

For the mayors recruited before the war, social or political movements were most frequently cited events connected with their recruitment. For instance, a French mayor recruited during the Popular Front period said,

> I remember the strikes in the region around Carmaux in 1934, before the Popular Front. One man was trying to break the strike and get to his place of work. The others wanted to stop him. He took out a gun and shot at the crowd. Then the people tried to overturn the car in which they had put him [PCF].

An Italian mayor's first political involvement took a somewhat different form. Now a Social-Democrat, he was asked what his first exposure to politics had been. He responded, perhaps ironically, "The beautiful days under fascism when you really believed in it all. The *ballilla,* the *avanguardisti,* all of the stuff; we really liked it" (PSU).

Other crisis-recruited mayors had been more personally involved in social and political conflicts. For example, a French Socialist said,

> I was 24 years old. I took part in the great demonstration of February, 1934, where there were two people killed, one of them a student, at Limoges. . . . When you came out of school there were demonstrations at least once a week that often ended up at the police station [SFIO].

And an Italian Communist said,

> I remember one night in 1924. The fascists came to my house to search for my father, who had fled to the woods, and wanted to break down the door and beat him up [PCI, father also a Communist].

The mayors recruited into politics during the war of 1939-1945 were even more deeply bound up with the great events of their day. A French résistant said,

> At the beginning, there were the refugees hiding in the forest, and we used to feed them. But you can't live forever in the forest. . . . So we gave them false identity papers so they could go and live in town. . . . Then we started to have contacts with the leaders of the Liberation, and finally [in 1944] we began to get arms, and I myself created a group of *maquisards* [Republican-Independent].

The Italian crisis-recruited mayors told equally vivid stories. One mayor said,

> I was formed politically in Russia, as a prisoner of war, by reading and by looking around myself, and listening to people talk about how things were in that great country. I came back to R . . . after eleven years of prison and right away joined the party to put into practice the ideas I had acquired [PCI].

The early postwar period was equally rich in such formative experiences. One Gaullist mayor spoke of having been an electoral worker for the RPF: "It was very exalting to be in politics at that time: You got beat up just for putting up posters and lots of nights we ended up at the police station" (UDR). An Italian mayor spoke of an exaltation of a different sort:

> Returning from a prison in 1946, I went to vote. It was something totally new, before there were none. There was a mass of people, it seemed like it was a party. It made a deep and positive impression on me[DC].

The role of intense partisan involvement was frequently highlighted in the crisis-recruited mayors' reports of their entry into politics. For example, one Italian mayor said,

> Politically . . . it was the 25th of July, in 1943. I was a university student in medicine in Padua. Not very enthusiastic about the regime, I offered resistance and ended up in jail after the 18th of September of that year. During the period of left-wing domination, I escaped, and in '45 I founded the local section of the Christian Democracy, which I directed until we took power here in '48[DC].

A French Communist was even more explicit. He said,

> It was just after the war. I was asked to be the local secretary of the Jeunesse Communiste when its name had just been changed to the Jeunesse Republicaine to attract more young people from other social groups. . . . It was full of enthusiasm, it is my most beautiful memory of political life.

But the role of national solidarity and even of anti-partisanship was occasionally also invoked. For example, when describing his participation in the Resistance, a conservative French mayor said, "For me it was different than for many others who had a political goal. For me it was simply as a Frenchman whose country was occupied by the Germans."

An Italian Socialist spoke similarly of his participation in the Resistance. He said, "I just found myself in it, and even though it is not my nature to get involved in politics, at the first post-war administrative elections, I found myself elected as a city councilman" (PSI).

Whether or not they were deeply involved in a clandestine resistance organization, a mass social movement, or a political party, for the mayors recruited into politics during years of crisis their entry into politics stands out in their memories as the most exciting episode of their public lives. But whether these experiences play a dominant role in determining their later beliefs and behavior is a different question, and one which we will now begin to explore.

CRISIS RECRUITMENT AND PATTERNS OF
POLITICAL INVOLVEMENT

We suggested earlier that recruitment during a historical crisis like the Resistance, the war or the liberation from fascism might have one or two main effects on a local political leader. Fueled by the impassioned ideological commitment of those times, he might remain closely linked to the party organization with which he identified at the outset, immerse himself in an ideological subculture, and continue to reflect a deep hostility to political opponents. Or, conversely, he might be led from the intense political solidarities characteristic of his period of recruitment to more routine involvements in politics and into greater satisfaction with the game of politics as it is played at his level of the political system.

To what sorts of indicators can we turn in testing these competing approaches to the attitudinal and behavioral correlates of crisis and non-crisis recruitment? First, we shall examine the mayors' partisan involvements, both in terms of their continuity of party membership, the extensiveness of their formal roles in party organizations and the intensity of their involvement in particular ideological subcultures. Second, we will look at their affect for the game of electoral and community politics, especially with respect to their contacts with leaders of other political tendencies. Third, we shall compare their reported satisfaction with and activism in both local politics and administration.

Partisan Continuity and Party Involvement

From the outset, in comparing these patterns of political involvement, we encounter a major contrast between the crisis-recruited local elites in each system: The Italians demonstrating a *higher* level of partisan involvement than their non-crisis-recruited colleagues, while the French reveal somewhat *less* involvement in parties and ideological subcultures than their non-crisis-recruited colleagues.

First, the French mayors who entered politics during times of crisis are significantly less likely than their colleagues to have retained the partisan identification they had at the beginning of their careers. In contrast, the Italian crisis-recruited mayors are significantly more likely than their colleagues to have the same party identification now as they did at the beginning. These relationships, which are presented in Table 8.6, may reflect the greater degree of partisan realignment that has occurred in France since the start of the Fifth Republic. That it is the *crisis*-recruited mayors who are most likely to have switched parties suggests that they are more closely associated with the volatility and low partisan identification of the French party system than are others who were recruited during calmer periods.[15]

Second, French crisis-recruited mayors are less deeply involved in party organizations than their non-crisis-recruited colleagues. The situation is exactly the reverse in Italy, where the crisis-recruited mayors have a higher average score on a composite index of party organizational experience than their colleagues.[16] As can be seen in Table 8.7, the differences in mean scores on

TABLE 8.6
PERCENTAGE OF CRISIS- AND NON-CRISIS-RECRUITED MAYORS
REPORTING A PRESENT PARTY ATTACHMENT
DIFFERENT FROM THEIR INITIAL ONE, BY COUNTRY

	Crisis-Recruited	Non-Crisis-Recruited
Italy	15.5	24.5
France	27.3	16.3

TABLE 8.7
MEAN SCORES ON INDICES OF PARTISAN INVOLVEMENT,
CRISIS- AND NON-CRISIS-RECRUITED MAYORS,
BY COUNTRY

	ITALY		FRANCE	
Index of:	Crisis-Recruited	Non-Crisis-Recruited	Crisis-Recruited	Non-Crisis-Recruited
Party Organizational Experience[a]	8.17	7.60	5.59	6.42
Involvement in a partisan subculture[b]	8.88	8.52	7.00	7.10

[a] Scores on the Index of Party Organizational Experience range from 3 to 22.
[b] Scores on the Index of Involvement in a Partisan Subculture range from 4 to 13.

the index of party organizational experience vary in the same direction as the party identification data reported above, with the crisis-recruited Italian mayors *more* likely, and the French crisis-recruited mayors *less* likely to be deeply involved in party organizations than their colleagues in each country.

Third, isomorphic, but slight differences are found between the two groups of mayors on an index of involvement in a partisan subculture that was also built out of the questionnaire items.[17] Although the differences are far from significant, it is enticing to consider that, many years after their initial recruitment, Italian mayors who were recruited during periods of crisis are more deeply involved, on the average, in partisan subcultures than their non-crisis-recruited colleagues; most of whom were more recently recruited into politics.

The durability of Italian partisan involvements emerging from past crises is revealed in a particularly dramatic way by a Christian Democrat mayor:

> In 1919, I had joined the *Partito Popolare*, the predecessor of today's DC, and I remained secretary of the local section for 6 years. In my thoughts, I never ceased to be a member, and when, after the Second World War, the DC was formed, I just joined what was, for me, only the historical continuation of the *Partito Popolare*.

But a *non*-crisis-recruited mayor from the same region, who joined the DC in the 1950s told a very different story: "I joined because they asked me to and since it wasn't a very great sacrifice and didn't mean much to me. In any case, I accepted the invitation and I joined."

However, the fact that the differences between the two groups of mayors on this psychological dimension of partisanship are so insignificant indicates that the intensity of subcultural partisan involvement of the Italian crisis-recruited mayors may have declined drastically as a result of their involvement in public life over the years.

Political Affect and Political Contacts

Does the crisis-recruited mayor retain the bitter partisan hostility of his period of recruitment, or has his initially intense political involvement been transformed into a positive affect for politics in general?[18] When the crisis-recruited mayors in Italy were compared with their colleagues along an index for affect in politics,[19] they scored slightly higher than their non-crisis-recruited colleagues, as can be seen in Table 8.8. In France, in contrast, the crisis-recruited group scored slightly lower in political affect. The differences in the means reported are not, we should add, statistically significant. However, they portray the Italian crisis-recruited mayors as more affectively involved in routine political life than their French colleagues, an

TABLE 8.8

MEAN SCORES ON INDICES OF POLITICAL AFFECT AND
POLITICAL CONTACTS, CRISIS- AND NON-CRISIS-RECRUITED MAYORS,
BY COUNTRY

	ITALY		FRANCE	
Index of:	Crisis-Recruited	Non-Crisis-Recruited	Crisis-Recruited	Non-Crisis-Recruited
Political Affect[a]	10.65	10.22	9.10	9.62
Political Contact[b]	11.00	10.65	8.66	9.00

[a] Scores on the Index of Political Affect range from 3 to 16.
[b] Scores on the Index of Political Contacts range from 3 to 12.

image which appears to lend more support to the "exchange" model of involvement than to the "subcultural" one in Italy.

Conversely, in France, many of those who entered politics during periods of crisis reveal both less affect for the game of politics and lower partisanship than those who entered public life during more normal times. As one French mayor, who joined a Resistance group during the German occupation, and was thrown into prison for it, said of his experiences, "But that wasn't really politics . . . it was patriotism. I have never really been involved in politics or supported a tendency."

What kinds of political behavior are associated with these different affective orientations? Liking the game of politics is no doubt associated with a broader network of political contacts and with an emphasis on the interpersonal aspects of political life. Hostility to politics is more likely to be found alongside an attempt to avoid the personal entanglements and commitments of the political game. Table 8.8 shows that, when the mayors were scored along an index of their political contacts,[20] the differences in the mean scores were consistent with the differences in political affect described above, with the Italian crisis-recruited mayors claiming to have a broader network of political contacts than their colleagues, and the French claiming fewer such contacts than their non-crisis-recruited counterparts.

At this point, we begin to clearly see the imprint of the national institutional differences described above. If the French who were recruited during periods of crisis have greater hostility to the political game than the Italians, is this not the result of the generally low party involvement we encounter everywhere in France? And if the Italian mayors' partisanship does not inhibit them from engaging in broad political exchanges, is this not the result of the general importance of party as a medium of exchange in the Italian party system? Clearly, as Table 8.8 shows, both crisis- and non-crisis-recruited mayors in Italy reveal higher levels of both political affect and of political contacts than either the crisis-recruited or the non-crisis-recruited mayors in France.

The differences in the mayors' institutional roles can explain an important part of these variations. In France, where a strong system of center-periphery linkages connects local government to the state, overt partisanship is discouraged, and those who have been in the system longest—almost by definition the crisis-recruited—may have turned away from partisanship and political exchange purely as a matter of practicality. In Italy, where the bureaucratic ties between center and periphery are weak and inefficient, the partisan and the politically active mayor has a better chance to capture resources for his community than one whose political contacts are few. Thus, the differences between crisis- and non-crisis-recruited mayors, which were fairly strong when we looked at partisanship and partisan continuity, are increasingly eroded as we move toward the mayors' involvement in their roles in local government.

Affect and Activism in Local Administration and Politics

How do these differences in attitudes, affective orientations, and political contacts relate to the mayors' orientations to their roles? The measures we have available to analyze this question are three: First, an index of the mayors' satisfaction with the administrative side of their roles; second, an index of their activism in using their offices to achieve projects and grants for their communities; and, third, an index of their more purely political and electoral activism in local public life.[21] These measures are presented for the crisis- and non-crisis-recruited mayors in each system in Table 8.9.

If crisis recruitment acted as a brake on integration into the administrative system, then we might expect the crisis-recruited mayors to score lower than their colleagues on the index of administrative satisfaction; that this is somewhat the case in Italy, but not in France, suggests the strength of involvement in administrative roles as a leveller of different personal orientations in France. But if crisis recruitment inhibited involvement in administration, it would no doubt express itself in lower levels of administrative activism among the crisis-recruited mayors. That this is somewhat the case in France, but not in Italy, may be due to the greater age, and resulting inactivity, of the French crisis-recruited mayors, compared to the greater youth and vitality of their Italian counterparts. On the index of political activism, the results are isomorphic with what we saw before. In Italy, crisis recruitment is associated with greater political activism—this time significantly—and in France with less, than is the case among the non-crisis-recruited mayors. In this case,

TABLE 8.9
MEAN SCORES ON INDICES OF ADMINISTRATIVE SATISFACTION AND
OF ACTIVISM IN LOCAL ADMINISTRATION AND POLITICS,
CRISIS- AND NON-CRISIS-RECRUITED MAYORS,
ITALY AND FRANCE

	ITALY		FRANCE	
Index of:	Crisis-Recruited	Non-Crisis-Recruited	Crisis-Recruited	Non-Crisis-Recruited
Administrative Satisfaction[a]	6.38	6.76	7.34	7.37
Administrative Activism[b]	4.68	4.36	5.24	5.40
Political Activism[c]	8.85	7.98	9.61	9.98

[a] Scores on the Index of Administrative Satisfaction range from 3 to 9.
[b] Scores on the Index of Administrative Activism range from 1 to 9.
[c] Scores on the Index of Political Activism range from 4 to 18.

the greater age of the mayors in the French crisis-recruited group may combine with the institutional effects we described above to constrain their political activity outside their offices, while in Italy, youth combines with the inducements of the politicization of the Italian administration to increase the level of political activism of the Italian crisis-recruited mayors.

These findings are ambiguous and once again show greater cross-national than intranational differences, indicating the increasingly great effect of the mayors' institutional roles as we move closer to their administrative and political activities. But two inferences can nevertheless be drawn from the findings on the relevance of the subcultural and exchange models of political involvement to French and Italian local politics. First, partisanship is no guarantee of sectarian closure; the positive affect for politics and higher levels of political contacts that we posited from the standpoint of the exchange model of involvement are more characteristic of Italian mayors with their greater involvement in party organizations. Second, nonpartisanship does not necessarily imply openness to political exchange; in the French crisis-recruited mayors, it goes hand in hand with hostility toward the political game and repugnance for compromising political contacts. In Italy, perhaps because of the omnipresence of the party, the intense partisanship of crisis-recruitment has lost its edge and has been transformed into an involvement in everyday political exchange. In France, parties have declined in importance since the postwar period and the once deeply partisan crisis-recruited mayors have shifted their sphere of activity to administration rather than to political exchange.

FAMILY BACKGROUND, AGE OF POLITICAL ENTRY AND IDEOLOGY AS CORRELATES OF POLITICAL INVOLVEMENT

Before turning to some of the broader implications of the impact of crisis recruitment on the structure of political cleavages in Italy and France, it would be worthwhile to attempt an explanation of the differences in the patterns of political involvement between crisis- and non-crisis-recruited mayors in these two political systems in terms of their own socialization and ideological formation. In doing so, we turn from a macro-political approach which stresses the historic circumstances at the moment of recruitment, to a micro-political perspective, which stresses individual variables such as the nature of the mayors' early family socialization, their age at the moment of recruitment, and their ideological formation, as possible explanations for the differences in political involvement we have found between the French and Italian crisis-recruited mayors.

Early Family Politicization

Do the most important socializing experiences take place early in childhood or during adult life? On this issue, much of the field of political behavior research remains divided, with one group adhering to a "primacy model" of socialization and the other to a "recency" model. "The first," writes Robert Weissberg, "asserts that fundamental and enduring attitudes, values and behaviors are formed *early* in childhood. . . . The underlying reasons for the primacy argument vary greatly, but agreement exists that early childhood socialization places enormous constraints and predispositions on subsequent development."[22] In contrast, the "recency" argument holds that "the closer a learning experience is to adulthood, the greater its influence and political relevance. . . . Because much of politics involves complex skills and concepts that are probably incomprehensible to most children, this recency argument has considerable appeal."[23]

This contrast between early and late political socialization raises an important question with respect to crisis recruitment. If an actor was intensively socialized into politics as a pre-adult, then recruitment during a crisis may have a consolidating or reinforcing effect on his political involvement, fixing it permanently at a high level of militancy. If, in contrast, recruitment during crisis was the first important political event in the actor's life, it may act as a surrogate for earlier socialization in politicizing him. But to the extent that the "primacy" model of socialization holds true for those who have not received a socialization in childhood, such "late" socialization cannot permanently shape their attitude toward public life, since it has no foundations on which to build. Thus the actor's level of political commitment will drop sharply once the crisis is past and routine problems again absorb the political elite. One possible explanation for the different levels of political involvement of the French and Italian crisis-recruited mayors is that the entry into politics of the French was not preceded by a primary socialization sufficient to lay the groundwork for a permanently high commitment and level of activity in public life. By examining the early socialization experiences of the French and Italian mayors, we may be able to determine whether the relative *apolitisme* we found among the French is in any way related to a lack of prior political foundation-building in childhood.

In turning to the early socialization experiences of the men in our samples, we find that many of them in both countries received an early political formation well before the systemic crises whose impacts we have been studying took place. From the interview schedule, an index of childhood family socialization was constructed.[24] When this index was trichotomized, as we can see in Table 8.10, it appeared that over sixty percent of the Italians and seventy percent of the French came from families where there had been at least some political activity, while thirty-two percent in Italy and thirty-eight percent in France had come from *highly* politicized families.[25]

These findings seem to concur with Prewitt's observation from a California study that a large proportion of "politically socialized" local elites gained their first consciousness of politics at home, with many coming from families that had been reservoirs of political talent in the past.[26] However, the character of this family socialization in Italy and France appears to have been more intense than what Prewitt describes, bordering, at times, on what must have been a family political tradition. For example, one French mayor said, "From my most tender youth . . . I was the son of a man of politics. My parents kept a café where all the meetings of the Socialist party were held"(PCF).
And another remembered,

> The first time I went to the école laique; there were only two of us in the village . . . all the others went to the parochial school. They even offered my father money to pay for my studies if I would go to the church school like everybody else, but he refused[SFIO].

TABLE 8.10
MAYORS' EARLY FAMILY POLITICIZATION
BY COUNTRY

	Low	Medium	High	Total %	(N)
Italy	39.7	28.2	32.1	100.0	(131)
France	27.3	34.2	38.5	100.0	(117)

Similar memories could be found in Italy. For example:

> When I was little, I remember my father's tirades against the priests and the Church, with my mother sitting quietly and saying he oughtn't to say such things in front of me. . . . In 1945, I joined the party amid an enormous feeling of enthusiasm around here. I took part in meetings, I listened to the discussions, the stories of ex-partisans, and in the same year I joined the Young Communists' Federation[PCI].

Even more marked was the early political formation of this mayor, who remembered the following incident: "It was 1924, I was called, with a friend of mine, to the fascist party headquarters and they demanded that we join the PNF. But we wouldn't do it, because we were antifascists"(PSI).

When we compare the crisis- and non-crisis-recruited mayors in each country in light of the "primacy" model of political socialization, a partial explanation of lower levels of later political involvement suggests itself for the French. For while, in Italy, entering politics during a historic crisis was more likely to follow a high level of prior family socialization, in France it was not. As Table 8.11 shows, in Italy, forty-two percent of the crisis-recruited mayors and only twenty-four percent of the non-crisis-recruited came from highly politicized family backgrounds; in France, thirty-eight percent of the former and an almost identical proportion of the latter received an intense politicization in the family. Moreover, one-third of the French crisis-recruited mayors, compared to twenty-one percent of their colleagues recruited during more normal times, came from totally nonpolitical family backgrounds. Here is one possible explanation for the decline in the political involvement of the crisis-recruited in France during their later public life: For many, political activism lacked underpinning of a primary political formation in the family.

TABLE 8.11
EARLY FAMILY POLITICIZATION
CRISIS- AND NON-CRISIS-RECRUITED MAYORS,
ITALY AND FRANCE

	Low	Medium	High	Total %	(N)
ITALY:					
Crisis	27.8	30.5	41.7	100.00	(72)
Non-Crisis	50.0	26.0	24.0	100.0	(50)
FRANCE:					
Crisis	33.3	28.8	37.9	100.0	(66)
Non-Crisis	20.9	41.9	37.2	100.0	(43)

A second feature stands out about the Italian sample. For as well as revealing a greater proportion of early-socialized mayors among them, these differences are heightened when we consider the historical context of family political socialization during their childhood. Since the majority who entered politics during the period from 1939 to 1948 were less than thirty at that time, they must have grown up during the most oppressive period of fascism, when to speak of politics within the hearing of outsiders could mean imprisonment or death. That their parents brought up many of these crisis-recruited mayors to have political ideas suggests a political commitment involving a great deal of courage. In contrast, the French recruited into politics during the 1930s or 1940s grew up in the relatively liberal atmosphere of the Third Republic. Needless to say, conflict was rife in France during this period, as many of our interviews testify, but repression of unorthodox or outspoken political ideas was relatively rare.

Thus, even the French crisis-recruited mayors who received a political socialization in the family may have been socialized into the relatively calm culture of local politics that characterized much of provincial France during the 1910s and 1920s. We have no direct evidence that demonstrates the quality of politics in the villages, towns, and cities of that time, but we need not exaggerate its bucolic quality to recognize with writers like Maurice Bedel, that many of the conflicts in local politics at that time were inspired by local notables for their amusement or social gain, and followed by a skeptical peasantry which was often inured to the game of politics.[27] Far different was the quality of local political life under fascism.

The evidence reported in Table 8.12 is largely consistent with such an interpretation of the historical circumstances of each country as they imposed themselves on the family socialization of the two groups of crisis-recruited mayors. The Italian evidence reported there lends much support to the "primacy" argument outlined above. Among those Italian crisis-recruited mayors who came from politicized families, consistently higher levels of adult involvement are found than among those who came from less political backgrounds. However, in France, a linear relationship between family politicization and adult involvement levels exists for the crisis-recruited mayors only with respect to the index of administrative effect. Table 8.12 shows very little variance in the mean scores on the other indices for those French mayors who came from families with high, medium and low levels of politicization.

TABLE 8.12
CRISIS-RECRUITED MAYORS, MEAN SCORES ON
POLITICAL AND ADMINISTRATIVE INDICES
BY LEVEL OF EARLY FAMILY POLITICIZATION
AND COUNTRY

Index of:[a]	ITALY			FRANCE		
	Low	Med.	High	Low	Med.	High
Party Organizational Involvement	6.85	8.36	8.90	5.91	4.42	6.20
Party Subcultural Involvement	7.93	8.56	9.68	7.67	6.36	7.05
Political Affect	10.76	9.81	11.22	9.00	9.00	9.24
Political Contacts	10.32	10.81	11.57	8.89	8.31	8.75
Administrative Affect	6.25	6.35	6.50	6.75	7.28	7.91
Administrative Activism	4.10	5.41	4.53	4.73	5.74	5.32
Political Activism	8.25	8.82	9.27	10.23	9.26	9.32

[a] For range of scores on indices see Tables 8.7, 8.8, and 8.9.

Age Cohort

A second aspect of the "primacy" versus "recency" argument takes us further in explaining the differences in political involvement of the two crisis-recruited samples of mayors. It seems reasonable to suppose that an experience such as recruitment during a political crisis would have a deeper and more lasting impact upon youth than upon men whose personal development was already well advanced. Indeed, for a very young man, crisis recruitment might be a primary experience in itself, capable of setting the pattern for later political involvement. Thus, high levels of political involvement later would be more commonly found among those who were recruited into politics when they were young than for men who entered public life when they were more fully formed.

Table 8.13 shows that this is indeed the case for France, but not for Italy. When the crisis-recruited mayors were divided into those who entered political life before the age of twenty-five and those who entered politics at a later age, we find no significant differences among the Italians for any of the measures of political and administrative involvement. (Indeed, on the two administrative measures, both affect and activism were found to be higher, on the average, for the Italian mayors who entered politics later in life than for the younger ones.) But in France, the mayors who entered politics before the age of twenty-five scored higher—in some cases significantly so—than their colleagues who entered politics later on five of the seven measures of involvement. On a sixth—administrative affect—there are no differences between the two groups, and on a seventh—political contacts—the older French crisis-recruited mayors scored higher than their younger colleagues.

TABLE 8.13
CRISIS-RECRUITED MAYORS,
MEAN SCORES ON POLITICAL AND ADMINISTRATIVE INDICES,
BY AGE COHORT AT TIME OF RECRUITMENT
AND COUNTRY

	ITALY		FRANCE	
Index of:[a]	25 years or younger	26 years or older	25 years or younger	26 years or older
Party Organizational Involvement	8.28	8.30	6.50	5.04
Party Subcultural Involvement	9.09	8.86	7.84	6.42
Political Affect	10.56	10.91	10.17	8.43
Political Contacts	11.07	11.00	8.06	8.94
Administrative Affect	6.22	6.66	7.30	7.36
Administrative Activism	4.49	5.00	5.71	4.97
Political Activism	8.90	8.77	10.50	9.09

[a] For range of scores on indices see Tables 8.7, 8.8, and 8.9.

These findings take on added interest when we recall that the French crisis-recruited mayors were far more likely to have entered politics at an advanced age than either their Italian counterparts or their French colleagues. Half were over thirty when they were recruited, compared to thirteen percent of the Italian crisis-recruited mayors and fourteen percent of the non-crisis-recruited French. It is obvious, therefore, that—in dealing with France—we have a crisis-recruited sample that entered politics at a later stage of the life cycle than any of the other groups of mayors. The evidence in Table 8.13 shows that, had the age of the French mayors been distributed more "normally," their levels of political and administrative involvement might have been higher, and they would have resembled the Italian crisis-recruited mayors more in this respect.

But, of course, the French crisis-recruited mayors' later political entry is a political reality, and not merely an artifact of the sampling process that can be factored out by the administration of appropriate controls. That a number of French mayors were catapulted into local political life in their thirties, forties, and fifties by a major national crisis testifies to the catalytic function of such crises and to its capacity to bring into politics individuals who might otherwise have remained in private life. More than one observer of French politics has noted the system's tendency to attack change through a series of fits and starts, with long periods of relative political stalemate succeeded by sudden moments of crisis during which pent-up energy is released, overdue policy changes are brought about, and, inter alia, the political elite is renewed. What stands out about our sample of French local elites is:

(1) that even as late as 1970, the bulk of crisis-recruited mayors were products of the central crisis of the nation from the mid-1930s to the late 1940s;

(2) that leaders recruited during more recent crises—most notably, those of 1958 and 1968—have, as yet, failed to dislodge them in large numbers from local power positions and,

(3) that the crises that brought our sample into public life were sufficiently severe to energize older men into beginning a political career after their basic lifestyles had been formed.

It is partly the presence of these older men that helps give French local politics much of its suffocating air of *apolitisme*, an air that—if normal generational forces continue uninterrupted—will perhaps be dissipated as younger age cohorts, formed politically at an earlier age and during different crises, begin to take their place in local politics. At the national level, with the passing of de Gaulle and the recent defeat of his successors, the modernization of French political life is already under way.

Ideology, Institutions, and Political Involvement

The mention of de Gaulle and national politics in general may puzzle those who are accustomed to thinking of French politics as distinct from national life. But there is a parallel between the two which serves to bring together several strands of the explanation we have offered for the lower level of political involvement of the French crisis-recruited mayors and of the higher level of the Italians. We saw earlier that half the French crisis-recruited mayors were centrists or conservatives, compared to the almost two-thirds of the Italians who are associated with conservative groups or parties. In contrast, as we saw in Table 8.2, among the non-crisis-recruited in each country, left-wing mayors were far more common, and mayors associated with the majority party were in a distinct minority.

When we compare the scores of the crisis- and non-crisis-recruited mayors in each country on an index of ideological radicalism,[28] we find the mean scores to be almost identical in Italy, while in France the crisis-recruited are more conservative, despite the fact that there are more mayors who identify with conservative parties among the Italians. In other words, despite a greater frequency of conservative party identifiers, the Italian crisis-recruited group is identical in ideological coloration to non-crisis-recruited colleagues, while the French, with more left-wing party identifiers among them, score substantially lower on the index of radicalism than their non-crisis-recruited compatriots. These ideological contrasts are underscored in Table 8.14 where we compare the mean scores on the index of radicalism of the crisis- and non-crisis-recruited mayors in each country. Within each political category—Communist, non-Communist Left, Center-Right, and apolitical—the crisis-recruited in France are more conservative than the others, while in Italy, the scores of the corresponding groups vary in a far less predictable fashion.

TABLE 8.14
MEAN LEVEL OF IDEOLOGICAL RADICALISM
CRISIS- AND NON-CRISIS-RECRUITED MAYORS
BY COUNTRY AND POLITICAL CATEGORY

Political Family	ITALY		FRANCE	
	Crisis-Recruited	Non-Crisis-Recruited	Crisis-Recruited	Non-Crisis-Recruited
Communist	14.3	14.7	13.7	13.9
Non-Communist Left	13.2	11.5	10.4	12.3
Center-Right	9.1	8.9	6.5	6.6
Apolitical	—	—	7.3	8.2
Total	11.1	11.0	8.9	10.3

Is it merely the higher age of the French crisis-recruited mayors which explains their greater conservatism? There is a significant negative correlation between the age of the mayor and his score on the index of radicalism in France, just as there is an association between age and conservatism for most population groups in most countries. But the association is stronger, in France, for the *non*-crisis-recruited mayors (-.41) than for their crisis-recruited counterparts (-.29), indicating that factors other than age are more powerful in explaining the greater conservatism of those French mayors who were recruited during periods of crisis.

Without in any way resolving the paradox, let us suggest an interpretation of both the greater conservatism and of the lower levels of political involvement of the French crisis-recruited mayors. Ideology is all too often taken to be equivalent between similar ideological groupings in different countries, when, in reality, its content can differ considerably. In Italy, where the dominant political party has for thirty years been the Christian Democrats, conservatism means above all fidelity to the Church and opposition to the Left, but it also implies an obligatory connection to the organized political subculture that the Church and the DC have constructed. Conservatism, in Italy, means many things, but its common denominator is the massive machine of patronage and religious affiliation built up by the Christian Democratic organizations since the war. Those Catholics who joined the Christian Democrats either from the Catholic Resistance or after the Liberation did so through a party organization or a Catholic affiliate, such as Catholic Action or the Christian trade union movement. Hence, for them, conservatism and political involvement of a highly partisan kind are unambiguously linked.

In France, this was not to be the case. The Resistance movement headed by General de Gaulle never gave rise to a coherent political organization, and many of the *resistants* recruited under the banner of the Cross of Lorraine were left to relapse into relatively unorganized political activity at the local level with the disintegration of the *Rassemblement du Peuple Francais* (RPF) in the early fifties. By the time the *Union pour la Nouvelle Republique* (UNR) appeared on the scene in 1958, most of these men—particularly those who lacked a prior political formation—had either retreated into private life or had become involved in local political roles of a decidedly nonpartisan cast. The Right, in France, has always been less well-organized politically than the Left, and with the failure of the Gaullists to build a serious party organization after the war—in no small part due to the ideological preferences of de Gaulle himself—a local politician with conservative sentiments who had been recruited into public life by the Gaullist resistance movement had no logical party to join. Hence, conservatism—at least of a Gaullist variety—was almost synonymous with a low level of party organizational involvement. This merged with an older tradition in French political culture which denied the efficacy of *all* political parties, and elevated the individual into the basic unit of politics. For these reasons, for local conservatives in France, particularly those recruited during the Resistance, nonpartisanship and conservatism are intricately linked.

But this is only part of the story, for it is not only on the Right that the crisis-recruited mayors in France revealed lower levels of political involvement. To explain this, we must turn to the factors discussed earlier—to the greater age and experience of the French crisis-recruited sample, to the weaker bases of their politicization in childhood, and in particular, to the institutional effects of a system of local administration that provides greater rewards for administrative activity than for the cultivation and manipulation of political resources. In Italy, in contrast, the crisis-recruited mayors are younger, less experienced, and—given the nature of the bureaucratic blockages between the local and national levels—better rewarded for their efforts if they engage in active politicking than if they stay in their offices all day filling out dossiers. Indeed, there is evidence that there is a great deal of *latent* partisanship in French local government among mayors who have a political identification and would act on it if the constraints of their role in the French administrative system did not sanction it. There is also a significant degree of *reluctant* partisanship among the Italian local elite, among mayors whose partisan commitment is slight, but who must engage in active politics in order to get resources for their communities where party is the major vehicle of political allocation.[29]

SOME OBSERVATIONS ON CRISIS RECRUITMENT AND POLITICAL CONFLICT

While the differences in political involvement presented above are not always statistically significant, or even unidirectional, they describe an overall pattern that can hardly be random or accidental. Compared to their non-crisis-recruited peers, the Italian crisis-recruited mayors are more likely to have had steady party identification, to be more deeply involved in a partisan subculture and more actively and effectively involved in political life, and to have more contacts with higher elected officials. Compared to their non-crisis-recruited colleagues, the French crisis-recruited mayors are more likely to have switched parties at one time or another, less likely to be deeply involved in partisan subcultures or active in and enthusiastic about political life, and are likely to have fewer contacts with higher elected officials. While the overall level of political involvement is higher in Italy, the variations between crisis- and non-crisis-recruited mayors move in opposite directions in each country.

Where then lies the impact of crisis recruitment in the system of political conflicts and cleavages that mark the face of French and Italian politics today? We might begin by noting the differential incidence of crisis-recruited mayors in French and Italian communes at different levels of economic prosperity. If these were mayors who governed large and thriving communes, the imprint of crisis might continue to play a direct role in structuring local political conflict in the future. But a brief inspection of the kind of communities they were elected to lead suggests the opposite inference. In Italy, crisis-recruited mayors are still in power mainly in smaller towns with declining populations that still tend to be heavily engaged in agricultural pursuits, and where the recent increase in nonagricultural employment has been minimal. In France, the crisis-recruited govern slightly larger towns with a growing industrial base, but there, too, the rate of population growth is lower than average and the shift into industry is taking place more slowly than elsewhere. Thus, the incidence of mayors recruited during the historic crises of the past is greater today in the backwaters of French and Italian politics than in the rapidly growing towns or more industrialized cities of each country.

Secondly, even if such leaders were more widely distributed in each country than they are now, we still could not assume that an initiation into politics in the crucible of past crises would produce an inclination to return to a politics of confrontation and near-civil war. It is true that recruitment during a historic crisis can remain among the most cherished memories of a political actor. As a city councillor from the South of France—recruited as a *résistant* in Paris many years before—recalled:

> Those times were really impassioned. You would put your life in the hands of someone whose name you didn't even know . . . whom you would probably never even see again. It was a very exciting time.

On the other hand, we have seen that, particularly for individuals recruited at an advanced age, initiation during a political crisis does not always leave the heritage of a high level of politicization and involvement. Indeed, not only advanced age at political recruitment, but age and experience in general can leave a mixed heritage of feeling with respect to a possible return to the conditions of crisis politics. When passions are inflamed and conflict heightened in the political system in general, friends become enemies, ordinary policy issues are infested with ideology, and the often-delicate equilibrium of local political life can be severely unbalanced. One conservative French mayor, himself recruited during the Vichy period and subsequently purged by the Left, put this most firmly: "The prefect helps this community because there are no longer any *histoires* here, and as long as I remain mayor, this is the way it is going to remain."

An Italian mayor led up to a similar point, by recalling an incident from the time of his own recruitment:

> I remember it well . . . too well. It was the end of the war. There was hunger and grain was rationed. They discovered a case of black-marketing here, and precisely in grain, with truckfuls of contraband wheat brought in from France. The crowd was in a fury, everyone in town poured into the square. Not knowing who to blame, they went to grab the town clerk, a poor guy who hadn't done anything wrong.

Thus the mayor reveals why he would scarcely contribute to a new state of crisis in his community:

> I won't tell you what a shock it was for me. The anonymous mob is a fearful thing, the individual in a crowd loses his head, he becomes a beast. There is nothing more frightening and more dangerous than the mob[PSI].

A French Communist was also deeply marked by the crisis of May-June 1968. But when asked to describe his greatest disappointment in public life, he said, "That you can struggle and struggle to help the people and then they turn against you like they did in June, 1968 with de Gaulle." He concluded with a surprising metaphor, given his partisan identification: "It was like Christ carrying the cross and being stoned by the people he was trying to help."

That conservative mayors should recall the bitterness of past crises with dread, and fear their revival, is understandable. But the responses of mayors on the Left are perhaps more difficult to interpret. In reflecting upon the cautious reaction of the official French and Italian Left to the popular uprisings of the past five years, many have interpreted their policies in rather diabolical terms. More basic may be the fear of a return to a state of crisis which, in the past, has never been beneficial to the Left in either country. From the Italian crisis of 1919-1921, fascism emerged the victor, and after the crises of 1958 and 1968, Gaullism was strengthened in France. More than anything, perhaps, it is the traumatic fear of a return to fascism that has sparked the recent Italian Communist call for a new "historic compromise" between the forces of the Left and of the constitutional Center-Right.

Thus, crisis-recruited politicians are not the source of continually renewed political conflict that they may seem to be at first glance. Indeed, to the extent that they continue to structure their images of politics along historical cleavage lines, they may exert a *conservative* influence in local politics, allowing the new issues of the environment, the modernization of urban services and administrative decentralization to penetrate the local governing class only with difficulty.

The really destabilizing influence of the heritage of crisis and conflict in Italy and France is far less direct. Because neither country has, thus far, succeeded in developing an ideologically neutral myth of its own past, historic crises continue to survive as axes of cleavages even as the personnel which lived through them are retired, gain in conservatism, or become tangential to the currents of change in the society. If each new crisis that comes along—and there have been many since the crisis of the 1940s—is instinctively poured into the vessels of the old, then a new crisis generation, which may lack organizational or even ideological ties with older cohorts of crisis-recruited leaders, cannot help being identified with its positions or against those of its enemies.

The paradox, as well as the irony it implies, was brilliantly pointed out by

Pierre Vidal-Naquet, in his introduction to the English edition of the *Journal de la Commune Etudiante.* "In France and in Italy," he wrote.

the very fact that there exist large workers' parties which are revolutionary in speech if not in practice . . . gives the student movement extraordinary confidence in the capacity for action of a working class "betrayed" by the unions and the political parties, and allows it to present itself as the University detachment of a revolutionary workers' party that does not exist.[30]

The heart of the irony underscored by Vidal-Naquet is that neither the new crisis generation nor the old one—despite their mutual suspicion—can escape this marriage that history has imposed upon them. And this situation will continue until such time as each nation develops an ideologically neutral myth of its own past, a development which may take some time in coming, if the intensity of present conflicts is any guide.

NOTES

1. Francois Mentré, in *Les Generations Sociales* (Paris, 1940), writes, p. 47: "All the men of a generation feel themselves linked by a community of standpoints, of beliefs, of wishes. Have they not been witnesses of the same events, have they not read the same books and applauded the same plays, have they not received the same education and observed the same deficiencies in society?" A more somber and analytical conceptualization of the notion of political generations is found in Rudolf Heberle, *Social Movements* (New York, 1951), chapter 6.

2. Thucydides, *The Peloponesian Wars,* Modern Library translation (New York, 1934), 184-185.

3. Because of the characteristics of local political recruitment in Italy and France, the number of mayors who entered politics during the crises of the late 1950s and 1960s was too small at the time of the interviews (1969-1972) to form a sizable enough cohort for analysis. But note that this to some extent reflects the weighting of our samples toward small towns, where turnover is somewhat lower than average. There is evidence that in the municipal elections of 1971, the first to follow the events of May 1968, in France, there was a significant degree of leadership turnover in the local political elite in larger French cities.

4. Indeed, one of the few well-documented findings in recent research about the adult consequences of childhood political socialization is that people who enter politics tend disproportionately to have come from families in which political activity was already present. See Kenneth Prewitt, *The Recruitment of Political Leaders: A Study of Citizen-Politicians* (Indianapolis and New York, 1970), chapter 4.

5. For a cogent analysis of some of the current problems of political socialization research, see Fred I. Greenstein, "A note on the ambiguity of 'political socialization': definitions, criticisms and strategies of inquiry," in Journal of Politics 32 (November 1970), 969-978. For a recent critique of the work on socialization in the family, especially in the United States, see R. W. Connell, "Political socialization in the American family: the evidence re-examined," Public Opinion Quarterly 36 (1972), 323-333.

6. Heinz Eulau has recently argued that intervening and adult experiences are more critical than earlier ones in determining adult political roles. Reflecting upon his own earlier work, he writes, "We sought to test the developmental hypothesis that predispositions brought to the adult role from prior

experiences account for adult political behavior. The evidence did not support the hypothesis. We therefore speculated that experiences intervening between early socialization and adult conduct, such as those stemming from recruitment and induction into politics, might be more relevant." *Micro-Macro Political Analysis* (Chicago, 1969), ix. Eulau's conclusion was perhaps prematurely pessimistic. Our data suggest some interactive effects between early socialization and the conditions of recruitment, rather than the absolute primacy of the latter over the former.

7. A major aim of the study was to investigate the strategies of local political elites on the periphery of centralized administrative systems in responding to rapidly changing economic conditions. Large cities were, therefore, underrepresented in the sample, and metropolitan areas were not studied at all. Details of the study and the sample will appear in Sidney Tarrow, "Integration at the Periphery: A Study of the Grassroots in Italy and France." For preliminary reports, see Tarrow, "Partisanship and Political Exchange in French and Italian Local Politics," Sage Professional Papers in Contemporary Political Sociology (Volume 1, 1974); Tarrow, "Local constraints on regional reform: a comparison of Italy and France," Comparative Politics 7 (October 1974), and "Local Activists in Public Life," in Donald L. M. Blackmer and Sidney Tarrow, eds., *Communism in Italy and France* (Princeton: Princeton University Press, 1975).

8. Subcultural models of political involvement are the bases of much of the work on mass party systems done in the 1950s and 1960s. For a survey of some of this literature and its ambiguities, see Tarrow, "Partisanship and Political Exchange," pp. 7-11. An excellent analysis of this literature is Arend Lijphart's "Typologies of democratic systems," Comparative Political Studies 1 (April 1968) 13-16.

9. Theories of political exchange can be found in a formalized version in Sidney Waldman, *Foundations of Political Action: An Exchange Theory of Politics* (Boston: Little, Brown, 1972) and in a less systematic, but perhaps richer form in Warren Ilchman and Norman T. Uphoff, *The Political Economy of Change* (Berkeley and Los Angeles: University of California Press, 1969).

10. A discussion which stresses the biases introduced by institutional role structures can be found in Tarrow, "Local constraints on regional reform." For a discussion of role theory and its applicability to comparative analysis, see John Wahlke, Heinz Eulau et. al., *The Legislative System: Explorations in Legislative Behavior* (New York and London: John Wiley, 1962), chapter 1.

11. For instance, the "crisis of penetration," the subject of an essay by Joseph La Palombara in Leonard Binder et al., *Crises and Sequences of Political Development* (Princeton, 1972), would probably not have been completed successfully under the French *ancien regime* had too many French nobles been aware of what the Capetians were up to. An elaboration of this point is found in Herbert Luethy, *France Against Herself* (New York, 1955), chapter 2.

12. Ten experts were canvassed for each system. Eight Italian experts and seven French experts responded. Among both groups, unanimity was approached only on the wartime years. A rate of agreement of six experts out of eight in Italy and five out of seven in France was considered sufficient for a particular year to be included in the "crisis" category. Note that economic criteria were not used in defining crises because of our assumption that economic crises do not affect different parts of the public with the same degree of uniformity as major political crises.

13. But note that at the national level, an Italian study shows, only a relatively modest proportion of the Communist Party's *personale dirigente* still in office during the early 1960s had been recruited during the 1940s. See Gianfranco Poggi, "Aspetti della composizione del personale dirigente del PCI e della DC (1945-1963)," in Instituto di Studi e Ricerche Carlo Cattaneo, *L'organizzazione partitica del PCI e della DC* (Bologna, 1968), 510.

14. Prewitt, *The Recruitment of Political Leaders*, 65-69.

15. There is now a tradition of interpretation of the low partisan identification characteristic of recent French politics, beginning with Philip Converse and Georges Dupeux's "Politicization of the electorate in France and the United States," Public Opinion Quarterly 26 (Spring, 1962), 1-23. A newer study that summarizes the literature since then, as well as making an empirical contribution, is Bruce A. Campbell, "The future of the Gaullist majority: an analysis of French electoral politics," in

American Journal of Political Science 18 (February 1974), 67-94. For a discussion of partisanship and nonpartisanship in rural France, see Tarrow, "The urban-rural cleavage in political involvement: the case of France," American Political Science Review 65 (June 1971), 341-357.

16. The index of party organizational involvement was constructed from the following information gathered from the interview protocols: (1) number of years of party attachment; (2) number of functions held in party; (3) highest function ever held in party organization.

17. The index of partisan subcultural involvement was constructed from the following categories of interview responses'; (1) the partisanship of group memberships before entering public office; (2) the number of partisan media sources regularly read; (3) the importance of political party in the mayor's concept of political activism; (4) the intensity of political discussion in the mayor's family.

18. For an interesting discussion of the relationship between political hostility and political generations, see Robert D. Putnam, *The Beliefs of Politicians; Ideology, Conflict and Democracy in Britain and Italy* (New Haven and London: Yale University Press, 1973), chapter 11.

19. The index of affect for political life was constructed from the following interview items: (1) affect for electoral campaigns; (2) affect for community meetings; (3) affect of first memory of political life.

20. The index was based upon the mayors' reports of the extensiveness of their contacts with politicians at higher levels of the political system: provincial councillors (conseilleurs généraux in France), parliamentary deputies and senators.

21. The index of administrative satisfaction is based on the following interview categories: (1) level of affect for the job of mayor; (2) desire to become mayor; (3) desire to continue as mayor. The index of administrative activism is based upon a variety of criteria: (1) preference for the administrative aspects of the role of mayor; (2) help sought and received from administrative officials at higher levels of government; (3) nature of projects sought for the community; (4) administrative character of most satisfying political experience. The index of political activism is based upon the following categories of interview responses: (1) number of group memberships before taking office; (2) number of local meetings organized; (3) holding office in a group at the present time; (4) level of electoral activity.

22. Robert Weissberg *Political Learning, Political Choice and Democratic Citizenship* (Englewood Cliffs, N.J.: Prentice-Hall, 1974) 24-25.

23. Ibid., 25.

24. The index of family politicization was constructed from interview responses on the following subjects: (1) whether politics was discussed at home during childhood; (2) father's level of interest in politics; (3) relatives having held public office; (4) whether father identified with a party and/or political tendency.

25. The definition of "highly politicized" was determined by the highest score on at least three of the four interview items included in the index and listed in note 24, above.

26. Cf. Prewitt, *The Recruitment of Political Leaders,* 68.

27. For discussion of this mode of local politics in provincial France, see Henri Mendras, *The Vanishing Peasant* (Cambridge, Mass.: MIT Press, 1970), chapter 7. Maurice Bedel writes of a village in the Limousin, "There are a rightist and a leftist blacksmith. One shoes pious horses, the other unbelievers. It is good that right-wing plows do not think like left-wing plows. This is what saves the village from boredom, what preserves this minimal activity" *Géographie de Mille Hectares* (Paris, Grasset, 1937), 114.

28. The index of ideological radicalism was constructed from the following interview items. "Do you agree or disagree that (1) strikes against the public services should be banned? (2) if the young people of today rebel, it is because there is insufficient discipline in their families? (3) state subsidies to private (religious) schools should be stopped? (4) France (Italy) is in need of a strong army? (5) large-scale industries ought to be nationalized?"

29. See Tarrow, "Partisanship and Political Exchange," 22-23.

30. Alain Schnapp and Pierre Vidal-Naquet, eds., *The French Student Uprising, November 1967-June 1968: An Analytical Record* (Boston: Beacon, 1971), 17.

Chapter 9

THE RECRUITMENT MARKET OF THE
GERMAN POLITICAL ELITE

WERNER KALTEFLEITER

Christian-Albrecht University

THE PROBLEM

The study of the German political elite has always been confronted with a basic political question: Does this elite represent the "ruling class" of a traditionally autocratic political culture, which today is acting behind the facade of a formally democratic constitution? Or is it an integrated part of an open and democratic society based on effective political competition, equal opportunities, free interchange among elites and non-elites and intergenerational mobility?

The scarcity of relevant empirical studies[1] reflects in part the recent development of modern social science in the Federal Republic of Germany. The methodological problems of sampling[2] an elite and the extremely high costs of such studies should also be mentioned. It can easily be explained, therefore, why the first studies concentrated either on certain segments of the elite or were limited to an analysis of the available aggregate data.[3] Finally, as E.K. Scheuch has pointed out, the word "elite" acquired an ideological connotation as a result of its abuse in the Nazi period, thus preventing serious analysis. Indeed, even today the danger of being misunderstood by using the term "elite" is real. "Fuehrungsschicht" (leading social class) or "Inhaber von Fuehrungspositionen" (top position holders) are often-used terms that avoid the historically problematic term "elite."[4] Whatever relevance this argument may have for the explanation of research development, it illustrates the basic question which is now being asked about the German political elite: Is it an instrument of an autocratic society and government, or an instrument of democracy?

The recruitment of the political elite is at least one variable in the answer to this question.[5] Of course, the political elite is not a homogeneous group, either in Germany or in other countries. Political party leaders, the legislature and top executives, on the state and federal level, constitute the hard core of the political elite. But top leaders in the economic system (big business, industrial organizations as well as trade unions), the civil service and the mass media cannot be excluded because of their involvement in the political decision-making process, and because of the actual behavior of these elites. In addition, by comparing these "neighboring" elites with the hard core of the political elite, the particular characteristics of the hard core may be more clearly delineated. In a competitive system the political elite cannot be isolated from the leading personnel in other sectors. The degree of interchange between the different strata of the elite is a relevant variable in answering the question of the political elite's openness or accessibility.

For several years discussions of the German political elite have focused on the question of the degree to which the elite had been transformed at the end of the Nazi regime. In fact, this happened neither in the Federal Republic nor in the German Democratic Republic,[6] and counting and comparing the number of "old" members of the elite in both political systems constitutes one of the futile exercises of contemporary politicians, commentators and analysts. As long as societies do not want to pay the price of heavy and prolonged frictions, the continuity of a highly sophisticated political, social and economic system requires the continuity of large parts of the elite, even if the political order changes dramatically, as it did in Germany after 1945.

The functional definition of an elite is based on professionalism. This implies a rather large recruitment reservoir for elites in an industrial society with a highly developed educational system. This reservoir, however, is restricted by the motivation of potential recruits—i.e., their willingness and propensity to compete and take risk in contests for certain top positions.

Additionally one should not overlook the fact that industrial societies require much more leadership in specific, differentiated functions.[7] There was in postwar Germany no real alternative to the continuity of large parts of the elite in the 1950s and early 1960s. This situation changed at the beginning of the 1970s. Twenty-five years are sufficient for intergenerational change; the changes in the governing coalition in 1966 and again in 1969 offer an opportunity to analyse how the composition of the political elite has been influenced by the changing results of elections and coalition bargainings.

The process of recruitment may analytically be divided into the processes of socialization and selection. In reality these are two sides of the same coin. The socialization process leads to the internalization of values and to the basic ability to adapt. Furthermore, the motivation to seek or qualify for an elite position is also a result of the socialization process. These are the main variables which make a person eligible and fit to fulfill a given position among the elite. The selection process consists of choosing adequately socialized individuals under certain conditions. The whole process may be described by three different dimensions:

(1) The reservoir dimension, which includes the opportunity for interchange between elites and non-elites.

(2) The qualificational dimension, which includes formal qualification, formalization of the patterns of upward social mobility and so on.

(3) The normative dimension, which includes adaptation to the norms, values and moral standards of the respective elites.

These three dimensions may be restated as three simple questions:

Where do the elites come from?
What stations do they pass before becoming part of the elite?
What do they know and believe?

The answers to these questions describe the relevant aspects of the recruitment process.

(1) The degree of intergenerational vertical mobility describes the reservoir as well as the degree of openness of the elite.

(2) High formal qualifications describe a functional elite. The question remains, how open the access to these qualifications is.

(3) The way to the top describes the patterns of success and reflects the structure of the communication and influence system of a society.

Empirical data to answer these questions have been taken from a study among 1,825 members of the German elite,[8] representing about sixty percent of a total of 3,000 defined by means of the positional approach.[9] The interviews were conducted in the spring of 1972.

THE SOCIAL PROFILE OF THE GERMAN ELITE

In 1965, both E. K. Scheuch[10] and Ralf Dahrendorf[11] pointed out—on the basis of research done by Wolfgang Zapf—that about fifty percent of the German elite are recruited from the upper or upper middle class, which altogether constitute only five percent of the total population, and two-thirds of the elite come from social groups which constitute ten percent of the whole population. The picture of a highly closed elite was very clear.

In 1968, however, in the first general elite study based on personal interviews,

Rudolf Wildenmann and his associates found that only about thirty percent of the elite were recruited from the upper and upper middle class.[12] The 1972 study generally confirmed this finding; the differences are the result of sampling: large sections of the German elite recruited from the middle class (e.g., the economic sector and the administration) were underrepresented in the 1968 study. Nearly forty percent of the 1972 elite described the positions of their fathers as "middle class" (Table 9.1). Of course, with only twelve percent among the elite, the lower class is still underrepresented. Even given the difficulties of comparing the different data, the trend is obvious: from a highly upper-class recruitment to a middle-class recruitment, which slowly tends to become open to the lower class.

More detailed description shows significant differences between the respective segments of the elite: next to the trade unions with forty-five percent lower-class recruitment (34% lower-middle class and 11% lower class), the political elite, in a narrow sense, shows the highest degree of lower class recruitment: twenty-four percent (Table 9.2). A strong tendency towards upper and middle class recruitment is still to be found in the economic sector, the bureaucracy and the mass media. But in these segments too, the percentage of lower- and lower-middle-class recruitment seems to be high enough to indicate a tendency toward

TABLE 9.1
SOCIAL BACKGROUND OF GERMAN ELITES AND POPULATION[a]
(in percentages)

Class	Elites				Population	
	1925 N = 244	1955 N = 251	1965 N = 800	1972 N = 1825	1955 N = 385	1968 N = 14,375
Upper/ upper middle	47	43	32	35	5	6
Middle	—	—	29	37	—	11
Lower middle	18	22	27	11	39	38
Lower	5	10	11	2	52	45
Not coded	30	25	—	15	5	—
	100	100	100	100	100	100

[a] The figures for 1925 and 1955 are based on the criteria developed by M. Janowitz, "Soziale Schichtung und Mobilitaet in Westdeutschland," *Koelner Zeitschrift fuer Soziologie* 10 (1958); those of 1968 are based on the slightly modified scale of G. Kleining and H. Moore, "Soziale Selbsteinstufung als Instrument zur Messung sozialer Schichten," *Koelner Zeitschrift fuer Soziologie* 20 (1968). The 1972 elite data and the 1968 population data are based on the Kleining-Moore scale. The most important difference between the Janowitz and the Kleining-Moore definitions is that Janowitz understands "gehobener Dienst" (high grade civil servants) as part of the upper-middle class, while according to Kleining-Moore they belong to the middle class.

TABLE 9.2
SOCIAL BACKGROUND OF ELITES (in percentages)

	Upper class/ Upper middle class	Middle class	Lower-Middle class	Upper lower class/ Lower class	Not coded[b]		Total
Politics[a]	26	35	19	5	15	= 100%	353
SPD	24	22	32	10	12	= 100%	123
CDU	25	44	11	3	16	= 100%	124
CSU	27	38	15	—	20	= 100%	48
FDP	32	42	11	—	16	= 100%	57
Administration	36	41	8	1	14	= 100%	549
Economic sector	45	34	7	1	13	= 100%	392
Trade unions	7	35	34	11	13	= 100%	62
Mass media	32	35	11	1	21	= 100%	264
Others	38	42	6	1	14	= 100%	205
Total N =	629/35	681/38	202/11	42/2	271/14	= 100%	1825

a Respondent of the political elite without party affiliation.
b This rather high percentage follows from the fact that respondents were asked about the father's social position at the age when they left school. At the time 180 (9.9%) of the fathers had already died, 40 (2.2%) had retired.

a more open elite. The differentiation according to father's occupation recon-firms these data, further emphasizing the distribution (table omitted). This difference between the political and nonpolitical elites may be explained by the former's lack of a formalized career path in contrast to most other elites (with the exception of the mass media, which are a very special case). The social cleavage between SPD and CDU/CSU is reflected in the social background of their respective elites:[13] Social democratic political leaders three times as frequently come from lower middle and lower class families as do CDU/CSU leaders; among the latter, the middle and upper-middle class is overrepresented. This is not surprising at all; what is important is that quite a few SPD leaders are recruited from the middle and upper-middle class and that about fifteen percent of CDU politicians are of lower-middle and lower-class origin.

Thus the major German parties are not exclusively class-based parties. The fact that they represent various social strata is reflected in both the social background of their elites and in the structure of their electorate.[14] This tendency toward an open elite is equally distributed between age groups. Lower-class recruitment is not stronger among the younger elites (table omitted).

Education is one of the most important avenues of vertical mobility in a modern society. Does an educational cleavage divide the German elite from non-elites? Indeed, 27.5 percent of the fathers of the present elite have a university degree (master or Ph.D.) or at least graduated from high school (14.6%). But more important seems the fact that fifty-four percent of the fathers of the present elite had no higher education (table omitted). This, of course, reflects the general tendency toward higher education in modern industrialized societies. Indeed, with respect to the father's education the figures for the population are very similar, with a slight tendency that a higher education of the father increases the likelihood of becoming a member of the elite. This was to be expected; what is important is that the differences between the total population and the elite is so small: 64.3% of the respondents' fathers had only primary school education, 12.9% had a university degree and 8.1% at least graduated high school.[15]

Vertical intergenerational mobility is highest among the political elite—second only to the trade unions. Among big business elites the percentage of people from a family with low educational background in remarkably high. Only in the civil service is the intergenerational change comparatively low, both with regard to the general level of education as well as the specific content of the education: Father and son usually went to law school to become members of the top administration.[16] Intergenerational mobility is reconfirmed by a comparison between fathers' and respondents' education: Nearly all members of the present elite with a highly educated family background received a high education themselves, but also more than seventy percent of those with father of only primary school education received a high school diploma (Table 9.3).

Considering the overall configuration of social background characteristics, three more or less typical recruitment patterns of the German elite emerge:

(1) The political elite: diversity in recruitment with certain strongholds among the middle class, heterogeneous professions of the father and high intergenerational mobility in education.
(2) Labor elite: lower-class recruitment with a high degree of intergenerational professional homogeneity and high mobility in education.
(3) Civil service and business elite: upper-class recruitment with high degree of educational and professional continuity.

Among other groups, academics come close to the third category, and the mass media approximate the first type.

ASPECTS OF THE SOCIALIZATION PROCESS

Religion has been traditionally an important source of cleavage in German society.[17] The elite was dominated by Protestants in a country that was between thirty-three percent (Weimar Republic) and forty-five percent (Federal Republic) Catholic. As far as religion as a political elite recruitment variable is concerned, the underrepresentation of Catholics has been decreasing since the beginning of this century. In postwar Germany, Catholics temporarily dominated among the top political elites in Adenauer's cabinets.[18] The 1972 data do not reconfirm these findings: a slim overrepresentation of Protestants exists among the political elite (table omitted).

TABLE 9.3
FATHER'S EDUCATION AND RESPONDENT'S EDUCATION

Father's Education	Respondent's Education					
	Elementary	Secondary	High	No Answer	Total	
Elementary	12%	15	71	2 =	100%	(646)
	76%	63%	30%	32%		
Secondary	3%	7	88	2 =	100%	(340)
	10	15	19	16		
High	*%	3	95	2 =	100%	(769)
	3	13	48	42		
No Answer	16%	18	60	6 =	100%	(70)
	11	9	3	10		
Total	100%	100%	100%	100%		
	(102)	(150)	(1535)	(38)		(1825)

TABLE 9.4
POLITICAL ENVIRONMENT OF PARENTAL HOME

	Politics N = 353	Administration N = 549	Economic sector N = 392	Trade Unions N = 62	Mass Media N = 264	Others N = 205	Total N = 1825	Population[b]
A. Parents politically affiliated?								
Yes	71%	64%	55%	74%	59%	57%	62%	23%
No	25%	33%	40%	26%	36%	39%	34%	77%
NA	4	3	5	0	5	4	4	0
	100%	100%	100%	100%	100%	100%	100%	100%
B. Politics discussed at home?								
Yes	69%	64%	65%	77%	65%	68%	66%	25%
No	31%	35%	35%	23%	34%	31%	33%	75%
NA	a	a	a	0	a	a	a	0
	100%	100%	100%	100%	99%	99%	99%	100%
C. Politics disagreed over?								
Yes	28%	26%	27%	15%	36%	31%	28%	
No	70%	73%	71%	85%	62%	68%	71%	
NA	1	1	1	0	2	1	1	
	99%	100%	99%	100%	100%	100%	100%	
If yes, between:								
Parents	18%	16%	12%	—	15%	14%	15%	
Generations	38	49	51	33	43	46	46	

[a] Less than one per cent in cell. [b] Data for 1972. See Social Research Institute of the Konrad Adenauer Stiftung, unpublished paper, Alfter 1973.

Religion is a discriminating variable in voting behavior between SPD/FDP and CDU/CSU voters.[19] With the catholic vote as an important factor in the CDU/CSU electorate, these parties always attempted to balance the relation between Protestants and Catholics in political office. The present coalition (SPD/FDP) has no relevant catholic constituency and, therefore, does not need to achieve a religious balance. The effect is that the Protestant-Catholic ratio in these parties has become similar to that in other segments of the elite. The balancing tendency in the 1950s and 1960s was more or less artificially achieved by conscious political decisions. When there is no need for such a balancing policy, the Protestant dominance among the elites has characterized the political elite as well.[20]

A more relevant indicator of the socialization process is the parents' political orientation. Roughly two-thirds of the German elites—in contrast to only one-fourth of the non-elites, report that their parents had a particular political affiliation. Among the political elite and the trade union leaders this percentage is even higher (Table 9.4A). The same significant difference exists in regard to the perception of political conversation at home: sixty-six percent of the elite, but only twenty-five percent of the non-elites did remember political discussions at home (Table 9.4B). The political consensus in the parental family was also significantly high—about three-fourths of the present elite have not experienced political dissensus at home; those who did stated conflicts between the generations more often than between their parents (Table 9.4C).

The development of the German party system from a multiparty system in the Weimar Republic and the "Kaiserreich" into a nearly two-party system in the recent elections in the Federal Republic of Germany is reflected in the elite's perception of the political orientation of their parents. The old liberal, conservative and Catholic parties on the one hand, and the SPD on the other hand, characterize the political orientation of the parents of the present elite. In the perception of the present elite, there was no significant sympathy for National Socialism among their parents.

The socializing effect of the political orientation of the parents is shown in Table 9.5. Forty-seven percent of the present SPD oriented political elite follow the political lines of their parents; forty percent of the CDU/CSU oriented political elites have parents among the Catholic or Protestant parties of the Weimar Republic or the Kaiserreich, and another substantial part (16%) is recruited from a conservative family.

Political interest and orientation in the family is one of the important socialization variables. Even against the background of the German party system's complete reconstruction after World War II, political affiliation shows a remarkable intergenerational continuity, highest among Social Democrats and trade unionists. But this continuity does not mean homogeneity, although, statistically, certain political groups dominate the respective segments of the

TABLE 9.5
POLITICAL ORIENTATION OF PARENTS

Sector	Christian parties	Liberal parties	Left parties (SPD)	Conserva- tive parties	Radical left parties	Radical right parties	Others	No answer	Total	
Politics Total	22%	7	18	12	1	2	11	27	352	100%
SPD	4%	7	47	2	2	—	11	27	123	100%
FDP	4%	23	5	18	2	9	14	26	57	100%
CDU/CSU	40%	3	2	16	—	2	9	28	172	100%
Administration	18%	7	11	19	—	5	7	34	549	100%
Economic sector	12%	7	6	24	—	5	5	41	392	100%
Trade unions	19%	3	36	5	7	2	2	27	62	100%
Mass media	18%	5	10	13	1	6	5	41	264	100%
Others	20%	2	2	21	2	7	6	40	205	100%
Total N =	320	114	199	316	14	87	119	655	1824	

elite: no segment of the elite is politically closed. There is a significant trade union leadership without socialist parents and a big business elite with social-democratic background. Again, the picture which emerges is one of an elite that combines a background of continuity and diversity.

PATTERNS OF SUCCESS

Social background and the socialization process produce the reservoir from which the elite is selected. What personal qualifications, however, are required to be selected from this large pool?

High formal education is the first prerequisite for success. Eighty-four percent of the present elite graduated from high school, with trade union leaders displaying the only major deviation; two-thirds of the latter managed to reach the top on the basis of primary and secondary school education (but became well trained by a sophisticated internal trade union educational system). By contrast to figures from a representative sample (25% with high school and 15% with university degrees—table omitted), high formal education is the prerequisite for the recruitment of the elite. Even among the trade union elite the percentage of university degrees is higher than among the total population.

Among the political elite about a three-fourth, among the bureaucrats close to one hundred percent, earned a high school degree. About sixty percent of the political elite received university degrees, which is a rather low proportion in comparison with the administrative and economic elites, but remarkably high in comparison with the labor elite. There is also a significant difference along party lines: only forty-four percent of the Social Democrats, but more than seventy percent of the CDU/CSU elites had a university education. High education, therefore, seems to be an important but not exclusive criterion for access to the elite.

Among various educational fields the former law school students are still dominant, particularly among the civil servants, but also to a remarkable degree (47%) among the political elite. Dahrendorf has already pointed out that the more important a position is in the hierarchy, the greater is the likelihood that it is in the hands of a law school graduate.[21] Consistent with the data on educational background, the dominant position of former law students is lowest among Social Democrats. Nevertheless, the educational background of the political elite is too heterogeneous to indicate one specific educational pattern characteristic of "professional politicians" (in contrast to the civil service and academics, who constitute rather closed elites with respect to education).

Next to formal education, occupational experience is an important criterion for selection to the elite. The first research done on this subject in Germany indicated that the respective segments of the German elite are rather isolated from each other and that there is no effective interchange between different types of the elite. This means that climbing up along the lines of a specific occupational career pattern is the typical way to success.[22] This is still true for the administrative elite, because of persisting traditional career patterns. Nevertheless, inside recruitment is decreasing. Big business, trade unions and mass media still show considerable inside recruitment, but they cannot be characterized as isolated, autonomous segments of the elite.

The political elite, on the other hand, does not follow these patterns at all. It is recruited from a variety of occupational sectors. Training in other jobs and being successful in other fields, seem to be important conditions for political success. Two explanations can be advanced for this distinctive pattern of recruitment. On the one hand, the achievement of positions in executive functions is to a high degree dependent on parliamentary experience and success.[23] On the other hand, there is a certain interdependence between individual professional success and political eligibility.[24]

Practically all members of the political elite had experience in other fields, more than forty percent of them in three different sectors (Table 9.6). Along with the high rate of crossing other political sectors (60%), the percentage of politicians with experience in the judicial and administrative branches as well as in economics and in the educational system, is remarkably high (Table 9.7).

The high proportion of former bureaucrats among the political elite may be explained by the fact that the social and economic security attached to civil servant status is not lost by winning elective office. According to German law, a civil servant who is elected goes on leave and subsequently returns to his office—usually at a higher level—if he is defeated in an election.

The economic sector offers similar guarantees to its employees who are willing and capable of representing group interests inside parliament. The economic sector is represented among the political elite mostly by managers rather than entrepreneurs. The increasing representation of scientists is obviously the result of the increased importance of scientific experts in political decision-making, as well as of the high prestige of this group which parties use for their own purposes.

Within the political elite, the largest difference between the major parties refers to previous positions in the trade unions: 22 percent among Social Democrats, in contrast to only 2.4 percent among CDU/CSU politicians (table omitted). Crossing different sectors is less frequent among other parts of the elite. The highest percentage of single-sector careers was found among the business and mass media elites: More than fifty percent had no cross-sectoral experiences. (Table 9.6).

Table 9.8 shows the fields in which members of the present elite started their careers. The political elite is most frequently recruited from the economic and judicial sectors. This reflects the still dominant position of the law school

(text continued on p. 254)

TABLE 9.6
OCCUPATION IN VARIOUS SECTORS[a]

	in 1 (own) Sector	in two Sectors	in three Sectors	in more than three Sectors	no answer		Total
Politics total	7%	45	41	6	1	= 100%	353
S P D	3%	40	53	3	1	= 100%	123
C D U	7%	48	37	5	3	= 100%	124
C S U	11%	48	31	10	—	= 100%	48
F D P	14%	49	28	9	—	= 100%	57
Administration	30%	45	20	5	—	= 100%	549
Economic sector	51%	31	13	4	1	= 100%	392
Trade unions	5%	55	35	5	—	= 100%	62
Mass media	57%	33	8	1	1	= 100%	264
Other	27%	56	14	3	—	= 100%	205
Total N =	602/33%	761/42	379/21	74/4	9/1	= 100%	1825

[a] See H. Neumann, B. Steinkemper, Consensus . . ., p. 21

TABLE 9.7
SECTORS CROSSED DURING CAREER[a]
(in percentages)

Sector	Politics	Law	Administration	Business	Professional organizations	Trade Unions	Mass media	Education and science	Number of respondents
Federal/State governments	62[b]	26	31	36	—	7	8	23	84
Federal parliament	65	15	31	34	—	6	7	15	88
State parliaments	61	15	21	46	2	8	5	18	61
Federal/State parties	59	12	25	29	—	3	9	19	120
Administration	8	24	91	16	—	2	2	12	549
Economic sector	4	14	14	92	—	—	1	10	392
Trade Unions	3	5	24	44	3	77	—	10	62
Mass media	2	2	5	14	—	—	97	5	264
Others	4	7	19	41	2	1	4	33	205
Total									1825

[a] Last two and first positions. See Neumann/Steinkemper, Consensus . . ., p. 24
[b] Percentage for each category based on number of respondents; because of multiple responses, the rows in this table do not add up to 100%, but more than 100%.

TABLE 9.8
SECTOR OF FIRST POSITIONS[a]
(in percentages)

Sector	Politics in general	Party politics	Administration	Law	Economic sector	Trade unions	Mass media	Education Science	Other positions	Number of respondents
Federal/State Government	1	1	11	25	25	—	5	17	6	84
Federal Parliament	7	6	17	14	23	—	5	9	22	88
State Parliament	5	5	15	12	28	—	3	13	12	61
Federal/State Parties	—	17	13	9	19	1	8	15	17	120
Administration	1	—	35	22	11	1	1	12	19	549
Economic sector	—	—	7	13	59	—	1	8	11	392
Trade unions	—	—	18	5	40	15	—	7	13	62
Mass media	—	—	3	—	15	—	70	3	9	264
Others	—	1	8	6	24	1	2	24	35	205
Total										1825

[a] See Neumann/Steinkemper: Consensus . . ., p. 21.

graduates, whose first position will usually be in the judicial field before moving into other sectors. Many members of the political elite also start their career in the universities and in the bureaucracy.

The percentage of recruitment from the same sector among the political elite is extremely low, given the large number of party employees at different levels of the party organizations. Only about seventeen percent of the present party elite and about one to five percent of the various executive and legislative elites started their career as party employees. Nevertheless, this may be understood as the beginning of the development of a new profession in politics.

On the basis of their interchange ratio, the different sectors may be divided into "elite sellers," "elite buyers" and "self-sufficient systems."[25]

    (1) The political elite—and this is independent of party identification—is the most important buyer. The sector demands personnel from all other sectors, mainly from business and the civil service, but also from academics.

    (2) Business and the civil service fulfill a distributing function for all sectors. They sell and buy personnel most frequently.

    (3) Unions, media and academic sector are rather self-sufficient systems; they sell some personnel, but the largest part of their elite is recruited from their own reservoir.

The following figures demonstrate these selling and buying functions of the different segments in relation to the political elite:

Figure 9.1 – SECTORS OF FIRST POSITIONS OF THE POLITICAL ELITE*

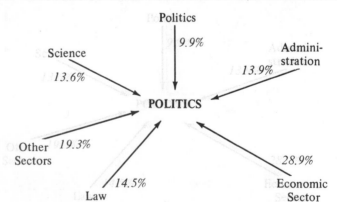

* Neumann/Steinkemper: Consensus. . . , p. 21

The distribution of the sources of recruitment does not change considerably when all the positions in the career of the present elite, rather than the first position, are taken into consideration (Figure 9.2).

There is no substantial difference in this respect between the political parties, with the exception of the fact that the Unions deliver their personnel almost exclusively to the SPD. Consequently recruitment from other sectors of society is higher for the CDU/CSU and FDP. A different distribution obtains when the analysis is restricted to those who already belonged to some elite before they reached their present position. Figure 9.3 shows that nearly seventy percent of the present political elite with experience in other elite positions were recruited from political positions. Given the fact that the top administrative positions are filled predominantly according to political considerations,[26] the twenty percent recruited from this sector demonstrate that the circulation of the political elite (at the top levels) is almost exclusively an internal circulation. Different sectors are crossed on the way to the top, whereas at the top internal circulation is dominant. These findings contradict Scheuch's observation[27] that inter-elite exchange occurs at the top levels, but not during the career stages leading to the top.

Figure 9.2 – SOURCES OF RECRUITMENT OF THE POLITICAL ELITE

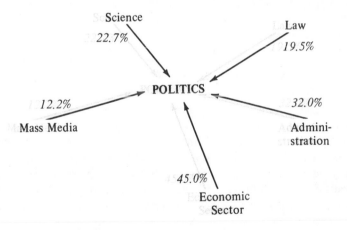

Figure 9.3 – POLITICAL ELITES WITH EXPERIENCE IN TOP POSITIONS

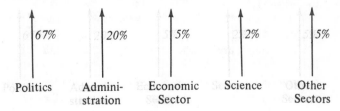

The average age of the elite in the different sectors helps explain the direction of these exchanges. The youngest elite is found among the political parties, followed by the legislative elite at the lower (state) level. Close to the average are the elites in the executive branches, the federal parliament and the trade unions. The oldest elites predominate in the civil service and in the economic sector (Table 9.9).

TABLE 9.9

AVERAGE AGE AND TIME OF REACHING FIRST TOP POSITION[a]

	Average Age	First top position Reached after years (average)
Politics	48	15
Federal/State	50	18
Federal parliament	52	17
State parliament	50	15
Federal/State parties	45	11
Administration	56	18
Economic sector	54	16
Trade unions	52	19
Mass media	48	15
Others	52	20

[a] Neumann/Steinkemper, Consensus . . ., p. 16

This reflects, on the one hand, the rather formalized career patterns in the civil service and (somewhat surprisingly) in large parts of the economic sector where people reach the top at the end of their career. On the other hand, the very open and unformalized patterns of advancement among the political elite explain their relatively low age. It is very likely that the rather low age of the political elite follows partially from the change in the governing coalition in 1969, which brought in a rather young elite and started the process of personnel turnover within the new opposition. In an alternating party system the age of the political elite tends to go up and down with the length of the period a party stays in office. The significant difference between the age of the party and state legislative elites on the one hand, and the federal legislative and executive elites on the other hand, is indicative of a political career pattern. The positions with the highest prestige are at the federal level—executive and legislative, and they will be reached only after some experience has been gained in other fields, often in party or state politics.

Similar results are obtained on the basis of the length of time the members of the elite had to wait until they reached their present positions (Table 9.9). For governmental elites, civil servants and trade union leaders, the waiting period was longer than for party and state parliamentary elites.

This leads to the question of continuity and change within the elite of one generation. Table 9.10 shows that on the average a member of the present German elite spends no longer than six years in office, with the political elite in the executive displaying the shortest time in office.[29] The data only partially reflect this fact since the research was done two and a half years after the change in the federal coalition of 1969, and it also included state executives. The turnover among parliamentarians and the members of the civil service is also remarkably high, demonstrating as high a competitiveness among the latter as in the party system. Table 9.10 also demonstrates the impact of a change in the governing coalition on the bureaucratic elite. The present elite in this sector entered in three waves: the first (today the smallest) consists of holdovers from the old CDU/CSU/FDP coalition; the second was appointed during the CDU/CSU/SPD coalition (1967-1969), and the largest fraction (40%) entered under the new SPD/FDP coalition. It is not surprising therefore that eighty-five percent of the present SPD members and eighty-seven percent of the FDP members[30] in top administrative positions were appointed after 1969.

PERCEPTIONS OF ELITE POSITIONS

One way of assessing the "openness" of an elite is to inquire whether the holders of elite positions view their advancement to these positions as the result of strong competition. A large percentage of office holders perceiving ascent to the elite as involving a "hard struggle" or strong competition would indicate that there is a large reservoir of candidates and, consequently, that the elite is perceived as accessible. Furthermore, the harder the struggle to maintain an achieved position (in the perceptions of the elite), the more likely it is that incumbents can be seriously challenged. Although responses to questions pertaining to personal success and to security in office are often determined by self-serving motivations, a comparison across different sectors of the elite can shed some light on the relative openness of these sectors.

Thus, whereas among nonpolitical elites only fifty-four percent mentioned that they had to fight hard for their success, the frequency of this response rose to sixty-six percent among federal and state government officials and to seventy-five percent among members of the federal legislature. Similarly, only twenty percent of the non-political elites, but thirty-seven percent of the federal legislators, believed that they have to "struggle" constantly or frequently in order to maintain their positions (Table 9.11).

Political positions, appointive and elective, seem therefore to be more highly contested than those in other areas of the German elite. This is perhaps not surprising in a competitive party system. However, it is indicative of the fact that only those who are sufficiently motivated to engage in this "hard struggle"

TABLE 9.10
TIME OF ENTERING THE PRESENT POSITION[a]
(in percentages)

Sector	Since 1970	1967-1969	Before 1967	No answer	%	Average time span of the present position	Number of respondents
Federal/State							
Governments	42	27	30	1	= 100%	4.2 years	84
Federal parliament	6	46	41	7	= 100%	6.7	88
State parliament	44	20	33	3	= 100%	5.4	61
Federal/State parties	43	19	37	1	= 100%	5.9	120
Administration	37	34	28	1	= 100%	4.7	549
Economic sector	18	25	57	1	= 100%	8.0	392
Trade unions	13	36	51	—	= 100%	7.0	62
Mass media	30	25	44	1	= 100%	6.4	264
Others	49	19	30	2	= 100%	4.4	365
Total/Average	31	28	39	2	= 100%	5.9 years	1825

[a] Neumann/Steinkemper, Consensus . . . , p. 16, 25

TABLE 9.11
STRUGGLE FOR THE TOP POSITION
(in percentages)

	Number of respondents	Hard struggle for ascent				Struggle to maintain position			
		Yes	No	No answer	Total	Constantly frequently	Sometimes never	No answer	Total
Politics	353	64	32	4	= 100%	33	64	3	= 100%
Federal/State Government	84	67	27	6	= 100%	37	61	2	= 100%
Federal Parliament	88	75	22	3	= 100%	38	60	2	= 100%
State Parliaments	61	57	38	5	= 100%	29	66	5	= 100%
Federal/State Parliaments	120	58	40	2	= 100%	29	68	3	= 100%
Non-political Elite	1472	54	40	6	= 100%	21	76	3	= 100%
Total/Average %	1825	56	38	6	= 100%	23	74	3	= 100%

are potential candidates for recruitment from the pool of eligibles into the political elite.

People who have this motivation are the reservoir of the elite. If they are coming from a middle class and well educated family, they have a better chance of climbing up the ladder, although the small proportion of elite members with a low-class social background indicates that access to the German elite is not altogether restricted by social background. Parental interest or involvement in politics seems to be an important facilitating factor.

Qualification is the next filter, which candidates from this reservoir have to pass. This includes firstly formal qualification, a training in college or university. Here again we find a preponderance of members of the middleclass, but also a remarkable intergenerational upward mobility. In addition to that, high qualification includes experience in various sectors of society, which leads back to motivation: bearing the risk of changing the job and being willing to fight. These are the important variables in the recruitment of the political elite of the German Federal Republic. The recruitment process, which demonstrates tendencies towards an open and highly competitive elite, operates according to the theoretical assumptions of a democratic system.

NOTES

1. See K. Sontheimer, *Grundzuege des politischen Systems in der Bundesrepublik Deutschland* (Muenchen: Piper, 1971); K. D. Bracher, *Die Aufloesung der Weimarer Republik* (Stuttgart: Ring Verlag, 1957); R. Dahrendorf, *Gesellschaft und Demokratie in Deutschland* (Muenchen: Piper, 1965); R. Dahrendorf, "Eine neue deutsche Oberschicht?," *Die neue Gesellschaft* 1 (1962); W. Zapf, *Wandlungen der deutschen Elite* (Muenchen: Piper, 1966); E. K. Scheuch, "Fuehrungsgruppen und Demokratie in Deutschland," *Die neue Gesellschaft* 13 (1966); R. Wildenmann, *Eliten in der Bundesrepublik* (Mannheim, 1968, Tabellenband); E. Enke, *Oberschicht und politisches System der Bundesrepublik Deutschland* (Frankfurt-Bern: Lang, 1974); K. W. Deutsch and L. J. Edinger, *Germany Rejoines the Powers* (Stanford, Cal.: Stanford University Press, 1959).

2. See H. Palme, "Criteria for the Selection of Sectors and Positions in an Elite Study," paper presented at the ninth congress of the International Political Science Association in Montreal, Canada, 1973.

3. K. v. Beyme, *Die politische Elite in der Bundesrepublik Deutschland* (Muenchen: Piper, 1971).

4. E. K. Scheuch, "Continuity and Change in German Social Structure," unpublished paper (Koeln, 1965), 45.

5. R. Aron understands recruitment as one of four general and central themes of elite analysis: social background, recruitment, attitudes on society, and homogeneity. See R. Aron, "Classe sociale, class politique, class dirigeante," *Europaeisches Archiv fuer Soziologie* K/2 (1960), 260-261. Dahrendorf adds the aspects of fluctuation within the elite. R. Dahrendorf, "Recent changes in the class structure of European societies," Daedalus (1964), 225-270.

6. After 1945 the attempts of the allies to wipe out the Nazi-affiliated elite failed. Therefore the assertion of L. J. Edinger, "Posttotalitarian leadership—elites in the German Federal Republic," American Political Science Review 54 (1960), that in a totalitarian political system a counter elite is developing, has to be modified. See H. D. Lasswell and A. Kaplan, *Power and Society* (New Haven: Yale University Press, 1950), 267.

7. See S. Keller, *Beyond the Ruling Class* (New York: Random House, 1963), 108.

8. W. Kaltefleiter and R. Wildenmann, eds., *Westdeutsche Fuehrungsschicht.* Tabellenband, by U. Lange, H. Neumann, H. Palme, B. Steinkemper (Kiel-Mannheim, 1973).

9. For a discussion see Palme op. cit., 2. The top positions were defined as follows—*politics:* ministers, parliamentary state secretaries, chairmen of political committees and parties at the federal and state levels, and party leaders; *administration:* state secretaries, heads of the federal and state departments, heads of local administration; *business:* industrial organizations, chairmen of boards of directors, chairmen of directorates; *trade unions:* chairmen at the federal and state levels; *mass media:* managing superintendents, administration and program directors, editors-in-chief, publishers, and department heads of national newspapers or radio and television networks; *science:* heads of universities and other scientific organizations.

10. See Scheuch, "Fuehrungsgruppen," 362.

11. Dahrendorf, *Gesellschaft und Demokratie.* 279; also W. Zapf, *Wandlungen.* 180.

12. Enke, *Oberschicht.* 75.

13. Beyme, op. cit., 40.

14. See W. Kaltefleiter, *Zwischen Konsens und Krise: Eine Analyse der Bundestagswahl 1972* (Koeln: Heymanns, 1973), 144.

15. Representative sample, June 1971, Social Science Research Institute of the Konrad Adenauer Foundation.

16. The dominant position of law school graduates, the so-called "Juristenmonopol," has only marginally been challenged since the end of the 19th century: constantly about two-thirds of the top positions in public administration are held by civil servants who are law school graduates. See R. Dahrendorf, "Ausbildung einer Elite—Die deutsche Oberschicht und die juristischen Fakultaeten," Der Monat 166 (1962). See Zapf, op. cit., 177; J. A. Armstrong, *The European Administrative Elite* (Princeton: Princeton University Press, 1973), 171.

17. Max Weber, *Die protestantische Ethik und der Geist des Kapitalismus,* in *Gesammelte Aufsaetze zur Religionssoziologie,* Vol. I (Tuebingen: Mohr, 1947), 17.

18. See Zapf, op. cit., 175; Beyme, op. cit., 28.

19. See E. Blankenburg, *Kirchliche Bindung und Wahlverhalten* (Freiburg: Walter Verlag, 1967). For the recent elections, see Kaltefleiter, op. cit., 159.

20. There is much literature in Germany dealing with the problem of Catholic underrepresentation among the elite, which goes back to the sociology of religion literature, particularly: Weber, op. cit.; A. Mueller-Armack, *Religion und Wirtschaft* (Stuttgart: Kohlhammer, 1959). Zapf, op. cit., 176, has pointed out that in contrast to protestant values the impact of the catholic religion is lower motivation toward individual success.

21. See Dahrendorf, op. cit., 264.

22. Scheuch, "Fuehrungsgruppen, 365.

23. Beyme states that about 90% of the executive elite has made its way by occupying parliamentary positions; op cit., 91.

24. Ibid., 76.

25. See Neumann-Steinkemper, "Consensus," 20.

26. B. Steinkemper, *Klassische und politische Buerokraten in der Ministerialverwaltung der Bundesrepublik Deutschland* (Koeln: Heymanns, 1974), 45.

27. Scheuch, "Continuity," 59.

28. Zapf's findings are in the same direction: the more formalized a career pattern, the older the top position-holders. Zapf, op. cit., 170.

29. In the first theoretical analysis of the parliamentary system Walter Bagehot had already pointed out that continuous changes of ministry are one of the prerequisites of a well-working parliamentary government. See W. Bagehot, *The English Constitution* (1867).

30. See Steinkemper, op. cit., 52. A heavy turnover in office also characterizes the military elite; none of the present military elite were in their present positions three years ago. This does not reflect the political change of 1969; it follows from the formal patterns of the military career which normally require a change in military position after three years of service.

Chapter 10

CRITICAL ELECTIONS, CONGRESSIONAL RECRUITMENT AND PUBLIC POLICY

MICHAEL R. KING
Pennsylvania State University
a n d
LESTER G. SELIGMAN
University of Illinois

Twice during the past century, in 1896 and 1932, presidential elections realigned the social and geographic distribution of electoral support for both major political parties. Such elections are called "critical" or "realigning" because they were significant turning points in periods of electoral change and realignment. During such periods of realignment, a new pattern of voting was established which persisted until the next realignment, although an occasional election, such as 1912, 1916, 1952 and 1956, deviated from this pattern.[1]

The following characteristics distinguish elections during realignment periods:

(1) conflict within and between political parties intensifies and polarizes; (2) the percentage turnout of voters increases markedly; (3) in unprecedented numbers incumbent elected officials go down to defeat at the national and state levels; (4) new third parties arise; and finally (5) as a result of the new crystalization of public sentiment, the government embarks on new directions in public policy.

In a seminal paper published in 1955, V.O. Key first identified critical elections and presented data which substantiated the existence of this special category of presidential election.[2] Four years later, Key explained critical elections as an outgrowth of secular realignment, the result of long-term changes and processes that operate gradually, election after election, to form new party groupings.[3] Since then, Burnham,[4] Schattschneider,[5] Pomper,[6] Campbell,[7] and Jahnige[8] have further refined the concepts of critical or realigning elections.

Burnham,[9] McRae and Meldrum,[10] Rogin and Shover,[11] and McSeveney [12] have analyzed their incidence in various states.

A number of explanations of critical elections have grown out of this research. Walter Dean Burnham regards critical elections as acute expressions of

> tensions in society which, not adequately controlled by the organization or outputs of
> party politics as usual, escalate to a flash point; they are issue-oriented phenomena,
> centrally associated with these tensions and more or less leading to resolution
> adjustments; they result in significant transformations in the general shape of policy;
> and they have relatively profound after-effects on the roles played by institutionalized
> elites.[13]

Thomas Jahnige suggests that economic developments which destabilize and change the relative advantage of some groups cause critical elections. These changes weaken group party attachments and create opportunities for political leaders to forge new electoral coalitions through the skillful manipulation of class, ethnic and regional cultural symbols. A new alignment of voters results which becomes the dominant consensus and pattern of influence of the ensuing period.[14]

Despite such assiduous research, the explanations of critical elections remain ambiguous and incomplete. The thesis that critical elections result from the contradictions and/or gaps between social conditions and political institutions applies equally well to many kinds of protest movements—e.g., third parties, labor or nativist movements, and women's suffrage. Burnham's suggestion that critical elections are more issue-oriented than other presidential elections approaches the specificity we need, and his assertion that critical elections have far-reaching consequences for institutionalized elites points in a fruitful direction. Nevertheless, as it now stands, the analysis of critical elections seems poised between the richness of substantiating historical voting data, and its poverty as a predictive theory. It has not yet generated theory precise enough to explain and predict long-term change in American politics. When a presidential election is judged as "critical" it is a retrospective judgment made only after a voting realignment persists for a number of successive presidential elections. Yet if a theory of critical elections or political realignment is to fulfill its promise, it should identify the variables and processes that bring about such turning points in American politics.

It seems to us that the phenomenon of critical elections has been investigated with a focus too narrow and limited to yield predictive theory. Most research has concentrated exclusively on the behavior of the electorate during critical elections and has neglected the broader periods and processes of realignment of which critical elections are but a part.[15] The significance of the processes at work during periods of realignment reaches beyond changes in voters' preferences. In the wake of realignment, changes in both legislative representation and policy direction occur. In many congressional districts, voter realignment alters the party makeup and changes the progression of offices that define career paths to Congress. During the realignment period, the processes of recruitment which select individuals to Congress may change, indicating that the structure of political opportunity—the differential chances of people to run for political office— also has changed in some districts. The social, economic, and political influences which precipitate the realignment reduce the political opportunity of established groups and interests in the constituency and give such advantages to spokesmen of new ones.[16] In the aftermath of realignment, new congressmen are elected who are "new" in many respects. Thus, realignments for voters bring about realignments in recruitment patterns, career paths to Congress, legislative coalitions, and public policy. Examination of these broader aspects of change during periods of realignment may give insight into the linkages which tie together electoral change, elite turnover and public policy. In this regard, changes in policy, as well as changes in the membership of Congress (and the presidency and executive) which flow from electoral realignment deserve investigation.

This study is a modest step in this direction.[17] Despite our reservations about the usefulness of the concept of critical elections, we shall use critical elections as convenient bench marks for ascertaining the recruitment and policy consequences of electoral realignment. We shall examine the changes in the composition of Congress following the critical elections of 1896 and 1932, and compare them with changes after noncritical elections selected at twelve-year intervals between 1872 and 1956, namely the elections of 1872, 1884, 1908, 1920, 1944, and 1956. Then, as a test case, we will assess the legislative policy consequences after the 1932 election. In conducting this study of the impact of electoral realignment, we have two primary objectives: (1) to determine whether social background factors and recruitment experiences influence the voting decisions of new congressmen and incumbents after critical elections; and (2) to assess what part such congressmen's decisions play in redefining legislative policy.[18] By examing the composition of a sample of the new elites who assume office after critical elections we may discover the particular linkages among electoral realignment, turnover patterns, elite recruitment and policy changes which set apart critical elections from other presidential elections.

The focus on new congressmen illustrates the usefulness of cohort analysis in the recruitment of political elites. A cohort is an aggregate of individuals who experience the same event within the same time interval. A political cohort is "distinctly marked by the career stage it occupies when prosperity or depression, war or peace, impinge upon it."[19] A period of electoral realignment implants common outlooks and experiences on the newly elected congressional cohort which become the bases of political identifications in the hierarchically organized Congress. Not only the background characteristics of congressmen, per se, but also their common experiences in political ascent in the context of electoral realignment influence their policy outlooks and the way they vote on legislation. In combination, the common changes in constituencies which make the newly elected congressmen a political cohort, combined with their common recruitment experiences and social background characteristics predispose the new congressmen to collaborate on policy in Congress.

During the eras of electoral realignment, social and economic changes are particularly striking in some congressional constituencies, and the recruitment of new elites helps translate changes in public opinion into changes in public policy. Therefore, the analysis of the process and consequences of the recruitment of the congressional elite is an integral aspect of explanations of voting realignments. When significant realignments in voting take place, some congressional candidates are beneficiaries and others are victims in particular ways that differ from those which occur during other kinds of presidential elections.

POLITICAL PARTIES AND CRITICAL ELECTIONS

As we shall show, voter realignment gives rise to new, insurgent political leaders who challenge the entrenched leaders of one or both of the major political parties. The strategies of these insurgent leaders have varied with the particular critical election and the region of the country. In one-party congressional districts, insurgents turn to the minority party in some instances and wrest control of the party from its established old guard. The critical election then brings many new voters and activists to the minority party banner who breathe new life into the organization of the minority party. At some times, such as in 1932 when insurgents turned to the minority Democratic party in those major cities still dominated by the Republicans, the voting shift is so pronounced that the pre-election majority party becomes the minority party in the years after the critical election. In other instances, insurgents in the majority party challenge the old guard of their party for leadership. In the aftermath of 1896, for example, agrarian forces in the South retained their vigor, and their contest with the old guard Bourbon elements of the Democratic party has persisted, in some respects, to the present. In still other instances, insurgent leaders successfully gain control of the emerging national majority party organizations in districts where the party is in a competitive or dominant position. The critical election then strengthens such organizations. Constituencies which were competitive before the critical election then become one-party districts, and one-party districts show even more lop-sided returns. Many incumbents from such districts are returned to Congress with unprecedented pluralities, as was the case in areas of established Democratic strength in 1932, for example.[20]

In general, after a realignment, the new majority party becomes a broader and more incompatible coalition than before. In Congress this is manifest in the cleavage between many older incumbents of the majority party and new men elected during the critical election. For example, in 1896, the victorious Democrats from the plains states, Far West, border states and South joined with Populists and some newly elected Republican congressmen to oppose both the conservative Republican majority and the Democratic old guard.[21] Similarly, a growing cleavage between the Northern urban Democratic congressmen and the alliance of older Southern Democrats and younger Republicans elected in 1938 and 1946 eroded the New Deal coalition elected in 1932-1936.[22]

As a result of the critical election, the older leaders of the former majority party go down to defeat not only in Congress, but in state and local offices as well. Usually, congressional candidates of the opposing party replace them, although occasionally younger challengers within their own party defeat them for the nomination. The defeat of the veteran incumbents and the resulting crisis in confidence opens up vacancies on party tickets which attract younger political aspirants, even though the party is now in a minority. The younger aspirants blame the older leaders for the party defeat and demand a change in party leadership. Such generational conflicts occurred within various state Democratic parties during the period of Republican dominance from 1896 to 1932.[23] The same conflict took place after 1932 and 1936 in the Republican party. The younger Republican congressmen and senators who were elected in 1938 and 1946 were members of this younger vanguard.

In Congress, the turnover between parties during noncritical and critical elections differs substantially. Noncritical elections usually cause only marginal change in the party balance in Congress. Party control of one or both Houses of Congress may change, but such shifts reflect either short-term reactions to current events and issues, or fluctuations in presidential popularity. But after critical elections, a sizeable turnover occurs, a new party balance is struck, divisions over issues become sharper, prevailing public policies are challenged, and new policies are pressed with greater urgency. The new people elected to Congress are vigorous spokesmen for the claims of new groups challenging the political status of older groups and interests.

Table 10.1 shows turnover in Congress at twelve-year intervals since 1872, including the critical elections 1896 and 1932. The six noncritical elections run the gamut of types of presidential elections. They range from Harding's landslide in 1920 (a *reinstating* election) when the coattail effect was operative in many congressional races, through the elections of 1872 and 1884 (Grant's second administration and Cleveland's first), two *maintaining* elections during the competitive period of the latter part of the nineteenth century; the 1908 election of Taft and the 1944 election (Roosevelt's fourth administration), two maintaining elections during the eras of Republican and Democratic dominance respectively, to the 1956 election (Eisenhower's second administration), which was a *deviating* election in which a Republican won the presidency, but the Democrats made new gains in Congress.[24] The data in Table 10.1 include measures of the percentage of congressmen replaced at each election and electoral defeat. The former indicates the magnitude of turnover from all causes (e.g., defeat, retirement, death), after controlling for the effects of reapportionment and the admission of new states.[25] The percent defeated measures turnover owing to electoral defeat,[26] either through failure to secure renomination or defeat by an opponent of the other party.[27]

TABLE 10.1
TURNOVER IN CONGRESS SINCE 1872,
INCLUDING THE CRITICAL ELECTIONS OF 1896 AND 1932

Election	(1) % Replaced	(2) % Defeated	(3) % of all Turnover Due to Defeat (3 = 2/1)
1872	50.2 (151)	14.7 (44)	29.1
1884	44.3 (144)	15.4 (50)	34.7
1896	42.6 (152)	20.5 (73)	48.0
1908	23.0 (90)	11.2 (44)	48.9
1920	31.0 (134)	15.7 (68)	50.7
1932	36.8 (160)	27.1 (117)	73.1
1944	12.9 (56)	10.8 (47)	83.9
1956	10.8 (47)	10.2 (44)	93.6

Clearly, the rate of defeat has not paralleled the steady and substantial decline since 1872 in the percent of new congressmen who assume office after each election. The rate at which congressmen retire has diminished as seniority in Congress has acquired greater importance and a congressional career has grown more attractive relative to the declining prestige of state and local office or a career in business.[28] But the percent of congressmen who go down to defeat at each election has not changed appreciably since 1872. Regression analysis shows that *only during critical presidential elections does the rate of electoral defeat increase substantially* (Table 10.2). After such elections, the rate of defeat drops to the levels that prevailed before the critical election.[29]

Critical elections institute long-lasting changes in the pattern of turnover in Congress. Each critical election changed the proportion of turnover attributable to electoral defeat, and established a new pattern that persisted until the next critical election (see Table 10.1, above). Prior to 1896, electoral defeat accounted for roughly one-third of all turnover. In 1896, the figure rose to approximately fifty percent and stabilized until the critical election of 1932, when it climbed to over seventy percent to remain there through 1956. Thus, sizeable shifts in the *proportion* of turnover attributable to defeat follow in the wake of critical elections. Such shifts are independent of the rate at which congressmen leave office from all causes, and the rate of electoral defeat, considered separately (Table 10.2). Critical elections, more than other factors, account for the increasing

TABLE 10.2
MULTIPLE REGRESSION ANALYSIS OF TRENDS IN THE RATE OF DEFEAT
AND PERCENTAGE OF ALL TURNOVER DUE TO DEFEAT

% DEFEATED

Dependent Variable	Independent Variables
Y = Percent Defeated	X_1 = Critical/Non-Critical Elections (a dummy variable where 0 = non-critical elections and 1 = critical elections)
	X_2 = Percent Replaced

Results of Multiple Regression: $Y = 9.61 + 9.51X_1 + 0.12X_2$

Hypotheses	b	Standard Error of b	p	R^2	p
$\beta X_1 > 0$	b = 9.51	2.31	<.01		
				.85	<.01
$\beta X_2 > 0$	b = 0.12	0.07	>.05		

% OF ALL TURNOVER DUE TO DEFEAT

Dependent Variable	Independent Variables
Y = % of All Turnover Due to Defeat	X_1 = Eras of Partisan Politics (a dummy variable where the presidential elections from 1860 to 1892 = 0; 1896 to 1928 = 1; and 1932 to the present = 2)
	X_2 = Percent Replaced
	X_3 = Electoral Turnover

Results of Multiple Regression: $Y = -0.98 + 32.44X_1 + 0.39X_2 - 1.43X_3$

Hypotheses	b	Standard Error of b	p	R^2	p
$\beta X_1 > 0$	b = 32.44	15.40	<.05		
$\beta X_2 > 0$	b = 0.39	1.06	>.05	.94	<.01
$\beta X_3 < 0$	b = -1.43	1.77	>.05		

importance of electoral turnover and the diminishing significance of retirement as reasons for departure from Congress since 1872.

Such findings shed new light on the changing institutional patterns in Congress over the past century. Some research suggests that since 1900 or 1910, the rate of voluntary retirement in Congress has declined gradually, marking the advent of the seniority system and the increasing specialization and decentralization of congressional leadership. These institutional changes are variously explained as responses to the expanding scope of the national government, especially the executive branch, which are in turn responses to the problems of industrialization, urbanization, and technological growth;[30] as gradual adjustments to the electoral reforms of the Progressives such as the direct primary, which made congressmen more dependent on their local electorates and thereby strengthened local, specialized outlooks in Congress;[31] or as long-term reactions to the abuses of strong leadership in Congress during the latter part of the nineteenth and early twentieth centuries.[32]

Our findings call such explanations into question. Institutional change in Congress, to the extent that it is reflected in declining retirement rates and increasing seniority, has not been incremental, but constitutes periodic or cyclical responses to the new issues, outlooks, recruitment patterns and voting identifications that gave rise to the critical elections of 1896 and 1932. At present, we know little of the mechanisms which translate the influences at work outside of Congress during critical elections into important changes in the internal structure of Congress.

CRITICAL ELECTIONS AND THE PARTY BALANCE IN CONGRESS

After critical elections, the party balance in Congress always shifts substantially from one party to the other. This shift results primarily from electoral defeat; the rate of voluntary retirement declines during critical elections (see Table 10.1). On occasion, major shifts in party strength occur during noncritical elections, such as the Republican gains in 1920, but the defeat of incumbents is not the primary cause. Such shifts occur when an unusually large number of the incumbents of one party retire, and newcomers of the other party replace them disproportionately.[33]

Table 10.3 shows the party composition of the House of Representatives before and after the eight elections. With the exception of the Harding landslide of 1920, the party balance in the House changed only marginally after noncritical elections. After both critical elections, Republican congressional strength declined substantially. In 1932, Democrats gained wherever Republicans lost. In 1896, the realignment in Congress was more complex. Both major parties declined in the Senate as the Populists gained eight seats.[34] In the House, Republican losses were taken up almost equally by the Democrats and several minority parties, notably the Populists and the Silverites.[35] Thus, in 1896, opposition to the Republicans was scattered among the Democrats and several minority parties based primarily in the South, great plains and West. Such Populist parties represented farmers and mining interests which had fared badly during the late 1880s and especially during the Panic of 1893. Although the Populists focused their demands on government regulation of monopoly and easy credit policies, many of them also espoused restoration of traditional rural values and rejected the alien values they associated with industrial Eastern cities, now teeming with new immigrants.

It goes without saying that critical elections change not only party representation in Congress, but also party coalitions in the electorate. The 1896 election was the threshold that inaugurated full-blown sectional politics in America. During the period immediately after the Civil War, the Republican party in the South showed considerable strength, derived primarily from the votes of newly emancipated Black voters. The Democrats, entrenched in the South, also had strongholds in the North, and only Northern Democrats were nominated for president in the elections between 1872 and 1892. The 1896 election shattered the last vestiges of Republican strength in the South, and converted most of the remaining bastions of the Democrats in the North into Republican positions. Threatened by the Populists, Northern Conservatives exploited Civil War sentiment and alleged Populist hostility toward foreign immigrants and urban labor to rally a broad coalition of business, labor, the middle classes, and the Protestant ethnic minorities, and promised unprecedented prosperity through sound currency and high tariffs. Southern Conservatives used the fear of Black political influence and coopted the Populist position on currency to counter agrarian populistic protest. In this way, Populist agitation in the South, Great Plains, and Border states was quashed.[36] Anti-slavery supporters in the Northeast, Midwest and the Far West were brought solidly into the Republican camp, where they remained (with some vacillation) until 1928 and 1932. Thus, the two parties, acting in their customary fashion as consensus builders, amalgamated diverse groups into two sectional political parties.

The critical election of 1932, another threshold, shattered the sectional pattern and divided the voters of the non-Southern states according to their social and economic status, which overlapped, in good measure, with urban-rural residence. The 1932 election ushered in the New Deal, a series of policies, neither programmatic nor consistent, which made the Democratic party a "concert of interest" of the metropolitan majorities and the rural (then "solid") South. The core support for the New Deal, as Lubell and others pointed out, was a coalition of metropolitan labor and a new generation of ethnic voters.[37]

TABLE 10.3
CHANGE IN THE PARTY COMPOSITION OF THE HOUSE OF REPRESENTATIVES
AT 12-YEAR INTERVALS SINCE 1872 INCLUDING
THE CRITICAL ELECTIONS OF 1896 AND 1932

ELECTION	REPUBLICANS			DEMOCRATS			MINORITY PARTIES		
	Pre-Election	Post-Election	% Change[a]	Pre-Election	Post-Election	% Change[a]	Pre-Election	Post-Election	% Change[a]
1872	134	194	b	104	92	b	5	14	b
1884	118	140	+6.8%	197	183	−4.3%	10	2	−2.5%
1896	244	204	−11.3%	105	113	+2.2%	7	40	+9.1%
1908	222	219	−1.0%	164	172	+2.0%	—	—	—
1920	240	301	+14.1%	190	131	−13.6%	3	1	−0.5%
1932	214	117	−22.5%	220	310	+20.8%	1	5	+0.9%
1944	208	190	−4.1%	218	242	+5.5%	4	2	−0.5%
1956	203	200	−0.7%	232	233	+0.2%	—	—	—

Source: HISTORICAL STATISTICS OF THE UNITED STATES: COLONIAL TIMES TO 1957 (Washington, D.C.: U.S. Government Printing Office, 1960), p. 691.

[a] Change is computed as a percent of total House membership. The increases in percent by one party are not always exactly matched by declines in the other if one or more seats were vacant before or after the election.

[b] Percentage change cannot be computed for 1872 because, as the first election following the Census, the number of seats in the House was increased, following the practice that was customary until the number of seats in the House was fixed at 435 early in the 20th Century.

CRITICAL ELECTIONS AND CHANGES
IN CAREER PATHS TO CONGRESS

Critical elections alter the existing pathways to Congress. During the years between critical elections, congressional career paths become routinized and institutionalized. In the various districts, the successive offices held by individuals who became congressmen represent career models which would-be congressmen emulate.[38] But in a number of these districts, the electoral realignment brings new men into power who were blocked from the "normal" channels of entry and advancement. The electoral tide defeats the incumbents in such districts and sweeps challengers into office who bring with them social and political credentials different from the pre-election majority officeholders.

Shifts in career paths are most evident in districts where party dominance changes as a consequence of the critical election. Similar changes in career paths occur in constituencies which change from control by the pre-election majority party to two-party competition after the election, or from competition to dominance by the new national majority party in the wake of the critical election.[39] In such districts, the critical election establishes new career patterns which persist at least until the next electoral realignment a generation or so later.

Nevertheless, changes in career paths to Congress do not occur in most, or even a majority of districts during critical elections. It is more accurate to say that permanent changes in the party identification of small, but decisive elements of the electorates in no more than ten to twenty percent of all congressional districts can alter the party balance in Congress. In most congessional districts, the opportunity structure for congressional office remains unchanged. Career paths remain relatively stable in the remaining strongholds of the party that lost the critical election, as do career patterns in districts that the new national majority had controlled.

For such reasons, critical elections result in small, yet far-reaching changes in the social and political profiles of each party's congressional contingent. Such changes stem, of course, from turnover of all kinds, and show up most clearly when we compare the backgrounds of defeated congressmen and their replacements. During critical elections, contrasts between the social and political credentials of losing incumbents and new congressmen symbolize the rise and decline of various interests, changes in political career paths, and the salience of new issues. By contrast, the differences or variations in backgrounds during other, noncritical elections, if they have import at all, indicate only transitory responses to a president's coattails or ephemeral issues which do not change the structure of political opportunity in a congressional district.

Comparison between critical and noncritical elections shows contrasting patterns of change in the background characteristics of defeated and victorious congressmen. *Noncritical elections maintain and often enhance the differences in social origins and political experiences which differentiate congressional contingents of the two parties. But critical elections disproportionately bring new men to Congress from both parties who share common backgrounds.* The critical election expands political opportunity in both parties, even though one party is the major beneficiary of the national electoral realignment. New congressmen are elected because of their positions on the key issues of the critical election. Most of the victorious freshmen are of the new majority party and have won their seats by defeating incumbents of the opposite party and a few old guard members of their own party. A few newly elected congressmen are of the minority party. They have withstood the realignment that devastated their party nationally by defeating conservatives of their own or the opposite party.[40] In the aggregate, the new congressmen resemble one another more closely than the incumbents they defeated, irrespective of party. In short, critical elections bring changes in background that cut across party lines.

We collected background data on congressional winners and losers for every fourth presidential election from 1872 to 1956. Information was gathered about (1) candidates' experiences in pre-congressional political offices (i.e., local, state, national) (2) the character of such offices (i.e., elective, appointive, party); and (3) the average number of different offices held by each congressman before his election to Congress. In addition to such data, we tabulated information on the social and economic origins of the congressmen, including educational attainment; age at date of their election; occupation; and geographic mobility—i.e., whether the congressman was elected from the region he was born in, or another region of the country to which he migrated.

Table 10.4 summarizes the pre-congressional political activities of winning and losing congressmen of each party during the eighty-four years. It is evident that little difference exists between critical and noncritical elections in the number or magnitude of changes in the political backgrounds of winning and losing congressmen. Although sizeable changes in such experience occurred after 1896 and 1932, several noncritical elections, notably 1872 and 1920, showed changes as great or greater. Such findings suggest that the number and magnitude of changes in background characteristics in a given election have little meaning unless we know whether or not they stem from electoral realignments in the various constituencies. Only then can we begin to separate short-run from long-run fluctuations in the background characteristics of congressmen which may affect representation and public policy.

We hypothesized earlier in the paper that critical elections stand apart from other elections because they show similar changes in the background profiles of congressmen of both parties, whereas after other types of presidential elections, the background characteristics of each party's congressional contingent change independently of one another. In Table 10.4, whenever similar changes in background profiles occur in both parties, the signs (+ or -) are the same;

TABLE 10.4
CHANGE IN THE POLITICAL BACKGROUND CHARACTERISTICS
OF LOSING INCUMBENTS VS. WINNING REPLACEMENTS, CONTROLLING FOR
PARTY AT 12-YEAR INTERVALS SINCE 1872
(in percentages)

| | NATURE OF PRIOR POLITICAL POSITIONS | | | | | |
ELECTION	None	Elec-tive	Appoin-tive	Party	Total	N^a
1872						
Losing Republican Incumbents	5.4	78.4	13.5	2.7	100.0%	(37)
Winning Republican Freshmen	6.8	50.7	31.5	11.0	100.0%	(73)
% Change: Republicans	(+ 1.4)	(−27.7)	(+18.0)	(+ 8.3)		
Losing Democratic Incumbents	13.5	61.5	21.2	3.8	100.0%	(52)
Winning Democratic Freshmen	3.8	65.4	19.2	11.6	100.0%	(26)
% Change: Democrats	(− 9.7)	(+ 3.9)	(− 2.0)	(+ 7.8)		
1884						
Losing Republican Incumbents	2.4	64.3	19.0	14.3	100.0%	(42)
Winning Republican Freshmen	1.2	69.8	16.3	12.7	100.0%	(86)
% Change: Republicans	(− 1.2)	(+ 5.5)	(− 2.7)	(− 1.6)		
Losing Democratic Incumbents	2.9	71.0	20.3	5.8	100.0%	(69)
Winning Democratic Freshmen	3.3	76.7	8.3	11.7	100.0%	(60)
% Change: Democrats	(+ 0.4)	(+ 5.7)	(−12.0)	(+ 5.9)		
1896						
Losing Republican Incumbents	8.5	50.9	18.9	21.7	100.0%	(106)
Winning Republican Freshmen	2.7	48.6	29.7	19.0	100.0%	(37)
% Change: Republicans	(− 5.8)	(− 2.3)	(+10.8)	(− 2.7)		
Losing Democratic Incumbents	10.0	50.0	16.7	23.3	100.0%	(30)
Winning Democratic Freshmen	5.3	50.5	28.3	15.9	100.0%	(113)
% Change: Democrats	(− 4.7)	(+ 0.5)	(+11.6)	(− 7.4)		
1908						
Losing Republican Incumbents	3.0	50.0	19.7	27.3	100.0%	(66)
Winning Republican Freshmen	3.3	45.9	34.4	16.4	100.0%	(61)
% Change: Republicans	(+ 0.3)	(− 4.1)	(+14.7)	(−10.9)		
Losing Democratic Incumbents	3.6	69.1	10.9	16.4	100.0%	(55)
Winning Democratic Freshmen	5.7	71.7	5.7	16.9	100.0%	(53)
% Change: Democrats	(+ 2.1)	(+ 2.6)	(− 5.2)	(+ 0.5)		
1920						
Losing Republican Incumbents	0.0	42.8	28.6	28.6	100.0%	(21)
Winning Republican Freshmen	13.0	35.9	30.4	20.7	100.0%	(92)
% Change: Republicans	(+13.0)	(− 6.9)	(+ 1.8)	(− 7.9)		
Losing Democratic Incumbents	5.4	40.5	39.6	14.5	100.0%	(101)
Winning Democratic Freshmen	9.1	31.8	31.8	27.3	100.0%	(22)
% Change: Democrats	(+ 3.7)	(− 8.7)	(− 7.8)	(+12.8)		
1932						
Losing Republican Incumbents	16.6	39.6	21.9	21.9	100.0%	(169)
Winning Republican Freshmen	4.8	47.6	19.0	28.6	100.0%	(42)
% Change: Republicans	(−11.8)	(+ 8.0)	(− 2.9)	(+ 6.7)		
Losing Democratic Incumbents	12.8	41.0	23.1	23.1	100.0%	(39)
Winning Democratic Freshmen	4.2	44.6	22.6	28.6	100.0%	(168)
% Change: Democrats	(− 8.6)	(+ 3.6)	(− 0.5)	(+ 5.5)		

TABLE 10.4 continued

NATURE OF PRIOR POLITICAL POSITIONS

ELECTION	None	Elec-tive	Appoin-tive	Party	Total	N^a
1944						
Losing Republican Incumbents	10.3	50.0	30.9	8.8	100.0%	(68)
Winning Republican Freshmen	7.1	57.1	14.3	21.5	100.0%	(14)
% Change: Republicans	(−3.2)	(+7.1)	(−16.6)	(+12.7)		
Losing Democratic Incumbents	13.6	36.4	36.4	13.6	100.0%	(22)
Winning Democratic Freshmen	4.1	46.9	36.7	12.3	100.0%	(98)
% Change: Democrats	(− 9.5)	(+10.5)	(+ 0.3)	(− 1.3)		
1956						
Losing Republican Incumbents	12.2	41.5	31.7	14.6	100.0%	(41)
Winning Republican Freshmen	8.1	43.2	37.8	10.8	100.0%	(37)
% Change: Republicans	(− 4.1)	(+ 1.7)	(+ 6.1)	(− 3.8)		
Losing Democratic Incumbents	11.9	28.6	42.9	16.6	100.0%	(42)
Winning Democratic Freshmen	12.8	25.5	40.4	21.3	100.0%	(47)
% Changes: Democrats	(+ 0.9)	(− 3.1)	(− 2.5)	(+ 4.7)		

LEVEL OF PRIOR POLITICAL POSITIONS

							AVERAGE NUMBER OF PRIOR POSITIONS	
ELECTION	None	Local	State	Nat-ional	Total	N^a	$\overline{X}$	N
1872								
Losing Repub. Incumbents	5.4	10.8	59.5	24.3	100.0%	(37)	2.2	(16)
Winning Repub. Freshmen	6.8	21.9	42.5	28.8	100.0%	(73)	2.2	(32)
% Change: Republicans	(+1.4)	(+11.1)	(−17.0)	(+4.5)			(0.0)	
Losing Democ. Incumbents	13.5	17.3	51.9	17.3	100.0%	(52)	1.5	(28)
Winning Democ. Freshmen	3.8	26.9	50.0	19.3	100.0%	(26)	2.1	(12)
% Change: Democrats	(−9.7)	(+9.6)	(−1.9)	(+2.0)			(+40.0)	
1884								
Losing Repub. Incumbents	2.4	33.3	38.1	26.2	100.0%	(42)	2.2	(18)
Winning Repub. Freshmen	1.2	34.9	34.9	29.0	100.0%	(86)	2.9	(29)
% Change: Republicans	(−1.2)	(+1.6)	(−3.2)	(+2.8)			(+31.8)	
Losing Democ. Incumbents	2.9	42.0	42.0	13.1	100.0%	(69)	2.1	(32)
Winning Democ. Freshmen	3.3	31.7	43.3	21.7	100.0%	(60)	2.8	(21)
% Change: Democrats	(+0.4)	(−10.3)	(+1.3)	(+8.6)			(+33.3)	
1896								
Losing Repub. Incumbents	8.5	33.0	34.9	23.6	100.0%	(106)	1.9	(57)
Winning Repub. Freshmen	2.7	37.8	37.8	21.6	100.0%	(37)	2.0	(17)
% Change: Republicans	(−5.8)	(+4.8)	(+2.9)	(−2.0)			(+5.0)	
Losing Democ. Incumbents	10.0	30.0	33.3	26.7	100.0%	(30)	1.9	(16)
Winning Democ. Freshmen	5.3	36.3	36.3	22.1	100.0%	(113)	2.0	(56)
% Change: Democrats	(−4.7)	(+6.3)	(+3.0)	(−4.6)			(+5.0)	

TABLE 10.4 continued

LEVEL OF PRIOR POLITICAL POSITIONS

ELECTION	None	Local	State	Nat-ional	Total	N^a	AVERAGE NUMBER OF PRIOR POSITIONS $\overline{X}$	N
1908								
Losing Repub. Incumbents	3.0	12.1	50.0	34.9	100.0%	(66)	2.7	(24)
Winning Repub. Freshmen	3.3	18.0	32.8	45.9	100.0%	(61)	2.8	(21)
% Change: Republicans	(+0.3)	(+5.9)	(−17.2)	(+11.0)			(+3.7)	
Losing Democ. Incumbents	3.6	29.1	40.0	27.3	100.0%	(55)	2.2	(20)
Winning Democ. Freshmen	5.7	30.2	41.5	22.6	100.0%	(53)	2.2	(23)
% Change: Democrats	(+2.1)	(+1.1)	(+1.5)	(−4.7)			(0.0)	
1920								
Losing Repub. Incumbents	0.0	31.8	28.6	33.3	100.0%	(21)	1.9	(11)
Winning Repub. Freshmen	13.0	42.4	23.9	20.7	100.0%	(92)	1.7	(57)
% Change: Republicans	(+13.0)	(+4.3)	(−4.7)	(−12.6)			(−10.6)	
Losing Democ. Incumbents	5.4	35.1	42.3	17.1	100.0%	(101)	1.5	(57)
Winning Democ. Freshmen	9.1	27.3	45.4	18.2	100.0%	(22)	1.6	(11)
% Change: Democrats	(+3.7)	(−7.8)	(+3.1)	(+1.1)			(+6.6)	
1932								
Losing Repub. Incumbents	16.6	33.7	30.2	19.5	100.0%	(169)	1.7	(98)
Winning Repub. Freshmen	4.8	38.1	30.9	26.2	100.0%	(42)	1.9	(14)
% Change: Republicans	(−11.8)	(+4.4)	(+0.7)	(+6.7)			(+11.8)	
Losing Democ. Incumbents	12.8	33.4	30.8	23.0	100.0%	(39)	1.5	(19)
Winning Democ. Freshmen	4.2	39.9	32.7	23.2	100.0%	(168)	1.9	(103)
% Change: Democrats	(−8.6)	(+6.5)	(+1.9)	(+0.2)			(+26.7)	
1944								
Losing Repub. Incumbents	10.3	41.2	32.4	16.1	100.0%	(68)	1.7	(35)
Winning Repub. Freshmen	7.1	42.9	35.7	14.3	100.0%	(14)	1.7	(08)
% Change: Republicans	(−3.2)	(+1.7)	(+3.3)	(−1.8)			(0.0)	
Losing Democ. Incumbents	13.6	27.3	40.9	18.2	100.0%	(22)	1.7	(12)
Winning Democ. Freshmen	4.1	35.7	36.7	23.5	100.0%	(98)	2.4	(39)
% Change: Democrats	(−9.5)	(+8.4)	(−4.2)	(+5.3)			(+41.2)	
1956								
Losing Repub. Incumbents	12.2	41.5	36.6	9.7	100.0%	(41)	2.3	(23)
Winning Repub. Freshmen	8.1	40.5	27.0	24.4	100.0%	(37)	2.4	(19)
% Change: Republicans	(−4.1)	(−1.0)	(−9.6)	(+14.7)			(+4.3)	
Losing Democ. Incumbents	11.9	28.6	40.5	19.0	100.0%	(42)	2.3	(21)
Winning Democ. Incumbents	12.8	25.5	38.3	23.4	100.0%	(47)	2.3	(25)
% Change: Democrats	(+0.9)	(−3.1)	(−2.2)	(+4.4)			(0.0)	

a In the tables on nature and level of prior political positions, "N" represents the number of prior positions held by the Congressmen, not the number of Congressmen.

Source: BIOGRAPHICAL DIRECTORY OF THE AMERICAN CONGRESS 1774-1961
(U.S.: G.P.O., 1961).

whenever the background characteristics of congressmen of the two parties change in opposite directions, the signs are opposite. Thus, when the signs of the changes for a particular background category are the same in both parties, our hypothesis is supported, whereas when the signs are different, the hypothesis is refuted.

The findings in Table 10.4 and Figure 10.1 support our hypothesis. During noncritical elections, the differences between winners and losers of one party in the pre-congressional political experiences are randomly related to changes in the other party. For example, in 1956, the percentage of Republicans with no previous political experience declined, while the percentage of Democrats increased. Similarly, the proportion of Republicans who had held elective or appointive office before they entered Congress increased, while the proportions for the Democrats declined. After critical elections, the shifts in political background cut across party lines and affect each party in the same way. In 1932, for example, the number of congressmen from both parties with no previous political experience declined, the number who had been elective or party officeholders increased, and the percent with experience in appointive office decreased.

The proportion of like-signed pairs of changes to all signed-changes is a rough measure of whether an election increases or diminishes the differences in the background profiles of the two parties, or affects both parties in a way that crosscuts party lines. The greater the proportion of like-signed pairs, the greater the incidence of crosscutting change. Figure 10.1 graphs the percentage of all pairs of changes which have the same sign for the eight elections and indicates the elections where the probability is significant that changes in background characteristics cross party lines. Such probabilities show the odds of getting the observed number of like-signed pairs, assuming that change in background characteristics is random in all elections (i.e., P (like-signed changes) = P (unlike-signed changes) = .5).[41]

Figure 10.1 shows that background changes are randomly distributed during noncritical elections. If anything, the differences in political background between congressmen of the two parties tend to increase slightly. Critical elections disproportionately bring new men to Congress in both parties who have experienced common types of political apprenticeship in their political ascent to national office. As we will see below, these men often vote together, acting as generational cohorts, and play a central role in altering the voting patterns in Congress.

THE SOCIAL BACKGROUND OF ELECTED AND DEFEATED
CONGRESSMEN IN CRITICAL ELECTIONS: 1896

After each critical election, the social composition of Congress has changed in ways that mirror the issues and interests in conflict during the election. The

Figure 10.1

PATTERNS OF CHANGE IN POLITICAL BACKGROUND CHARACTERISTICS
IN CRITICAL AND NONCRITICAL ELECTIONS

Changes in Political Background Which Cross Party Lines
As a Percent of All Instances of Change
(Like-Signed Pairs of Changes as a % of All Pairs)

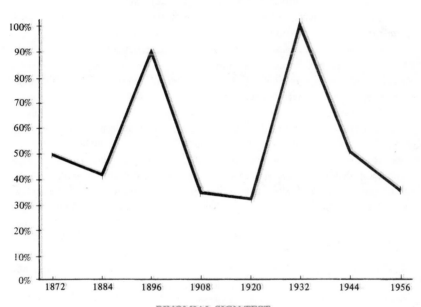

BINOMIAL SIGN TEST

	Binomial Distribution[a]	Findings	Probability of Crosscutting Change
I. 1896 and 1932 Critical Elections Sub-Tables:	B(18, .5)	17:18	>.999
1896	B(9, .5)	8:9	>.98
1932	B(9, .5)	9:9	>.998
II. Non-Critical Elections Sub-Tables:	B(50, .5)	21:50	<.95(n.s.)
1872	B(8, .5)	4:8	<.95(n.s.)
1884	B(9, .5)	4:9	<.95(n.s.)
1908	B(8, .5)	3:8	<.95(n.s.)
1920	B(9, .5)	3:9	<.95(n.s.)
1944	B(8, .5)	4:8	<.95(n.s.)
1956	B(8, .5)	3:8	<.95(n.s.)

[a] Cases where there was no change between the background characteristics of defeated and incoming Congressmen in one or the other party were not included in the calculations.

McKinley-Bryan campaign of 1896 crystallized issues that arose out of the Panic of 1893 and the farm revolt. Although the Republicans captured the Presidency and control of both Houses of Congress, the last ditch efforts to fuse a coalition of the Populists, Silverites, Silver Republicans and trans-Mississippi and Southern Democrats nearly cost the McKinley Republicans their legislative majorities. Indeed, the election of 1896 marked the peak of Populist strength in Congress. In the House of Representatives, the number of Republicans diminished, and in the Senate, the newly elected Populist senators held the decisive votes, which gave them influence out of proportion to their numbers.[42]

In the Congress as a whole, the 1896 election strengthened Western, Great Plains and Southern farmers and mine owners at the expense of Midwestern farmers and Eastern business and manufacturing interests. The alliance of farmers and mining interests was a wedding of necessity because both interests wanted an abundant supply of currency for easy credit. The mining interests advocated free coinage of silver and, indeed, the abandonment of the gold standard. Farming interests concurred in such demands because they sought the expansion of credit such changes would bring. The farmers were concerned with monetary policy because subsistence farming had been declining steeply in the Great Plains and South since the Civil War as the railroads brought access to Eastern and European markets. By 1870, the small farmer or rancher in the South or Great Plains no longer resembled the self-sufficient yeoman that Jefferson had glorified, but had become an entrepreneur engaged in the business of farming. By shifting from subsistence farming to cash crops, such farmers found that they were at the mercy of fluctuating commodity prices, the balance of trade, tariff policy, and the questionable practices of the railroads, grain speculators, and livestock wholesalers. In addition to their support for low tariffs and free silver, the Populists demanded an end to alien ownership of land, the revocation of title to most public lands granted the railroads, a graduated income tax, and various schemes designed to provide low interest loans to farmers using nonperishable products as collateral. Currency reform and free trade, plus the other Populist demands offered the small farmer relief from heavy mortgages and low farm prices.[43]

Opposing the Populist and Southern Democratic coalition of farmers and miners were the Republicans and the Eastern "Gold Bug" wing of the Democratic party who had bolted after Bryan was nominated on a free silver platform. The anti-Populist forces favored high tariffs and a sound currency. Such policies would protect infant industry from overseas competition, assure cheap labor and foster low prices for raw materials at home and from abroad.

During the decades of the 1870s and 1880s these issues became more insistent—the currency and tariff question, farm prices and agrarian indebtedness, the rise of labor and its relations with capital, the emergence of big business and monopoly. But for the most part they developed below the surface until the 1890s when they erupted into politics and shook prevailing political outlooks and behavior.[44] Although the Republicans successfully withstood the Populist revolt, Democratic and Populist gains in 1896 made possible policy measures favorable to farming and mining interests after 1896. For example, the remnants of the Populists, in coalition with Southern Democrats and agrarian Republicans from the West, Midwest and plains states were instrumental in enacting the Newlands Act of 1902 which made the federal government responsible for reclamation and irrigation. Several historians have linked a number of measures enacted during the Progressive era to the combined influences of Populist voters and former Populist leaders working later within the two major parties. These include, for example, the Aldrich-Vreeland Act of 1908 which authorized an emergency currency, to be lent to banks during financial crisis; the Federal Reserve Act of 1914; the Warehouse Act of 1916; the establishment of the Federal Trade Commission and strengthening the Interstate Commerce Commission; the Clayton Antitrust Act; such electoral reforms as direct primaries and direct election of Senators; and the graduated income tax, all of which, in one form or another, had been included on the Populist agenda.[45]

Ironically, the most pressing Populist demands for free coinage and low tariffs were satisfied through coincidental technological developments and historical events in the years immediately after 1896. Crop failures abroad in 1898 raised farm prices and the discovery of gold in Alaska and South Africa, together with the development of the cyanide process for extracting gold from ores previously regarded as unprofitable increased the amount of currency and boosted farm prices. In the era of Republican domination after 1896, industrialization proceeded with little outcry from the miners and farmers who had been so vocal during the critical election of 1896. The issues of monopoly and labor protest reappeared with renewed vigor in the Progressive era, and became pressing questions during the late 1920s and early 1930s when business regulation and the right of labor to organize became incorporated in the agenda of the New Deal.

The Populist Revolt, then, was a catalyst that inaugurated full-blown sectional politics in America. In fusing with the Populists, the Democratic party made an abrupt about-face from a *laissez faire* to a government interventionist stance on some economic issues. To withstand the Populist challenge, and to preserve the very existence of their party, Southern Democrats were forced to embrace the Populist platform in its entirety, including the provisions that would restrain the monopolistic economic powers of the East. In the bargain, the Democrats won the West for the first time, but lost the East. As Binkley observes,

> never has the South been so solidly Democratic as New England had become Republican. Industrial workers, unsympathetic with the agrarians, had voted for their jobs, which they believed to be threatened by free trade and free silver. Already the 'Democratic' depression of the nineties had planted firmly and for a generation

the conviction that a Democratic victory meant famine, starvation, and soup kitchens. . . . The Eastern farmers, dairy, truck and fruit producers who supplied the urban workers, feared the effects of Bryanism on their section.[46]

Nevertheless, the remnants of the agrarians, in concert with Progressive Republicans, witnessed the enactment of many of the proposals voiced by the Populists in the two decades that followed the McKinley-Bryan campaign.

The social characteristics of the congressmen elected in 1896 reflected a change in the relationship between social status and recruitment opportunity. The data on geographic mobility of each congressman make this clear. In the West, great plains, and certain areas of the South, many of the congressmen who lost in 1896 could be classified as "pioneers." As children or young adults, they had been among the earliest arrivals in these areas of new settlement, and had risen to wealth and prominence as successful ranchers, farmers, mine owners, and the like. In 1896, they were defeated by younger men of somewhat lower social status who were born in the regions they represented in Congress. These new congressmen were the scions of families who moved to the region several decades after the original pioneers. From the biography of each representative, we learned whether the state he represented was the same as the one in which he was born, or one to which he had moved and when. If he had moved from a region of older settlement to a region of newer settlement, he was classified as "mobile," although "pioneer" would be a more apt description prior to 1870. If he had not moved, he was included in the category called "stable." We took into account that pioneer settlements varied throughout history. Thus, migration from Pennsylvania to Missouri in 1825 was regarded as equivalent to migration from Missouri to Oregon in 1849.

The data show that defeated congressmen disproportionately were "mobiles" of relatively high educational and occupational attainment who had moved into an area during the earliest period of settlement (Table 10.5). Such individuals had been elected in increasing numbers at least since the 1872 election. In 1896, much younger men who had been born in the region, and whose families had arrived in the "second wave" of migration, defeated the older, high-status original settlers. These new congressmen were less educated and had lower status occupations than the men they defeated. For the most part, the victorious congressmen were small-town lawyers, local business, farmers and mine owners, in that order. Congressional representation shifted from the upper echelons of the local communities in these areas to middle-class farming and commercial interests. Political opportunity expanded when this second generation of settlers became eligible for public office. The expectation that a congressman should be a native of the state or region he represents took root in 1896 as the number of geographically mobile congressmen declined. This expectation has persisted to the present.

TABLE 10.5
CHANGE IN THE SOCIAL BACKGROUND CHARACTERISTICS
OF LOSING INCUMBENTS VS. WINNING REPLACEMENTS, CONTROLLING
FOR PARTY AT 12-YEAR INTERVALS SINCE 1872
(in percentages)

ELECTION[b]	OCCUPATIONAL BACKGROUND						
	Lawyer-Read[a]	Lawyer-Degree	Other Profes.	Govt. Related[a]	Business	Farming	Total
1872							
Losing Repub. Incumbents	37.5	6.3	18.7	6.3	18.7	12.5	100.0% (16)
Winning Repub. Freshmen	43.8	18.8	15.6	0.0	12.5	9.3	100.0% (32)
% Change: Republicans	(+6.3)	(+12.5)	(-3.1)	(-6.3)	(-6.2)	(-3.2)	
Losing Democ. Incumbents	60.7	17.9	7.1	3.6	10.7	0.0	100.0% (28)
Winning Democ. Freshmen	25.0	25.0	0.0	0.0	33.3	16.7	100.0% (12)
% Change: Democrats	(-35.7)	(+7.1)	(-7.1)	(-3.6)	(+22.6)	(+16.7)	
1884							
Losing Repub. Incumbents	55.6	11.1	0.0	0.0	11.1	22.2	100.0% (18)
Winning Repub. Freshmen	34.5	13.8	17.2	13.8	20.7	0.0	100.0% (29)
% Change: Republicans	(-21.1)	(+2.7)	(+17.2)	(+13.8)	(+9.6)	(-22.2)	
Losing Democ. Incumbents	46.9	18.8	6.2	3.1	21.9	3.1	100.0% (32)
Winning Democ. Freshmen	52.4	9.5	9.5	9.5	4.8	14.3	100.0% (21)
% Change: Democrats	(+5.5)	(-9.3)	(+3.3)	(+6.4)	(-17.1)	(+11.2)	
1896							
Losing Repub. Incumbents	33.3	12.3	14.0	21.1	17.5	1.8	100.0% (57)
Winning Repub. Freshmen	23.5	0.0	23.5	35.2	17.6	0.0	100.0% (17)
% Change: Republicans	(-9.8)	(-12.3)	(+9.5)	(+14.1)	(+0.1)	(-1.8)	
Losing Democ. Incumbents	25.0	31.3	6.2	25.0	0.0	12.5	100.0% (16)
Winning Democ. Freshmen	12.5	12.5	17.9	28.6	16.1	12.5	100.0% (56)
% Change: Democrats	(-12.5)	(-18.8)	(+11.7)	(+3.6)	(+16.1)	(0.0)	
1908							
Losing Repub. Incumbents	29.2	25.0	20.8	4.2	16.6	4.2	100.0% (24)
Winning Repub. Freshmen	28.6	19.0	9.5	14.3	23.8	4.8	100.0% (21)
% Change: Republicans	(-0.6)	(-6.0)	(-11.3)	(+10.1)	(+7.2)	(+0.6)	
Losing Democ. Incumbents	40.0	25.0	0.0	20.0	15.0	0.0	100.0% (20)
Winning Democ. Freshmen	26.1	30.4	13.1	4.3	17.4	8.7	100.0% (23)
% Change: Democrats	(-13.9)	(+5.4)	(+13.1)	(-15.7)	(+2.4)	(+8.7)	
1920							
Losing Repub. Incumbents	0.0	54.5	18.2	0.0	27.3	0.0	100.0% (11)
Winning Repub. Freshmen	14.1	33.3	12.3	14.0	21.1	5.2	100.0% (57)
% Change: Republicans	(+14.1)	(-21.2)	(-5.9)	(+14.0)	(-6.2)	(+5.2)	
Losing Democ. Incumbents	8.8	21.0	7.0	35.1	28.1	0.0	100.0% (57)
Winning Democ. Freshmen	9.1	27.3	9.1	45.5	0.0	9.1	100.0% (11)
% Change: Democrats	(+0.3)	(+6.3)	(+2.1)	(+10.4)	(-28.1)	(+9.1)	

[a] "Lawyer-Read" denotes individuals who read the law rather than taking degrees. "Government-Related Occupations" include, for example, states attorneys, judges, local and state bureaucrats, and the like.
[b] In 1884 and 1896, the "third" parties, i.e. Populists, Silverites and Fusionists, were lumped together with the Democrats. Farmer-Labor party Congressmen in 1932 were included with the Democrats.

TABLE 10.5 continued

OCCUPATIONAL BACKGROUND

ELECTION[b]	Lawyer-Read[a]	Lawyer-Degree	Other Profes.	Govt. Related[a]	Busi-ness	Farm-ing	Total	N
1932								
Losing Repub. Incumbents	5.1	19.4	16.3	37.8	19.4	2.0	100.0%	(98)
Winning Repub. Freshmen	14.3	28.6	14.3	14.3	28.6	0.0	100.0%	(14)
% Change: Republicans	(+9.2)	(+9.2)	(-2.0)	(-23.5)	(+9.2)	(-2.0)		
Losing Democ. Incumbents	10.5	10.5	21.1	31.6	10.5	15.8	100.0%	(19)
Winning Democ. Freshmen	14.6	24.3	17.5	19.4	15.5	8.7	100.0%	(103)
% Change: Democrats	(+4.1)	(+13.6)	(-3.6)	(-12.2)	(+5.0)	(-7.1)		
1944								
Losing Repub. Incumbents		40.0	8.6	5.7	40.0	5.7	100.0%	(35)
Winning Repub. Freshmen		50.0	0.0	25.0	25.0	0.0	100.0%	(8)
% Change: Republicans		(+10.0)	(-8.6)	(+19.3)	(-15.0)	(-5.7)		
Losing Democ. Incumbents		50.0	8.3	0.0	33.4	8.3	100.0%	(12)
Winning Democ. Freshmen		25.6	20.5	23.1	28.2	2.6	100.0%	(39)
% Change: Democrats		(-24.4)	(+12.1)	(+23.1)	(-5.2)	(-5.7)		
1956								
Losing Repub. Incumbents		65.2	0.0	0.0	30.4	4.4	100.0%	(23)
Winning Repub. Freshmen		47.4	5.3	5.3	42.1	0.0	100.0%	(19)
% Change: Republicans		(-17.8)	(+5.3)	(+5.3)	(+11.7)	(-4.4)		
Losing Democ. Incumbents		57.3	14.2	14.2	9.5	4.8	100.0%	(21)
Winning Democ. Freshmen		52.0	20.0	12.0	8.0	8.0	100.0%	(25)
% Change: Democrats		(-5.3)	(+5.8)	(-2.2)	(-1.5)	(+3.2)		

ELECTION	Average Years of Schooling		Average Age When Elected		% Geographically Mobile	
	X̄	N	X̄	N	% Mobile	N
1872						
Losing Repub. Incumbents	12.9	(16)	44.4	(16)	37.5	(6)
Winning Repub. Freshmen	13.7	(32)	46.4	(32)	25.0	(8)
% Change: Republicans	(+ 6.2)		(+ 4.5)		(-12.5)	
Losing Democ. Incumbents	14.2	(28)	46.4	(28)	15.4	(4)
Winning Democ. Freshmen	13.6	(12)	52.9	(12)	33.3	(4)
% Change: Democrats	(- 4.2)		(+14.0)		(+17.9)	
1884						
Losing Repub. Incumbents	14.8	(18)	49.0	(18)	33.3	(6)
Winning Repub. Freshmen	13.9	(29)	50.2	(29)	34.5	(10)
% Change: Republicans	(- 6.1)		(+ 2.4)		(+ 1.2)	
Losing Democ. Incumbents	14.8	(32)	47.2	(32)	31.3	(10)
Winning Democ. Freshmen	15.1	(21)	46.8	(21)	28.6	(6)
% Change: Democrats	(+ 2.0)		(- 0.8)		(- 2.7)	

Source: BIOGRAPHICAL DIRECTORY OF THE AMERICAN CONGRESS 1774-1961
(U.S.: G.P.O., 1961)

TABLE 10.5 continued

ELECTION	Average Years of Schooling		Average Age When Elected		% Geographically Mobile	
	$\overline{X}$	N	$\overline{X}$	N	% Mobile	N
1896						
Losing Repub. Incumbents	15.4	(57)	59.5	(57)	52.7	(30)
Winning Repub. Freshmen	13.9	(17)	41.2	(17)	23.5	(4)
% Change: Republicans	(- 9.8)		(-25.8)		(-29.2)	
Losing Democ. Incumbents	16.6	(16)	54.0	(16)	62.5	(6)
Winning Democ. Freshmen	14.9	(56)	41.2	(56)	37.5	(21)
% Change: Democrats	(-10.2)		(-23.0)		(-25.0)	
1908						
Losing Repub. Incumbents	15.3	(24)	54.8	(24)	25.0	(6)
Winning Repub. Freshmen	13.6	(21)	48.8	(21)	19.0	(4)
% Change: Republicans	(-11.1)		(-10.9)		(- 6.0)	
Losing Democ. Incumbents	14.9	(20)	47.7	(20)	15.0	(3)
Winning Democ. Freshmen	15.4	(23)	44.6	(23)	13.0	(3)
% Change: Democrats	(+ 3.4)		(- 6.5)		(- 2.0)	
1920						
Losing Repub. Incumbents	16.5	(11)	58.3	(11)	18.2	(2)
Winning Repub. Freshmen	16.4	(57)	58.3	(57)	22.8	(13)
% Change: Republicans	(- 0.1)		(0.0)		(+ 4.6)	
Losing Democ. Incumbents	17.5	(57)	59.9	(57)	22.8	(13)
Winning Democ. Freshmen	17.1	(11)	56.6	(11)	18.2	(2)
% Change: Democrats	(- 0.2)		(- 6.6)		(- 4.6)	
1932						
Losing Repub. Incumbents	17.3	(98)	72.3	(98)	28.6	(28)
Winning Repub. Freshman	16.1	(14)	50.4	(14)	28.6	(4)
% Change: Republicans	(- 7.0)		(-30.3)		(0.0)	
Losing Democ. Incumbents	17.4	(19)	71.0	(19)	21.1	(4)
Winning Democ. Freshmen	16.7	(103)	49.9	(103)	21.4	(22)
% Change: Democrats	(- 4.1)		(-29.7)		(+ 0.3)	
1944						
Losing Repub. Incumbents	16.4	(35)	55.4	(35)	5.7	(2)
Winning Repub. Freshmen	17.1	(8)	46.7	(8)	0.0	(0)
% Change: Republicans	(+ 4.3)		(-15.7)		(- 5.7)	
Losing Democ. Incumbents	16.5	(12)	53.3	(12)	0.0	(0)
Winning Democ. Freshmen	16.4	(39)	56.8	(39)	15.4	(6)
% Change: Democrats	(- 0.6)		(+ 6.6)		(+15.4)	
1956						
Losing Repub. Incumbents	17.2	(23)	61.3	(23)	21.7	(5)
Winning Repub. Freshmen	15.7	(19)	56.9	(19)	0.0	(0)
%Change: Republicans	(- 8.7)		(- 8.6)		(-21.7)	
Losing Democ. Incumbents	17.0	(21)	59.3	(21)	14.3	(3)
Winning Democ. Freshmen	17.4	(25)	57.2	(25)	12.0	(3)
% Change: Democrats	(+ 2.4)		(- 4.3)		(- 2.3)	

1932

The Democratic victory in 1932 recorded a protest against the Depression of 1929 and the failure of the "remedies" of the Hoover administration. From 1896 to 1929, high tariffs and *laissez faire* policies of an almost unbroken succession of Republican administrations stimulated unprecedented industrial growth. Economic concentration increased despite the trust-busting efforts of the Progressives. By the late twenties, the wealthiest five percent of the population received a third of all personal income, and industry was even more in the hands of a few corporate giants.[47]

The working man, and especially the farmer, received increasingly smaller shares of the general prosperity. By 1929, the right of unions to bargain collectively was still not recognized, and union membership, after substantial growth during World War I, declined from over five million in 1920 to less than four and a third million in 1929 as a result of a crusade for the open shop led by business leaders.[48] Working conditions remained poor in many industries, notably coal mining and the Southern textile industry, and wages remained substandard.[49] Farm prices dropped sharply during the 1920s and farm protest, dormant since Populist days, re-emerged during the late twenties. This time the leaders were the owners of large farms working through the American Farm Bureau Federation.

The election of 1928 presaged the critical election of 1932. In 1928, the Northern Republican coalition consisting of the middle classes, commercial and industrial interests, and the urban, especially Protestant, working classes, showed signs of disintegration. The Democrats nominated Alfred E. Smith, then governor of New York, to oppose Herbert Hoover. Smith evoked greater loyalty and hatred from the electorate than any candidate since William Jennings Bryan. Millions of urban voters, many of them immigrants and Catholics in the Northeast, regarded the Irish-Catholic, urban-bred Al Smith as their spokesman and broke their ties with the Republicans to vote for him. But he was anathema to a majority of Southern Democrats who bolted their party and voted for Hoover. His candidacy caused the first major defection in some cities of Northern Black voters from the party of Lincoln.[50]

Such defections increased and contributed to the diversified Democratic coalition that elected Roosevelt in 1932. The Democrats forged a new electoral coalition of urban workers, recent immigrants (1880-1917), Northern Blacks, and small farmers who had been hardest hit by the Depression. Hoover's defeat repudiated economic individualism and conservatism in favor of positive government intervention in behalf of economic recovery and reform.

The changes in the social and economic backgrounds of new congressmen elected in 1932 reflect the social changes and the shifts in voters' preferences that led to the critical election of 1932. Although the number of geographically mobile congressmen remained virtually constant in both parties, the mobile incumbents who were defeated disproportionately were native born or of Canadian or British origins. The newly elected congressmen included many of Irish or Southern European background who had moved to America early in life and had worked their way up the party hierarchy in the major cities, notably New York and Boston.[51] In both parties, the proportion of congressmen that had pursued full-time careers in local or state politics prior to their election declined. They were displaced by new congressmen, most of whom were lawyers, elected to Congress without previous elective office experience (see Table 10.4). The percentage of businessmen, farmers, and nonlegal professionals remained roughly the same, but in the category of "other professionals," college professors replaced journalists and school administrators. Whereas most defeated attorneys were educated in law schools and were members of major law firms, the incoming lawyers were for the most part small town practitioners of lower status who became lawyers through apprenticeships to an attorney. Thus, after the critical election of 1932, the number of upper-middle class professionals in Congress increased, but at the same time opportunity had broadened as the election opened the doors of Congress to more marginal members of the professions, ethnic minorities and political neophytes. In their occupations, the newly elected legislators were more diverse than their predecessors.

CRITICAL ELECTIONS AND GENERATIONAL SUCCESSION IN THE HOUSE OF REPRESENTATIVES

The data in Table 10.5 indicate that critical elections foster a generational cleavage within Congress which corresponds, in some ways, with a generational cleavage in the electorate.[52] After both critical elections, the new congressmen were much younger than those they displaced, whereas after noncritical elections, the victorious and defeated congressmen of both parties were almost the same age.[53] In fact, in some instances, notably 1872 and 1920, the freshmen were actually older than the incumbents they defeated. Thus, during critical elections, younger candidates, usually of the opposite party, defeated older congressional veterans. In 1896, for example, the average age of defeated congressmen was fifty-eight, while the new congressmen averaged forty-one years. The age difference in 1932 was even more striking: The losers averaged seventy-two years, while the newly elected had an average age of fifty.

To be sure, it is no surprise that new congressmen are younger than veteran ones. Oleszek found that congressmen elected to the House of Representatives for the first time are usually between the ages of forty and forty-five.[54] Taking into account the expected prior service in state legislatures or local offices, it is between the ages of forty and fifty when a candidate is regarded as "ready" to contest for a congressional seat. But after critical elections, the considerable age differences between the incoming and outgoing contingents of each party have special political importance because they correspond to differences among congressmen in political and social background and policy outlooks. The age changes after critical elections mark the advent in Congress of the kind of political generation to which Karl Mannheim referred, a cohort with a particular political outlook.[55] Only during critical elections did substantial age differences show up which parallel the differences in the social and economic characteristics of the incoming and outgoing congressmen, just as only following critical elections did changes in social background, like the changes in political career paths, cut across party lines (Figure 10.2). In this way, after both critical elections, the social and political profiles of the younger congressmen who won resembled those of other winners, the more elderly veteran congressmen who lost resembled one another, and the two groups differed from one another, irrespective of party.

Thus, during critical elections, changes in representation are not confined solely to shifts from one party to the other. The new congressmen reflect changes in relative political opportunities in constituencies of *both parties*, but especially within the former minority party. The minority party offers a home to the dissident interests, who acquire new influence and representation in Congress because of the electoral realignment. Some of the incumbent representatives of the new majority party in Congress are also challenged from *within* their own party, though most withstand such challenges and are swept back into office by the electoral tide that defeats many of their colleagues of the opposite party.

By contrast, during noncritical presidential elections, incoming and outgoing congressmen of the same party have much the same social, economic and political characteristics. During both the 1920 and 1956 elections, for example, newly elected Democrats resembled in their social and economic backgrounds the Democrats who were defeated more than either the incoming or outgoing Republicans; freshmen Republicans likewise had much the same background experiences as the veteran Republicans who were defeated.[56] *Thus, noncritical elections reaffirm, even enhance the differences in background and outlook that divide the two parties, whereas the electoral realignment during critical elections modifies the established recruitment procedures, opportunities, and interest in each party.* Yet the minority party, which has undergone the greatest change, is more open to dissident interests at the local level, and thus becomes the major beneficiary of the shifts in status and influence among the voters that inaugurated the crisis.

Figure 10.2

PATTERNS OF CHANGE IN SOCIAL BACKGROUND CHARACTERISTICS
IN CRITICAL AND NONCRITICAL ELECTIONS

Changes in Social Background Which Cross Party Lines
As a Percent of All Instances of Change

(Like-Signed Pairs of Changes as a % of All Pairs)

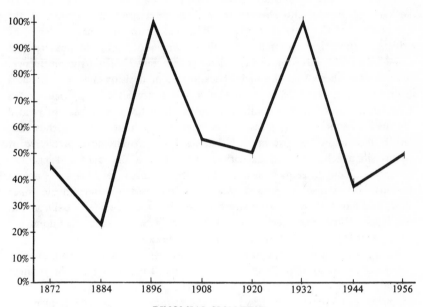

BINOMIAL SIGN TEST

	Binomial Distribution[a]	Findings	Probability of Crosscutting Change
I. 1896 and 1932 Critical Elections	B(16, .5)	16:16	>.999
Sub-Tables:			
1896	B(8, .5)	8:8	>.99
1932	B(8, .5)	8:8	>.99
II. Non-Critical Elections	B(51, .5)	22:51	<.95(n.s.)
Sub-Tables:			
1872	B(9, .5)	4:9	<.95(n.s.)
1884	B(9, .5)	2:9	<.95(n.s.)
1908	B(9, .5)	5:9	<.95(n.s.)
1920	B(8, .5)	4:8	<.95(n.s.)
1944	B(8, .5)	3:8	<.95(n.s.)
1956	B(8, .5)	4:8	<.95(n.s.)

[a] Cases where there was no change between the background characteristics of defeated and incoming Congressmen in one or the other party were not included in the calculations.

CRITICAL ELECTIONS AND CONGRESSIONAL LEGISLATION

During critical elections, the social, economic and political composition of Congress changes. The crises which precipitate such elections provoke sharp conflicts between competing coalitions of social and economic interests who seek to maintain or capture control of government by electing their spokesmen to Congress and the Presidency. Such conflict brings the influence of social background factors into sharper focus because a generational shift in the composition of Congress takes place. The congressmen and senators elected by critical elections figure prominently in the enactment of legislative measures that change the policy direction of the federal government. Tracing such influences tests the hypothesis that the social background of decision makers influences their decision making behavior. Research which attributes voting behavior in Congress to the social and political backgrounds of lawmakers has not yielded convincing results.[57] As a result, the social background hypothesis has been largely discounted because other influences have proven more predictive of congressional behavior—e.g., seniority, party, region of the country, delegation, caucus, and committee membership. However, the historical evidence is not all in. Most of the social background research on Congress has been conducted since 1932, and has dealt with issues which arose when the New Deal coalition was dominant. What part background factors play when such coalitions are disaggregated and/or reconstructed has yet to be examined.

Before a critical election, new issues crystallize which challenge the prevailing policies of the majority in Congress. In the contest for nomination, the younger candidates define their differences with the old guard of their own party. After capturing the nomination the new candidates wage an ideological contest with the congressional incumbents of the majority party.[58] Thus, a double generational battle occurs, one within the parties, and the other between the nominees of both political parties. After the critical election, the new majority in Congress formulates a new policy agenda. The success they achieve in enacting new legislation stems both from their numbers,[59] and from the formation of a bloc of cohorts in Congress.

We selected the critical election of 1932 to test whether age differences and changes in the social and political characteristics of incoming and outgoing congressmen correlate with changes in congressional policies. The Roosevelt victory in 1932 proved an especially appropriate test case. After the 1928 election, Democrats in Congress intensified their demands for reform legislation. As a result of the onset of the Depression in 1929, Democrats won a majority in the House of Representatives in the 1930 congressional election, although the conservative Republican coalition retained control of the Senate. The Seventy-

Second Congress (1931-1933) considered a number of bills that were forerunners of legislation enacted later during the New Deal: The Norris-LaGuardia labor reform bill, unemployment and farm relief, banking reform, and the Reconstruction Finance Corporation Act. These measures constituted early legislative response to the Depression, steps in the government's new commitment to regulation of the economy.

We compared such issues during the sessions of the Seventy-Second Congress when the Republican coalition in the House was still intact, with the votes on comparable measures enacted during the Seventy-Third Congress (1933-1935) when the New Deal majority was in power. We tabulated roll calls for such measures during the pre- and post-1932 Congresses and selected three pairs of major new bills that were considered in both Congresses. The issues were unemployment relief, agricultural relief, and industrial recovery.[60] The votes on such bills showed that virtually the same congressmen favored all three proposals, and another group of congressmen opposed all three issues in the Seventy-Second Congress. The same was true in the Seventy-Third Congress. We could thus collapse the vote distributions and make them a composite of average votes cast pro or con.[61] In Table 10.6, the composite vote distributions on unemployment relief, agricultural relief and industrial recovery for the Seventy-Second and Seventy-Third Congresses are classified according to the status of congressmen as newly elected, defeated or reelected in the 1932 election. The votes of holdover Democrats and Republicans who served in both Congresses were compared with those of Republicans and Democrats who were defeated in 1932 and with those who replaced them.

TABLE 10.6
COMPOSITE VOTES ON REFORM LEGISLATION, PRE- AND
POST 1932, RELATED TO LEGISLATIVE TURNOVER PATTERNS

Seventy Second Congress (1931-1933)		
	For	Against
Holdover Democrats	84% (135)	16% (26)
Defeated Democrats	57% (8)	43% (6)
Defeated Republicans	71% (53)	29% (22)
Holdover Republicans	35% (37)	65% (69)

Seventy Third Congress (1933-1935)		
	For	Against
Holdover Democrats	93% (183)	7% (14)
Incoming Democrats	93% (87)	7% (7)
Incoming Republicans	86% (12)	14% (2)
Holdover Republicans	48% (43)	52% (47)

The data suggest that the incoming and outgoing contingents in 1932 were cohorts not only in age and background, but in policy outlooks as well. The defeated Democrats were more conservative and the defeated Republicans more liberal than the holdover contingents of their respective parties. In the aggregate, *the voting patterns of the departing congressmen, Republicans and Democrats alike, resembled one another more closely than they did the voting distributions of their own parties. Likewise, the incoming congressmen of both parties showed similar voting patterns.* The new congressmen were New Deal liberals who joined with the holdover Democrats to give Roosevelt his majorities on New Deal legislation. Thus, our findings show changes in voting distributions in Congress after the critical election of 1932 that cut across party lines.[62]

Thus, the election of 1932 purged the Republicans of their liberal wing and the Democrats of their conservative wing. In effect this turnover rid Congress of the moderates of both parties who had shown mixed voting records on reform legislation. The moderates were replaced by younger, New Deal Democrats of somewhat lower socio-economic status than their Republican opponents. The few freshman Republicans who won despite the Democratic upsurge were younger, of lower social status, and favored reform legislation more than their veteran Republican colleagues in the House. The holdover Republicans who were reelected in 1932 were members primarily of the conservative old guard, while the more liberal Republicans were defeated by younger, even more liberal Democrats, who also defeated conservative elements of the Democratic party. The 1934 off-year election and the Democratic landslide of 1936 ousted many remaining conservative Republicans and left them with little more than a corporal's guard who represented the Republican constituencies that resisted the Democratic resurgence.

The election of 1932 *was a phase* in the crystallization of a new electoral and congressional alignment.[63] The first signs of the realignment appeared in 1928 (some would contend 1924), when a small group of liberal Democrats were elected to Congress. The liberals increased in number in the 1930 election; captured control of the Congress and the Presidency in 1932; and ousted the remnants of the old majority in 1934 and 1936. The 1932 election was the turning point when the new congressional recruits wrested power from the more venerable and vulnerable Republican and Democratic congressmen. It was such younger liberal Democratic congressmen, along with liberal Republican insurgents, who enacted the legislation of the New Deal. At each phase of the congressional realignment from 1928 to 1936 as the nation moved in new policy directions, social background influenced recruitment opportunities and the policy preferences of the new men elected to Congress.

CONCLUSION

Pareto and Mosca suggested that political innovation is the result of the circulation of political elites. Our study suggests that the changes in the membership of congressional elites that result when we examine electoral realignments play a significant part in congressional policy direction. Although we have not proven that the new members of Congress elected during a critical election are responsible for legislative innovation, we have shown that they are catalysts in such innovation. To say that critical elections and electoral realignments are turning points includes not only what "starts" them, but also what policy changes the new electoral coalitions *make possible* as a result of the changed complexion of congressional alignments.

We reiterate that the theory of critical elections has not yet become a predictive theory, nor is it likely to become one. The characterization of a presidential election as "critical" remains a retrospective judgment applied when the electoral realignment it reflects persists for the next thirty years or so. We have used critical elections as points in time to measure the effects of electoral realignment. In doing so, we have explored new dimensions: the impact of critical elections on turnover in Congress; the recruitment of new congressmen; and the policy consequences that follow therefrom. Unless such changes in leadership and policy are included in the analysis of electoral realignments we shall not understand their full significance, and the explanations of past critical elections will remain inadequate.

In the course of our analysis, we have found a number of variables that differentiate critical elections from noncritical elections which might serve as indicators of the advent of a critical election before or immediately after it occurs. During critical elections, incumbent congressmen are defeated in unprecedented numbers. After a critical election, the ratio between those who retire from Congress and those defeated changes dramatically to a new level which remains stable until the next realignment. When we examined changes in the social composition of the House of Representatives following critical elections, we found significant differences in the generational composition of Congress. The new men have followed different career paths, exhibit different patterns of social and geographic mobility, and hold occupations somewhat different from the incumbents they displaced. *Thus, a critical election makes manifest new patterns of elite socialization and recruitment. In a sentence, critical elections for voters are also critical elections in the recruitment of their political representatives.*

The changes in Congress reflect changes in the congressional recruitment processes and their outcomes in some congressional districts. Younger men are elected with backgrounds different from those of both the established party leaders on the local level and the older congressional incumbents they displace. The realignment taking place on the national level is reflected in microcosm in particular congressional districts, where shifts in party balance and changes in the succession of party leadership accompany the critical election. This occurs only in a small number of congressional districts, but such changes affect the coalitions and factions in Congress and legislative policy.

What do our findings contribute to a theory of electoral realignment? If a new cohort is being elected in a number of congressional districts, then we have a sign of a critical election, which increases the likelihood of new legislative policies in Congress. A realignment occurs because major cumulative issues polarize the electorate.[64] The new cohort which is elected to the House of Representatives gives voice to new viewpoints on these issues and helps to shift legislative policy in new directions. Such covariance adds a new dimension to the analysis of critical elections and electoral realignment.

The question arises, under what social and economic conditions will such combinations of change occur? We have little to add on this point. It puts too much weight on recruitment variables to make them solely responsible for the decision making behavior of congressmen. We suggest, however, that the break-up of established political opportunity patterns should be a focus for analysis. Under what conditions does insurgent leadership arise? What determines how it articulates with the established party leadership in the local community? Under what circumstances do older majority parties weaken because their leadership and public officials lose their responsiveness? The answers lie in responses to social and economic changes, whether they stem from industrialization, technological developments, urbanization, immigration, social mobility, or other factors that generate new issues. Indeed, it is possible that the *emergence of new leadership may be one determinant of electoral realignment and the subsequent changes in policy direction.*

The idea of critical or realigning presidential elections ought to be liberated from notions of cyclical "inevitability." Electoral realignments are significant even if they do not recur with the regularity of ocean tides. When electoral changes result in changes in the processes of leadership recruitment (and *vice versa* as we are suggesting), then we can predict significant policy changes. *In the final analysis, the changes in leadership and public policy make us call some presidential elections "critical."* In this regard, we might say that congressional critical elections also occur when turnover and the gains for one party are so great that congressional orientations toward policies change. For example, 1946 and 1958 might prove to be what we have called congressional (midterm) critical elections. The subject awaits further exploration, as do the wave-like rates at which local, state, and presidential votes respond to one another. Generational waves in political leadership at local levels will have their "ninth wave" in national politics sometime later and presidential candidates inspire new generational sets of aspiring politicians on the local level.

A viable theory of electoral realignment would be nothing less than a dynamic theory of American politics, for it would identify the variables that explain intervals of accelerated and extensive realignment and their consequences in American politics, as differentiated from more normal periods. The scope of such a theory would reach beyond changes in voting patterns alone. We have suggested another dimension, i.e. leadership recruitment, that should be examined because when new leadership emerges, this dimension reflects changes. Moreover, in American politics, the democratization of the recruitment of political elites has been historically more important than the democratization of suffrage. In England and Western Europe it was the other way around, and the legal struggles for the equalization of suffrage were intense and protracted.

Clearly, more extensive historical investigation of recruitment processes and trends would yield more insights into critical elections and the processes of change in American politics. The mechanisms and linkages that tie together social and economic changes, voter realignment, the social background and recruitment experiences of elites, and public policy are yet to be discovered. In this regard, we must move beyond simple analysis of aggregate historical voting data. The virtue of most research on critical elections—i.e., its reliance on systematic aggregate voting data, is also its greatest limitation. Such data does not allow valid inferences about the influences at work at middle levels of politics—interest groups, party organizations, and state and local officials. We suggest that the wealth of available historical data on social and economic development, elite backgrounds, recruitment patterns, and legislative behavior in the Congress should be examined for its theoretical and empirical promise.

NOTES

1. Portions of this study appear, in different form, in the authors' "Continuities and Discontinuities in the Recruitment of the U.S. Congress: 1870—1970" in Mattei Dogan and Juan Linz, eds., *Political Elites and Social Structure in Parliamentary Democracies: A Comparative and Historical Analysis* (Cambridge: MIT Press, forthcoming 1976).

2. V. O. Key, Jr., "A theory of critical elections," Journal of Politics, 17 (1955), 3-18.

3. Key, "Secular realignment and the party system," Journal of Politics, 21 (1959), 198-210.

4. Walter Dean Burnham, *Critical Elections and the Mainsprings of American Politics* (New York: W. W. Norton, 1970).

5. E. E. Schattschneider, *The Semi-Sovereign People* (New York: Holt, Rinehart & Winston, 1960), chapter 5.

6. Gerald M. Pomper, *Elections in America* (New York: Dodd, Mead, 1968), chapter 5. See also Pomper, "Controls and influence in American elections," *American Behavioral Scientist* 13 (1969), 219.

7. Angus Campbell, Philip E. Converse, Warren E. Miller, and Donald E. Stokes, *The American Voter: An Abridgement* (New York: John Wiley, 1964), 274-279.

8. Thomas P. Jahnige, "Critical elections and social change," Polity 3 (1971), 466-500.

9. Burnham, op. cit.

10. Duncan McRae, Jr., and James A. Meldrum, "Critical elections in Illinois: 1888-1958," American Political Science Review 54 (1960), 669-683.

11. Michael P. Rogin and John Shover, *Political Change in California* (Westport, Conn.: Greenwood, 1969).

12. Samuel T. McSeveney, *The Politics of Depression: Political Behavior in the Northeast, 1893-1896* (New York: Oxford University Press, 1972).

13. Burnham, op. cit., 10.

14. Jahnige, op. cit.

15. A prime example of the small but growing body of literature which focuses on broader realignment periods rather than critical elections is James L. Sundquist, *Dynamics of the Party System* (Washington, D.C.: Brookings, 1973). Sundquist has analyzed three periods of realignment, and has stressed the impact of new political issues and the ways the political parties adapt to them as primary causes of realignment.

16. For more comprehensive discussions of the concepts of political recruitment and political opportunity, see Lester G. Seligman, "Political Parties and the Recruitment of Political Leaders" in Lewis J. Edinger, ed., *Political Leadership in Industralized Societies* (New York: John Wiley, 1967), chapter 10; and Lester G. Seligman, Michael R. King, Chong Lim Kim, and Roland E. Smith, *Patterns of Recruitment: A State Chooses its Lawmakers* (Chicago: Rand McNally, 1974), chapter 2.

17. See our "Continuities and Discontinuities in the Recruitment of the U.S. Congress: 1870-1970," op. cit. for a more detailed discussion of the continuities which have provided the foundation for the transformations inaugurated by critical elections. In that paper we emphasize the electoral structure, party system, opportunity structure, and constitutional system which have remained relatively unchanged in the face of economic and social changes in America and a succession of foreign and domestic political crises.

18. See Lewis Edinger and Donald Searing, "Social background in elite analysis: a methodological inquiry," American Political Science Review 61 (1967), 444-445.

19. Norman B. Ryder, "The cohort as a concept in the study of social change," American Sociological Review 30 (1965), 858. See also Bennett Berger, "How long is a generation?" British Journal of Sociology 2 (1960), 557-568; Richard Jenson, "Quantitative Collective Biography: An Application to Metropolitan Elites," in Robert P. Swierenga, ed., *Quantification in American History* (New York: Atheneum, 1970), 402 and throughout.

20. Although there has been no broad-gauged study of the rise of insurgent leadership in the years immediately prior to a critical election, numerous case studies document the insurgent-old guard battles which occurred in the years between 1888 and 1900 in both the Democratic and Republican parties, depending on the region of the country in question. Similar factional battles arose prior to 1932 in the Democratic party. The classic study of the rise of the Populist movement and the origins, rise and decline of its national and state leadership is John D. Hicks, *The Populist Revolt: A History of the Farmers' Alliance and the Peoples' Party* (Minneapolis: University of Minnesota Press, 1931). Hicks' groundbreaking work includes analyses of the roots of agrarian discontent in the South and trans-Mississippi West and deals in considerable detail with the origins and ultimate fate of leading Populist and Farmers' Alliance leaders in the South and Plains states.

21. The breakdown in Congress following the 1896 election was as follows:
Senate:

"Sound Money" Republicans 43

"Silver" Republicans 4

"Silver" Democrats and Populists 42

House:

"Sound Money" Republicans 180

"Sound Money" Democrats 2

"Silver" Republicans 24

"Silver" Democrats and Populists 151

Source: *Philadelphia Evening Telegraph,* November 6, 1896. Of the new legislators in 1896, 78.9% came from the Far West, Plains, Border, and Southern states. Of these, 86.7% were Populists or Democrats.

22. See V. O. Key, *Southern Politics,* 374-378.

23. See Hicks, op. cit., 410-412.

24. The classification of elections as "critical," "deviating," "reinstating," or "maintaining," is taken from Key's "A theory of critical elections," op. cit., as modified by Campbell et al., op cit., 274-279.

25. The measure of percent replaced is taken from Morris P. Fiorina, David W. Rhode, and Peter A. Wissel, "Remarks on Historical Changes in Congressional Turnover," (University of Rochester, Department of Political Science, mimeo, 1970), 4.

26. The percentage replaced was adjusted in 1944 to take into account the sizeable number of congressmen who retired to enlist in the armed forces during World War II. In all, nineteen congressmen left the Seventy Eighth Congress in this manner and all but three were returned to Congress after the war in 1946 or 1948. Considering the unusual circumstances, such "retirements" were considered atypical and were excluded from the percent replaced measure.

27. Data regarding electoral defeat were drawn from the biographical material in the *Biographical Directory of the American Congress, 1774-1961* (Washington: Government Printing Office, 1961), and were cross-checked against historical election returns supplied by the Inter-University Consortium for Political Research, Ann Arbor, Michigan.

28. Nelson W. Polsby, "The Institutionalization of the U.S. House of Representatives," American Political Science Review, 62 (1968), 146.

29. As Table 10.2 shows, only critical elections are significantly related to the rate of electoral defeat. Changes in the general rate of replacement of congressmen are essentially unrelated to the rate of defeat. The partial correlation between critical elections and electoral turnover is .87; the figure for percent replaced and electoral turnover is .28. The zero order correlation between critical elections and percent replaced is .35.

30. See Nelson W. Polsby, op. cit.; and Polsby, Miriam Gallaher, and Barry Spencer Rundquist, "The growth of the seniority system in the U.S. House of Representatives," American Political Science Review 63 (1969), 806-807.

31. James Holt, *Congressional Insurgents and the Party System 1909-1916* (Cambridge: Harvard University Press, 1967).

32. See Polsby, Gallaher and Rundquist, op. cit., 791, 798-802; George B. Galloway, *Congress at the Crossroads* (New York: Thomas Y. Crowell, 1946), 187; George Goodwin, "The seniority system in Congress," American Political Science Review 53 (1959), 417; and James Holt, op. cit.

33. In 1920, 66 congressmen retired. Of these, 48 were Democrats and 26 of the newcomers who replaced them (54%) were Republicans. Only approximately 20% of the Republican retirees were replaced by Democrats.

34. The Republicans dropped from 47 to 43 Senators; the Democrats declined from 39 to 34. The minor parties increased from 4 to 12 Senate seats.

35. The minor party membership in the House in the Fifty-fourth Congress (1895-1897) was nine People's Party members (Populists), one Fusionist, and one Silverite. The figures for the Fifty-fifth Congress (1897-1899) were 19, 7, and 3 respectively, with eleven other congressmen securing nomination by both the Democratic and People's parties. There were three Populists and one Independent (Southern Democrat) in the Fifty-fourth Senate. The Fifty-fifth Senate had seven Populists, four Silverites, and the same "Independent" Southern Democrat. This Senator caucused with the "Silver" Democrats.

36. Richard N. Current, T. Harry Williams and Frank Freidel, *American History* (New York: Alfred A. Knopf, 1963), 528-535; Hicks, op. cit., chapters 13, 14, 15.

37. Samuel Lubell, *The Future of American Politics* (New York: Harper, 1952). See also Campbell et al., op. cit., 90-93.

38. See Joseph Schlesinger, *Ambition and Politics* (Chicago: Rand McNally, 1966). For similar findings at the American state level, see Seligman, King, Kim, and Smith, op. cit., chapter 6.

39. The relations between shifts in career paths and changes in the competitive structure of congressional districts is indicated roughly by the fact that over 55% of electoral defeat in 1896 occurred in districts where "permanent" changes in party control followed the critical election. The figure for 1932 is 69%. As we will see in the pages that follow, the new men elected from such districts contrasted in their social and political credentials with the incumbents they defeated.

40. See note 20, above.

41. Since instances of like-signed pairs of changes support our hypothesis and unlike-signed pairs disconfirm our hypothesis, we can use the resulting binomial distribution to compute the probability of obtaining the observed number of like-signed pairs if in fact change is random.

42. The Republicans captured 43 seats in the Senate, three less than a majority of 46 of the 90 seats. The Democrats captured 34 and the minor parties, 12 (seven Populists, four Silverites and one Independent). There was one seat vacant throughout most of the Fifty-fifth Congress.

43. See Current, Williams, and Freidel, op. cit., 712.

44. Current, Williams and Freidel, ibid.

45. Hicks, op. cit., 414-419.

46. Wilfred E. Binkley, *American Political Parties* (New York: Alfred A. Knopf, 1965), 320.

47. Current, Williams and Freidel, op. cit., 712.

48. Ibid., 695.

49. Ibid.

50. The first wholesale transfers by Black voters from the Republican to the Democratic party occurred in 1932, although the first signs were present in 1928. In 1932, the Black vote was delivered by urban Democratic machines in New York, Kansas City, and Pittsburgh. Black voters in Chicago did not follow suit until 1934, and the process was not fully completed in Philadelphia, Cleveland, Cincinnati, Baltimore, and Columbus until 1936. See Henry Lee Moon, *Balance of Power: The Negro Vote* (Garden City, N.Y.: Doubleday, 1948), chapter 1.

51. Two of the congressmen defeated in 1932 were immigrants, one from England and the other from Canada. Seven of the 22 incoming Democratic congressmen who were mobile (32%) were immigrants, and many more were first or second generation descendants of immigrant families. No incoming Republicans were foreign-born.

52. Campbell et al., op. cit., 93, discuss the notion of 1932 as an election which activated a new generation of voters for the first time.

53. See Walter Oleszek, "Age and political careers," *Public Opinion Quarterly* 33 (1969), 100-102.

54. Ibid., 101.

55. Karl Mannheim, "The Problem of Generations," in *Essays on the Sociology of Knowledge* (London: Oxford University Press, 1952), 291.

56. In 1872, 1884, and 1944, the differences between the parties were enhanced, since there were more unlike-signed pairs of change than like-signed pairs. In 1908, 1920 and 1956, change in background was virtually random.

57. See Heinz Eulau and Katherine Hinckley, "Legislative Institutions and Processes," in James A. Robinson, ed., *Political Science Annual 1966* (Indianapolis: Bobbs-Merrill, 1966), 114-122 for an extensive review and critique of this research.

58. See note 20 above for sources which describe insurgent strategies and campaign tactics.

59. See Marvin Weinbaum and Dennis R. Judd, "In search of a mandated Congress," *Midwest Journal of Political Science* 14 (1970), 276-302, for evidence that the size of a congressional coalition, more than any other factor, explains the passage of innovative legislation. The evidence pertains to bills enacted after the 1936 and 1960 elections.

60. The bills were selected as follows: we tabulated roll calls for the pre- and post-1932 Congresses, searching first for bills that dealt with essentially the same issue in both Congresses. The list was reduced by eliminating all unanimous or nearly unanimous votes. Three pairs of bills remained that dealt with major innovative issues, were nonunanimous, and were considered in the Seventy-second and Seventy-third Congresses. The bills were: *Unemployment Relief*—Seventy-second Congress, First

Session, H.R. 12445; Seventy-third Congress, First Session, H.R. 4606: *Industrial Regulation and Assistance*—Seventy-second Congress, First Session, H.R. 7360; Seventy-third Congress, First Session, H.R. 5755: *Agricultural Relief*—Seventy-second Congress, Second Session, H.R. 1036; Seventy-third Congress, First Session, H.R. 3855.

61. Less than three percent of all votes cast deviated from the bloc voting pattern.

62. Brady and Lynn have examined voting patterns in the U.S. House of Representatives during the sessions following the 1896 and 1964 elections. They analyzed the roll call behavior of congressmen from "switched-seat districts" (i.e., districts which switched in the direction of the landslide from Democratic to Republican in 1896 and from Republican to Democratic in 1964), and compared the votes of these congressmen with those of the remaining membership of the House on bills which elicited partisan votes, and also on bills which pertained to the major innovative legislation which was passed during the sessions immediately after the two elections. They found that: (1) congressmen from switched-seat districts showed considerably higher party support scores than other members of the House; and (2) congressmen from switched-seat districts were more supportive of policy change than other congressmen.

It is not entirely clear whether Brady and Lynn's findings complement or contradict our own. We can point to certain similarities: the victorious Democratic freshmen in 1932 voted for reform legislation at least as frequently as their holdover colleagues, and more frequently than the remainder of the House as a whole. Since all issues we examined were also party votes, the same applies to the party support levels of the incoming Democrats in 1932. But not all incoming Democrats were from "switched-seat" districts in 1932, and not all incumbents from "switched-seat" districts in 1896 and 1964 had defeated their opponents. These and other differences in the data bases of the two studies cast doubt on the comparability of the findings. The level of party support or support for innovation among newly victorious Democrats and Populists in 1896, and among freshman Republicans in 1964 needs to be examined before we can assess whether the crosscutting pattern of party voting we found in 1932 also occurred in 1896 and 1964. See David W. Brady and Naomi B. Lynn, "Switched-seat congressional districts: their effect on party voting and public policy," American Journal of Political Science 17 (1973), 523-543. See also Brady, *Congressional Voting in a Partisan Era* (Lawrence: University Press of Kansas, 1973).

63. See James T. Patterson, *Congressional Conservatism and the New Deal* (Lexington: University of Kentucky Press, 1967).

64. Benjamin Ginsberg, "Critical elections and the substance of party conflict," *Midwest Journal of Political Science* 16 (1972), 603-625.

NOTES

NOTES

NOTES

NOTES

NOTES

DATE DUE

HIGHSMITH 45-220